CITIES OF LIGHT AND
SONS OF THE MORNING

Books by Martin Green

A MIRROR FOR ANGLO-SAXONS

REAPPRAISALS: SOME COMMONSENSE READINGS IN
AMERICAN LITERATURE

SCIENCE AND THE SHABBY CURATE OF POETRY

THE PROBLEM OF BOSTON

YEATS'S BLESSINGS ON VON HÜGEL: ESSAYS ON
LITERATURE AND RELIGION

CITIES OF LIGHT AND SONS OF THE MORNING

CITIES OF LIGHT AND SONS OF THE MORNING

A Cultural Psychology for an Age of Revolution

BY MARTIN GREEN

LITTLE, BROWN AND COMPANY
Boston and Toronto

124554

LIBRARY OF CONGRESS CATALOG CARD NO. 76–161858

FIRST EDITION

T05/72

The author is grateful for permission to reprint selections from his
material which was originally published in periodicals in slightly different
form. The articles are: "Writing and the Revolution in Havana" from
London Magazine, October 1969; "Goethe and the Faculty Club"
from *London Magazine,* December 1969 © London Magazine 1969.
And "Revolutionary Cuba" from *The Month,* January 1970.
© Peter Hebblethwaite, 1970.

The author also gratefully acknowledges permission to reprint quotations
from the following sources: *The Armies of the Night* by Norman Mailer.
An NAL book. Copyright © 1968 by Norman Mailer. Reprinted by
permission of the World Publishing Company. *The Autobiography of
Malcolm X* written with the assistance of Alex Haley. Reprinted by
permission of Grove Press, Inc. Copyright © 1964 by Alex Haley and
Malcolm X; Copyright © 1965 by Alex Haley and Betty Shabazz.

Chapter 6, "American Literature, 1780–1820: The God Who
Neglected to Come," by Martin Green, is taken from volume 8
of the Sphere *History of Literature in the English Language,*
edited by Marcus Cunliffe. It is reproduced here by permission
of the publishers, Sphere Books Ltd., London.

*Published simultaneously in Canada
by Little, Brown & Company (Canada) Limited*

PRINTED IN THE UNITED STATES OF AMERICA

TO BERNARD AND LUCY MC CABE
In love and admiration

The Noontime Carillon at Tufts
"As I was going to Strawberry Fair"

Moderate   English

As I was going to Strawberry Fair
Singing, singing, buttercups and daisies,
I met a maiden taking her ware
Fol de dee
Her eyes were blue and golden her hair,
As she went on to Strawberry Fair,
Ri-fol, ri-fol, tol-de-riddle-i-do
Ri-fol, ri-fol, tol-de-riddle-dee.

The carillon rang grapes in decorator clusters
Slow dying punctures of the warm March grayness
Plaintive blobs of melting unmeaning
Lime jello salad and angel food cake
Hesitant mimicry, mechanically faulty
Musical entropy, patterned over Boston
Bleeding away significance and meaning
Severing sweetly ligatures and muscles
Rosily pouring wax along the arteries
Sprouting bridgework from all the orifices
Prostheses linking man to man to building
                              Ringing, ringing,
                              Somerville and Medford

While hesitant snowflakes glided thickly
Melted quickly on warm pathways
And students sloshed along in silence
Gathering grades and carrying napalm
And the bells rang out the liberal illusion
                              Pastel, plastic,
                              buttercups and daisies

Down in the city there are busts and bombs and trashings
Up on the hill we conjure up ideas
Summon in our circle the mind's Homeric heroes
Materializing the approved that's immaterial
Homunculi in glass and Christ in aurum potabile
Structures of meaning to compete with concrete
                              Ri-rol, ri-fol,
                              alchemy and H-bombs

And the bells of St. Philomela
Last fading bugle of the Lawrence Welksound
Last light that shakes across the lakes of Disney
Rang me in to a strawberry class
On Keats's Ode to a Nightingale.

> *Your cherries soon will be wasted away*
> > *Singing, singing, buttercups and daisies,*
> *Your roses wither and never stay,*
> > *Fol de dee*
> *'Tis not to seek such perishing ware*
> *That I am tramping to Strawberry Fair*
> > *Ri-fol, ri-fol, tol-de-riddle-i-do,*
> > *Ri-fol, ri-fol, tol-de-riddle-dee.*

CONTENTS

ILLUSTRATIONS

PART ONE

1 — AUTOBIOGRAPHICAL REFLECTIONS AND EXPLANATIONS: AN INTRODUCTION

The days of the old order are numbered. When capitalism goes under, it will go in a crash. We must rise up and help destroy the power structure root and branch. For the first time in history mankind is capable of living free, without the chains of repression or alienation. The present oppression, this totally evil system of war, poverty and exploitation, is doomed. The revolution that is coming will transform all life and culture as we have hitherto known it.

We are not in a riot but in a revolution. All the established institutions must be destroyed.

Réforme non, Révolution oui.

*What the world needs today is not the making of Art nor the making of Music, but the making of Revolution — everywhere in the World.**

Autobiographical Reflections in an Age of Revolution

Written December 1969–February 1970, Boston

First of all, why was this book written? To stop me feeling so badly about myself-and-the-world. My present circumstances present me

---

* All quotations were spoken in 1968 and are from articles on Revolution by Melvin Lasky in *Encounter*, October 1968, January and October 1969, and March 1970. The first, by a student representative to the Conference of Revolutionary Youth in London, June; the second, by a student leader in the Berlin demonstrations, April; the third, by Dany Cohn-Bendit at the Sorbonne demonstrations; the fourth, by Hans Werner Henze.

with invitations, challenges, duties, which I do not take up. So I feel, like many other people in these circumstances, paralyzed and guilty. I want to describe those feelings and circumstances in the first chapter, and then analyze parallel sets of circumstances (or diametrically or rectangularly opposed sets) in other places or times. That analysis will, I hope, give me an understanding of the problem that will interpret my circumstances differently — differently enough to make for different feelings.

We are living in an age of revolution; that is, an age when the fact of revolution is so imaginatively present to all men of reflection that they must stand up and say that they are either for it or not, and if not, why not. These are the circumstances and the challenges referred to, this is the problem. Not that Boston in 1969 is yet like Paris in 1789 or Moscow in 1917, but 1969 is perhaps like 1788 or 1916. It is like early 1848, both in England where the revolution did not finally occur, and in France, where it did. To be liberal, worse yet to be apolitical, is to be less than a man. Those who are for the revolution, the serious about life, have more respect for those who are against it than for those who don't know.

However, Are you for the revolution? is only the Idea of the questions we all individually face. My individual question is to be defined in terms of the conflict my situation creates in me.

AS A COLLEGE ENGLISH TEACHER

We are all anxious these days — anxious about what our society has been and is, as well as about its future — but college teachers of English maybe more than most. We are more anxiously anxious. Having made ourselves the cultural conscience of others, the accusers of our society, we now see ourselves in moral jeopardy. We are coming to the end of our seven fat years, which have been about twenty-five, and we suspect that we have misemployed them. 1945–1970 seems to have been our fat period — fattest of all in the last ten years — so that you feel as if there was a steady intensification through the whole, especially if the curve of your career, like mine, reached its apogee at the end. This was a period when we could think that the brightest students majored in English, and the best departments in most colleges were their English departments, and the best years of the students' lives were the years they spent

The Brandeis faculty plod through the mockery of their students on
their way to Commencement, June 1969. Here we see the two groups
that constitute the modern university, the modern city of light, confronting each other and both characterizing themselves in terms as
differentiated, in roles as opposed, as the two bands of settlers in Hawthorne's story "The Maypole of Merrymount." But then the cast-iron
Protestant Puritans expelled the revelers from their traditional gaieties.
Now, in modern New England, it is the skeptical-agnostic players of
the game of learning who figure as Puritans. And insofar as there is
any thought of one group's dispossessing the other and dispelling its
frail illusion of a life-style, the initiative, the threat of brutal realism,
now lies with the motley and antic students. (Courtesy of the *Boston
Globe*.)

with us, before the world got at them. We could not *feel*, despite what we thought and said, that such a period and such a culture was wholly bad.

As for fat life-style, living off the fat of the land, college teachers at rich colleges have perhaps been the true aristocrats of our age. Even when poor themselves, all they have lacked have been the vulgarities of wealth. They have had the vacations and the trips abroad — the Fulbrights, the Guggenheims, the Fords, the Danforths — and the conditions of work and the pace of life and above all, the people, the company, that money is best employed to buy. Their lack of power in the political sense, their lack of wealth in the crude sense, have been just enough to keep them innocent; they have not been involved in the crimes of American capitalism or imperialism. And the teachers at poor colleges felt themselves part of a proud and rising profession.

So much was true of teachers in general; and on those green-lawned, white-porticoed campuses — "summer school" evokes the whole pastoral-rococo atmosphere — the English teachers played their guitars perhaps louder than the rest, their brightly shirted students squatting round them, leaning back on their hands, in a circle, under the elm, drinking us in. Teachers of English felt themselves more the meaning of the whole thing than other teachers, closer to the heart of the mystery, subtler priests of knowledge, suppler acrobats of mind. They felt they did better than other disciplines at combining critical ideas relevant to contemporary society with free play of the imagination over material from all ages. They combined seriousness with delicacy. And with our monopoly of the Freshman Composition courses, we got the lion's share of the majors; it was only the boy or girl with a congenital calling to math or philosophy who did not feel some pull to English.

Of course there were bad teachers, and bad whole departments, but if this happened in good colleges it meant there was perversity somewhere. There were good teachers to be got; it was a profession of teachers; the act of teaching made most of them better than they otherwise were. In contact with their students, or talking about their classes, they were a good deal sharper and intenser than they were in other manifestations. Their scholarship, their Ph.D., P.M.L.A., J.G.P., selves, were pretty deadly, often. It was their teaching that counteracted that, and the counteraction was more effective in English than in other subjects, because the teaching of English called for the handling, the massaging, the physiotherapy of the students' ideas, and the teachers' ideas, about things powerfully personal, about marriage and death and manners. Quite often the student of Freshman English who complained that his teacher was putting him off literature for good, called pedantry what he could have called zeal. It was the teachers' missionariness, or at least the intensity of their reaction against certain things in their students' culture, which caused more trouble than that boredom with the course attributed to them. They were a minor order, a third order, the church in the world of the mind; perhaps they sometimes thought they were the ten just men for whose sake the Lord would spare the wicked city.

First of all . . the Freshman Composition teaching had really been the basis of that society he had discovered in Arbor Heights, that society which was what America had meant to him, his Columbia, his land of promise and opportunity. When they ceased to be teaching fellows, he realized, they would cease not only to know each other well, but probably to want to. What had bound them together was a community of position, their one to two thousand dollar salary range, their twenty-five to thirty-five age range, their division of time between course taking and course giving, their dependence on the same whims of the same professors. But it was much more, more importantly, a community of action, of teaching. It was the Freshman Composition teaching that called out in them, and made the common denominator between them, that one series of actions and reactions in which young psychic hypochondriacs and intellectual-novel-readers like them could be, he thought, unreservedly liked and admired and gone out towards.

The best reason they all had for becoming teachers and indeed for becoming English majors in the first place, was a need and a will to justify to the game-going rest of the world their difference from it; and Freshman English Composition was an arena dedicated to just that demonstration. Every day they descended into it, each doomed, whatever his mood of the moment, to try to persuade his section of twenty-three or twenty-four all-American adolescents to reject the bromides they had been nourished on all their lives, fed to them with embossed silver spoons, in favor of those tarter, chewier nourishments he, and he alone, peddled and praised and exemplified. He struggled to bring out from behind the black cloud of "cynicism" and "criticism" and "sophistication" in his students' minds, those perceptions and sympathies and dissatisfactions which were his own keenest pride and most personal possession, but which could not be recommended to his students by any of the words in the vocabulary of praise they used. And after every such hour the Teaching Fellows rejoined each other flushed with that battle in which their best selves had been engaged, exerted, endangered; and each recognized in the other then exactly that same flush, that same self. The most pedantic of them, the most elegant, the most irresponsibly rebellious, even the quite stupid, were all induced by their work into living from their best centers. Teaching the Medieval Lyric and getting published in P.M.L.A., after all, would not have the same effect. That would activate other centers in them.

That is an excerpt from a novel I wrote at least ten years ago, when the seven fat year period was in full swing. By connecting the teaching with the idea of America it suggests why the former meant so much to me, and why I have always attributed more importance to it than other people have. That chapter goes on to claim that the hero's very identity was constituted by the job — that it first gave a focus and interaction, a knotting together, of energies and aptitudes before then dispersed and centrifugal. It gave him an image of himself as the agent of Criticism, as subverter of the established order. This was admittedly subversion in the service of intellectual courage and imaginative vitality, not primarily a matter of active politics. But it seemed a genuine radicalism, an enterprise of the mind against society, and not to be dismissed as being theoretical as opposed to practical.

That was the fatness of the fat years for me — the quite existential reassurance, indeed, exultation, which I could get out of being an English teacher. That has diminished, disappeared — in phase with our political complacency. What we feel now is anxiety.

If Freshman English had prevailed, perhaps the hegemony of the English teacher would have prevailed also, and the seven fat years would have continued. (Perhaps. More likely not. The world has changed in ways that war against us.) But the Freshman English programs, quite generally, I think, began to decay before the English major did, and the English course offerings, and the English department. They decayed because young teachers in the pride of the New Criticism — the Spock children of their intellectual generation — began to demand to teach literature and not composition. As long as the bright young men were forced to cope with the weekly essay on "My Neighborhood" some intensity went into the teaching of composition. But then freshmen began arriving — at colleges like Tufts — much better prepared than they had been: already able, in most cases, to turn out a college paper passable enough in grammar and paragraph structure and footnotes. This undermined the case of the older men, and control passed to the Spock children. Instead of intensifying their idea of composition in response to the new situation, English departments reacted by offering the sonnet or the myth or some other exotic reading matter. And more recently, as the demand for relevance made itself heard, they added *The Communist Manifesto* and *Civilization and Its Discontents* and Marcuse. The New-Critical narrowness and rigidity has vanished, and I now find myself to the right of people I used to be to the left of. I am more conservative than they are, because I think they are reacting away from their old aestheticism toward no intellectual discipline at all. Relevance and revolution are guiding stars that lead on long journeys if one starts from English literature; they may seem to hover over the manger of, say, Blake, but when you get there you find they've moved on — toward action here and now. These two weaknesses, the aestheticism and the experimentalism by reaction, are our professional counterparts to the failures of liberal society as a whole.

The Tufts Freshman English course this semester offers sections on "The Demonic Strain in Literature," "The Concept of the Modern," "Identity, Black and White," "Myths Ritual and the Modern Mind," "Varieties of Radical Analysis," "Salem Witchcraft Trials," "On the Road in Quest of America," "Marx and Marxism," "Heaven and Hell in Literature," "Student Revolt and Academic Change." Last semester there were also "The New Free Woman," "The Conflict of Humanisms; Classical, Marxist, and Freudian," and "Revolutionaries, Marxist and Freudian." The last was my own section.

This course, though a great success, has two defects, potentially serious. It is not a course in composition primarily; though students do more writing for it than for other courses, most of their energy must go into the reading, the minimal understanding, of such material. And it is not properly a college course at all, since the people teaching it have not been professionally trained in the subject matter. These defects are potential rather than actual — well, that varies with the teacher, of course — because enthusiasm covers a multitude of sins. But they are still real defects because as long as we keep to the intellectual tradition (and we aren't seriously proposing to abandon it) we must feel uneasy at being so amateurish. We must be building up a reaction in ourselves and in others against "sloppiness." Sloppiness does occur even when the class goes well. We did, in my section, nibble on the edge of twenty-five huge ideas, and grant each other huge intellectual titles ("You're a Marxist"; "You're a Freudian") on the strength of very little knowledge. We did write a lot of papers that might have been called "Me and the Sexual Revolution" or "Me and the Emerging Nations" or "Me and Herbert Marcuse."

We need not have had these weaknesses if we had maintained any clear sense of and feeling for composition. Radical subject matter is manageable — just — even in a classroom, so long as it is kept in subordination to a severe discipline in reflection and articulation. When that discipline is the prime concern of the course one can handle any kind of subject matter, even the radical kind implicitly hostile to liberal studies. But composition had become identified, in most teachers' minds, with a set of utilitarian skills, to be learned — this was the absurd theory — by studying Aristotle and John Stuart Mill and John Henry Newman. However, the inappropriateness of the models is not the point, but the inadequacy of the aims. The art of orderly exposition cannot seem important enough to impose itself as a discipline on a mind fired by the idea of revolution. But if English departments had believed that composition meant more than orderly exposition, meant teaching — for example, how to write and to think like Orwell — had believed in the essay form as an expression of passionately reflected-on experience, they would have had just as full-time a job teaching it to well-prepared freshmen today — to freshmen interested in revolution — as they had in the age of conformity. Used that way, the essay form was in fact to become a major form in our decade, as Mailer has shown, but the bright young men in English departments believed in the fictive and the mythical and "form." The composition men believed in teaching the students to write like the rhetoric manual examples. The American academy has never had even as much of a common culture tradition as the British academy — minor though that tradition is there — and we did not build it up when we had the chance. We squandered our strength, we threw away the advantages of our position; and now we find ourselves in a situation that would anyway be difficult — having to blame ourselves. We in Academia, as well as They in Washington, have something to expiate.

But this is all accusation of others, since I myself always believed in composition. There are other problems for the profession, other causes of the English teacher's unease, for which I must accuse myself equally. We have most of us played the radical, and now find we never meant it. There are too many things radicalism legitimately can mean which, now we are faced with them, we find we don't like. Constant critical response, constant challenge to the teacher, can impede the educational process; particularly that public, classroom, part of it which is our job. Just as constant testing of ideas against experience, against action, can impede the intellectual mastery of those ideas. The typical English department member has been a crypto-liberal, disguised as a radical, a sheep in wolf's clothing.

This makes it difficult to say and do radical things now, especially when everyone is competing in radicalism. Moreover, our subject matter has lost status. Nowadays the bright, committed, serious students — *our* students — major in political science, sociology, anthropology; and when they come to us for a course they find — we find — no way to ally our subject matter with their concerns. Our once radical novels and poems no longer even criticize society effectively. By the standards of revolutionary social action, all literature belongs together — it is *literature*.

Our social role has changed. Our task as responsible teachers is no longer to urge our students to take up more boldly radical positions, to let go of traditional safeguards, intellectual, moral, social; it is to ask them to be more cautious, to be sure they have really read the book, to give what they condemn a fair hearing, to go slower, to distrust their own passion. We no longer lead, we hold back. We no longer stand on the opposite side of them from their parents. Like America in the world, we have lost our democratic-cowboy glamour, our radical-progressive denim. We stand revealed as liberals, the most shameful kind of nakedness, because liberals are eunuchs.

With the whole discipline of college relaxed (there is less regular attendance at classes, etc.) our identity as teachers is emasculated. The initiative now lies with the students in matters where it used to lie with the faculty. In our department, we have now abolished all requirement of courses for the major. We now only suggest certain sequences of courses. We make ourselves available for consultation; and our triumph is the feminine one of being sought out; failure is to be left alone in our office, a wallflower. Empty chairs in the classroom now condemn the teacher, not the absent students. The responsibility lies with the teacher to make himself attractive, and keep himself attractive, to each new class he meets. No wonder we are anxious.

In that situation, the teacher who wants to keep in touch with his students has to renounce the authority he used to derive from just being teacher, from the mere machinery of the academy and ultimately of society. He must now derive his authority from his personal qualities directly, either by making each class self-justifying intellectually, or by sheer size of personality. For many teachers — for me — justifying each class hour as it goes along means narrowing the margins of freedom crucially. It means reading a verdict in the students' eyes every twenty minutes instead of every two weeks. That this should happen is of course the ideal of the radical students; they exhort the others not to accept what a teacher says and does just because he is a teacher, but to criticize, to object, to demand something relevant. This admirable principle, which I myself have no doubt recommended in the past, is what when now put into practice prevents me from relaxing sufficiently with a class to give them the best benefit of what I know. I live in nervous solicitation of their approval.

So we are anxiously anxious, with a quasi-sexual anxiety, and we protagonize all the other anxious and guilty sectors of society. We were a part of it; we had our counterparts for its past failings, and for its present ineffectuality. The gold which turns to feces in the hands of our pupils' parents is like the books which go dead on our shelves. Criticism was not enough. Our neglect of composition was like the whole society's neglect of quality-of-life. Our pseudoradicalism was like its pseudoegalitarianism.

So for us too the future promises decline and diminution, and the past, even while we yearn back for it, implies a condemnation. We enjoyed our fat years stupidly. We did not provide for the winter. We let a bland complacency falsify our politics, and an unreal radicalism dandify our cultural gestures. And in consequence we are confronted by three great specters of reproach: Youth, corporate Youth, rioting, occupying our buildings, protesting our war; the Blacks, in their ghettos, discovering our slavery, their violence coming out of our violence; and the Radicals, people like Mailer, who protested clamorously at a time when we thought such protests exaggerated.

This book is an attempt to deal with those three specters. Not by the classic method of either beating them or joining them. I cannot pass myself off as either young, black, or radical. And I am not ready to attack, at least not head on. I am looking for other ground to stand on, that would justify my being different from them, justify my being liberal. Some of their condemnations I must accept, but some of the recommendations, the exhortations, which they attach as by necessity to the judgment, I want to reject. Naturally, if I succeed in finding that other ground, I shall have turned their flank, and so attacked, laterally. I shall have created not only the liberal position, that elliptical shape disallowed in radical geometry, but a new, total space which does allow it, and so reduces radicalism to one mode among many, which denies the porro unum necessarium.

AS A LIBERAL

I take it for granted here that a liberal position, or what that was and would be but for radical pressure, is inadequate today. My interest here is to explain how I came to be liberal by temperament.

It is clear now that I always was a liberal, and yet in my youth I used to think of myself as being rather radical — about literary and cultural matters, at least. But my position was better described as liberal, because it was an ellipse, with two foci, two centers of energy. Every man's position is likely to have at least two such centers, perhaps, whether he is liberal or not. But the metaphor of the ellipse belongs to the liberal position, because it means that the two foci are significantly far from each other but have equal power. And though one focus of my position (which I imitated from F. R. Leavis when I was his student at Cambridge) was recognizably radical, and potentially political, the other was primarily aesthetic and potentially conservative, or apolitical. This last was his concern for both imaginative purity, freedom, and for cultural continuity, tradition. These two things, freedom and tradition, go together for a Leavisite, and his concern for them is balanced against a concern for Puritan values in cultural things, a distrust of the elegant, the worldly, the amoral, the frivolous. Because he finds that second focus of concern so forcefully developed in D. H. Lawrence, as well as the concern for freedom and tradition, Lawrence is his exemplary author even more than James or Eliot. And these literary preferences carry with them a whole range of left-wing opinions, or tendencies to opinion, in political and social matters, which I more or less adopted. This was the position which I mistook for radical.

In those days, in the forties and fifties in England, Leavis seemed radical. In the alternative position (we associated it with Bloomsbury) both foci were implicitly conservative; its counterpart for Leavis's Puritanism was an anti-Puritanism, a love of the worldly, the elegant, the amoral, the frivolous. But, more important, Leavis *sounded* radical. He was a radical *personality*. He was a force for radicalism even when he was saying reactionary things, as he did in the Two Cultures controversy. These positions must always be matters of temperament as well as of ideology, and for some cases it is worthwhile to separate those two ranges of meaning, because the one has much more explanatory power than the other. In some cases, we see how fragments of ideology are cemented together by, and encourage the development of, secretions and spasms of personal feeling, to form a temperament that is more aggressively and consistently "engaged" than a man's actual opinions. Leavis was radical in that sense, and in the same sense I — like lots of others — was temperamentally radical during the years just after I left Cambridge; the years when I wrote my first book, *Mirror for Anglo-Saxons*. I shall keep coming back to these ideas, of position and of temperament, throughout the book, so I must define them with some care. They are to be organizing ideas for the whole argument. But, to avoid delay at this point, I have removed that definition to the end of the chapter, and put it together with other definitions and formulas, under the heading, "The Intellectual Machinery of the Argument." It will be found there, if anyone wishes to look ahead, in the form that suits the use just made of those terms.

To resume, I came to America seeming to myself to be a radical. But being here, in Eisenhower's America, which was provoking Mailer to such rage, pacified me. "The shits are killing us" is how he put it in *Advertisements for Myself*. But I came in 1952, and lived through the McCarthy era, yet what America meant to me was variety, freedom, gaiety, the release from the compulsion to be angry. This was because I was realizing how many resentful, indignant, even apocalyptic attitudes had been engrafted on me in England in the name of radicalism — attitudes to general public phenomena, but "spontaneous" attitudes, radically emotional, rooted in my unconscious life and secreting a bitterness quite unintellectual. The anger, to put it crudely, was my own; Leavis had attributed ideological values and functions to it; then America showed me an alternative interpretation. I resolved, unconsciously, to invest my energies in avoiding partisan roles henceforth, in seeing myself instead as part of a consensus, part of a cooperation of disparates.

I acknowledged how much someone like me depended on forms and divisions and order and rules, how much I benefited from belonging to a de facto society. However severely I might, as the agent of Criticism, hold at arm's length the Idea of that society, I embraced the fact as something to lean on and grow along. I realized how much I owed it even for being an artificial and repressive construct; how much of my inner life derived from my performing prescribed tasks and being rewarded for them; how much in me that people knew as me was socially constituted; how little I made of myself by really direct, unmediated impact on others. My life was largely a matter of intelligence, and of that self-alienated kind which operates best in the cool medium of books. It derived from self-alienation, and — by analogy — from an alienating society; in a truly "organic" society of wholly un-self-alienated people that intelligence would have a much-diminished value and function. I recognized a similarity between the mechanisms and prosthetics of that society, its failures in "organic" life, and those in my own personality. I acknowledged a kinship. I saw myself as belonging to that society as well as deriving from it, as criticizing it imaginatively rather than as subverting it politically.

The America with that message, the one I listened to, was the one Mailer denounced and contradicted, and when, nowadays, I read over his pieces of 1952, I realize that he was by and large right. He was saying that men of intelligence must, in America, as a moral duty, be alienated. In his "Our Country and Our Culture," reprinted in *Advertisements for Myself*, he called for an American genius, obviously intending to become it himself. "If and when he arrives may I speculate that he will be more concerned with 'silence, exile, and cunning' than a strapping participation in the vigors of American life." We all deserve one smile at the thought of Mailer practicing silence — and who has been more strapping than he? — but after that we must admit that he was right. He succeeded in becoming America's genius. Resolute and unrewarded denunciation of the status quo did prove truer to his and our deepest feelings than any other response.

However, to many British writers of about my age, America meant much the same thing as it meant to me; that is, an invitation to enjoy life and to slip the traces of old moral compulsions. My response was more than an individual phenomenon. It fitted into a marked cultural pattern. This has been expressed in a number of British novels in which the central character, who represents the novelist, comes to the U.S.A., responds reluctantly to its various challenges and invitations, gradually makes up his mind for it as opposed to England, but (usually) returns home nevertheless, feeling unable to meet those challenges adequately. I'm thinking of Malcolm Bradbury's *Stepping Westward*, Kingsley Amis's *One Fat Englishman*, Julian Mitchell's *As Far as You Can Go*, Andrew Sinclair's *The Hallelujah Bum*, and David Lodge's (somewhat different) *Out of the Shelter*. Taken together, these add up to a recognizable genre of British fiction in the fifties and sixties to which my own novel would also belong. Though they do not deny the tragic elements in the American situation, they respond more to the comic elements. They see even the tragic as comic, in the sense that it is another manifestation of the whole country's size and vitality, its oppositeness to the smallness and claustrophobia of Britain. These were all anti-Calvinist-radical, would-be Faustian-conservative novels. The radical, the serious, British fiction of the time was being written by Raymond Williams and Doris Lessing. And they were able to keep their seriousness only by resolutely turning their faces away from America. The price they paid for their purity (I'm not for the moment saying that it was excessive) is evident in their work.

In essay form, some of the later parts of *Mirror for Anglo-Saxons* (1960) express this same determination to take America as the land of comedy, as a guarantor of the playful approach to life in general. And in *Reappraisals* (1963) I backed Salinger and Nabokov as artistic exemplars of what I mean by comedy. Half of the spirit of *Reappraisals* is Leavisite, what Leavis should have said about American literature — a commonsense repudiation of the pretentious. The standardized rise and fall of Faulknerian fury seemed to me then (still seems to me) second rate in comparison with, say, Lawrence's denunciations of industrialism and technology. I rejected Faulkner as failing by the high standards of that crusade. But the other half of my book's motivation is a refusal of those standards, a refusal to swallow the American version, the American equivalent, of Lawrence's and Leavis's prophetic anger against "England." The pious obbligato of American critics responding to Faulkner's vatic intonings was something I seized the chance to challenge. Indirectly and unconsciously I was challenging my own old radical pieties — though that challenge was only literary-critical at the time. It is a relief to find how few of the particular judgments and arguments of that book I now have to disavow. But the taste from which they derived now does seem to me to some degree vitiated; foolishly bland, over-lyrical, lightweight, unserious — liberal in the bad sense.

But I can see why I, unlike Mailer, had to move in that direction, when I reread Orwell. Take this passage from "Inside the Whale."

To say "I accept" in an age like our own is to say that you accept concentration camps, rubber truncheons, Hitler, Stalin, bombs, aeroplanes, tinned foods, machine guns, putsches, purges, Bedaux belts, gas masks, submarines, spies, provocateurs, press censorships, secret prisons, aspirins, Hollywood films, and political murders.

Such a sentence puts one in an impossible position. One can't go on saying "I don't accept" to all those things. Indeed, what is called for is a stronger phrase, "I reject" or "I denounce." You can't go on saying that to so much of life, especially when your father (Orwell) said it before you. You find you like tinned foods and Hollywood films, you quite like aeroplanes and submarines, and aspirins have their uses. There was bound to come a contrary reaction in anyone who had tried to believe that.

It was not, obviously, bound to go in the direction mine took. It could have been a reaction like Raymond Williams's, toward a more radical and political temperament, with more uniform seriousness. But Orwell himself invited us to go in the direction away from political radicalism. In literary matters he was an Erasmian, and his imaginative sympathies went rather to Faustian than to Calvinist radicalism. In "Inside the Whale" he talks mostly about Henry Miller, whom he visited in Paris on his way to Spain to take part in the Civil War. Miller as man and artist fascinated Orwell just because he did accept "an age like our own." He accepted the end of Western culture in internalized terms as well as in terms of institutions and buildings; he had rejected the decency and the intense concern for values which Orwell so prized. Despite his rebelliousness, Orwell, like Leavis, believed very much in cultural continuity. He responded to a care for that even in political conservatives like Eliot, because in literary matters the temperament of both men was equally Erasmian, equally English. But, and this was more remarkable in an Englishman, he responded also to the opposite in Miller. We may even guess that he recognized a superiority in Miller's fiction over his own in imaginative vitality, and saw the connection between his own fictional failure and his preoccupation with decency. That guess seems legitimate because of Orwell's fascination with Joyce, and his comparison of his own novels with *Ulysses*. He said that put beside *that* novel, his own writing sounded like the singing of a eunuch who had taken a course in voice production and could pass himself off as a baritone. And the truth is that he was right. We literary men brought up on Orwell had that discovery waiting for us, to guide our reaction against his limitations, and with his sympathies, toward the omnivorous, apolitical modernism of Miller and Joyce. Brought up by Leavis on Lawrence, our first unguided, tottering step had to be toward recognizing the other Lawrence, the modernist author hidden by Leavis behind the English moralist. It was just because Raymond Williams offered us nothing comparable that we felt — and I still think that we were right — that his imaginative path led toward no exciting perspectives. It is Mailer's achievement to have shown us the way through that anti-decent, omnivorous modernism to his own kind, which is now *our* kind, of politics in art. On the whole, the English writers of this century, and the last, have refused to make the Faustian bargain out of which modernist art comes.

It is time to define what I mean by Faustian, and by Erasmian, and by Calvinist. My fuller definitions I have kept for the "intellectual machinery" section at the end of the chapter, but the crux of the three ideas is soon given. They are three temperamental types, corresponding to the three political positions, conservative, liberal, and radical, which I want to characterize as deriving each from its own kind of spiritual bargain, compact, or exchange. The Faustian, or diabolic, bargain is that by which a man of imagination sells his soul (his sense of his own decency, normality, morality) in exchange for giant powers, swollen organs, of personality and of intuitive knowledge. The Erasmian bargain is the normal growing-up exchange of appetitive and instinctive energy for intellectual and moral civilizedness. And the Calvinist is the compact of the saints, of the dedicated members of an ideologically radical party, to exchange their individual freedoms for a group identity which will enable them to save the people. The Calvinist and the Faustian bargains are the two standard ways for intellectuals to escape the diminishment and enfeeblement of experience, the two-dimensionalizing of the soul, which can accompany growing up, especially in men devoted to ideas, men who live by the life of the mind.

The immediate autobiographical application of this theory is that in my Cambridge days, I, like many other people, had been induced by Leavis (and Orwell and Lawrence) to establish my identity in his radicalism, his double repudiation of "civilization" — a civilization which had been identified for us with Bloomsbury — his double escape, in two opposite directions at the same time, from the feebleness of being merely literary. We identified ourselves both with Leavis's own Faustian splendors of personality — from most Leavisites their literary opinions come forth with the voice of a lion out of the mouth of a lamb — and also with the Leavisite saints' mission to redeem a fallen world and preserve a saving remnant. America taught me that I participated in both those temperamental styles only minimally, phonily, by mimicry — that I myself had never really transacted either bargain. My real identity was established in an Erasmian contract, and for that temperament the naturally corresponding position was liberal.

My "radicalism" was all of the Freshman English teacher type, circumscribing itself in the intellectual-imaginative sphere, limited by temperament to ineffectuality in times of crisis. It fostered a capacity for radical action in others, but not in myself. Like Erasmus's own radicalism, its most forceful expression was a bitter humor, which when confronted by an active attack on the abuses satirized, contracted into nervous silence. My mind's virtues all belonged to the liberal temperament: clarity, honesty, justice, flexibility. Of capacity for moral passion, as implemented by either a creed and group discipline, or by sheer personality power, I had very little.

My next book, *Science and the Shabby Curate of Poetry* (1964), gave me the chance to challenge Leavis more directly, and to disaffiliate myself from the education that had falsified me. It was written during a two-year return to England, when I was trying to acquire a smattering of the scientific culture. I claimed to trace (quite correctly, I still think) an imbalance of temperament, a readiness to denounce, an us-against-them psychology, to the literary-centered, science-hostile training which Cambridge had given me. And I sketched out for myself a different intellectual ideal, a humanism which would be equally committed to both art and science. This tension-free ideal, committed to the free play of the mind over all subjects, is of course an expression of the Erasmian temperament. I was extending the boundaries of my liberalism, strengthening its intellectual foundations, purifying it of its radical-aggressive taint. Unluckily for me, liberalism is an ideology for ages of peace and prosperity, of compromise and conformity and consensus. In an age of revolution, you have to change your ideology and — if you are to avoid acute discomfort — the temperament that goes with it. If you are heavily committed to the Erasmian temperament, you are in for trouble.

In 1965, after having taught for two years again in America, I went back to England to teach at the University of Birmingham. There I was forced to take account of the British New Left, the radical development of the heritage I had repudiated. This was of course an uncomfortable challenge. I was forced to take account, for instance, of how scornful a title my chosen label of "liberal" could be made to sound. I was then finishing *The Problem of Boston* (1965), a book only obliquely ideological, being an account of literature and society in nineteenth-century Boston, but still anti-radical in tendency, because it is directed against the condemnation of that society, and the despair over society in general, which is taken for granted by so many American Faustians and Calvinists. It was even positively liberal, in its endorsement of much of the early work of Yankee Boston, which was a corporate manifestation of the Erasmian temperament, repressing appetite and crude ego in order to put that energy into the pursuit of light of all kinds. I protested against that scorn for genteel values which comes so easily to both aesthetes and political puritans.

And in my last book, *Yeats's Blessings on Von Hügel* (1967), I tried to root this tensionless humanism in religion, finding the Erasmian temperament in Roman Catholicism itself — in one kind of Catholicism, that is. I related von Hügel and his liberal-humanist Catholicism to the Catholic humanism of St. Francis de Sales and Fénelon, and contrasted it with the reactionary Catholicism of Greene and Waugh, Mauriac and Bernanos. I also contrasted it with the Symbolist aestheticism of Yeats and Nabokov, and with the Socialist realism of Sholokhov. I thus again repudiated the Faustian as well as the Calvinist temperaments, and all mixtures of the two, like reactionary Catholicism — repudiated them as obligatory on men of letters and on me. I contrasted the advantages of humanism with the disadvantages of puritanism for the writer who belives in a totalitarian creed like Catholicism or Communism. And I said to myself that with that book I had finished a whole enterprise. I had defined my position, I had established my liberalism, I had established my identity.

And so, in 1968, I found myself returning to the U.S.A. after a three-year absence, determinately liberal, and resigned to meet, as I in fact met, a series of situations in which everyone's actions defined him as either radical or conservative; in which there was no option of action that could mark one as a liberal. But the disturbance of the meeting was more than my defined position, my established identity, could take care of. In discussing the daily news, as in the daily business of teaching, I found myself humiliated. If I had had a Faustian temperament, I could have retreated within the kingdom of my own personality, or within a mystical or nihilistic cynicism. If I'd had a Calvinist temperament, I could have joined, as my opinions impelled me to join, in the group movements, the strikes, the sit-ins, the marches, the committees, the moratoriums. But with an Erasmian temperament, one is conscious mainly of negations and unresponsivenesses. One feels constantly at fault and in lack and failing. One is too deeply implicated in the world which one is called on to attack.

But one is just as deeply committed to the principles and the logic by which one is called on to attack. The challenge to move outside that society, to re-form my temperament, comes most sharply from radical priests, like the Fathers Berrigan in this country, and Father McCabe in England. I shall have more to say about them later. Let me cite now instead — almost the whole radical Catholic movement makes the same impact — the trial of the Milwaukee 12, as reported in the *New York Review of Books*, September 25, 1969. They were on trial for having napalmed ten thousand draft records twelve months before, and the report forces the reader to identify with either them or the judge, the Court.

THE COURT: I shall not permit any testimony about the fairness of the draft or the fact that it discriminates against some, and as far as the Vietnam War is moral or anything else, it is not relevant here.

FRED OJILE: Oh for God's sake, don't give me that. What do you think we're playing, tiddly winks?

Mr. Ojile is described as "a wiry youngster whose sunken cheeks, abundant hair, and stalking stride give him a startling resemblance to Nureyev."

Howard Zinn gave testimony that "there's a vast difference between a person who commits an ordinary crime and a person who commits an act which technically is a crime, but which in essence is a social act designed to make a statement." . . .

(Wild clapping from the audience, a few shouts.)

THE COURT: I must stop you. There was an objection to that . . . did someone cry out back there?

FATHER MULLANEY: The whole American people are crying out, Your Honor.

A little later:

DOUG MARVY: Do you as a historian see any connection between the Declaration of Independence and the act which has brought us twelve defendants here today?

ZINN: Yes, I . . .

MR. SAMPSON: I object to that . . . Mr. Marvy knows that these questions are immaterial, and that he is just asking them to inflame the jury.

THE COURT: Objection sustained.

MARVY: I find that kind of a disgusting comment (the prosecution) is able to read my mind. I'm not asking these questions because I think they're immaterial — they are the most material things I can think of. Burglary, arson and theft are immaterial. The Court has ruled that screwdrivers are relevant and dead bodies aren't. What the hell!

Doug Marvy's voice was loud and threatening.

The moral advantage lay with the defendants all the time. The prosecuting D.A.s were both young and liberal, one Jewish, the other black, both supporters of McCarthy and opponents of the Vietnam War — but liberals. Mr. Jackson, the black D.A., finally declared: "It is impossible for the State represented by human beings to sit here any longer having it said that they believe in and of themselves that poverty and the war are irrelevant." His voice broke. "I just can't take it," he said.

But the defendants were merciless. "He's put out," Doug Marvy said, "and I think that's just plain tough. . . . He says he doesn't know what to do, and I see four doors in this room and that's a perfectly reasonable choice for him. He can quit any time."

Marvy, twenty-eight, the only Jewish member of the group, was a graduate student in mathematics at Yale and the University of Minnesota.

The judge, known as "Grandpa" to the defendants, also broke down, in the act of sentencing Father Mullaney. He is described as a "loyal, soft-hearted, sentimental man . . . more aggrieved than annoyed . . . a benign, gauche man in his sixties." As he began to sentence Father Mullaney, he "choked on that good Irish name, and fumbled among his black robes for a handkerchief. He wept for a few seconds, and then in timorous voice resumed sentencing the monk who stood before him triumphantly, dressed in clerical black, his arms folded as if he were the executioner."

When the sentences were read out there was great excitement in the audience. "We thank you, men and women of the jury," shouted Sister Joanna Malone of the D.C. 9 raiders, a nun who specializes in liturgical dancing, "for finding Jesus Christ guilty again." The nun's voice set off a burst of rhythmical applause by the two hundred people wedged into the courtroom, a chorus of sobbing and weeping, a melee of clenched fists and V signs. Dozens of spectators rose, linked arms through the courtroom, and swayed, singing, "We shall overcome . . ." "I pity the nation that fears its young," Father Mullaney blasted out.

In the hall outside the courtroom one hundred persons still milled about. Three young men burned their draft cards, and the supporters of the Milwaukee 12 made the sign of the cross on their foreheads with the remaining ashes. The trial ended, as it had proceeded, in a bizarre mixture of burlesque and religious fervor.

This is moral triumphalism, moral Faustianism, and challenged by it I feel what Erasmus did when challenged by Luther and the Lutherans. Clearly there is something morally and religiously splendid here; equally clearly, there are objections one might reasonably urge against it. But above all I feel the temperamental incompatibility of both those splendors and those weaknesses with the liberal mind. This has nothing to do with how right one judges those men to have been. As far as I am concerned, they were right, and the judge was wrong, as far as positions go. But as I read, my sympathies go reluctantly with the judge; by virtue of my temperament. Their mode of feeling and acting and being — so independent of institutional support, so defiant of "propriety" — derives from a psychic contract which is fundamentally unlike mine.

And so, instead of feeling free to write fiction, as I'd promised myself after my last book, I am compelled again to seek out historical examples, construct arguments, define positions. Drowning in uncertainty again, I try to nail together a raft out of flotsam and jetsam. It is flotsam because of my own fragmentariness, the incompatibility of aspirations and identities, which leaves gapings, leaks, shifts of level. My final formula, an Erasmian temperament but a radical position, is still trying to have things both ways. But the materials of my raft are of the noblest.

Already before I left England, I was finding myself drawn more and more to Goethe. Partly, perhaps, because he is the great authoritarian, the great political conservative, among literary figures; in times of revolution, a liberal starts to look for authoritarian conservatives to lean on. But also because Goethe is the ultimate source, as I gradually realized, for many of the large *liberal* ideas which I acquired in my clumsy retreat from radicalism. He is in some ways the greatest example of the liberal position in cultural matters. (The paradox of his being both conservative and liberal I try to explain in Chapter 4). He is the supreme exemplar of the arts-and-sciences humanism I aspired to in *Science and the Shabby Curate of Poetry*. He is the great inspirer of von Hügel and George Eliot and the other heroes of *Yeats's Blessings on Von Hügel*. I daresay even von Hügel's hobby of geology was a legacy from Goethe. Emerson, a hero of *Reappraisals*, learned almost everything from him. And Weimar, the Kulturstadt, the city of light, stood behind Carlyle and Emerson and nineteenth-century Boston. It also stood behind Arnold and therefore behind Leavis and both men's culture idealism and culture criticism; therefore, behind *Mirror for Anglo-Saxons*. Moreover, Goethe had lived through an age of revolution, *the* other age of revolution to which we may look back as a warning of what may well (though as yet it may not) happen to us.

Goethe and his city, Weimar, were the first thing I knew I had to explore in order to discover better where I stood and how to explain it. And opposite to it I set the challenging figure of Mailer and his city of New York. Though indeed Mailer is like Goethe in some respects — notably in his free ways with science and with religion — and they are not to be taken as opposites from every point of view. A better antithesis to Goethe is Blake. They too shared more than one would think at first glance, but their careers, and the policies those careers express, do diverge widely and do present us with a rich landscape of choice. Moreover, Blake's London, the radical London of the 1790's, promised a different set of fruitful comparisons with Mailer's and our New York. And in between Weimar and London it seemed interesting to set up for study the liberal city of Edinburgh in the same period, the city of Scott and the *Edinburgh Review* and the Encyclopaedia Britannica. Thus far, then, the book shaped itself as an investigation of four cities of culture — that is, of the cultural aspects, the cultural form and persona, of those cities — in ages of revolution; three of them in the age before our own; illustrating three different policies of cultural response to the facts of their revolution, so that we might compare their literary results, and apply their patterns to our own situation.

To explain why other elements get into the book, I had better pursue my autobiographical reflections into different aspects of my autobiography.

AS WHITE, ANGLO-SAXON, ETC.

As White. Like everyone else, I have a part of me now always alerted toward black people. Toward the ghetto and the South, toward Harlem tenements and tar-paper shacks. Toward Africa and the slave trade and colonialism, toward Frantz Fanon and Che Guevara, that other kind of white Negro, post-Marxist instead of post-Freudian. Toward Eldridge Cleaver, Claude Brown, Malcolm X, Leroi Jones.

Like other people I am alerted in lots of different ways, and not many of them generous. Those sullen black faces in class, armored into impersonality, joining themselves to all and only the other black faces, being their skins and not their minds; all that is a trial and a nuisance to me as teacher. And walking across campus, when two or three are gathered together, it is always in the name of blackness, and they constitute a phalanx. They are the elect, the party, joined each to each in a compact of the saints. They are locking themselves away from my kind of intelligence, which is so much a matter of flexibility and lightness of grip and readiness to let go; and for that I refuse to feel guilty. The guilt must be expiated by other means; the guilt *feelings*, now that they are socially required, are a campus miasma, poisonous to the life of the mind. I set out my wares as best I can, and since I know they won't buy for another decade at least, I must make myself some armor of my own to protect me from the drafts while I wait.

But behind them stand their leaders, who hold me, my mind, in subjection. Not as writers, festooned with the rave notices we have given them. As so often happens, the liberal segment of high culture is overenacting what it wants the culture as a whole to do, and creating a foolish parody, in some ways positively dangerous. But as nonwriters, as star speakers and actors and mimes in the resonant theater of our times, stars of the hot media. In an age of revolution the cool media go at a discount, and the bookman, poor worm, is limply impotent. He watches from his hole, congratulating himself if he is allowed to be — luckier than Erasmus himself — a spectator at this tragedy. Of course there are things to do. But when they are done — even while you are doing them — you are still a spectator. They tell you so, and they are right. At times you are even an enemy, and you must be alert to them the way a fat house dog is alert in a wood full of wolves. *His* feelings are not primarily generous.

Out of this alertness comes, principally, Part II of this book. There in a sense the black faces ring themselves round my native village in Shropshire. Also comes my trip to Havana, and my essay on Cuban literature and the revolution.

As Anglo-Saxon. The more we are all confronted by the blacks, the more the Anglo-Saxons feel themselves merely white, find themselves shoulder to shoulder with the Jews, the Italians, the

Irish, all those old-time antagonists, those former virtuosi of sex and sentiment. It is a moment of gentle triumph for us. We welcome them into the brotherhood. We have so much to teach them about how to feel uptight with resignation. We fully realize how hard it must come to be no longer figures of untidy passion or warmhearted eccentricity, but coldhearted, precise possessors, as anal as the next man. It is really very unfair. But that is the way it is. The Great Casting Director only wants black faces for Faustian roles now. The public demands it.

But things haven't gone all the way yet. Shoulder to shoulder with Robert Lowell on the march to the Pentagon, Norman Mailer still feels him a foreign body. And the three men who have most represented America to me since I came back this last time have been non-Anglo-Saxons; Sal Abbadessa, my landlord, Sol Gittleman, who teaches German at Tufts, and Father Fitzgerald, the Catholic chaplain there. Italian, Jewish, Irish, each one still derives some of his vitality from feeling himself not Anglo-Saxon. That is why they are so alike. They are all short, bouncy, broad-shouldered men, energetic, irritable, capable, round-faced, sunny-tempered; favorite sons, favorite brothers, favorite fathers; great creators of comedy, creators of life, wherever they go. This is of course the old liberal America, the land of comedy, the perfect home for an Erasmian exile; a great relief from England, where one must admit that such qualities are in shorter supply; but they play out these roles now against the background not of Beacon Hill but of Roxbury; their antagonist is no longer the prim Yankee but the violent black.

So there is not so much in this book that derives from my feeling Anglo-Saxon; but still my interest in Mailer and New York is an interest in Jewishness. What a relief it will be to bookmen soon not to have to measure themselves always against Jews.

As Catholic. The Church is another scene of revolution. Among intelligent and sensitive Catholics the hierarchy is anathema, the structure of the Church is evil, the ceremonial of the Mass, the institution of the priesthood, even the sacraments themselves, are under attack, while old shibboleths like Thomism haven't been mentioned in years. And the faces of a few heroic priests, as I've said, present the swordlike challenge of radicalism more authentically than anything else.

But by and large what is replacing the old Church around here is genteel and liberal — at its best sensitive and intelligent — rather than radical. We sing folk-songs to guitars; emancipated nuns do modern dance in the sanctuary; we give each other the kiss of peace; loving couples bring the bread and wine to the altar hand in hand, and go back down the aisle exchanging melting glances; the priest shares experiences with us, or induces a dialogue, at sermon time. Spontaneous petitions replace set prayers, priests talk angrily against Rome from what would once have been the pulpit, we have advances instead of retreats, and on them the participants are subjected to total media experiences.

All this, while upsetting to a conservative, might seem sure to feel innocuous, where not positively welcome, to a liberal. And it often does, taken bit by bit. Even taken as a whole, I am not ready to be apocalyptic about it — the old Church was so bad that one cannot see it go without relief — though the situation does of course induce anxiety. But what makes my kind of liberal more upset is the religious attack on the Erasmian temperament. All these new Catholic activities are calls to community — to the community of love.

The same call goes out in secular society in many forms of sensitivity training and T groups. Love is the ultimate perspective behind the short-term aims of those courses. In other words, you find the same range of aspiration, with the same range of varieties within it, inside the Church as outside it. But I am exposed to the aspiration and the call in its Catholic form. And it is an attack on the Erasmian temperament because it calls on men to give back their separateness, their identity as organs of judgment, their mental transcendence of their bodily and emotional selves (their habits of abstraction and criticism), in order to relocate their identities in their bodies, in their senses, in their merging with others. They must get in touch with themselves, and with others, and establish their identities in that touch.

At the price of yet more guilt, I have so far declined all these invitations. I could easily, of course, point out some ludicrous, and some dangerous, aspects to both the theory and the practice of sensitivity training; and of community loving. But suffice it to say that I see a more valuable vocation to remaining a liberal and an

Erasmian through such times as these, to maintaining an identity rooted in the mind as we have traditionally defined it.

So in this chapter, and again in Chapter 10, there is a good deal about my being a liberal, which derives from the loving pressure I feel on me from the new Church to become something else.

As Critic and Scholar and Full Professor and Married Man, etc. Two sections of the book derive from my activities as "scholar and professor." Chapter 6, on American cities in the period 1780–1820, is a version of a chapter in the Sphere books *History of American Literature*, though its organizing idea is new. And Chapters 7 and 8, "Other Cities, Other Ages, Other Revolutions" and "An Alternative for Intellectuals," both derive largely from courses I taught at Tufts this year. In this case too the relation between the book as a whole and this material was symbiotic. I chose to teach those courses in part because I was involved with these ideas. But those chapters came in the way they did because I am a professor.

Two other chapters take their form from my being a magazine writer. I wrote a piece on Weimar and another on Cuban literature and the revolution after visiting East Germany and Havana last summer; and some brief impressions of life in Havana. These have influenced the shape of Chapters 4 and 9. And to a less extent Chapters 3 and 5, on London and Edinburgh, were written as descriptions of a visit to those two cities, with the thought of making magazine pieces out of them.

And then there is a certain failure of passion I note, a fading of conviction in comparison even with my own earlier work, and which I attribute to age and establishment. One's opinions do get more "conservative" as one gets older, not out of cynicism about the world, but out of cynicism about oneself. If one makes use of the privileges and advantages that come with age, though still disapproving, still disassociating oneself from, the system that makes them come, must one not suspect one's disapproval — renounce it? If one does not in fact give up those advantages, must one not bring one's beliefs into conformity with one's behavior, however unintended? This is cynicism, because it makes a test of sincerity out of the willingness of an individual to oppose a whole system, which is severe. But a certain cynicism is as reasonable and honorable as idealism; and it is more natural after you have changed your opinions often, and seen that the opinions you are discarding were the expression of self-interest, of willful blindness, of resentment. You cannot henceforth be sure that the opinions you are adopting do not conceal the same worm in their bud. You necessarily hold them with some lightness of grip, some readiness to give them up. That is cynicism, and though it does not preclude passionate action, it does demand that mild opinions go with mild actions. And if so much is true of a change of opinions, and a discovery of false opinions, how much more results from a change of temperament and a discovery of false temperament, like mine?

As Myself. My argument asserts that we choose (affirm, confirm) our temperaments. But it perhaps implies, in certain passages and in its general shape, that they also choose us; that they are our fates, that we cannot change them. Now this is perhaps more true of me than of other people, more true in this one case than in general. The normal thing is that people can not only blend two temperaments, but alternate them — and alternate their blends. They can normally respond to the demands of a new age, even an age of revolution, with in effect a new temperament (assuming that they have some liberality of *mind*); in the same way as the social personality changes temperament to pass from work to play. But so to change is harder for some people than for others. Some temperaments are more of a conscious construct, have the rigidity of intentionality, are brittle. I myself seem to have embodied the negative principle so completely, so swallowed and retained the punishment cane of my early teachers; I so rejoice in negations, distinctions, separations, prohibitions, regulations, punishments, that I cannot think profitably about the largely affirmative and the freely joyful. I cannot make up my mind about nonpunitive teaching methods and nonrepressed children, because my touchstones ring false — I know *I* liked rules, but I suspect that I did so for bad reasons. Or, to take a political example, I resent people who demand a pay increase. I have so identified myself with the principle of self-restraint that I feel affronted when it is flouted. Both of these are of course generally Erasmian, up to a point. Negation and repression are the same thing, according to Freud. The grammatical forms of no and not, and the negative prefixes, un and dis and non, express the ability to repudiate something at the same moment as you apprehend it, to desire it and not desire it with the same impulse. Every Erasmian is by definition, by vocation, a negator. But mine seems to be an Erasmian squared, multiplied by itself, and reluctant to modulate into anything else. This may introduce an idiosyncrasy into my argument, an implication that these things are more rigidly separate than most people have found them to be, even people of Erasmian temperament. But it is not perhaps a disabling bias in a theoretician, because the man who feels himself restricted explores his confines, and may possess them in a way useful to others. That is, after all, the source of half the useful knowledge in the world.

So that is how and why the book is what it is.

What the Book Is Not

It is not a book which explains why I am not for the revolution. Luckily, I don't yet have to know whether or not I am for it, not knowing what "the revolution" means. Of course, people usually don't know, even at the moment when they have to declare themselves, but luckily that moment has not yet come for us.

This is a book about the *concomitants* of revolution and of revolutionariness, about the *consequences* of political radicalism in nonpolitical areas of thought. And nonpolitical modes of thought even about politics. It is about the difference between the radical position and the Calvinist temperament, and it is an argument for the value of the Erasmian temperament in those areas. Its focus is on feeling, not action; guilt feelings, not guilts; literature, not politics. There *is* guilt, and there is action which must be taken, but someone else must write that book.

One might say that Chomsky has written it — and God knows plenty of other people have tried to. I would like to think that my book could be added on laterally to *American Power and the New Mandarins*, that it is not, as it may seem to be, contrary in tendency. There is nothing in common — in my judgment — between what I mean by calling myself a liberal, and what he means by a Kennedy liberal. Nor between my college English teacher and his new mandarins. I at least do not feel myself condemned by his analysis, except insofar as we are all condemned. I admire very much what Chomsky has done. For college teachers he must be an exemplary figure, the scholar who turned from his specialty to devote his energies to public affairs when the times demanded it. I agree with much of what he says about politics and history. But I think that his writing shows that erosion of liberal-intellectual values which so often happens when an Erasmian (all scholars are Erasmians, by virtue of their training) takes up a radical position. In other words, I think that his book gives occasion for mine, makes room for mine to be added to it, because it suffers from the defects as well as the virtues of radicalism.

For instance, in his discussion of Gabriel Jackson's history of the Spanish Civil War, Chomsky repeatedly says that he is not criticizing Jackson for his liberal opinions, for his lack of sympathy with the anarchists, or for his preference for the forces of law and order. Chomsky insists that he criticizes only the historian's failure to be objective. But the reader is left remembering that Jackson is a liberal, writes liberal history; and feeling that being a liberal means being unfair to anarchists. The idea of a liberal historian who would transcend the limitations of his opinions, and not deserve Chomsky's criticism, is a hard one to focus in the field of Chomsky's ideas in general; and if one does focus it the tendency and movement of those ideas in general becomes blurred. To put it another way, under the impact of Chomsky's moral passion, the reader cannot value "objectivity" very highly. Chomsky's critique is essentially radical, but it observes a liberal decorum and rationale which hobble its stride.

He says, "Thus . . . a headline in the *New York Times* can refer to Indian capitulation to American demands concerning the conditions of foreign investment as India's 'drift from socialism to pragmatism.' With this narrowing of the range of the thinkable comes an inability to comprehend how the weak and dispossessed can resist our benevolent manipulation of their lives, an incapacity to react in human terms to the misery that we impose." But what he is attacking here is *not* an inability to comprehend or an incapacity to react, but a lie, a mystification, a self-deception. What he wants from us is not more flexible imagination but more inflexible indignation, more rigorous cognition. He wants to *narrow* the range of the thinkable in us, to make one interpretation, and one only, impose itself on our minds, the porro unum necessarium.

These faded liberal banners, these feeble slogans, have no real function in his critique. The true function of liberal-intellectual values in the service of such moral passion is to recognize it and present it for what it is, to make it more itself, to disengage it from such irrelevant respectabilities.

The rash of quotation marks over Chomsky's page is another sign of what goes wrong. He constantly quotes his enemies, but without taking any real interest in their arguments. It is not even the *interest* of hatred, though hatred is certainly there. He doesn't care *how* and *why* they say these things. He has no imaginative identification with them. He quotes partly because their words signal an automatic response. They bring together all those in his audience whose attention might have been straying, or whose sympathies might have lapsed; the quotation renews their sense of community and dedication. But he quotes also partly because it is a scholarly habit, to display the evidence, to let the reader make up his own mind, to make impersonal reason, not passion, prevail.

I need not argue that these two intentions contradict and confuse each other. And there are signs of something similar in his thought as well as in his rhetoric. In "The Revolutionary Pacifism of A. J. Muste," he says, "The prediction that the United States would emerge as the world-dominant power was political realism; to forecast that it would act accordingly, having achieved this status by force, was no less realistic." But if to act accordingly with its statutes is to act as the U.S.A. *is* acting, why the moral indignation? If the way it is acting is in accordance with its status, then surely it is "the nature of things" which is to blame. (There is that puzzling clause "having achieved this status by force," but I suggest that both syntactically and logically that is a phony alternative, a protective device provoked by a sense on Chomsky's part of the dilemma he was getting into.) This is a significant point because major differences between the liberal and radical positions derive from their different answers to such questions. The liberal assumes that there is a "nature of things" in politics which filters and forms moral judgments, including among other things a tacitly admitted and permitted level of sordidness, of behavior unlike its professed aims; that an individual action is to be seriously attacked only when it exceeds that level, and then is to be criticized "politically."

The radical insists on absolute moral standards and purely moral indignation.

In most cases today — certainly in the case of the Vietnam War — I think that Chomsky is right. Radical moralism is the right approach, in our decade, to American policies at home and abroad. But one reads Chomsky wondering how he adjusts his moral standards to his sense of realism when he has to judge other decades and other political cases. On occasion he will talk of China being "quite naturally" disinclined to honor a harsh treaty obligation, and of repressive governments denying revolutionary movements their "natural" course of development. This implies that there is such a "nature" in politics, which contains, which gives shape to, the moral passion. But if so, why cannot the U.S.A. invoke the protection of that nature against absolute moral criticism like Chomsky's? One suspects that he has not worked hard at the mutual adjustment of these two key ideas in his argument, and that he has not done so because his effort has been directed mostly to attacking others, that he has not much considered defending himself, or even rationalizing his position. The strategies and the virtues of apologia go with the liberal temperament, and are easily lost to the radical.

Several of Chomsky's convincing analogies between American and Japanese aggression in Asia amount to proofs that American behavior is no better, even though we talk as if it were. The nonbeliever's response to that might be "That's the nature of politics" or perhaps "Let's then talk as immorally as we act." Chomsky clearly wants our response to be "Let's then act as morally as we talk." But there is nothing in his argument to enforce that and preclude the other; nothing but naked moral feeling. The detail of his examples, the substance of his comments, imply a political realism which is at war with that naked moralism, and the two need to be reconciled before they can legitimately give birth to his conclusions.

His dominant note seems to me the accusation that "the American leaders regard themselves as having *the right to* strike where and when they wish . . . regard the world as an American preserve." In other words, "*They* think they can do what they like." Whereas in fact, he implies, America has no *right* to do anything but withdraw, cease to be. America has *no* rights anymore. This emphasis (I myself have done the italicizing, of course) seems to me his central assertion — an assassination of his enemy's moral persona, of that "America" which lyingly speaks and acts in his name.

By putting the point that way, by insisting on the moral passion that animates his position, I don't mean to diminish its rational dignity. I mean to bring out its radicalism, and to repeat my point that the rational structure at present surrounding it seems to me an ineffective combination of liberal with radical elements. I would like to put the virtues of the liberal temperament really at the service of the radical passion.

Of the student generation in the Movement we might take Paul Cowan as representative. His book, *The Making of an Un-American*, shows that he was on the scene everywhere at the right moment, in Israel and Cuba and Mississippi as well as Choate and Harvard, in the Peace Corps and the *Village Voice* and a kibbutz and a Freedom House. His book's vulnerability is obvious. It would be inappropriate to direct any severity of criticism against it. But the vulnerability, the innocence, of the persona within it, might be mentioned briefly, because it exemplifies something important about liberalism in relation to movement leaders. Such a warmth of self-congratulation encloses the gestures of radicalism which Paul Cowan reports; such a warm enclave of mutual admiration as alienates even the politically sympathetic. When Cowan and his friends meet cynicism and repudiation from the people they are trying to help they sometimes blame Washington policies when they might blame their own moral-psychological policies. Self-awareness, self-criticism, self-irony, the traditional liberal awarenesses, would have helped them.

Cowan talks of his heroes being civil rights workers instead of football stars:

But that game ended the night that Andy Goodman, Mickey Schwerner, and James Chaney disappeared in Neshoba County, Mississippi. Rachel and I were then still in training at Western College for Women in Oxford, Ohio.

A few hours after we had learned that they were missing, I heard a girl yell at her mother, who had phoned her in a sudden panic, "If someone in Nazi Germany had done what we're doing then your brother would still be alive."

And:

The project seemed to be a turning point in America's history. We were an army of love, and if we integrated Mississippi we would conquer hate's capital. But if we were repulsed that summer then racism would triumph everywhere. My brother, Geoff, summarized our mood in a sentence. "I'm going," he told our parents, "because I don't know how to tell my grandchildren why I stayed home."

As delivered, face to face, face to *family* face, these remarks would be more impressive, of course. It is in book form, in the cool medium of the liberal mind, that they ring false. Reportage is the only printed form appropriate to such gestures. But even *viva voce*, when no longer directed at parents but at blacks in Mississippi and Ecuadorians while in the Peace Corps, they met with cruel rebuffs. As they would have done also from ideologists Cowan and his friends much admire, men like Mailer and Marx. Both Faustian and Calvinist radicalism derive from depths and intensities of moral emotional life, experiences of hot shame and cold alienation, severe efforts of sustained consciousness, which refuse to be subdued by, subordinated to, exempla of virtuous naïveté.

I felt much closer to Rachel during training than ever before. It was such a rich emotion, so filled with subtleties, such a welcome relief from the preoccupation with my career which had separated us when we lived in New York that for the first several weeks in Albuquerque I spent much more time savoring it than I did worrying about the classes or the other trainees. If anything, our sudden isolation from New York, the skepticism we shared about our work, the desire we nevertheless found ourselves sharing to discover ourselves in its midst, allowed us to explore entire areas of each other, share portions of ourselves, that would have remained tightly closed if we'd remained part of the raucous, ambitious crowd at the Big Fiesta.

This rather bleating tone about one's personal life is exactly what Mailer said — and said some time ago, in *The Armies of the Night* — puts him off from "liberals." As I am using the term, however, it is a liberal, or an Erasmian, irony that would be the best guard against it. The tone of *The Strawberry Statement* is even more incongruous with radicalism. This is prep-school prose, thick with the cream of privilege and the sugar of self-love. Both belong to Strawberry Fair. This language in the mouths of so many *soi-disant* "radicals" today suggests that it may be time for our opinion-makers to start handling the terms a different way; shifting the tonal biases built into these smooth and deadly bowls from the skittle-alley of ideas.

But I began by saying that I hoped my book could be taken in conjunction with Chomsky's, as not contrary in tendency to radicalism. Clearly I have in fact criticized both Chomsky and Cowan quite severely, and according to a tendency of my own, which must be called different from theirs. But I still hope that the criticism is usable and that the tendency is a matter of temperament and sensibility, not of position.

The Intellectual Machinery of the Argument

The key terms I want to define are "position" and "temperament" and "temperamental contract"; and then I have to describe in more detail the three psychological types which I am offering as major categories; briefly compare them with the categories Karl Mannheim uses in *Ideology and Utopia*; and finally give an example of a man who embodied more than one of these temperaments in his life, who chose to be one of them, to make himself one of them, after having been another, and who therefore demonstrates that voluntary and self-creating factor within the idea of temperament which in most people remains hidden.

By "position" I mean to evoke a geometrical image to describe the ideological configuration of a person's or a group's opinions. "Focus" is therefore one center of such opinions or interests, and I want its meaning to merge into that of "source," to include a sense of genesis and dynamism. Very few people are perfect circles. Most have more than one focus. Most also have excrescences, lopsidednesses, that are not geometrical at all. The geometrical character of a position (its classifiability, from my point of view) corresponds to the ideological character of the opinions. Conservative, liberal, and radical, understood as loosely as usual, are the only three positions, or categories of position, that seem necessary for my argument.

By "temperament" I mean to evoke a physiological-psychological image to describe the instinctive and reactive aspects of a person's or a group's interests and opinions. Rather like the four medieval humors, sanguine, bilious, atrabilious, and phlegmatic, I am going to define three temperaments, the Erasmian, the Faustian, and the Calvinist.

As categories, they will be used in two different ways. First of all, they imply that some important people are recognizable as either one or the other, or some blend. But secondly, that everyone, all the different temperaments and positions in the world, can be divided into three groups, which can be associated with these three types. This second categorization is very loose. Sometimes Faustian means only "more-Faustian-than-Erasmian-or-Calvinist"; just as conservative often means only "more-conservative-than-liberal-or-radical." Which is to say that it means very little, and I have tried to guard against using the terms that way. But I haven't entirely succeeded (there are argumentative virtues to using them loosely) and I must here warn readers that in the stricter sense of these categories, they do not apply to everyone.

Though the three temperaments correspond to the three positions, they are quite separable from them, and the correspondence is not one to one. Temperament shows itself in quite nonpolitical ways. One might say that all theater people tend to be Faustian, all schoolteachers Erasmian, all priests Calvinist. A given temperament may take up any one of the three "political" positions; and all three positions may be traced in some people — in their attitudes to different subjects. But however intricately the forms interact — so I claim — when you trace them out in a person or a problem you understand the original complexity more clearly.

The word temperament points to the instinctive and reactive, the unplanned, the spontaneous, the purely feelingful. The intellectual and imaginative contract I speak of must — in order to be effective — be a rehearsal in the terms of consciousness of a dramatic action that really takes place in the preconscious. But because we are concerned with intellectuals and with their work as intellectuals, we are not in fact dealing with sighs and groans and grunts, but with highly articulated sentences. So temperament must be taken to refer to the background and accompaniment of conscious thought, the field of consciousness which surrounds the objects sharply focused. It is particularly appropriate, of course, to the world of the imagination and to works of art. It covers much that "sensibility" covers, but adds some effort to explain the same phenomena genetically, and some attribution of responsibility for them.

Since I am concerned with a man's body of imaginative and intellectual experience, the word as I use it need not refer to his temperament in social life — to his personality in the ordinary sense of the word. A man may have quite different temperaments in the two worlds, first of thought, and then of social life. It seems as if Elijah Muhammed were an example of this, at least in Malcolm X's account of him; in the world of thought, fiercely radical; in the world of social behavior, gentle, quiet, and moderate. And a man's primary sexual or "Freudian" temperament, contracted in infancy, may be very unlike that secondary temperament with which he thinks and feels about public issues — in Freud himself we get a case of that, which I shall describe later. But though separable logically, all a man's temperaments are linked genetically, and, when he makes himself an authentic individual, linked and similar also in fact. Normally, then, I shall speak of a man's temperament as a single entity, and take examples of its expression from all spheres of behavior indifferently.

One more preliminary word. To have a temperament is in the ordinary sense merely to have a recognizable pattern of instinctive preferences. But I am using the term primarily for those cases in which each of those preferences is imaginatively authentic, not merely received; when it issues from and results in valuable acts of intelligence and of will. It is only when intelligence and will mutually correct and reinforce each other that a man's preferences become authentic; when he likes what really corresponds to his deepest identity and what he has ponderingly, experimentally explored, not what he has been told to like. A temperament in this sense is the achievement of imaginative form; the actualization of one's potentialities; the clarification and intensification of a person's meanings. It is an achievement, and a rare thing. In most cases, the farther people get into an area like politics or literature, in terms of knowledge and sophistication, the less temperament they have. They like everything equally, or they run their personal taste as a status hobby. This stolidifying of the imagination is particularly the curse of the academic mind, but even among creative writers many are expert, in technique and in observation, who yet "have nothing to say." So in discussing individuals and groups this way, I shall have occasion to use the categories "no temperament" or "phony temperament."

But my main categories are the three temperamental types, Faustian, Erasmian, and Calvinist. They all derive their characteristics from psychic bargains, or exchanges of one set of possibilities of personal development for another. To use another metaphor, they are investment-transfers of one's psychic resources, capital and work-force, from one enterprise to another. This is important not so much because either capital or work-force is limited in quantity, as because the act of transference arouses and energizes the whole psyche. The mind has a self-consciousness, and is profoundly responsive to its own actions. The larger the action, the larger the responsive effect. This is not limited to the conscious mind, nor to the effects of conscious decisions on the whole. The unconscious itself makes such transferences of engagement, and intensifies itelf in so doing; romantic love experience is full of examples of that, from Romeo to Vronsky. Some of those transferences are very large in their compass, and have the character of being for life. Those are temperamental contracts.

Most people make many contracts, which compromise each other's intentions, in order to take care of all their needs to some degree. But though to make just one contract is to risk large failures, it is also to acquire large energies, because of the mind's power of self-excitation. This is what Nietzsche meant when he said that a man of just one virtue is stronger than a man of many.

The first is what is traditionally meant by the Faustian or diabolic or daimonic compact, in which a man sells his soul to the devil in exchange for forbidden knowledge and forbidden powers, giant faculties and forces.

The idea of excess in this contract may seem unconnected with that other idea of the incorporation of meanings, their appropriation to the body. The two are nevertheless connected, and the great demonstrator of the connection in Western literature is Tolstoy, who was himself a great Faustian temperament. Take Natasha in *War and Peace*; primarily and superficially, she exemplifies the second idea, and with such charm, such winsomeness, that to reproach her with Faustian excess seems very strange to most readers. But Tolstoy is concerned to point out that her vitality, her charm, her power to express moods and incorporate meanings, is at the expense of other values and other people, for instance of Sonia. Natasha is of course very unlike Faust. But it is not entirely inappropriate to her to speak of giant powers of personality, or of dangerous swings of mood which derive from the consciousness of excess. Something similar is true of Anna Karenina. This connection, between the expressive body and the excessive ego, is a constant theme in Tolstoy. These are not necessarily the forces or faculties of genius. Mabel Dodge possessed them as well as D. H. Lawrence himself. They are the forces and faculties which both of them shared, and which E. M. Forster and T. S. Eliot lacked.

Goethe took the title of his play from a sixteenth-century magician, and his imagination was fired by other such figures, like Giordano Bruno and Paracelsus. These men dealt in the forbidden knowledge of their times, magic, alchemy, astrology, and they denied or evaded the teachings of Christianity, as mediated to Europe through the churches. But by Goethe's own time it was science and rationalism which had to be denied or evaded in order to acquire new powers, as we see in the case of his own and Blake's attacks on Newton and Locke. They attacked Newtonian science and rationalist philosophy as major forms of the deadening discipline imposed on civilized man from on high, the blighting reign of Urizen. They were determined to make a world within which there would be free play for their own giant powers of intellect and imagination. Clearly, what I am saying applies to all Romantics to some degree, but some more notably achieved and expressed this temperament than others; early Goethe and Blake more than Shelley and Wordsworth. As for the price paid, in Goethe's case it is clear how much he felt he lost by his Faustian freedom, from his decision in Weimar to compromise the Faustian contract with a quasi-Erasmian counterpart. In the twentieth century, the Faustian bargain for writers has been typically, as we see in Mailer's books, the sacrifice of decency in exchange for indecent sexual and sensual knowledge; the senses of disgust and recoil — what a feast for the nose is the modern novel — and the sexuality of degradation and perversity. It is in all ages the selling of one's soul for one's body, and today for the possession in fullest imaginative detail of one's physical apparatus. Modern writers who have achieved power have done so by observing this bargain. When Bellow tries, as in *Herzog*, to have it both ways, to have the virtues of decency too, he fails.

The Faustian temperament will express itself in a conservative position if the power added to the individual personality is "paid for" by the imaginative endorsement, intensification, of social rules, limitations, and traditions. This can seem very like the Erasmian policy in such matters, but it is more self-affirmingly enforced, and its identification with social power is positive instead of negative. It very frequently happens in men of notably powerful persona; it happened in Goethe and the other Weimar personalities after their first Sturm und Drang phase. The rules and traditions endorsed are external to the individual, and leave a zone of freedom around his personality, but they guarantee the order of society in general against too much freedom. But if the forbidden power is not "paid for," compensated for, in this way, if it is rejoiced in as a universal and absolute good, then the Faustian temperament takes up a radical position — as Mailer does in "The White Negro."

Freud's essay on the *Moses* of Michelangelo gives us a glimpse of a great imagination studying the terms of the Faustian contract as they had been rendered in sculpture by another great imagination long before, and interpreting them to issue in the conservative rather than the radical position. Freud attached a profound personal importance to Rome and the Renaissance, as well as to Moses and Judaism — all of them themes of power for him — and Michelangelo's huge statue focused them all into one image.

How often have I mounted the steep steps of the unlovely Corso Cavour to the lonely place where the deserted church stands, and have essayed to support the angry scorn of the hero's glance! Sometimes I

have crept cautiously out of the half-gloom of the interior as though I
myself belonged to the mob upon which his eye is turned — the mob
which can hold fast no conviction, which has neither faith nor patience,
and which rejoices when it has regained its illusory idols . . .

It was in some sense the main drive of Freud's life — his main
moral ambition — not to be found one of that mob but to become
a hero like Moses. He says in *The Psychopathology of Everyday
Life,* "There is scarcely any group of ideas to which I feel so antag-
onistic as that of being someone's protege . . . I have always felt
an unusually strong urge 'to be the strong man myself.'" He
studies and interprets the statue as the expression of two such
strong men, Michelangelo himself and Pope Julius, whose gigantic tomb it was designed to adorn. As he does so, he is clearly testing himself against it. His contemplation is engaged and emotional.

I can recollect my own disillusionment when, during my first visits to
the church, I used to sit down in front of the statue in the expectation
that I should now see how it would start up on its raised foot, hurl the
Tables of the Law to the ground and let fly its wrath. Nothing of the
kind happened. Instead, the stone image became more and more
transfixed, an almost oppressively solemn calm emanated from it . . .

It is a figure of power, then, with its giant size, its horned brow, its
massive beard, its angry glance; a Faustian figure, ready to break
the Tables, as Freud himself was thought to have done. (We can
see in *Moses and Monotheism* what a strong fellow-feeling he had
for his great predecessor, the lawgiver of orthodox Judaism.) But it
is also, Freud convinces himself, a conservative figure, who will not
really break them.

[Michelangelo] does not let Moses break them in his wrath, but makes
him be influenced by the danger that they will be broken and calm that
wrath, or at any rate prevent it from becoming an act. In this way he
has added something new and more than human to the figure of Moses;
so that the giant frame with its tremendous physical power becomes
only a concrete expression of the highest mental achievement that is
possible in a man, that of struggling successfully against an inward passion for the sake of a cause to which he has devoted himself.

That is the Faustian conservative temperament defined in stoic
terms, and in the image of Freud contemplating *Moses* we see that

temperament being fostered as a result of having been expressed —
we see how it is transmitted by the means of art.

The American writers I picked on to admire in *Reappraisals,*
Emerson and Salinger, are not in the least Faustian. They are exemplars of a different temperament, the result of a different bargain, one in which a writer sells his body in exchange for freedom
of the spirit. This is the angelic pact, as opposed to the diabolic,
and I associate it with Erasmus — for reasons I will explain later —
as opposed to Faust, Bruno, and Paracelsus. Writers like Forster
and Trilling are good examples of this temperament, and to some
degree everyone at home in British literature as opposed to American belongs to it. This pact is the one every man enters into by the
process of maturation, by the very process of becoming human, as
described by Freud in *Civilization and Its Discontents.* It is the
exchange of sensual pleasure for mental, of immediate gratification
of appetite for indirect and subtle gratification, of nature for culture. It is repression, suppression, and sublimation. It causes the
uniformity and rationalization of civilized man, and that two-
dimensionality which so many intellectuals rebel against. Intellectuals, writers among them, enter into this contract more largely
than other people, are specially its beneficiaries and its victims.
They are its sponsors in society, and feel specially responsible for it.
They get more from it and lose more by it. They specially yearn for
the three-dimensional world of rich, full, free, vivid, unmediated
experience. They often contract, or try to contract, the Faustian
bargain as well, and are therefore often *its* sponsors, or would-be
sponsors, as against the Erasmian.

The Erasmian temperament is impersonal, and in personal relations likely to be insipid — lacking in force and fire. It is to be
associated with the elements of air and water rather than with fire
and earth. It is likely to be lacking in courage and passion, at least
in direct and unprepared encounters, just because it lacks a strong
instinctive sense of its own or any other individual's worth just as
an ego. In social life and in intimacy it is the decent thing to put
on a Faustian face — the lineaments of gratified desire — with intimations of a free and fiery spirit within. He has a bit of the devil
in him, people say of someone attractive, meaning that he promises
to break bounds, to trespass in the forbidden. And quite right; for

gaiety one should go to that temperament, not to Erasmians; scholars' gaiety is the obverse of scholars' melancholy, the saturnine humour inverted. The Erasmian virtues are justice, selflessness, understanding, scrupulousness — the virtues which result from subduing the id and the ego, and erecting the superego, identifying oneself with society in general. These are the qualities by which the world of the mind works. They are its machinery. But they do not produce the most splendid triumphs of the imagination. This temperament makes its contractors feel that they are two-dimensional.

Reminding ourselves of Michelangelo's *Moses* and Freud's learning from it, we find an equivalent for Erasmians within the visual arts in the portraits of Erasmus himself by Metsys and by Holbein. These paintings are wonderfully precise and patient and appreciative renderings of his face, his robe, his study, his life. Their atmosphere is absolutely clear and dry, their drawing absolutely steady, their coloring absolutely sober, their lines as sharp as the lines on Erasmus's own face. They are acts of worship of truth itself, in the interest of which Erasmus's pride of power, if he had had any, was implicitly sacrificed. Every weakness and ignominy, within the limits of decorum, is exactly inscribed. Secular Dutch painting of the fifteenth and sixteenth centuries can largely be seen as Erasmian. So can most eighteenth-century English painting, and favorites of that taste, like Canaletto. This is the fruit, and the seed, of the angelic contract.

For Calvinists the best equivalent in painting would perhaps be some anonymous group-portrait of Calvin and the elders of Geneva, in which both the artist and the art of painting had been subordinated to the symbol's social function of recalling that authoritative assembly to the minds of the faithful. But it could also be a collection of icons, or a fourteenth-century Sienese painting in which the saints' faces are all outlined and exalted in gold, or almost any kind of solemnly religious Pre-Raphaelite. The essential thing is that it should be an image of power.

For if the Faustian bargain is one way of escaping from Erasmian limits, the Calvinist bargain is the other, the opposite. While the first intensifies the powers of the individual as individual, personal power, personal intuition, and personal imagination, the other makes one participate in the intensified powers of a group, of the elect, the redeemed, the saints. By this social contract, this saints' bargain, one sacrifices individual freedom and gains party infallibility. I choose Calvin to entitle this temperament primarily because of Michael Walzer's interesting book, *The Revolution of the Saints*, in which he points out the similarity between the Calvinist reformers of the sixteenth century and the Marxist revolutionaries of our own times. The Calvinist saint, he says, was the first of those self-disciplined agents of social and political reconstruction who appear so frequently in modern history. What was new in them was party organization and methodical activity, leading to political opposition and reform, and ultimately to radical ideology and revolution. Conscience, work, and the organization of groups entered the political world together, under Calvin's auspices. Calvin was, unlike Luther, a man with no private life, and opposed to theological speculation, but committed to innovation, in moral conduct and social organization, and to systematization. Calvin thought that the key experiences of fallen men were fear and anxiety, disorder and war, and they therefore needed above all things order, system. The duty of a pastor is "By bringing men into the obedience of the Gospel, to offer them as it were in sacrifice unto God, not as the papists have hitherto proudly bragged, by the offering up of Christ to reconcile men unto God." He understood political realities in a very Hobbesian and Realpolitik way, because he saw human nature as totally corrupt. His achievement was an ideology rather than a theology or a piety; an ideology being a complex of ideas designed to change the world. The key image to associate with him is of a group of men working together to change the social structure, working in committees and cells cooperatively, methodically, wasting not a moment or a thought or a feeling, and working to some degree secretively, because their methods alarm and outrage the outside world insofar as they are known.

We do not often find this temperament among men of letters. The saints' contract involves some sacrifice of the free play of the imagination. Milton and Bunyan's major creative work was done after they ceased to expect or work for the kingdom of God on earth. Tolstoy did no more major novel writing after coming to believe that he must work for that kingdom — after activating that temperament in himself, and subduing the other, as best he could.

The literary work he did then do, in folktales and fairytales, is a good example of what such a temperament can produce with genius. Hopkins's verse, with its strange impersonality, perhaps shows the highest poetic achievement of such combinations of aesthetic ambition with Calvinist values. Hymns and prayers and exhortations to battle, pamphlets, constitutions, anything traditionally anonymous, are more ordinary examples. And one of the major images of the culture in which this temperament expresses itself is the military or popular parade in a Communist city, in Moscow or Peking or Havana, with great masses of people marching by, gazing up at a balcony on which are gathered the group of their leaders, more or less indistinguishable from each other, equally dedicated, equally anonymous.

It is clear that the radical position corresponds to the Calvinist temperament; and the liberal position to the Erasmian temperament; and the conservative position — and sometimes the radical — to the Faustian. Though, as I said, the correspondence is not one to one. In a man like Voltaire or Francis Jeffrey of Edinburgh the Erasmian temperament and the liberal position unite, but my most vivid example of that temperament, Erasmus himself, was profoundly nonpolitical. His love of books and his timidity about confrontations, however ideological, plainly both grow from the same root. From both the Diet of Worms and the Diet of Augsburg he was notably and fatally absent, barricaded behind books in his study. And this is a difference, let us note, between two intellectual types within the same temperamental category, not between social personalities. To take examples from Calvinist radicalism, there are differences in personality between the knife-edge narrowness of Calvin and the fieriness of Marx, not to mention the boisterous expansiveness of Castro. But the difference in intellectuality is rather that between Calvin and Marx taken together, "the systematizer," and Lenin and Castro, taken together, "the politician." But despite the variations possible within a given pattern, each one retains enough magnetic-cohesive power for any other matching of temperament and position, any matching that breaks the pattern, to be liable to breed problems. In an age of revolution a man with an Erasmian temperament may find himself holding radical opinions in politics, which will cause him difficulties. If he acts vigorously on those opinions, he will find that that induces a change, or a conflict, in his temperament. You can see that happen in the work of liberals-turned-radical today.

It is only, one might think, in times of revolution, of crisis, that temperament and position are likely to be painfully in conflict. But the definition of such periods is in part subjective, so they are occurring for someone all the time.

> I dreamed I dwelt in marble halls,
> And woke to find it true;
> I wasn't born for an age like this;
> Was Smith? Was Jones? Were you?

Orwell saw his own times as critical, and was forced, he felt, to a radical position in politics, while in literature, where he felt most "himself" and "at home," he remained an Erasmian liberal.

> A happy vicar I might have been
> Two hundred years ago,
> To preach upon eternal doom
> And watch my walnuts grow.

And though he had strong radical feelings about particular political issues, felt with all the strength of his childhood experience of oppression, he passionately distrusted the "dirty little orthodoxies" of the Calvinists, and his political attitudes are consequently tortuous.

Karl Mannheim's categories for analyzing "The Utopian Mentality" in *Ideology and Utopia* are quite close to mine. He too talks about "states of mind" instead of about positions. But his categories describe four stages in the development of the Utopian mentality in modern times. Thus he presents his states of mind as historically successive and leading on from one to another, while I see mine as alternative at a given moment, alternative ways of responding to a single set of pressures. Moreover, his interest is sociological, and relates political thought, etc., to social classes, not to highly individual imaginations. Nevertheless, his comments on his stages make them sound significantly like my alternatives. He has four categories to my three, because my Faustian temperament corresponds to both his "orgiastic chiliasm" and his "conservative idea." Obviously his scheme is much the clearer in this way. It is confusing to find radicalism and conservatism so linked. But my

scheme cannot afford to be clear at the expense of close contact
with the phenomena it offers to explain. I am dealing with imaginative writers, and from a psychological rather than a sociological
point of view. That is why the political terms are sometimes ambiguous.

Mannheim's first form of the Utopian mentality, the orgiastic
chiliasm of the sixteenth-century Anabaptists, corresponds to my
Faustian radicalism. In "The White Negro" Mailer describes that
mode with participatory enthusiasm. But in *The Armies of the
Night* and *Miami and the Siege of Chicago* he describes similar
behavior from a position of dissent and criticism. And yet he is
closer than any other major writer to that political option. That
ambiguity is a clue to why there is so little about orgiastic chiliasm
in this book, even though on the streets it is so prominent a feature
of today's scene. Writers, as writers, do not belong to it. *The Electric Kool-Aid Acid Test* gives a very vivid picture of that life; but it
seems clear that for Ken Kesey living that life was an alternative to
being a novelist; that while he was living it he was different, in
policy, in position, from while writing. That is why Faustian radical seems a better term to use for such a writer than orgiastic chiliast, because it gives him an identity that unites his activity of writing and his activities in living.

But many of Mannheim's comments on chiliasm are relevant to
contemporary radicalism of the Faustian or inverted Faustian kind
— by the latter phrase, I mean such things as hippie communes.
For instance, the identifying characteristic of chiliastic experience,
he says, is absolute presentness. The present is the breach through
which what had been inward bursts in and transforms the world.
The mystic lives in longing for, or memory of, ecstasy. Thomas
Muntzer, the sixteenth-century Anabaptist, said that all prophets
should speak only in the present tense. Another characteristic is the
inseparability for them of sensual experience from spiritual; everything is experience in immediately sensual terms. And revolution is
a value in itself, a creative principle. Bakunin, saying that the will
to destroy is a creative will, is a chiliast.

The second stage of the Utopian mentality Mannheim calls the
liberal-humanitarian idea, and it corresponds to my Erasmian temperament. He describes it as characteristically *rational*, as positively

accepting of *culture*, and as giving an *ethical* tone to human affairs. Ethics and intellectual culture, he says, have been the middle class's principal self-justification against the nobility. Its spirit is critical, not creatively destructive. It worships the world of the spirit, of ideals, "that other world" which, once absorbed into our moral conscience, inspires us. It has pursued a middle course between the vitality, ecstasy, and vindictiveness of the oppressed social strata, on the one hand, and the limited, concrete factuality of a feudal ruling class, on the other. Both the ideas and the art of this middle class, Mannheim says, are necessarily lacking in depth and color. The Erasmian temperament does indeed tend to these defects in its imaginative work, but that fact seems to me better explained by the dispositions of its temperamental contract, than by any middle-class origins.

The third form of the Utopian mentality is the conservative idea, which he describes as the idea of a class with no disposition toward theorizing, which discovered its own idea ex post facto, in reaction against the liberal idea. He points out that historical concepts emphasizing the uniqueness of events are likely to be the product of conservative elements in society, which we shall see verified in Herder's historicism, and he also compares such conservative philosophy of history with Goethe's botany and biology, with their stress on morphology and development. The conservative idea is oriented toward the past, not the future, and its lack of standards in political matters is quietist. All this has its relevance to Weimar, our example of conservatism, but again I think that the literary-intellectual product of that city can be understood more intimately in terms of temperament. While the fourth and final stage is the Socialist-Communist Utopia, corresponding to my Calvinist temperament, which he describes as a culture permeated by a point of view formed primarily in the political area, and which brings with it a new realism and a new sociology.

On the whole, these sociological ideas do not explain for me our political-literary complexes as suggestively as do my "psychic contracts." And in justification of that decision, and finally, I must now give something of a case history.

It is essential to my theory of such contracts that a man engages in one voluntarily — that is, he engages intention and imagination,

124554

however unconsciously, in the enterprise of becoming himself. But it needs to be demonstrated that "voluntariness" and "idea of one-self" are as relevant to the facts of temperament as to those of ideology; that is, to patterns of emotion and taste, of spontaneous reaction, of unconsidered feeling, of occasional self-betrayal; of be-havior in the genre of the management of the voice and the facial expression and the body posture; patterns which we usually treat as "natural" and "congenital." And for that demonstration we need a case in which a man changes temperamental type before our eyes, in accordance with a change in his *idea* of himself, and of his other *ideas*, theories, purposes in life. Rousseau is such an example, who makes it clear in which sense every man chooses his own tempera-ment.

Up to 1740, when he left Mme de Warens, Rousseau seems to have seen himself, and enacted himself, as Figaro-Cherubino, the charming rogue, incapable of sustained effort, susceptible to every tempting invitation, forever involved in rash adventures, impetu-ous, enthusiastic, timid, sentimental. And in the first six books of the *Confessions*, the settings are all rococo, the incidents are all out of operetta, the characters and their gestures are all variants of Mme de Warens having her stays laced by a visiting priest, erotico-religiose-playful figures, of marked innocence and marked sophisti-cation combined.

The *Confessions*, of course, give a shaped and colored version of those years, and other faces of Rousseau emerge in the documents of the time; more plaintive, more bedraggled, more desperate faces. But these are nearly all variants on the main image, excluded from the official record only because they were rather sordid, rather un-flattering, or unpleasant to acknowledge. They are all manifesta-tions of the same temperament — it was essentially a temperament — made up of weaknesses, talents, absurdities, and amiabilities. Within this quick, warm, clever, but not-to-be-taken-seriously per-sona, the man's capacity for hard work, his power of logic, his power of eloquence, his ambition, his moral fervor, all these ener-gies slumbered undeveloped.

One does not have so clear a picture of what Rousseau was like during his first years in Paris, but it must have been that those hitherto undeveloped potentialities were gradually aroused by his friendship-rivalry with Diderot and Grimm, while the form of his personality remained what it had been. Diderot must have known Rousseau as the amiable, rather dishonest enthusiast, the rather absurd compound of a thousand talents and a thousand weaknesses, which he had been. (It is worth noting that Diderot was the stronger personality "by nature"; worth noting because it reminds us that the intensity of personality we associate with Rousseau was the creation of his mind and intention. In his writings, his intellectual temperament, Diderot was an Erasmian liberal, and he therefore makes a more moderate impression.)

And then in 1749, on the road to Vincennes, Rousseau discovered a new personality for himself, a new temperament, a new self. He remembered that he was a citizen of Geneva, of a Protestant republic, of a city of virtue. That he was essentially different from these Parisians, and need not compete against them on their terms. He saw himself descended from early Romans, from Scythians, from Sparta, republic of demigods, where the arts and the sciences so valued in Paris were strictly forbidden. He saw that the arts and the sciences lay garlands on the iron chains that bind men, stifle in men the feeling of that freedom for which they were born. He who had begun his first phase by literally selling his birthright of Calvinist and Genevan citizenship, to buy the *fêtes champêtres* of Les Charmettes — Mme de Warens's whole establishment was a rococo limbo of such lost souls, all "converts" supported ultimately by pensions from despotic king and Catholic bishop — now saw himself as the boy who had read Plutarch to his father and had thrilled to images of the severest civic virtue. He who had rebelled against every constraint now longed for law.

I should have liked to live and die free, that is, so completely submitted to the law that neither I nor anyone could shake its honourable yoke: that sweet and salutary yoke which the proudest heads bear with all the more docility because they are made to bear no other.

With these opinions he changed his life-style, and his personality-style, began to wear different clothes and to do his hair differently; he signed himself Citizen, he became a Protestant, he left Paris for his Ermitage, he began to earn a meager living by copying music manually, to be like his father, who made watches. His literary style, even in letters to friends, grew marmoreal, lapidary, statuesque. Thus, to Mme de Créqui he wrote,

I have worked eight days, Madame, that is, eight mornings. To live, I must earn forty sols a day; there are, then, sixteen francs owing to me . . . On my return from Passy, I shall have the honour of calling on you; the copyist will receive his payment; Jean-Jacques, since he must, will receive from you the compliments you intend for him; and as regards the honour which His Excellency the Ambassador wishes to bestow upon me, we shall do what ever is pleasing to him and to yourself.

The incidents of his life no longer remind one of operetta. The letters and the speeches between him and Diderot and d'Holbach and Mme d'Epinay, the intrigues and the confrontations, are now reminiscent of Racinian tragedy, the pitch of emotion is so proud, the moral intensity so acute, the language so elegantly and fatally analytical.

One understands how false this tone, this whole performance, must have seemed to those who had known the old Rousseau. And the affair with Mme d'Houdetot and the abandonment of his children are sufficient reminders of how incompletely Rousseau could carry out his new idea. (His fantastic moral insensitivity in the second matter is an example of how a temperamental contract can work — how psychic energy invested in one form of sensitivity can be withdrawn from another.) But there are also powerful proofs of how completely he did carry it out, did appropriate this temperament. One such proof is the value, the authenticity, of what he wrote under this inspiration. Another, of a different kind, is the bitterness of both sides of his long quarrel with those who claimed they knew the "real" Rousseau. That giant battle must have been about something real.

But from the time he began writing his *Confessions*, a third Rousseau began to develop, who was no more the virtuous citizen than the rococo rogue. This is the self-knower, the spider at the center of the huge web of his own sensibility and his own experience, the man who remembers everything and can explain everything and re-create everything with hallucinatory vividness, the man with boxes of letters and papers of every kind; the individual pleading his cause at the bar of all mankind. This is the author of the second half of the *Confessions*, of the *Rêveries*, of *Rousseau, Juge de Jean-Jacques*, etc.; the man who tried to leave his manuscript on the altar of Notre Dame. With this temperament went his Armenian costume, and the delusions and persecution complexes, and the constant removings, of the last years of his life. To this model we can approximate many a *monstrum sacrum* of modernist art; for instance, Proust.

Around 1760 Rousseau made some interesting notes for a self-portrait, which illuminate our theory.

I am not anxious for people to notice me, but when they do, I am not displeased that it should be in some rather special way, and I would rather be forgotten by the whole of the human race, than regarded as an ordinary man . . . Homer and Virgil have never been called great men, although they were very great poets. During my life-time, some authors have gone out of their way to acclaim Rousseau the poet as the great Rousseau. After I am dead, Rousseau will still be a great poet, but he will no longer be the great Rousseau. For although it is not impossible for a writer to be a great man, it is not by writing books, either in prose or verse, that he will become one.

Rousseau made good his boast. He made himself a great man by the means of making himself a special case. But clearly he did so not by *not writing* books. He was in all his phases a notable example of the writer who absorbs the rest of life into his writing; take, for example, his reading his books out loud to Mme de Luxembourg as a substitute for conversation. He made himself a great man by writing books that were more than just that, books that were, unlike the *Aeneid*, supreme expressions of the author, of *him*, of his temperament. And he realized that his temperament, his identity, was something that he could, though not without a struggle, define for himself in defiance of all the world. It is because he put such passion into that struggle, that he makes us see the more limited but analogous way in which all writers, all intellectuals, choose and realize their own temperaments.

It is interesting that of his personas, the second was Calvinist, as we are using the term, and that it was Genevan in the literal sense. Cities can be, as we shall see, very powerful manifestations and propagators of a temperament. Once a form of life has been achieved in a city, it is often perpetuated there and gives birth to

new versions of the same idea even centuries after the first version
died. Rousseau returned from Paris to Geneva, became a citizen
again and a Calvinist Protestant, and wrote his *Lettre sur les Spectacles* of 1758, as a Genevan protesting against the idea of having
a theater in the city. The men of Geneva, like those of Sparta, are
real men; their games and contests are in military strength. (In the
Prosopopée de Fabricius, the latter calls on his Roman descendants
to smash their statues and burn their paintings, because "the only
talent worthy of Rome is to conquer the world and make virtue
reign.") He had the motto *Vitam Impendere Vero* inscribed on
his seal, and often added it to letters. He did not become a party
member, there being no party then, but he did adopt an ostenta-
tiously hidden, sober, quiet style of life and manners, and his writings attacked every manifestation of personality as well as of privilege. Free competition, consciousness of others' opinions, the
maintenance of private rights, all the social forms of the Erasmian
temperament were condemned. While pride and curiosity, the key
Faustian drives, were blamed for the fall of man in the *Discours
sur l'Inégalité*. The community is the highest moral value, and its
General Will must supplant the chaos of individual desires that
corrupts liberal middle-class society.

For Rousseau's first persona there is no equivalent among my
categories, but the third is recognizably literary-Faustian. It is
Faustian because it is an immensely hypertrophied personality,
manifesting itself in shameful self-knowledge and self-absorption,
and excessive, abnormal self-projection. But it is a literary triumph
in compensation for life humiliation; in a sense it is inverted-
Faustian, because its strength is shown in the revelation and analysis of weaknesses, in complaint and self-exposure. This is a pattern
found among many great modernist writers, but it will not occupy
us much in this book because it is apolitical in tendency.

It is because the first and third personas — though more authentically achieved as temperaments — were apolitical, that Rousseau
is not a major subject of this book, despite the completeness with
which he illustrates its theory. The second persona, which was political, expressed itself best in his position. To talk about Rousseau
as a Calvinist *temperament* involves one in too many qualifications
and redefinitions. It is also because he did not live in an age of

revolution that we pass him by. The men and cities we are going to study all have that additional relevance to our own dilemma. But we shall recur to Rousseau to remind ourselves how ineluctably temperament, just as much as ideology, is a matter of deliberate choice. We are all responsible for who we are, and how we stand as well as where we stand confronting revolution is something for which we must answer.

2 — NORMAN MAILER AND THE CITY OF NEW YORK: FAUSTIAN RADICALISM

As announced above the mind of Dr. Faustus was fain to love forbidden things, after which he hankered night and day, taking unto himself the wings of an eagle in order to search out the uttermost parts of heaven and earth; for his forwardness, lawlessness and wantonness pricked and goaded him to such a degree, that the time came when he decided to try out and put into action certain magic words, figures, characters and conjurations in order to summon up the devil before him.

And this apostasy was nothing more nor less than his pride and arrogance, despair, audacity and insolence, like unto those giants of whom the poets sing that they carried the mountains together and were fain to make war on God, yea like unto that evil angel who opposed God, and was cast off by God on account of his arrogance and presumption.

Quoth Faustus ragingly, I will know, or I will not liue, wherefore dispatch and tell me. *

Mailer and Politics

The city of New York is itself a Faustian temperament; in its buildings, in its street scenes, in its racial and political tensions, in its social harshness, it contains a series of violent reachings toward power, and excessive and forbidden power; which a visitor, even if

* All quotations taken from E. M. Butler, *The Fortunes of Faust*, Cambridge, 1952.

he arrives from another of the world's metropoles, can feel on his nerves as a dangerous stimulant and challenge. It is no wonder that now, at the climax of the city's world-career, a group of writers are to be found who express it, take its temperament as their subject, reenact that in their style and sensibility. And it is no wonder, though it could not have been predicted, that the genius among them should be the one who expresses his city, relates to it, represents it, in the most various ways — including straight political representation.

In 1969 Norman Mailer ran, with a Left Conservative program, as candidate for the Democratic nomination as mayor of New York. He offered the policy of making the city into the fifty-first state, and analogously, of giving power to its neighborhoods so that they could design community life-styles, each for itself. Some could be integrated, some segregated; some could make church attendance compulsory, some could practice free love. Financing would be made available so that slum areas could be rebuilt room by room, to the occupier's taste and with the occupier's participation. Once a month every machine except those absolutely necessary would be stopped for a "Sweet Sunday." There would be a monorail around Manhattan and a free jitney bus service. There would be craftsman training and pollution control, legalized gambling and neighborhood cable TV, vest-pocket neighborhood colleges and weekend wrestling jousts for adolescents in the public parks.

The idea of Mailer as mayor was a comic one for several reasons. The one most relevant here is that Mailer is a writer; and I mean that his ideas on political subjects and his performance in political affairs are those of a literary man. In *Armies of the Night* his theories of the Vietnam War, and of the march on the Pentagon, are in the style of D. H. Lawrence while his behavior over the weekend was in the style of Dylan Thomas or Brendan Behan. Both his principles and his practice are governed by a highly literary sense of what constitutes style and what constitutes authenticity, of what is offensive and absurd, and when things become boring, and which is the step you absolutely refuse to take. That is why it was funny for most of us to think of his becoming mayor. But it did not mean that his politics were invalid. He was running seriously in his own opinion, and by any objective standard of seri-

New York City in all its sinister glory, with its saving clause impishly rising over the skyline. (*Smog over New York City,* Courtesy of A. Devaney, Inc. Norman Mailer Photo by Jerry Bauer.)

ousness the other candidates had quite as much against them as he had. I at least found his proposals admirable; and if we couldn't imagine the voters taking them seriously, that could have caused sadness rather than laughter.

So the striking thing is that we should find the idea of a writer becoming mayor comic. It is true that Mailer is also, in his words, an egomaniac; which always gives rise to a certain amount of nervous laughter from others. But that brings us back to the same point, for only an egomaniac writer *could* run for mayor of New York. Anyone else would "realize" that he "shouldn't." And it is typical of Mailer's services to literature that he should break through such inhibitions, which are inhibitions with plenty of common sense and common sensibility to them, to be broken only with much expense of adrenalin and sweat and hot flushes of shame and rage.

But I don't want to deplore the sheepishness of our profession. My own voice is too close to a bleat to be a proper vehicle for that particular truth. I want to reflect on the special case Mailer presents, of a writer oriented toward the city he lives in, feeling a mission to save it, a radical and political mission. It is rare, surely, to find an important writer who is concerned about the political workings of his own city or country with the same passionate concern as he brings to his writing. Such a writer needs a range of gifts that goes beyond the strictly literary; and he must be aiming at being a great man. As Rousseau said, "Although it is not impossible for a writer to be a great man, it is not by writing books, either in prose or verse, that he will become one." In most of the writers we call great, as in Mailer, we can trace the effects of a Faustian bargain. But even among that group Mailer stands out as the one most directly related to politics. Lawrence and Tolstoy, though men with an immense range of gifts, are not comparable from this point of view. Neither had, for instance, Mailer's gift — so rare among literary men — for public political speaking.

Nor had Goethe, but it is Goethe I offer as the great predecessor and contrast for Mailer. (In fact as a young man Goethe *was* told by a phrenologist that he was born to be a public speaker; but this only alarmed him — or so he says — as meaning that all the professions he was actually considering would be wrong for him; because there was in Germany then no political career open to him in which he could have used those talents.) For more than fifty years Goethe took a hand in governing the city and the state of Weimar, and during the first ten he was in many ways the chief minister. He too might have described his political philosophy as Left Conservatism, and when he first came to office he was distrusted for the wildness of his personal behavior. He had opted, before he reached Mailer's age, for a much more conservative style than Mailer. But that was partly because there was an aristocracy for him to belong to — except under ducal patronage he would never have reached public office. And if there were an aristocracy to join today, would not Mailer join it?

The contrast between them — the standard images of the two men could hardly be more different — derives largely from Goethe's determination to cultivate other temperamental potentialities, to cancel the Faustian bargain and to abide by the standard civilized and cultural contract. Most notably when he abandoned Sturm und Drang for Weimar, but again and again later, he decided to live by the values of society and knowledge and culture. Mailer has always refused to do that. Though a man of learning and a leader of opinion perforce, he has established his identity in his acts of dissent and dissociation from everything established. But because there was an element of the daimonic in Goethe's conservatism, and an element of the conservative in Mailer's Faustianism, the two have some interesting similarities nevertheless. Neither man has any significant traces of a Calvinist or party-ideological temperament. The elements of radicalism in their politics are due much more to their Faustianism, which makes them both hostile to liberal moderation. One sees that in their fascination by great men, power-figures, as well as in their own performances. Take for instance Goethe's fascination with Napoleon; his identification with the imperial adventurer's cause as against that of the German liberals and nationalists. In Mailer's case, take his fascination with Lyndon Johnson and with Barney Oswald Kelly (of *An American Dream*). In both writers this fascination is a natural extension of their feeling for striking personalities and against worthy causes — for Karl August and Byron in Goethe's case, for Sonny Liston in Mailer's case, against liberal enthusiasms in both cases. Both men

study power in other personalities in order to acquire it for themselves; though they normally present themselves as powerful, in relation to someone yet more so they portray themselves as strikingly
naïve.

Wilhelm Meister is the story of a young man acquiring power of
personality by this kind of study in the world of the theater. (The
theatrical profession, because it teaches men how to appropriate
powerful meanings to their bodies, is a vocational arena for transacting the Faustian bargain.) In Mailer's case, take his imaginative
relation with Hemingway, or Sergius O'Shaughnessy's relation to
his tutors in *The Deer Park*. (You see the same thing in Kingsley
Amis, a similar temperament; the heroes of his early novels habitually oriented themselves toward older, masterful men, in appren-
ticeship; for instance Patrick Standish in *Take a Girl Like You*.)
The left elements in their politics derive not from any radical ambition to reform the world — any general uniformity of salvation
would disgust them — but from an Erasmian-humanist decency.
These elements are therefore not very emphatic.

Politics and Literature

One day no doubt Mailer will give us an account of his adventures in politics, whether or not he ever takes office. And that is
likely to make a very good book, because the subject matter is well
suited to the form he has made his own, and has made the characteristic literary form of our generation, the autobiographical narrative in which different voices and genres play against each other as
well as playing together. His two most brilliant successes in this
genre are *Advertisements for Myself* and *The Armies of the Night*,
though *Presidential Papers* and *Cannibals and Christians* are also
interesting books with brilliant things in them. In *Advertisements
for Myself* the contrast in voices and forms is most obviously a
contrast between on the one hand the essays and fiction he is re-
printing, and on the other the present-tense reflective narrative
that connects them. In *The Armies of the Night* we have first the
"History as a Novel" and then "The Novel as History." The dis-
continuity of forms is less striking, but there is the same thematic
contrast between the outrageously indiscreet and personal, and the
powerfully insightful and reflective. That contrast is primary be-

cause this is a Faustian form; in formal terms the contrast rehearses the Faustian bargain; by being outrageous one makes oneself insightful. The artistic success of the genre lies in the connection made between those two, the way they feed each other and stimulate each other and interact. This is what makes it possible, approaching literature even from the point of view of form, to call Mailer the most important writer of his time. He recognized *our* form; Mary McCarthy achieved her best book, *Memories of a Catholic Girlhood,* by virtue of that form. Mailer made something marvelous out of it.

His political style has a similar combination of the willfully indiscreet and the solemnly prophetic. That style marks the influence of his literariness on his politics; and the influence of his political engagement on his writing accounts for some of that substantiality which makes him superior to most people writing today. He has been more serious and more responsible in his relation to his city and his country than most of them have, than most of us. But Faustian is the crucial interpretive term here too; there are strong elements of nihilism and anarchism in his political outlook. One need only remember "The White Negro," still one of his most powerful and authentic pieces, to be convinced of that. Against his *New York Times Magazine* piece for May 4, 1969, "Why Are We in New York?" which opened his mayoral campaign, we must set something reported in the daily *Times* of March 4. This was a Theater for Ideas discussion of "The End of the Rationalist Tradition?" with Peter Gay and Jean Malaquais defending rationalism, and Mailer and Fiedler attacking it. Mailer's opening statement declared that the logical end of rationalism was the present pollution. "The only way to end smog is for the citizens to get muskets, get on barges, go to Jersey, and explode all the factories." And he insisted that this was not the fault of capitalism — that socialism would do exactly the same. It was not a matter of politics but the consequence of rationalism, of the Western *mind,* no matter what its political persuasion. Fiedler is reported as recommending a return to myths and to "the power of positive unthinking." "The new irrationality is not directed at building something where nothing was, but it is directed against the city, the university, against the antiseptic, therapeutic church. . . . Reason, although dead, holds us with an embrace that looks like a lover's embrace, but turns out to be a rigor mortis. Unless we're necrophiles, we'd better let go."

Clearly, neither man was at his most considered or serious in this debate. But then neither man sets great store by being considered or serious; they hope to reach significant truth rather by being excited and paradoxical. They are, as they say, irrationalist. It is a central part of Faust's bargain with the devil, according to Goethe, that he will give up the use of reason, inasmuch as it has to do with ratio and proportion; that he will exceed all bounds and limits in reaching for mysterious truths and powers. There is a fairly widespread school of such thinking today; Norman Brown and McLuhan are other representative names. So it is fair, I think, to take what they said seriously, and to note that even just before his mayoral campaign Mailer was ready to represent — only temporarily and fragmentarily, no doubt, but vatically — forces that defined themselves as hostile to the city, along with the university and the church.

Fiedler I want to associate generally with Mailer in this discussion, because I think he represents the same forces, the same temperament of mind, and represents it in the field of literary criticism and scholarship. By associating the two, I can exemplify the operation of that mind in literature as a whole much more variously. Fiedler projects the same overweening egotism — "I have heard from time to time reports of friend separated from friend or lover from lover by arguments over one or another of my essays" (No! In Thunder) — and is equally irrationalist. In Waiting for the End, for example, he predicts the end of the novel, on the grounds that the form cannot live any longer than that eighteenth-century faith — now dead — in the power of writers to subdue the unconscious to reason. Nowadays we know that the unconscious is much the more powerful of the two. The form that succeeds the novel will be nonliterate, he predicts, and with the end of literacy and rationalism will come the end of conscience, moral individualism, and all of liberal culture. He sees the white Negro as the child of the love match between Huckleberry Finn and Nigger Jim, and endorses this orgiastic chiliasm as a solution to American society's ills.

Mailer and Fiedler are among the most scathing of all rejectors of liberalism. This is natural, since liberals are essentially men of reason and men of the city. That is why these two are the men my argument must immediately engage with, in order to show where it stands, how it defends itself, in calling itself liberal. From several diatribes by Mailer, let us take an early example, from the 1962 *Esquire* piece on the Patterson-Liston fight.

I could even wonder . . . whether the entire liberal persuasion of America had rooted for Floyd in the same idle, detached fashion as myself, wanting him to win but finding Liston secretly more interesting, in fact, and indeed, demanding of Patterson that he win only because he was good for liberal ideology. I had a moment of vast hatred then for that bleak gluttonous void of the Establishment, the liberal power at the center of our lives which gave jargon with charity, substituted the intolerance of mental health for the intolerance of passion, alienated emotion from its roots, and man from his past, cut the giant of our half-awakened arts to fit a bed of Procrustes, put Leonard Bernstein on the podium, John Cage in silence, offered a National Arts Center which would be to art as canned butter is to butter, and existed in a terror of eternity which built a new religion of the psyche on a God who died, old doctor Freud, of cancer.

Practically all of Mailer's case against liberalism gets mentioned there, its hostility to passion, to the arts and to religion, and its worship of mental health — its anti-Faustianism, its Erasmianism of temperament. It is true that there is a moral puritanism in the original self-condemnation; that he, as a liberal, had supported Floyd in an "idle, detached fashion"; he had not scrutinized his motives with sufficient severity. But honesty with oneself is only one half of his remedy against the fault, and the other half is less reassuringly old-fashioned; a commitment to the life of the senses and to those emotions not preprogrammed and preguaranteed by the superego. That is the Faustian remedy, and dangerous enough.

Faustianism and Jewishness

Of course Mailer and Fiedler are liberals themselves to some degree. Professional writers, men who spend their lives writing books on intellectual subjects for intellectual readers, could hardly not be. Their antiliberalism is in part self-exhortation and self-exorcism of that liberal self. And in their case this is closely connected with their being Jewish. Mailer speaks in *The Armies of the Night* of the one aspect of his own personality, the one persona, he finds absolutely insupportable — "the nice Jewish boy from Brooklyn . . . Something in his adenoids gave it away — he had the softness of a man early accustomed to mother-love." His theory of Jewishness and its love-and-power conflicts is like that of Günter Grass in *Dog Years*. But whereas Grass sees Jewishness as part of the German problem, Mailer sees it as part of America's, and above all, of Mailer's problem. It is clear which side of the divide he belongs on in this dichotomy of American types.

All the dull kids, too stupid to study, ovulating turgid fantasies in the back row, all liveliness sunk in premature sapience of burgeoning young meats, and up front, the bright middle-class children, little intellectual drills, their mental voracity driving them to further, better, higher critiques of the public material before them until — Vietnam!

His understanding of America is all patterned by the confrontation and opposition between clever, middle-class, big-city kids — typically Jewish — and mean, tough, supermales of the working class, from small towns. Those are the two forces he saw confronting each other at the Pentagon. The marchers, whether hippies or fraternity boys, all belonged to the first, the soldiers and marshals and jailers and sidewalk watchers all belonged to the second. Here nothing will do but a long quotation.

If the troops were relieved that a pullulating unwashed orgiastic Communist-inspired wave of flesh did not roll right over them, and that in fact the majority of demonstrators right there before them were not unlike in appearance the few quiet long-haired cool odd kids they had never quite gotten to know in high school, the demonstrators in their turn were relieved in profounder fashion that their rank of eyes had met the soldiers, and it was the soldiers who had looked away. They looked across the gulf of the classes, the middle classes and the working classes. It would take the rebirth of Marx for Marxism to explain definitively this middle class condemnation of an imperialist war in the last Capitalist nation, this working class affirmation. But it is the urban middle class in America who always felt itself most uprooted, most alienated from America itself, and so instinctively most critical of America, for neither do they work with their hands nor wield real power, so it is never their lathe nor their sixty acres, and certainly it is never their command which is accepted because they are simply American and there, no, the urban middle class was the last class to arrive at respectable status and it has been the most overprotected (for its dollars are the great nourishing mother of all consumer goods) yet the most spiritually undefended since even the concept of a crisis in identity seems most exclusively their own. The sons and daughters of that urban middle class, forever alienated in childhood from all the good simple funky nitty-gritty American joys of the working class like winning a truly dangerous fist fight at the age of 8 or getting sex before 14, dead drunk by 16, whipped half to death by your father, making it in rumbles with a proud street gang, living at war with the education system, knowing how to snicker at the employer from one side of the mouth, riding a bike with no hands, entering the Golden Gloves, doing a hitch in the Navy, or a stretch in the stockade, and with it all, their sense of elan, of morale, for buddies are the manna of the working class: there is a God-given cynical indifference to school, morality, and job. The working class is loyal to friends, not ideas. No wonder the Army bothered them not a bit. But the working class bothered the sons of the middle class with their easy confident virility and that physical courage with which they seemed to be born — there was a fear and a profound respect in every middle class son for his idea of that most virile ruthless indifferent working class which would eventually exterminate them so easily as they exterminated gooks. And this is not even to mention the sense of muted awe which lived in every son of the urban middle class before the true American son of the small town and the farm, that blank-eyed snubnosed innocent, bewildered, stubborn crew-cut protagonist of all conventional American life; the combination of his symbolic force with the working class was now in focus here.

Standing against them, the demonstrators were not only sons of the middle class of course, but sons who had departed the middle class, they were rebels and radicals and young revolutionaries; yet they were unbloodied, they felt secretly weak, they did not know if they were the simple equal, man for man, of these soldiers, and so when this vanguard confronted soldiers now, and were able to stare them in the eye, they were, in effect, saying silently, "I will steal your elan, and your brawn, and the very animal of your charm because I am morally right and you are wrong and the balance of existence is such that the meat of your life is now attached to my spirit, I am stealing your balls."

That is, Mailer says, what really happened at the Pentagon. It is because no one knew that that was it, that these were ignorant armies clashing by night. At a second level of meaning of the title, the organizers of the march like Dellinger, and its Marxist analysts like Teague, were equally ignorant. In his own analysis, I want to point out that when he says urban middle class he is thinking primarily of the Jewish middle class; and that the silent speech of the demonstrators is a dramatization of the Faustian bargain — not, of course, with the size or significance it has for certain Faustian individuals, for Mailer himself, but still the Faustian bargain as it figures in the lives of a lot of people.

This theory of America, that its real men live by that unspoken and unwitting bargain, appears again and again in Mailer's essays and stories, and presumably derives from his early experience. In 1944, at the age of twenty-one, after entering Harvard at sixteen, and writing a novel while an undergraduate, he was put into an army unit full of southwesterners. This was his first big experience of America outside New York and Cambridge, Mass., outside school and college and the middle class, outside polite and gentle and liberal people. In *The Naked and the Dead* he dramatizes some of that confrontation in the figures of Joey Goldberg and of Sergeant Croft. And in *Why Are We in Vietnam?* he names the two figures D.J. and Tex Hyde, and makes the Faustian encounter and transaction for them (and between them) directly sexual. It is partly because Mailer sees his own achievement of manhood in these terms that it occurred to him to describe himself as Lyndon Johnson's dwarf alter ego in the speech reported in *The Armies of the Night*.

Fiedler takes a great interest in the same problem from the same point of view, particularly in *Waiting for the End*. He argues that the great development in American writing since the war has been the release of Jewish writers from the constrictions of Jewishness. The most powerful mechanism for effecting this has been for Jewish writers to imagine themselves as sexual heroes — to abandon the traditional Jewish qualities of patience, humor, intelligence, irony, wisdom, and to acquire the goy qualities of violence and potency — which is to say, to transact the Faustian bargain. His two great examples are Mailer's character Sergius O'Shaughnessy, who appears both in *The Deer Park* and in episodes from an as yet unfinished novel which are printed in *Advertisements for Myself*; and Saul Bellow's character, Eugene Henderson, who appears in *Henderson, the Rain King*. Fiedler points out that both characters are big, blond, dangerous, sexually potent, goy heroes, who find adventure very much in the style of Hemingway's heroes and of Hemingway himself. O'Shaughnessy has been a bullfighter, Henderson goes to Africa. Fiedler says that both writers are reacting to Hemingway's portrayal of the Jewish victim-figure in Robert Cohn in *The Sun Also Rises*. Mailer has of course been explicit about his modeling himself on Hemingway, his stealing the very animal of Hemingway's charm. Henderson goes to Africa, Mailer (in "The White Negro") to the ghettos, in search of black models and tutors in manhood. Moreover, Sergius, in Mailer's unfinished novel, is a figure in a dream dreamed by a mild Jewish minor writer called Sam Slabovda. While in Bellow's *The Victim*, Fiedler suggests, the aggressive WASP, Kirby Allbee, has some character of being dreamed or imagined by the mild Jewish Leventhal. Both writers, and both heroes, Fiedler points out, see the good life as passionate, genital, anti-intellectual, impulsive. (This explanatory account of the transformation of the Jewish writer seems to me more satisfactory than the much more detailed, sober, verifiable accounts given by, for instance, Norman Podhoretz in *Making It* and Alfred Kazin in *A Walker in the City*. As explanations, their accounts are both liberal-humanist, whereas Fiedler's is Faustian — that is to say, mythical, wildly ambitious, unverifiable, self-parodying. A period when even explanations succeed better in the Faustian mode is a Faustian period indeed.)

In *Herzog* Bellow reverted to an earlier pattern for Jewish writers, making his hero an infinitely lovable clown. The contrast figure, Valentine Gersbach, also a Jew, is superior to him in power of emotion, and yet is to be rejected by the reader. This is of course an anti-Faustian theme, and it is worked out in interesting detail. It is much the most interesting part of the novel.

> Valentine loved to use Yiddish expressions, to misuse them, rather . . . "You're a ferimmter mensch." Moses, to save his soul, could not let this pass. He said quietly, "Berimmter."

Note the exaggeration of that "to save his soul" — Moses is forced, in his contest with Valentine, to play the role of the man of exact knowledge and refined taste, the genteel pedant, the Erasmian temperament, and to resign all claims to "soul" to the other man.

Dealing with Valentine was like dealing with a king. He had a thick grip. He might have held a sceptre. He *was* a king, an emotional king, and the depth of his heart was his kingdom. He appropriated all the emotions about him, as if by divine or spiritual right. He could do more with them, and therefore he simply took them over. He was a big man, too big for anything but the truth. (Again, the truth!) Herzog had a weakness for grandeur, and even bogus grandeur (was it ever entirely bogus?).

We shall see, in other cases of the Faustian temperament, that the criterion of bogusness is not crucial. Every big man, every king, is likely to have something bogus about him. I remember being bewildered, as an Erasmian myself, by this quality in my first American Jewish friends.

And Moses recognized that under his own rules the man who had suffered more was more special, and he conceded willingly that Gersbach had suffered harder, that his agony under the wheels of the boxcar must have been deeper than anything Moses had ever suffered . . . His great, his hot sorrow! Molten sorrow!

Tears were not relevant. The cause was too perverse, altogether too odd for all concerned. And then, too, Gersbach was a frequent weeper of distinguished emotional power. The hot tear was often in his magnanimous ruddy-brown eye. . . . So evidently, thought Moses, he's fucked up weeping for me, too.

These are Moses' own rules, we note, by which Gersbach is his superior and has the right to expropriate him from his own emotions. Indeed, they are the rules of all the characters in the novel, most notably of all the Jews in it. But the argument of the novel is that those rules are wrong; that Herzog, the figure of discrimination, is to be preferred to Gersbach, the figure of power. It is directed against all those more-or-less Faustian novels in which the supreme value is intensity of emotion, power of personality; (an interesting exercise in the negative mode of this Faustian form is Santayana's *The Last Puritan*). In Bellow's novel, the memory of Jane Austen, of Forster, of Erasmus himself, rises like a moon over the riotous sunset of Jewish-Faustian emotionalism. But *Herzog* is not very successful as a whole. The central character is finally a hero of sensibility more than anything else, and of that old sensibility which the novel is trying to repudiate. Our preference must go to Mailer, who is perhaps — being Bellow's cruder competitor for a long period of their careers — his ideological Gersbach.

Some Historical Backgrounds

An interesting example of the Jewishness which both Mailer and Bellow have tried to escape is to be found in the figure of Moses Mendelssohn, as presented in F. H. Hedge's *Prose Writers of Germany*, of 1847. He was born, we are told, the son of a very poor schoolteacher in Dessau, and carried wrapped in a cloak to attend the seminary (having been roused at 3:00 A.M.) from the age of seven on. He attributed both his cultural prowess and his physical deformity to his early study — he grew up small, feeble, and humpbacked. He said, "Maimonides is the cause of my deformity, he spoiled my figure and ruined my constitution; but still I doat on him for many hours of dejection, which he has converted into hours of rapture. And if he has unwittingly weakened my body, has he not made ample atonement by invigorating my soul with his divine instructions." This is a classic statement of the Erasmian contract, the subordination of body to mind.

At the age of fourteen, when he was living alone and extremely poor in Berlin, a rabbi got him free lodging and two days' a week board from a philanthropist. He taught himself Latin translating Locke, and earned money copying Hebrew. Then a wealthy Jewish manufacturer took him in, made him tutor to his children, and finally partner. He became a friend of Lessing, according to Hedge playing a very Jewish role in the friendship. "Lessing loved Mendelssohn for his excellent heart and highly cultivated understanding, and Mendelssohn was no less attached to Lessing for his inflexible consistency and his transcendent abilities." It is remarkable how quasi-sexual the terms of characterization are.

Mendelssohn's most popular work was a translation of Plato's *Phaedon*, accompanied by much additional material on the immortality of the soul. He is described as having a big nose, a gentle smile, big bright eyes, and "so much kindness, modesty, and benevolence portrayed on his countenance that he won every heart at first sight. . . . From sensual gratification he abstained firmly to the end." When he died, all Berlin mourned him. "No man has done more to soften the rigor of that hostility which embittered the lot of the German Israelite, a century ago . . . no one has better deserved the commendation, 'An Israelite, indeed, in whom there is no guile.' " * One could wish for no better representative of the Erasmian temperament, and no clearer explanation of why Jewish writers today have sought the Faustian bargain that would help them escape it.

In *Armies of the Night*, Mailer describes his own feelings about those virtues. "He could feel himself becoming more and more of a modest man as he stood there in the cold with his hangover, and he hated this because modesty was an old family relative, he had been born to a modest family, had been a modest boy, a modest young man, and he hated that, he loved the pride and the arrogance and the confidence and the egocentricity he had acquired over the years, that was his force and his luxury and the iron in his greed, the richest sugar of his pleasure. . . ." He is perfectly conscious of this aspect of his personality. It is the expression, the achievement, of deliberate policy. It is the intellectual and individual version of the silent speech of the demonstrators at the Pentagon.

Moses Mendelssohn, besides representing Jewish modesty, is also a figure of Jewish learning, of the rabbinical tradition of the servants and expounders of the sacred texts, the guardians of the moral law. Mailer, Fiedler, the modern Jewish writers in general, belong rather to the opposite Jewish tradition, to the line of Cabbalists. They aim at the qualities of Moses de Leon and Nathan of Gaza, or Sabbatai Zevi, Jakob Frank, and Simon Magus, rather than those of Moses Maimonides. If we use I. B. Singer's novel, *Satan in Goray*, as a dramatization of the conflict between the two traditions, Mailer and Fiedler align themselves with Mordecai Joseph and Reb Gedaliya and Rechele, not with Rabbi Benish Ashkenazi. The Cabbala, with its imaginative splendor and obscurity, its sexu-

* He inspired Lessing to create the figure of Nathan the Wise, and that image, blending together with Spinoza, begat the line of saintly-Jewish-scholar images in fiction, by impregnating the imaginations of Erasmian novelists like George Eliot.

ality and mystic obscenity, was not only forbidden knowledge of its time, but very like modern imaginative writing. *Back to China,* Fiedler's novel of 1965, has a thematic design in common with *Satan in Goray,* but with the sympathies almost reversed. Baro Finkelstone, his wife Susannah, and the man who gets her pregnant, Rodney Danichek, form a thematic complex very like Rechele, Reb Itche Mates, and Reb Gedaliya.

Mailer has always been interested in the occult, in magic and alchemy and drugs. His theories, of cancer and the nature of God and the tendency of the universe, all bear the stamp of mysticism in the loose sense. And his city, New York, is a city of the occult, though also of technology. The two things complement each other and blend in a certain sort of city, which I want to call the metropolis; a great, brutal, discordant city, full of race, creed, and class conflicts, crudely lacking in both moral and intellectual integrity, hideously unlike either the city of faith (Jerusalem) or the city of culture (Athens) and yet much more the template of subsequent Western cities than either of the two officially touted models. An apt emblem of this sort of city, and its worship of the-occult-and-technology, is the mechanical theater of Hero of Alexandria, which gave performances of "The Apotheosis of Dionysos" in the second century A.D. This was a religious mystery in which the altar moved and burst into light, by means of hydraulic machinery, and Dionysos came to life before the audience-congregation's eyes, gestured, spoke, poured liquids from his goblet and thyrsus, and cymbals clashed and Bacchantes danced, all by machinery. The audience could appreciate the technical ingenuity while they underwent the religious frisson, and could remain all the time radically uncommitted. The Egyptians had long been fascinated by animated statues. It is said that already in the third century B.C. there was a Dionysos in Egypt who could pour wine from a goblet. And the Hermetic manuscripts make much of the secret rituals by means of which statues could be built by men and yet acquire divine life and prophecy — after the right incantations, the right music, the burning of the right herbs, etc.

The great world-prototype of this sort of city is Alexandria, the city, like New York today, of Jews in exile and cultural eclecticism; of Cabbalism, gnosticism, magic, alchemy, of every exotic religious doctrine and practice. It was a great center of commercialism-and-gnosticism, a factory of the dissociated sensibility. And in all its main outlines New York belongs to this Alexandrian type of city. *An American Dream*, Mailer's rendering of New York in fiction, is an Alexandrian novel, full of machines and magic, full of telephone conversations with the moon and with the wind. It is a compendium of superstitions, incantations, irrationalisms, a compendium of gnoses. It portrays a city where, as one character puts it, there is a maniac buried underground who runs the communal mind of the eight million citizens, and sets up the mad coincidences of its life.

The citizens of Alexandria were mostly Greek, and the language was Greek, but there were large Egyptian and Jewish (and many other) minorities, and of these the Jews were the most active in intellectual affairs. It was the greatest Jewish city in the world, and the center of Jewish learning, where the Septuagint was translated into Greek, and where Philo and his followers interpreted the Old Testament by elaborate allegorical methods, to make it yield intuitive, mystic, and Hellenic meanings. When one reads of the Museum, an academy where learned men of every description were maintained at the state's expense, one is bound to think of New York's universities and of the allegorical interpretations being developed around American literature — by, for instance, Fiedler — in those classrooms. The library is said to have contained seven hundred thousand volumes at its height, and the white marble lighthouse of Pharos stood four hundred feet high; but the city was full of racial and social conflict, and its streets were frequently the scenes of mob battles between religious and ethnic groups. The character of Alexandrian poetry is suggested by the name of Theocritus, and of its science by Ptolemy and Euclid. It is to be contrasted with Athens at *its* height of development in much the way New York is to be contrasted with Emersonian Boston; for both the elaborated and sophisticated ingenuity of its intellectual products, and the brutal racial conflicts within its social substance.

Imperial Rome was another of the great wicked metropoles. And so — despite its smallness — was Elizabethan London. The latter's brilliant Renaissance styles of individuality at court, in dress, in theater, in food, in sex, in conspicuous consumption, everything that made the Puritans hate men like Raleigh, remind us of New

York. The Puritan style was plain of speech, methodical, purposive, ordered, disciplined. This is what Mailer conjures up in the figure of Teague the Marxist in *The Armies of the Night*, and it is plain that Mailer, like Raleigh, represents opposite qualities. He belongs to New York, the wicked city to which he is yearning to return all through the weekend.

The Body and the City

I defined the Faustian pact before as a way of coming into imaginative possession of one's body. There is something similar in Mailer's way of coming into imaginative possession of his city. He knows his body in extraordinary sensual detail, in an extraordinary series of sensual epiphanies and hallucinations — its sexual life, its intestinal life, its excremental life, every secretion of every gland, even the life of individual cells is dramatically vivid to his imagination. In this he just goes further than writers like Updike, Roth, Bellow, and Fiedler; the modern novel is suffused in body odors and body sensations, in body; it is because Salinger won't join them in that enterprise — and because that enterprise is crucial these days to a writer's temperamental contract — that he is silenced. But Mailer is more individual in the way in which he knows his city — which is by the same mode of knowledge. He knows its smells, he knows its secretions, he knows its shames, he knows its fevers. He knows its sexual life, he knows its intestinal life, he knows its excremental life. In both *An American Dream* and his movie *Beyond the Law* he portrays on the one hand the city of the Mafia and the police, and on the other the city of Andy Warhol and Susan Sontag's "Notes on Camp." In both cases it is the underground city, the city of the night. Of course he knows the aboveground city too; he knows everything, but his mode of knowledge is to be characterized as bringing out, giving relief to, the underground and the night truths.

This is no doubt because Mailer's whole life-style is imitative of New York's life-style. No writer has ever been more of the moment and of the scene. No one before ever wrote *Advertisements for Myself*; advertising not only his own personality, but the fact of his imitation of Madison Avenue, his desertion of the ivory tower for the most contemporary and commercial of circus stands. Few writers have had such acquaintance with a city's jails and asylums, its precinct offices and gang rumbles, its divorce courts and rich parties. He has lived the life of the city in the sense the newspaper editors give to that phrase — the headlines are his natural habitat. Most writers' lives suggest to some degree pastoral retreat and innocence, Wordsworthian quiet, a primrose by a river's brim, or at least the quiet of a library and a study. Mailer's suggests the opposite; rich, overspiced, overbourboned food in overexpensive restaurants; punching policemen, stabbing a wife, delivering drunken and obscene speeches in theaters and public parks. He has in some sense incorporated into himself the forces of his city, imaginatively appropriated and mastered them by imitating them.

The Faustian as Phallic Narcissist

But we have to return to the point we made before — that his kind of relation to the city, imaginatively serious though it is, includes within it highly destructive forces, forces of hatred, and derives much of its energy from them. He is a man who has encouraged those nihilistic tendencies in himself inseparable from the Faustian temperament, and who has reached not only his insights but his being, his self-hood, by that means. What he has achieved of course justifies those means, insofar as we have any right to judge him. But it is an irregular achievement, bulking much larger on the artistic-imaginative side than on any other. The man of the past whom Mailer most resembles is Byron, a man not only attracted to the Faust story but clearly living out some version of the diabolic pact in his own imaginative life. I have argued elsewhere that Kingsley Amis is another example of the same type, and that the results can be seen clearly in the same virtues and vices of style; great energy, great authenticity, great crispness, paid for in slanginess and occasional vulgarity, and long stretches of rhetorical overinflation (Byron and Mailer are guilty of this rather than Amis). All three are men with a very acute eye and ear for contemporary fashion, in feelings and ideas as well as in clothes and talk. All three articulate the worldly point of view, the antiliberal, antigenteel, antimoralist view on issues of the time, with imaginative authority. All three are sympathetic to the military point of view, are fascinated by the experience of command and killing and war in general.

I also argue that all these characteristics derive from an insistent sexual identity which all three share. They project an insistent masculinity — though they have strong feminine traits — which means, among other things, that they don't *want* to write as well as possible, writing well being for liberals, who are ideologically speaking neuters; they want to write only as well as is compatible with being always themselves. This insistent sexual identity is a kind of phallic narcissism, a flamboyant assertion and enjoyment of one's sexual performance, which assigns to all women a radically other and subordinate status as people. And the stresses and strains of this sort of sexuality bring with it a strong sense of sin, of guilt. "Sex to Mailer's idea of it was better off dirty, damned, even slavish! than clean, and without guilt. For guilt was the existential edge of sex. Without guilt, sex was meaningless. One advanced into sex against one's sense of guilt, and each time guilt was successfully defied, one had learned a little more about the contractual relation of one's own existence to the unheard thunders of the deep — each time guilt herded one back with its authority, some primitive awe — hence some creative clue to the rages of the deep — was left to brood about."

This sense of sin is one of the things Mailer claims makes him most incompatible with all liberals, and with the whole spirit of the march on the Pentagon. "His deepest detestation was often reserved for the nicest of liberal academics, as if their lives were his own life but a step escaped. . . ." The girls at their parties were "innocent, decent-spirited, merry, red-cheeked, idealistic, and utterly lobotomized away from the sense of sin." He is yearning all the time to get back to New York to a party which promises to have someone very rich and very social at it. This is the kind of party he enjoys; a party without a wicked lady in the room is like an opera company without a large voice. In this he is exactly like Kingsley Amis, in whose personal myth rich and wicked ladies play a prominent part. Elizabeth Gruffydd-Williams in *That Uncertain Feeling* is a good example; she is what sexual excitement means to the hero just because she is wicked, and at the end he has to run away from a woman who promises the same, in order to preserve his marriage and his self-respect and his socialism. Since then Amis's novels have dealt with heroes who did not run away from that opportunity, while Byron is one of the most notorious yielders to the importunities of rich and wicked ladies. Phallic narcissism as a whole is perhaps the sexual mode most appropriate to the Faustian temperament, though only a subdivision of Faustian writers fit that category without qualification.

"Phallic narcissist" is in fact the label Denise attaches to Sergius O'Shaughnessy in Mailer's brilliant story "The Time of Her Time." Her final taunt is to tell him that he is in flight from "the homosexual that is the real you." And clearly this sexual identity does involve an alert orientation toward men; close sexual companionship and calibration and appreciation, a sense even that they are sexually more interesting than women. Though to use the word "homosexual" for that orientation is to signal the final demise of that exhausted term. A more meaningful sexual label is suggested by the central action of the story, Sergius's anal rape of Denise, and the orgasm she finally, and for the first time, and furiously, achieves by that means. This motif of the sodomizing of a resistant woman occurs in other places in Mailer; for instance, the hero of *An American Dream* sodomizes the German maid. This is doubly interesting because the sexual scandal that broke Byron's marriage was, according to Wilson Knight and others, Byron's sodomizing of his wife. The practice recurs in *Lady Chatterley's Lover*, one of the finest of phallic narcissist novels. It is at least a vivid emblem of the phallic narcissist's relation to women and to sex, in its flamboyantly aggressive and even sadistic generosity, and in its impulse to simultaneously desecrate and consecrate the sexual organ.

There is a political style that corresponds as naturally to phallic narcissism as the literary style discussed before. The reason behind the frequent clashes between Women's Liberators today and their radical allies is that the latter are mostly Faustian by temperament, and so committed to sex as a power game. The natural allies for Women's Liberators would be the liberals. Calvinist radicals — such of them as there are — are distrustful of personal and sexual emancipation, while Faustians are phallic narcissists at root — they have derived from that sexual role the energy to defy society, though they can use that energy for conservative gestures as well as radical. Amis could call his politics Left Conservatism, and Byron could have called his that. Its features are a mixture of radicalism and Burkean reaction, with a stress on manhood, including of course sexual manhood, as a prime political value. There is also an addiction to Realpolitik, to the brutal facts of power, to all that contradicts anxious liberal ameliorations of those facts. And an attraction to the aristocratic style, by which the men of power treat with each other. Mailer describes himself and Lowell, isolated at the liberal party before the march, as poor damn émigré princes, and grands conservateurs. At the same time, all three maintain a strong sympathy for really anarchic radicalism, and even more a strong dislike for the Establishments of their societies. They are not really Burkean, because their strongest temperamental affinity is for fire and explosion, not for organic growth. The Faustian temperament is always radical underneath its conservatism.

Let me add only that they are all three sensationally, flashily handsome men, and rather flashy personalities, addicted to publicity. Both Amis and Mailer have been newspaper columnists, and frequently on TV; and can one doubt that Byron would have too if he had had the chance?

Many of the things I have said about these three would apply to all men of the Faustian temperament. But I think of these three as a subdivision within the group. Tolstoy, Lawrence, and Goethe, for instance, do not have the same stylistic character or limitations. Though all three had something of the same sexual assertiveness, the feminine elements in their temperaments are interwoven with the masculine in ways that make for more variety and more continuity, ways that make possible that Protean creative fecundity that marks them. Mailer and Amis and Byron belong rather with Waugh and Hemingway and Faulkner, writers of much more narrow and self-emphatic range, prone to self-caricature, novelists whose characters are often sketches that illustrate a part of an idea, instead of absorbing autonomous creations like the characters of the three greater writers.

Part of the point here of this connection (this temperamental identity) which I am asserting between Mailer and Byron, is that it enables me to draw more connections between Mailer and Goethe.

Byron was a very important figure to Goethe, as Professor Butler has established. He admired him more than any other of their contemporaries, and saw in him a man following the path he himself had turned away from. When Goethe was twenty-six he went to Weimar, and allied himself with the Duke and the hierarchy there; when Byron was twenty-six he got married, and the disasters of his subsequent life followed from that step as inevitably as the safeties of Goethe's did from his. At thirty-six Goethe slipped away from Weimar and official duties to travel to Italy, where he dedicated himself to "classicism"; understanding that as a taste in the art of the past, as an artistic policy for his own work, and as a life-style of clarity and calm transcending the urgencies of the moment. At thirty-six Byron went to Greece, took command of the uncoordinated forces insurgent against the Turkish rulers, caught fever, and died. He threw away his life as assiduously as Goethe conserved his. Goethe brooding over Byron — a frequent spectacle of his later years — is the man who has put his faith in the Erasmian compact mourning and admiring the man who abided by the Faustian. Admiring as well as mourning; it seems to have been Byron who inspired much of Goethe's theory of the daimonic, which he discussed often with Eckermann in his last years, and which is in some sense a recantation of his own moral conservatism. If we accept the identity of Mailer and Byron, we may see Goethe confronting Mailer there.

Gothic Form and Faustian Meaning

Like "Manfred," and the Urfaust, *An American Dream* is in the Gothic mode. This is Mailer's most successful piece of full-length fiction (though "The Time of Her Time" is his most brilliant and perfect thing in itself) and it is so because it is in that mode. It is an American romance, the fictional genre appropriate to a world in which Jackie Kennedy marries Aristotle Onassis. Everything in it is exaggerated, by the standards of the Great Tradition, or by those of any other expression of the liberal-Erasmian temperament. Everyone and everything is chosen from among the most extreme examples of their kind. Barney Oswald Kelly is not just rich but fantastically rich; Deborah is not the scion of one great American family, but of three; Rojack sodomizes the maid *immediately* after murdering his wife; his new sweetheart has been the mistress of his wife's father; more recently she has been the mistress of a black man who is a brilliant singer and also a killer; Rojack not only talks to the moon, the moon talks back to him; and so on.

This American Gothic form is an idea explored and recommended by Fiedler more prominently than anybody else. He has guaranteed its legitimacy by reinterpreting its nineteenth-century precedents to have sexual and mythical meanings. He reinterprets the whole of American literature in the service of this idea in *Love and Death in the American Novel.* This is a really brilliant book, and the major achievement so far in the field of criticism and scholarship of the same mind that Mailer's books express in more directly imaginative terms. Its mission, as a cultural enterprise, is to reconquer the past of American literature for present-day readers and writers, whom it assumes to share the same mind as Mailer and Fiedler. It rescues all those books from their original writers and readers, and from traditional critics and scholars, all of whom were either feminine-genteel in character or liberal-neuter. It repossesses all that territory of the imagination in the name of the proudly phallic consciousness, the mind of the phallic narcissist. Fiedler attributes to their books the unconscious meanings they would have had if he had written them in his sleep, if he had dreamed those plots and those characters. And because he is an intelligent man and an authentic temperament, those meanings are more interesting than the original books, by and large.

One of the most vivid treatments of the Faustian theme in contemporary fiction is the portrait of Maurice Stoker in John Barth's novel, *Giles Goat-Boy.* The book is one we probably owe to Fiedler — in the sense that his critical gospel called for such a novel to be written — and the figure too in a different sense. Maurice Stoker is the figure of sexual potency in the novel, but also of personality power in general, including the power of moral ascendancy over others. He is the figure of diabolism, sexually, politically, and morally; and yet he is not to be condemned; he is part of the moral economy of the universe. He looks, we are told, strikingly like Giles himself, the Christ figure. At the end Giles offers him "Candidacy," and comments on his refusal of the offer, "Had he not refused me, I should have had to refuse him; denial is his affirmation, and from that contradiction he — indeed, the campus — draws strength." He is the obverse of, and half-brother to, Lucky Rexford the President-Chancellor, the prince of light. Stoker's locus is the Furnace Room, underground, where he is surrounded by minor devils, all grotesquely lustful, in an atmosphere of fire and smoke and sweat and steam and smells and explosions. He is the power figure: the Power Plant, we are told, is his domain; WESCAC appointed him to control it. " 'Talk about *power*; all the power on this campus comes from here! The same power that runs the University!' " Stoker's heat supplies Lucky's light.

The novel is one that Fiedler has praised highly. It represents the future direction of American fiction as Faustian criticism understands it, as he predicts and wants it. It is a very Jewish novel, with a false Messiah, Harold Bray. It is a very bodily and sexual novel, its Christ figure a goat boy. And it is, with its parodic obscenity and scatology, a very full expression of the particular sexual temperament we have been discussing, the phallic-narcissist personality. Stoker is associated with Hell's Angels on his first appearance, which is heralded by:

. . . snarlings in the nearby forest, which grew to a roar and burst upon the beach with half a dozen bright lights, flashing red or blinding white. . . . As they drew nearer, the firelight revealed a party of humans in black leather jackets, variously ornamented with silver studs and bright glass jewels. Goggled and helmeted, each was mounted upon a gleaming black machine with side car attached. . . . With pounding heart I regarded our adversary, who had removed his helmet and goggles and was calmly blowing the smoke from his pistol-barrel: ruddy-cheeked, short-statured, and heavy-set he was, but not fat, with black curls on his head, hands, and finger-tops . . . a not unhandsome face withal, and the more striking for the clear eyes that flashed from so swart a field. . . . The man replied with a raucous fart ("Hear hear!" his cohorts cheered), raised his pistol again, and with incredible calm aimed it at my heart. I understood then that he himself was Maurice Stoker.

One is tempted to associate the figure of Maurice with Fiedler perhaps most of all because of the former's relationship with his wife, Anastasia. She represents all the passively Christian and feminine virtues, in their most conventional and silly but attractively provocative form. She provokes him to his most crudely masculine and pagan and diabolist brutalities. She is American literature of the nineteenth-century, genteel WASP culture. He is Leslie Fiedler in *Love and Death in the American Novel*.

Talking of American poets in *Waiting for the End*, Fiedler defines the "suburban" poetry of Richard Wilbur as characterized by its denial of three major characteristics of great poetry: the assertion of sexuality, the flaunting of madness, and the triumph of the ego. It is of course the Faustian temperament he is describing. And in *The Return of the Vanishing American* he manifests that temperament in more extreme opinions than ever before. In this book he extends his mythical explanation of America, and predicts the future as well as interpreting the past. He sees the Western as the crucial American literary form, in which the significant art of the future will get written. So far, Fiedler admits, the only successful literary attempts at the form have been grossly parodic, and he implies that they will continue to be so. Parody, as I pointed out before, is the literary effect toward which the phallic narcissist inevitably tends.

There is very little evidence that American writers are now turning to "Western" themes, or that, when they do, those themes and that form fire their imaginations to make them produce specially significant works of art. But evidence has never been what Fiedler worked from. He has always been a prophet, one who compels our assent by the brilliance of his phrasing, the challenge of his thesis, the accuracy of fragmentary insights, his general knowledgeability and superiority to ordinary method. He would betray his ideological manhood by following reasonable, liberal-humanist method. He simply attributes to every American writer both the Faustian temperament and a kind of phallic aggressiveness toward his literary material.

Here, in this last book, his prophecy is pointing away from New York Jewishness, putting the future of the American imagination in the opposite direction. But it is still the same New York Jewish temperament, his and Mailer's Faustian temperament, which he is calling to possess these themes and forms. He is calling for Jews to become cowboys, just as in *Waiting for the End* he was calling for them to be black. And if there he was thinking of "The White

Negro," here he is thinking of *Why Are We in Vietnam?* He and Mailer are always in step.

A Way Out of the Contract

Another brilliant exponent of this New York Jewish mind is Susan Sontag. But her most interesting work so far has taken the form of an attempt to escape from that psychic patterning, to escape the compulsion to egotism, madness, and the flaunting of sex as proof of imaginative authenticity. In *Trip to Hanoi* she identifies the America she hates, the America which makes war on North Vietnam, with her own segment of it, with Jewish-intellectual New York. That is, she asserts the indivisibility of the two. (By doing so, she shows up something unsatisfactory in Mailer's analysis in *Why Are We in Vietnam?* which by implication puts the blame on the other America, on Texas.) The first thing she discovers in Vietnam is her bad faith — "that I long for the three-dimensional, textured, 'adult' world in which I live in America." She had thought that all "America" meant was corrupt capitalist culture, something she had long ago taken the measure of, which she could take or leave. But she finds that her own consciousness, "reared in that 'big' culture, is a creature with many organs, accustomed to being fed by a stream of cultural goods, and infected by irony." To live in Vietnam would impoverish her American sensibility, which she must now admit that she treasures. We note the bigness, the adultness, the three-dimensionality she attributes to American culture, all typical images for what the Faustian temperament aims at.

She comes to hate the abrasive and aggressive egotism she took for granted in New York. She acknowledges "the grim view, popular where I come from, that 'real people' are dangerous, volatile; one is never altogether safe with them." She comes to see that politeness need not mean, as it is instinctive with her to assume, insincerity. Talk need not be "a brilliant, ambiguous, self-sufficient substitute for action; half an aggressive act, half an attempted embrace." She observes that "the phenomena of existential agony, of alienation, just don't appear among the Vietnamese — probably in part because they lack our kind of 'ego' and our endowment of free-floating guilt." Our kind of ego is of course the Faustian kind.

It is expressly with the Jews that she contrasts the Vietnamese in their style of suffering.

The Jews' manner of experiencing their suffering was direct, emotional, persuasive. It ran the gamut from stark declamation to ironic self-mockery. It attempted to engage the sympathy of others. At the same time, it projected a despair over the difficulty of engaging others.

What attracts her in Vietnam is an opposite ethos, an ethos of discipline and modesty, of politeness and self-restraint and self-sacrifice, but also of gaiety and simplicity, so that the self-restraint and self-sacrifice are not perilously achieved against powerful opposite impulses. What attracts her is not only the opposite of Texas and Lyndon Johnson's America, but the opposite of her own New York, of the mind she herself expressed in *Against Interpretation* and her novels.

Clearly the culture of North Vietnam as she describes it — and as it made impact upon her — was a cultural manifestation of some blend of the Erasmian and Calvinist temperaments. (By her account of it, Confucianism is as much a cultural institutionalization of the Erasmian temperament as Communism is of the Calvinist.) She says that in it shame plays the key role which in American culture is played by guilt. This guilt is something she lays great stress on, rather puzzlingly at first reading. But it is of course the natural accompaniment of the loud, aggressive, brilliant, challenging personality she identifies with New York. It is what Mailer means by sin. This is exactly the aspect of America which fascinates visitors from England, a more Erasmian culture. See, for instance, Malcolm Bradbury's *Stepping Westward*, Julian Mitchell's *As Far as You Can Go*, Kingsley Amis's *One Fat Englishman*, Andrew Sinclair's *The Hallelujah Bum*. This is the America which heroes of those novels recoil at, aspire to, fail to match, retreat from. It is a personality which is based on exceeding limits, on outsizeness, on outrageousness. A Faustian personality.

If that describes New York, who better to represent it than Mailer? His whole performance in *The Armies of the Night* exemplifies what Susan Sontag means by "American"; not only the behavior he describes but his way of describing it.

Susan Sontag ends *Trip to Hanoi* with the resolve to love her country, and not to fall back into her old state of alienation from it. But every reader is conscious, as she is herself, of the immense difficulty, the unlikelihood, of her being able to maintain that resolve. Not only because of the pressure on her from outside, but because of the nature of her mind. The kind of political responsibility and moral health which the New York Jewish mind can achieve is going to continue to be alienated. It is going to be less well represented by *Trip to Hanoi* than by *Why Are We in Vietnam?* and above all by *The Armies of the Night*.

That last book is more than a brilliant performance. It tells the truth about the march on the Pentagon, and about much of American politics. It is full of valuable insights, and is more really responsible in its politics than twenty-five more solemn books all added together. Nevertheless, its responsibleness, like Mailer's whole balance of personality, is an eccentric, a partly accidental achievement. It is a Faustian version of responsibleness; a balance only achieved after and despite a wholehearted pursuit of imbalance, or of things that implied imbalance necessarily. There are other things Mailer wants far more than political balance of judgment, and tomorrow that achievement might have to be sacrificed in pursuit of an authenticity he felt he was losing in his present stasis. He is still bound by his Faustian compact, and his politics, his relation to his city, is still, in important ways, nihilistic.

But my main interest is to claim that that relationship is representative, that New York is a *city* of Faustian temperament, a stronghold of imaginative phallic narcissism, over whose towers the face of Norman Mailer floats like a banner. The Faustian face typically has beautiful curly hair (Mailer, Fiedler, Byron, Amis) and the lineaments of gratified desire. It is the face of the sexually conquering hero. By contrast, Erasmians seem pale heroes of renunciation, Lambert Strethers all, though in fact there are better candidates than him to be found in the Great Tradition. Mr. Knightley is an Erasmian hero of fulfillment in the measure appropriate, and Emma Woodhouse and Anne Elliot of *Persuasion* and Mary Garth of *Middlemarch* are his heroines. In the performing arts today it is hard to find a face to represent these qualities adequately; the best I can offer is Alec Guinness, or Dirk Bogarde in his performance as the estranged husband of a Faustian heroine in "I Could Go On Singing" (both British). But the Calvinist hero quality is surprisingly available among Hollywood stars, especially in the war films made between 1945 and 1960. John Wayne, Gary Cooper, Gregory Peck, a dozen more, have portrayed the captain of a ship or plane or army unit in danger, fulfilled entirely in the service of his cause, his group. His tensely noble features relax at the end as he clasps some perfunctory starlet to his bosom, but it is clear that his private life is a matter of convention, run like a car-heater off the powerful engine of his command. Of these three types, thick curly hair, straight and fine, short and grizzled, the New York of the imagination surely belongs to the first. It is the city neither of a balanced liberalism, nor of an organized political radicalism, but of an experimental and explosive extremism.

3 — RADICAL LONDON IN THE 1790'S

*For 200 years "Radical London" has always been more heteroge-
neous and fluid in its social and occupational definition than the
Midlands or Northern centers grouped around two or three staple
industries . . . And the agitation of the 1790's, although it lasted
only five years (1792–6) was extraordinarily intensive and far-
reaching. It altered the sub-political attitudes of the people, affected class alignments, and initiated traditions which stretch forward into the present century. It was not an agitation about France,
although French events both inspired and bedevilled it. It was an
English agitation, of impressive dimensions, for an English democracy.**

Explanatory

There are several historical parallels to New York today, and London in the 1790's is probably not the closest. I shall in fact compare
London then with London now, and those two cultural situations
seem to me more alike than London then and New York now. In
both eras London is/was not the real world-center and potential
storm-center which was Paris then and New York is today. But
closeness is not the only thing that makes a parallel useful. I examine London in the 1790's after New York now, first because the
radicals there were particularly interesting — Blake, Paine, Godwin, Mary Wollstonecraft; and second because, besides their individual predicaments, they had a group predicament and fate which
is instructive when one is thinking about the problems of radicalism in literature. It is not the *same* predicament as that of Mailer,

* E. P. Thompson, *The Making of the English Working Class*, New York,
1963, pp. 21, 102.

Goodman, Fiedler, Susan Sontag — theirs is not the same radicalism, as we shall see — but to study it promises to illuminate our
understanding of our own writers.

However, I want to discuss this case, as I shall discuss the others
to come, as much for the various interests it offers in itself as for its
special value as a contrast with our own times. The illuminations of
our present position which I strike off by juxtaposing it with past
events are — judged by the standards of intellectual *method* — almost fortuitous. I have followed a method in choosing the cases,
and I devised that method to produce these illuminations, but it is
still very loose. The cases are roughly similar, and each is also interesting in other ways; that is all. I am hoping that that combination
of method and randomness will allow intuition free play and so
produce fruitful speculation.

The New York writers' situation is different for one thing because they have been so successful with the educated reading
public. Blake is the most striking example of the London writers'
failure in career, but he is not the only one. Once the tide of English opinion turned against the French Revolution, Godwin's brief
succès d'estime was snuffed out completely. He sank out of sight
intellectually, and underwater financially. Tom Paine's success with
the educated public was even briefer, and thereafter he was despised as a writer and as a thinker. The New York writers have had
comparatively immense rewards of money and prestige.

Mailer's success, both financial and prestigious, finds a parallel in
the earlier period only in the success of Walter Scott. I am not
hinting that Mailer is a liberal. The times are different. Unlike
liberal Edinburgh, in New York today genuine radicalism is still
acceptable — in intellectual circles you might say it is *de rigueur*.
The American government has not yet begun a policy of intellectual repression, nor has educated opinion in America yet turned
against revolution. Our talk has the atmosphere of London in
1789, not in 1798. Moreover, whatever political charges you might
bring against Mailer's position, his temperament is clearly antithetical to that of the Edinburgh liberals or any other true liberal. He
has far more in common with Blake than with Scott.

But it is significant that while some American writers have had
to flee their country just as Paine did — for instance, Eldridge

Cleaver and Stokely Carmichael — these do not include the men I have discussed. Cleaver and Carmichael are radicals in a sense that does not apply to Mailer and Fiedler. Their radicalism is that of a movement, a Party, and closer to the Calvinist in type — and by that token closer to Paine's kind of radicalism.

This brings me to the major difference relevant to my argument between London then and New York now. Whereas all the New York writers are of this same temperament, as a group, the radicalism of the London writers was of different temperamental kinds; Paine's being very unlike Blake's, and Godwin's unlike either. There was no group, in that sense. Moreover, whereas the whole New York skyline masses itself around Mailer's face — to the eye of the imagination — London belonged much less to Blake and Godwin. Though I have implied that London was a radical city, it was really, by the rules I have followed elsewhere, Tory. It was ruled by a Tory government and a ruling class either Tory or liberal, and there was no solid, lasting, radical opposition by the standards of the solid liberalism of Edinburgh or of the solid Faustianism of the arts in New York. When we come to discuss Havana today we shall see what a radical city is really like, and what it means for literature. But it seemed worthwhile to break the rules, in this case, because radicalism usually is just as diverse in kind as it was in London then, and usually does possess its city incompletely. Within the limits of Western culture, that is. Radicalism usually — that is, most often — has been fragmentary, soon forced into silence or shrill repetition, its parts eccentrically interrelated, and tending to separate centrifugally. Indeed, it is not to be expected that *any* position will dominate, or even completely characterize, a given city. The perspective we took on New York gave us a rather artificial impression of that city's uniformity, and a rather false standard for others.

In fact, the same perspective *could* be taken on London. If we imagined ourselves in the mind of the fifteen-year-old Hazlitt as he walked the streets of London in 1793, a student at the Hackney Dissenting Academy, we should see a city that belonged to the radicals of that time as much as New York belongs to Mailer, a city skyline that massed itself around the faces of Paine and Godwin and Holcroft and the Revolution Society. But that would be a

Portraits of

Will.ᵐ Blake

at the ages of 28 & 69 years.

Born November 20ᵗʰ 1757.   Died August 12. 1827

Ætat: 69.

Blake's second profile, his spiritual and daimonic self, is from my
point of view what he achieved by means of his Faustian contract,
is what he might have seen as his promised reward flickering in the
flames conjured up by Mephistopheles if he had followed the old-
fashioned scenario. (Undated self-portraits by William Blake,
from the Collection of Mr. and Mrs. Paul Mellon.)

forced and artificial vision for us now. All we can see now — or try to see, as we walk around London today, looking back — is Pitt's London, with glimpses of Blake's in odd corners and upper stories, and out of the corners of our eyes.

So the two situations and the two groups of talents are just roughly parallel. These are ages of revolution in great world-cities, and these are the writers most immediately and imaginatively responsive to that fact. But the London radicalism was fragmentary beside New York's.

Different Radical Temperaments

It is Blake more than any other of these radicals who interests the literary reader now. He is one of the few writers whose works gain in interest and vitality from the context of today's events. While our other jewels shrink paler and dimmer, Blake glows deeper and brighter with each passing month.

Like Mailer, Blake was very much a man, and a writer, of his city. He has to be explained in terms of it. His imagination received its education there and — more important — he deliberately possessed it, incorporated it into himself.

Loud sounds the Hammer of Los and loud his Bellows is heard
Before London to Hampstead's breadths and Highgate's heights,
To Stratford and old Bow and across to the Gardens of Kensington
On Tyburn's Brook; loud groans Thames beneath the iron Forge
Of Rintrah and Palamabron, of Theotorm and Bromion, to force the
*   instruments*
Of Harvest, the Plow and Harrow to pass over the Nations.

But unlike Mailer Blake was never a candidate for election as mayor of his city; and that was because he was never successful at being a public figure in London. Not because he did not want to be. He too tried to teach his fellow citizens saving truths, and he too had a vivid sense of himself as a prophet, but he became — perforce — one of the most private of all figures in English literature. He possessed his city most typically by transfiguring its names and places with his prophetic vision of the future. Mailer reveals his city in its current actions and figures, its television personalities and Mafia leaders and police captains; and Byron gives us the contemporary equivalent of that in "The Vision of Judgment." Blake

most often saw his city, Lambeth and Paddington and Putney, as it
might yet be or spiritually was. He recited its names in an incantation to make it become what he wanted.

But Blake was like Mailer a great egotist of the imagination. He
saw himself, as Milton, returning from heaven to earth in order to
redeem Albion. And like Mailer he acquired this faith in himself
by a spiritual bargain which repudiated the ordinary cultural bargain, the ordinary social identity assigned him.

> Thou, Mother of my Mortal part,
> With cruelty didst mould my Heart,
> And with false, self-deceiving tears
> Didst bind my Nostrils, Eyes, and Ears:
> Didst close my Tongue in senseless clay,
> And me to Mortal life betray.
> The death of Jesus set me free:
> Then what have I to do with thee?

He was in essence demonic. To be just human, to be a London
dissenting tradesman's son and an engraver's apprentice, would be
to accept limitations which he repudiated as fervently as Mailer
repudiated his fate as a modest, ironic, humorous Jew.

> My mother groan'd! My father wept.
> Into the dangerous world I leapt:
> Helpless, naked, piping loud;
> Like a fiend hid in a cloud.

He continued to see himself as a fiend; to judge by Mrs. Blake's
drawing of him, so like some of his own "ideal" drawings, he seems
to have intended himself in some of those radiantly golden-haired
figures of joyful rebellion he drew. What other people saw of him
was only a deception.

> Struggling in my father's hands,
> Striving against my swadling bands,
> Bound and weary I thought best
> To sulk upon my mother's breast.

He defied the limits set him by common sense and common decency, in the forms of established philosophy, science, religion, and
morality.

I am more famed in Heaven for my works than I could well conceive. In my Brain are studies and Chambers filled with books and pictures of old, which I wrote and painted in ages of Eternity before my mortal life; and those works are the delight and Study of Archangels . . . I find myself more and more that my Style of Designing is a Species by itself, and in this which I send you have been compelled by my Genius or Angel to follow where he led; if I were to act otherwise it would not fulfill the purpose for which alone I live . . . 13 years ago I lost a brother and with his spirit I converse daily and hourly in the Spirit and See him in my remembrance in the regions of my Imagination. I hear his advice and even now write from his Dictate. Forgive me for Expressing to you my Enthusiasm which I wish to partake of Since it is to me a Source of Immortal Joy: even in this world by it I am the companion of angels . . .

Blake affords us an interesting example of how the Faustian temperament can nurture itself within the cultural traditions of Protestant Christianity. By his language as well as by his choice of heroes like Milton, he affiliated himself clearly to the Puritan-Dissent line in English culture, and yet made that serve his artist's purposes of self-aggrandizement:

. . . for that I cannot live without doing my duty to lay up treasures in heaven is Certain and Determined. . . . The Thing I have most at Heart — more than life, or all that seems to make life comfortable without — Is the Interest of True Religion and Science, and whenever anything appears to affect that Interest (Especially if I myself omit any duty to my Station as a Soldier of Christ) It gives me the greatest of torments. I am not ashamed, afraid, or averse to tell you what Ought to be told: That I am under the direction of Messengers from Heaven, Daily and Nightly; . . . Art in London flourishes . . . Yet no one brings work to me . . . Yet I laugh and sing, for if on Earth neglected, I am in heaven a Prince among Princes, and even on earth beloved by the Good as a Good Man.

We see the mental freedom of Blake's, this self-creativity, in his quite speculative and rational dealings with occult philosophy and in his quite modernist sexual theories, as well as in his visions, his angels, and his voices. What he learned from Swedenborg, and Boehme and Paracelsus, put him in touch with that stream of forbidden knowledge which flows underground through European culture, and so rarely — especially in Anglo-Saxon countries —

comes to the surface in the work of distinguished artists. Blake managed to combine that imaginative tradition with evangelical Christian piety to form food for a Faustian temperament. Goethe also combined the two strains of thought, but his Faustianism fed also on other sources, which we don't know about in Blake's case.

Paine was the great Calvinist among those radicals, and one of the best representatives of that temperament in all of literary history. Representatively, he was not a poet, nor any other kind of "creative writer." The Calvinist is likely to make his contribution to myth by the life he lives; to inspire heroic poetry rather than to write it. Hazlitt and his fellow students at Hackney wrote poems about Paine. He himself shows, in the last of his *Crisis* papers, the subordination of literature to politics which he thinks appropriate. Discussing what service his writings may have done the new nation, he says, "if, in the course of more than seven years, I have rendered her any service, I have likewise added something to the reputation of literature, by freely and disinterestedly employing it in the great cause of mankind, and showing that there may be genius without prostitution." He was indeed a genius, if a vain one, and a hero; both for what he got done, what he contributed to the history-in-crisis of first the United States, then Great Britain, and then the French Republic, but also for the acts of his private life. For instance, he actually lost money on the best-seller, *Common Sense*, because he had given the copyright to Congress. And in Paris, in the revolution there, he took the place of an imprisoned Englishman he had never seen before, on the promise that the latter would return and stand trial after delivering some important documents to his firm in Birmingham.

Paine had also the weaknesses of a hero, a Calvinist hero. His life lay in his idea of it, in his intense relation to his ideology, his connection to his cause. When that was broken, he was broken. When he could no longer act for his cause, because he was isolated in prison, or because he was in disgrace with his party, he could collapse into complete inertia, and personal squalor, and overindulgence in stimulants like brandy and snuff. This happened to him at the end of his life, but also when he was disowned by Congress in 1778, and again in Paris after his release from prison. During such periods he often fell positively ill. He needed to be a member of a party, of a cell of activists, even though — like Calvin himself — he had his own uncooperativeness, his own touchy vanity and autocratic irritableness. He argued by contradiction, interpreted by moral condemnation, and conversed by monologue. He could not bear to be interrupted while speaking, and preferred not to speak at all; at the Society for Political Inquiries in Philadelphia he is said never to have opened his mouth. He was extremely on guard to defend the privacy of his private life. In America he refused to admit that he had been married, though he had had two wives in England. The second marriage had been dissolved because he refused to sleep with his wife, and in general he seems to have been lacking in intimate relations. His personality did not lack warmth, but it was a warmth directed toward the cause, and toward the group that fought for that cause. Everything in his life ranged itself around that center, that source of value, and anything else that could not or would not do that withered away, became vestigial. Porro unum necessarium can make for a very simple and unaffected style of heroism. One can compare Paine with Che Guevara today, in personal style and in revolutionary performance. Franklin had said, "Where Liberty is, there is my country." Paine improved upon him radically: "Where is not Liberty, there is mine." Like today's heroes, he and Lafayette carried the torch of rebellion across the Atlantic into lands not their own. Paine set the pattern of bookman-turned-liberator which was followed by Shelley in Ireland and Byron in Greece.

Paine was thirty-seven when he went to America in 1774, and until then his life had been marked outwardly only by bankruptcies, failed marriages, lost jobs; and there is no reason to suppose that it had been marked by distinction inwardly. He was called to intellectual life by the coming of the age of revolution, and his writing has a kind of vitality and distinction which is different from those of the liberal culture's man of letters, a kind that would figure more prominently in a radical culture's chart of literary values. And, as we have seen, when the life of revolution was cut off from him, he lapsed back into inertia. But as long as that life circulated in his veins, he wrote and thought with the sort of sparkling verve which illustrates one of the simpler meanings of "intellectual temperament." As tirelessly as Calvin himself, he reduced all the complexities of cultural tradition to simple alternatives, with an equally simple choice to be made between them. His schematic analysis turned all history and all experience into transparent streams of tendency, each making its moral character clearly legible within it. And for every problem he had a constitutional solution, a legal or political or economic answer that everyone could understand and assent to. The American constitution, he once said, is to liberty what grammar is to language.

How one feels about Paine determines one's sensibility in important ways. He was a real revolutionary hero. If words ever led to deeds, his did. If deeds ever changed the course of history, those he inspired did. And if one believes in man's capacity to take a conscious stride forward, deliberately to abandon old habits, because he thinks them bad and before he has acquired better ones — if, that is, one believes in revolution — then Paine is one's hero; and, therefore, whatever one believes in, he is as significant a piece of history as Burke. Within the world of letters, where we have few representatives of the Calvinist ideology, and where we overvalue the kinds of complexity he lacked, he needs special attention.

The intellectual career of Godwin, too, was promoted by the revolution. To some extent, of course, this was true of Blake, too, and of the others. All radicals need the impelling and compelling stimulus of a period when revolution is in the air. Ages of conformity breed the liberal and conservative tendencies in us. But among radicals it is the Calvinists who need, more than Faustians, a calling to something specific, by someone specific, as we see in the case of Calvin himself. It seems clear that the age of revolution intensified in Godwin a strain of heroism which otherwise would never have found such expression as it did. Trained though he had been in a Calvinist religious culture, he had made his way toward the intellectual virtues of an Erasmian as he came into possession of himself, in the 1780's. He had left the ministry for literary hackwork, and, in temperamental terms as well as vocational, was clearly in the process of turning himself into a man of letters. But then, under the pressure of the events of 1789–93, he produced *Political Justice*, one of the purest examples of Calvinist rhetoric and logic in the service of Erasmian ideals. Godwin has no strain of the Faustian. His dream is of perfect freedom for every individual, with no interference, and no compulsion — practically no contact — the quintessential liberal ideal. But no Erasmian liberal could have written *Political Justice*, because of the ruthlessness, the radicalism, with which it defines and idealizes that freedom, repudiates all compromises, rejects all the social institutions that traditionally have been allowed to limit it. Once the excitement of revolution passed, Godwin reverted to his previous pattern of quite narrowly Erasmian virtues of the mind. His "Essay on Sepulchres," one of his most successful late productions, is a mild, learned, low-temperature *essay*. His radicalism, like his marriage to Mary Wollstonecraft and his political pamphleteering, was a phenomenon of an age of revolution.

Even in the heart of that period he remained an individualist and private man of the most extreme tendency, as we see in this note on the year 1789, from his diaries.

I never for a moment ceased to disapprove of mob government and violence, and the impulses which men collected together in a multitude produce on each other. I desired such political changes as should flow purely from the clear light of the understanding, and the erect and generous feelings of the heart.

His educational theory quarreled with even Rousseau's because the latter allowed for the teacher's manipulation of the pupil's mind. Godwin insisted on absolute candor between the two. And his political theory differed from Rousseau's on similar grounds. Rousseau allowed for benevolent deceit of the ruled by the rulers. The Frenchman was being realistic about politics, but he was more importantly idealistic, in the mode appropriate to the Calvinist intellectual temperament, as we see in Calvinist politics from Plato to Marx. Whereas Godwin's politics were an Erasmian hallucination of perfect freedom from every kind of compulsion, interference, and compromise. He must be a unique case, the Erasmian radical, an animal one would have thought against nature. (Though today again we see a recurrence to philosophical anarchism, in men like Chomsky.) But as such he neatly completes the range of radical temperaments to be found in the London of the 1790's.

Places in Blake's London

Parallel with Carnaby Street, two blocks to the east, runs Marshall Street, where a towering modern structure calls itself William Blake House, because on that site, on 28 November 1757, he was born. On one side of this building is a shop with the sign, "Cranks Health Foods," and on the other, "The craftsmen potters shop." They might seem to constitute together a mildly sardonic comment on Blake's career; but far more clamantly sardonic are the signs of all those Carnaby Street shop windows, full of pornographic fancy-dress; vestries for the pansexual orgy, temples of the prostituted ephebe, altars of the glorified anus. A strange setting, it might seem, for short, short-necked, broad-shouldered Blake, big chinned and bulging eyed, with wide, tremulous lips compressed; devotee of the Bible and Swedenborg, illustrator of Dante and Job. "Regency" is a Carnaby Street period, a Carnaby Street style, but Blake was not of *that* Regency. He belonged to the second great layer of British cultural history, the stream that flowed under the Establishment surface from Bunyan to D. H. Lawrence. Even in the days of Beau Brummel (to *him* Carnaby Street might fairly claim some affiliation) this antiestablishment strain of English puritanism ran strong.

On the other hand, as the name of Lawrence might remind us, that Puritanism is not to be identified with a distrust of sensuality. Extreme Puritan sects in Bunyan's time believed that the Gospel announced the redemption of the whole man, including his senses. Man was now free. Everything was now lawful; to the redeemed man. This was sometimes called the Everlasting Gospel, and Blake's poem of that name seems to make it clear that he had inherited this tradition. He is one of literature's great spokesmen for "the body," and one of the authorities most cited by present-day Faustian anarchists like Norman Brown. "There is no energy except of the body" and "Energy is eternal delight." Brown, who is perhaps the most brilliant of our modern Blakeans, has united traditions of evangelical Protestantism and occult speculation in the same way as his master.

Moreover, Blake *was* of his period, in the matter, and even the manner, of his sensuality. Directoire might be a better word than

Regency for Carnaby Street, and A. L. Morton has pointed out that Blake's female figures in transparent shifts are wearing versions of the Directoire style fashionable at the time. Or take the nakedness in which Blake and his wife are said one afternoon to have received friends in their garden; the anecdote has been questioned, but Blake's friend Holcroft certainly practiced nudity. So indeed did Benjamin Franklin. And Blake's belief in polygamy, and his proposal to add a concubine to his household, is very like Mary Wollstonecraft's proposing herself to Mrs. Fuseli as a new inmate to her household. She admitted that the idea "arises from the sincere affection which I have for your husband, for I find that I cannot live without the satisfaction of seeing and conversing with him daily." It was a period of wild experiment, in all modes of behavior and sensibility. Carnaby Street, in its character of acted-out fantasy, its repudiation of sober, prudent, common-sense self-management, is not so antithetical to Blake as it first seems.

But the parallels between London then and now are something to take up later. For the moment I want only to locate some parts of London which can be looked at in such a way that the signature on them of the radical imagination of those days reemerges. The Carnaby Market area, down as far as Golden Square, has many associations with Blake. He lived with his father in Broadwick Street as a young man, and after his father died returned to live next door to the family home, then occupied by his brother. Later he lived in Poland Street, which is no distance away. This was, in Blake's time, a district full of painters, sculptors, engravers, etchers, etc. We get many references in Blake's letters to the rapid growth of these trades in London during his life, and to the growth of art. Thus he writes to Cumberland in 1800:

It is very extraordinary that London in so few Years from a City of meer Necessaries or at least a commerce of the lowest order of luxuries should have become a City of Elegance in some degree and that its once stupid inhabitants should enter into an emulation of Grecian manners. There are now, I believe, as many Booksellers as there are Butchers and as many Printshops as of any other trade. We remember when a Printshop was a rare bird in London and I myself remember when I thought any pursuits of Art a kind of criminal dissipation and neglect of the main chance, which I hid my face for not being able to abandon as a Passion which is forbidden by Law and Religion, but now it appears to be Law and Gospel too, at least I hear so from the few friends I have dared to visit in my stupid Melancholy.

This was only one aspect of the general and rapidly increasing prosperity of the great metropolis in that period, but it was the aspect which most affected Blake, both as a purveyor of art-objects and as a practitioner of the arts. In 1801 he wrote to Flaxman:

> I rejoice to hear that your Great Work is accomplish'd. Peace opens the way to greater still. The Kingdoms of this World are now become the Kingdoms of God and his Christ; and we shall reign with him for ever and ever. The Reign of Literature and the Arts commences. Blessed are those who are found studious of Literature and Humane and polite accomplishments. Such have their lamps burning and such shall shine as stars.

Some of the very un-Faustian diction and ideas, here, are presumably to be credited to Flaxman, via Blake's idea of Flaxman. But these social facts, and theories, have much to do with Blake's own vocation, with his very exalted ambitions for art, and his tragically intense disappointment over the failure of both the personal and the general ambition. He mixed up together his religious, political, and artistic hopes. These facts and theories also mark a difference between the Puritan radicalism of the seventeenth century and Blake's; they mark a likeness between radicalism today and in his day. In our times also the arts are flourishing commercially, and also allying themselves with politically subversive ideas.

It was in this area of London that the practitioners of the arts mostly lived. Canaletto stayed here when he came to London. Fuseli, the Swiss engraver, lived in Broad Street from 1780 on. Flaxman, the classical sculptor, lived in Wardour Street for a time. These two were Blake's closest friends in the great world of (comparative) success. Angelica Kaufman lived in Golden Square, and Benjamin Haydon, another visionary of the reign of the arts in London, again in Broad Street. Nowadays Golden Square has only one house left which one can associate with those days, Number 11, but in the middle of the square there is still a statue of George II, in Roman wreath and toga, carved by John van Nost in 1753.

In the Carnaby Market area the pattern of the streets, narrow and crowded alleys between three- and four-story brick houses, is still very evocative of Blake's period. Most of the other areas we associate with him are now absolutely blank to the eye — for instance, St. Paul's Churchyard, now completely of the 1960's, all giant modern concrete and glass. This is the street to associate with Blake the radical, because it was here that Joseph Johnson, the publisher, kept his bookshop and gave his weekly dinner parties, Godwin, Mary Wollstonecraft, Dr. Priestley, Fuseli, Horne Tooke, etc. — all the leading radicals of London then.

At least the Cathedral itself is as it was in Blake's time, and one can conjure up memories of him in those large, cold, ceremonious spaces. They do not belong to him, Heaven knows. They belong to the state and the court, to England's great soldiers and statesmen; but there are Blakean moments latent in their structure.

> 'Twas on a Holy Thursday, their innocent faces clean,
> The children walking two and two, in red & blue & green,
> Grey-headed beadles walk'd before, with wands as white as snow,
> Till into the high dome of Paul's they like Thames' waters flow.
>
> O what a multitude they seem'd, these flowers of London town!
> Seated in companies they sit with radiance all their own.
> The hum of multitudes was there, but multitudes of lambs,
> Thousands of little boys and girls raising their innocent hands.
>
> Now like a mighty wind they raise to heaven the voice of song,
> Or like harmonious thunderings the seats of Heaven among.
> Beneath them sit the aged men, wise guardians of the poor;
> Then cherish pity, lest you drive an angel from your door.

Of course the *Songs of Experience* has its antithetical treatment of this theme, particularly of the "wise guardians of the poor," which is also a Blakean moment in the imaginative structure of St. Paul's.

> Is this a holy thing to see
> In a rich and fruitful land,
> Babes reduc'd to misery,
> Fed with cold and usurous hand?

This announces Blake's sense that he did not belong to the Cathedral, any more than it belonged to him. But in Johnson's bookshop, so close, if it had not been destroyed, we would have found the world of Blake himself, the small shops and the sharp minds and the strong talk of London Dissent denying the great world of the establishment.

Joseph Johnson (1738–1809) is an interesting enigma in the complex of the radical English intelligentsia of his time. He has footnote fame for the help he gave Cowper; both taking the latter's first book of poems at his own risk, and offering many suggestions for their revision, which Cowper followed. But his later work as encourager of the radical writers of the nineties may have been even more important. Mary Wollstonecraft spoke of him as the father and brother Nature had denied her, and he looked after her, finding her lodgings, putting her up in his own house, dealing with tradesmen for her, finding her work, and nursing her through her writing of, for instance, *Vindication of the Rights of Man.* When Tom Paine, equally unworldly, had to be moved to new lodgings for his safety, Johnson found them for him, and picked up Paine and his belongings and transported them to the new address and installed him.

Johnson was born into a Baptist family in Everton, Liverpool, and came to London at the age of fourteen. At twenty-two he took a bookshop, and when that burned down in 1772, he took this more famous shop in St. Paul's Churchyard, that was the setting for his dinners. According to Gilchrist, he was a man of plain tastes and strict probity, who lived in his shop and for it, as well as by it. His authors were all on the left, or Evangelical-Dissenting, wing of British intellectual life. In 1772 he began to publish Mrs. Barbauld, the writer for children, and Dr. Priestley, the scientist and theologian. He was the earliest publisher of Erasmus Darwin, as well as of Cowper. He also brought out Maria Edgeworth and Horne Tooke, the friend of John Wilkes, a radical of rather a different kind. As Leslie Stephen puts it, Horne Tooke was a City of London patriot, hostile to the Whig aristocratic establishment, but certainly not for total revolution. He went to prison for a year in 1775, because his society had raised money to support the American rebels, but he always hated Paine's political theories.

There were at least three centers of interest to the books John-

son published; the scientific, especially books on medicine and sur-
gery, the politically radical, and the educational. Mary Wollstonecraft worked on the second and third types of book; one of her
children's books, *Original Stories from Real Life*, was illustrated by
Blake. Johnson brought out (at least it got as far as proof) the only
book by Blake ever published in this ordinary way — *The French
Revolution*. But Johnson, we read, wanted cheap books and wide
circulation for his authors. He was an enemy to the "typographical
luxury" which became the vogue among booksellers and publishers
around 1780. Presumably that cut down his employment of Blake.

Via Johnson, his authors acted on each other, and not only in
conversation at dinner. Between 1788 and 1799 he brought out a
magazine, *The Analytical Review*, for which all his writers reviewed, and in which they commented on each other. He also
passed their manuscripts among them for comments. Thus Fuseli
was asked to read that part of Cowper's translation of the *Iliad*
which the poet sent Johnson as a sample, when he proposed doing
a complete version. Fuseli made many criticisms, which Cowper
followed, and in fact Fuseli was consulted throughout the work.
Bonnycastle, the mathematician, was given *The Rights of Man*,
Part II and advised Johnson against publishing it. Mary Wollstonecraft read manuscripts for him, and wrote letters of advice to
authors.

Several of Johnson's guests were writers who made their living
doing hackwork for him. Mary Wollstonecraft translated from
French, particularly contemporary political pamphlets, which she
also reviewed for *The Analytical Review*. Holcroft translated from
French (his greatest coup the pirating of *Figaro* by memorizing it
in the Paris theater where it was being played) and later from German. Godwin began his literary career with novelettes, summaries
of the year's events, and even indexing. Johnson's dinners were not
exactly Grub Street functions, but many of the guests were, or had
been, publishers' hacks; theirs was a Grub Street radicalism.

Around this time publisher-booksellers seem to have played a
particularly important role in literary history, especially those with
radical sympathies. For instance, Richard Phillips, who went to jail
for selling *The Rights of Man*. Blake was very urgent with Hayley

to accept the editorship of a new radical magazine which Phillips was proposing. And Holcroft went to dinners like Johnson's at his own publishers, Robinsons', who had paid Godwin the very large sum of a thousand pounds for his *Political Justice*.

Nearly all the guests at Johnson's dinners were later imprisoned or arrested on political charges. When Johnson's own turn came, in 1798 (he was sentenced to nine months in jail for selling a subversive pamphlet), he continued to give his dinners each Tuesday, in the Marshal's house of the King's Bench prison.

The conversational and social star was Fuseli, who was also Johnson's closest personal friend. He continued to attend those prison dinners. Fuseli's work, both as painter and writer, has only historical interest now, but it seems clear that he was a genuinely remarkable man, and in touch with much of what was most lively in the ideas of his time. He won more than anyone else of Blake's esteem. Born in Switzerland, he had had to leave because of his radical politics. He, with others, had written a pamphlet against a corrupt magistrate who belonged to a powerful family. One of the others involved in this exploit was Lavater, whose friend Fuseli was. They had been ordained together into the Protestant ministry, and later, in England, Fuseli sponsored the publication of both Lavater's *Aphorisms* and his Physiognomy. These were important books to Blake, as to Goethe. Fuseli also corresponded with Rousseau, and wrote a defense of him when, after his quarrel with Hume, he was so much attacked in England. And he translated Winckelmann into English, another source of ideas important to both Blake and Goethe.

Thomas Holcroft was probably not present at many of Johnson's dinners, but he was a great friend of Godwin's, and a member of the same political organizations as Horne Tooke and the others. He spoke up for Godwinian gradualism and pacifism — against Thelwall, who attacked Godwin by name — in the London Corresponding Society, when pressure built up in the Society for more immediate and more militant action. This was the political society which the Government considered most dangerous of all. It was founded by Thomas Hardy in 1792, and was reputed to have thirty thousand members across the country before its suppression in

1797. Hardy was put in the Tower, charged with high treason that year, and Holcroft, Horne Tooke, Thelwall, and others, were all committed for trial with him.

The Old Bailey is another of the places in London still to associate with the radicals. The present building, the Central Criminal Court, was only put up in 1902, but part of the old Newgate Prison wall is built into it. At the time of Holcroft's trial, that Newgate had only been completed, after rebuilding, twelve years. It had been set on fire during the Gordon Riots, that harbinger of the age of revolution, the first public event in which Blake was involved. Lord George Gordon himself had just died, of Newgate jail fever, in 1793. Defoe and Penn had been prisoners there, and in the street, The Old Bailey, Milton's "Tenure of Kings and Magistrates," a defense of the execution of Charles I, was burned by the public hangman in 1660. There were thus many memories to inspire the prisoners of 1794, and in fact the prosecution was quickly defeated. Godwin's "Cursory Strictures," a pamphlet showing the illegality of the government's charges against them, played a large part in securing their acquittal. The moment Holcroft was free to leave the dock, he crossed the court and took his seat beside Godwin.

Holcroft was also a friend of Blake's; he edited *The Wits' Magazine* while Blake did the illustrations. Holcroft was perhaps the most attractive figure among all these radicals, and the closest to representing the submerged classes of England. He was the son of a peddler, and was a peddler himself as a child, before being apprenticed to a jockey, and later a shoemaker. An actor, a singer, a hack playwright, before his literary career proper began, he was yet the most committed and "philosophical" of men. He was self-made himself, and believed in the omnipotence of mind — even physical pain need not be felt if only one's mind and will are pure enough. He would have fitted well into Diderot's circle in Paris.

But after Blake, Godwin was the most important man at the dinners, for intellectual and literary history. (It was at Johnson's that he met Mary Wollstonecraft.) Born in 1756, he was the son and grandson of Dissenting ministers, and there were close connections between Dissent and political radicalism in the eighteenth century, which the careers of Dr. Price and Dr. Priestley exemplify.

At Hoxton Dissenting Academy, moreover, he had come under the influence of Jonathan Edwards, and his own writing has sometimes an Edwards-like mixture of logical stringency and emotional fervor. Under the stimulation of an age of revolution, this heritage expressed itself in a heroic and idealistic posture. Take, for instance, his letter to Joseph Gerrald when the latter was on trial in Edinburgh, urging him to observe the conditions of bail and stand trial and suffer for the cause; all in the grand tradition of Rousseauistic-Racinian analytical rhetoric. Like Rousseau in his Calvinist phase, Godwin, in the equivalent phase of his life, was easily intoxicated with abstract nouns, and wrote pages which promise a nobility of behavior which he knew in soberer moments he was unlikely to deliver. Both of them had, in these phases of their lives, images of Spartan, Roman, and Genevan virtue glowing on their mental screens, and projected themselves on it too, in purple tunic and laurel wreath, talking blank verse. Like Shelley, he was a great patron of rebellious youth, forever aiding even schoolchildren to throw off the bondage of tyrannical teachers and fathers. (In Godwin's case, it was boys and young men he aided; in Shelley's case, typically, it was young girls, from Harriet Westbrook to Emilia Viviani.) But his philosophy, too, though quite impersonal, was equally extremist and idealist. *Political Justice* is full of the most extraordinary leaps of destructive and creative imagination about social experience, all armored in logic and even in "realism" about existing institutions. Every relationship, private as well as public, must be made dissolvable at will. Marriage is only a form of legal contract, and by pretending to be more only becomes the most oppressive of injustices. And in all Godwin's novels, the hero is an individual pursued by society, one pitted against all the rest.

Tom Paine we have seen helped by Johnson in his practical and domestic affairs. To set him in the imaginative context of this group as a whole, we can recall the story that Blake warned him against government arrest just in time to save his life by flight to France in 1792. And it was Godwin and Holcroft and another man who formed a committee that saw *The Rights of Man* through the press in his absence. Two months after Paine had been condemned to death for his book, Godwin sent to the printers his preface to *Political Justice*, which calmly challenged the same treatment.

It was against Paine that the anger of the Tories was concentrated. (It is worth remembering that *The Rights of Man* came out the same year as Boswell's *Life of Johnson*. The two books are not merely contrasts but alternatives, exemplars of opposite literatures.) Paine was outlawed and burned in effigy in place of Guy Fawkes. Rhymed lampoons about him were sold in the streets. Crockery jars were made in his image so that they could then be smashed. His initials were set in nails on boot soles, so that they could then be stamped on.

His turn for imprisonment came not in England but in France, after he had opposed Robespierre by protesting against the king's execution. He came much closer to death than the others in England, and spent more time in jail than they, where he kept writing *The Age of Reason*. But he did not change his revolutionary allegiances in consequence. He continued to despise and denounce British tyranny rather than French. Blake, who had allegedly worn the *bonnet rouge*, the liberty cap, in the streets of London, got into trouble only in the country village of Felpham, where he was accused of insulting king and country. He was acquitted, but the momentary brush with retributive authority left a scar on his courage. Dr. Priestley suffered from the unofficial arm of the government, the magistrate-incited mob. In 1791, in the Birmingham Bullring, the mob rioted against him for his sympathies with the French Revolution, and sacked his house and destroyed his scientific apparatus. He left England for good, to settle in Philadelphia, like Paine.

Blake and his wife (and also Dr. Price, and Thomas Hardy, among those we have mentioned) were buried in Bunhill Fields, the Dissenters' burying ground, in Finsbury. They lie there today, alongside Bunyan, and Defoe, and Isaac Watts, and just across the road is Wesley's house and chapel. (Susannah Wesley's grave also is in Bunhill Fields.) This cemetery, a burying ground from 1685 to 1852, unites all the great men of Dissent in England, and some late Puritans. For instance, Milton, who died in the next street, Bunhill Row, in 1674, might have been buried there if he had lived another decade. The Commonwealth was only a memory when it came into existence. Sixteen eighty-five is almost the date of the Glorious Bloodless Revolution, which brought with it a consensus that gave Establishment status to some Dissenting attitudes. But buried in Bunhill Fields are the men who preserved the mummy-seed of revolution until it could sprout again, explode again, at the end of the century. It is a fitting place to end a meditative visit to the radical London of the 1790's.

There are corners, perspectives, moments, when one can see the city which Blake must have seen. But as compared with Mailer's New York, Blake's London has disappeared. And though this is mostly the result of the passing of nearly two centuries, it is partly the mark of those writers' failure to possess their city, of the ruling class's dispersal of the radicals, of the resolution into a conservative stasis of the age's manifold tensions.

London Then and Now

It was, half way through its career from 1788–98, a period very like our own; and we are bound to ask ourselves if the second half of our age will also be like Blake's. For the Establishment imagination today the emblematic and catalytic social group is the crowd of blacks, gathering on ghetto streetcorners on hot summer nights; or the group of long-haired students plotting violent protest. The equivalent for the 1790's was the revolutionary club, whether in England or France or America, where tailors and shoemakers encouraged each other to sack palaces and rape princesses. And for the seventeenth-century Puritan period, it was the conventicle of illiterates, intoxicating themselves on biblical rhetoric of vengeance, and misapplying prophecy to the established church and state. There are differences between those images, but also an important likeness. These are all new political groups, hitherto without power, and without the experience and training thought necessary to precede power, beginning to call into question the exercise and the bases of authority in the community, and whipping themselves up into the fury of seizing it. The presence of such groups, real or imagined, profoundly affects the thinking and the life-style of even those who do not belong directly with them; and especially of those intellectuals who would be on the side of change and protest in any age. It is these last I am particularly thinking about. They are the ones who in an age of revolution create a radical literature.

There was the intoxicating example of revolution in the air in 1790; the equivalent for us is the Cuban Revolution, and the promise of something similar in the South American countries, and to some extent the Third World as a whole and the resistance of North Vietnam in particular. This generated enthusiasm for a revolution at home, the promise of it among enthusiasts, which immediately countergenerated the threat of repression by the authorities, and almost immediately, among the radicals themselves, the threat of skepticism about that promise. But first came the enthusiasm.

What an eventful period is this! I am thankful that I have lived to it; and I could almost say, "Lord, now lettest thou thy servant depart in peace, for mine eyes have seen thy salvation." I have lived to see a diffusion of knowledge, which has undermined superstition and error. I have lived to see the rights of men better understood than ever; and nations panting for liberty, which seemed to have lost the idea of it. I have lived to see Thirty Millions of people, indignant and resolute, spurning at slavery, and demanding liberty with an irresistible voice; their king led in triumph, and an arbitrary monarch surrendering himself to his subjects. After sharing in the benefits of one Revolution, I have been spared to be a witness to two other Revolutions, both glorious. And now, methinks, I see the ardour of liberty catching and spreading.

The diction is pietistic on the whole, but the final metaphor is of fire. That is a paragraph from Dr. Price's *Discourse on the Love of Our Country*, which provoked Burke's *Reflections on the Revolution in France*. Burke treated Price as a figure out of the past, Hugh Peters redivivus, a ghost of the old Puritan rabblerousers, which in a sense he was — a reintroducer of the political enthusiasms of Putney in 1647. But Burke meant by doing this to dismiss Price from serious consideration the way Dryden dismissed Titus Oates; but this was the end of an age of consensus, not the beginning; in fact Price's enthusiasm, and the various reactions against it, dominated the intellectual London in which Blake and his friends lived.

The pressures of the times called London radicalism into being in the 1790's. But so did the pressure of the city itself, the greatest commercial and banking mart in the world, and the traditional home in England of the democratic liberties, restive under the heavy hand of Pitt, which grew heavier as the government grew increasingly alarmed at the course of events in France. The Gordon Riots of 1780 had been in the name of Liberty and Wilkes, the London radical, and they had seemed to Blake to manifest the spirit of the American Revolution which had crossed the Atlantic. Wilkes was the patron of that Republican Art to which Blake affiliated himself; large public paintings, meant to decorate public places, on heroic, historical, and ideal themes. This was the kind of painting which the flamboyant Mortimer and Barry had attempted to popularize, in opposition to the profitable portrait painting of Reynolds and Gainsborough. The first two painters, Blake's masters, had claimed the protection of Wilkes and Burke, and later of Fox, leaving Tory patronage to the hirelings of the aristocracy. Wilkes did in fact propose a National Gallery as early as 1777, and Blake lived all his life in hopes of seeing such a gallery established and favorable to his kind of painting, just as he hoped for a revolution which would be a natural development of that spread of liberty in British society which was the work, as they believed, of the congeries of London dissenting radicals to which he belonged.

But the course of the times was unfavorable to everything republican, and to most of the radical traditions of British liberty. In the 1790's laws were passed forbidding trade unions, repealing Habeas Corpus, banning public meetings, etc.; and along with them went measures in encouragement of all respectable religion. Even Methodism and Catholicism were recognized as allies of the established church, against the dangerous new doctrines of the age of revolution. In 1798 the Lord Chancellor refused to hold any more dinners on Sunday. In 1805 Wilberforce persuaded Pitt to forbid military drilling on Sunday. In 1809 Spencer Perceval stopped assembling Parliament on Mondays, in order not to encourage Sunday travel. The imaginative clock was being put back, as far and in as many ways, as the government could force it. This was the later London of Blake and Godwin and Holcroft, and up to 1797 of Paine and Mary Wollstonecraft.

That these radical writers did not accomplish more is then to be explained by the savage repression exerted by the British governments between 1790 and 1820. But equally important was the fail-

ure of the French Revolution to develop into the society of freedom, equality, and fraternity which it had promised to become. In
England the climate of opinion even among radicals changed,
affecting the very principles of political understanding, even in
people previously committed. The group became disoriented; individuals reoriented themselves in mutually opposed directions. One
can trace this quite clearly in the career of Godwin's reputation. In
1793 and 1794 he was every intellectual's hero. Southey, Coleridge,
and Wordsworth, for instance, were his devoted admirers. But
soon after that he began to be attacked both by conservatives and
by the more militant radicals in the London Corresponding Society, as a traitor to the radical cause, because he would not support
activism. Godwin was a very philosophical anarchist — an Erasmian — which is one reason why so many unlike people could
briefly unite to admire him; he was the hero of the movement at
that moment before action need be taken, and when the movement needs to be comprehensive more than anything else.

By 1799 the radical movement was fragmented, and the conservative reaction was in full swing. James Mackintosh, a personal
friend, delivered a series of recantatory lectures, "On the Law of
Nature and Nations," repudiating radicalism in general, and Godwin in particular. And next year, another friend, Dr. Parr, made his
Spital sermon an attack on Godwin by name. The publication of
his novel, *St Leon*, was the signal for a literary-critical attack by
Southey, Scott, and d'Israeli. A new conservatism and a new respectability had become fashionable among intellectuals. The prosecution of radicals was initiated not only by the government, but
by the Society for the Suppression of Vice, which was headed by
William Wilberforce, the liberal conscience of the age, the man
who was working to abolish the slave trade.

After 1798 the London radicals ceased one by one to be radicals.
Paine was the only exception, and he died not only exiled from his
native country, but rejected and dishonored by that adopted country he had helped create. The radicals' fate can again be shown in
miniature in Godwin. He began writing books for children in 1805,
using noms de plume, because of the ill repute attaching to his real
name. The series was called the Juvenile Library, and round it collected the scattered remnants of this old group, now no longer es-

saying major or political themes. There was Hazlitt's *English Grammar*, which was based on the philological theories of Horne Tooke, and Lamb's *Tales from Shakespeare*, which had illustrations by Blake. As happened on other occasions to the radical line in British culture, it went underground, into the servants' quarters, became ancillary to the establishment culture. Its serious enterprises waited out the Victorian Age to be rediscovered. The immediate future was to be the era of Carlyle and George Eliot, of the conservatives and liberals, who descend from Weimar and Edinburgh much more than from radical London.

But even in 1815 one could see writers like Hazlitt and Shelley forming a "second generation" by means of which radical ideas would be handed down. In 1811 Shelley "discovered" — so dead was the general hero worship of 1793 — that Godwin was still alive, and wrote to him, and visited him. He married Godwin's daughter, as he had already married his theories.

There were marked differences between the two men's personalities, their modes of behavior and emotion in social and intimate relationships, and even in the world of ideas. Shelley allotted a big place in his scheme of things to romantic love, and to the young hero figure, both of them highly sexual, in however ambiguous a manner, and both related to himself; whereas Godwin — no human skylark he — was a dull, clumsy, routine-bound pedant. Hogg tells about his own first meeting with Godwin, arranged by Shelley, at which the latter, who was always late, this time never appeared. Godwin kept consulting his watch with increasing puzzlement throughout the evening, quite unable either to understand Hogg's hints or to accept Shelley's defection. But if we think of strictly intellectual temperament, we see that that Godwin-Edwards syndrome of qualities — stringency, fervor, and idealism — was strikingly developed in Shelley, and in him related to Godwin's ideological position. The two men's styles have the same disembodied energy, their ideas have the same independence of experience, and the same enthusiastic intellectuality. Both men had, of course, rebelled against their fathers very bitterly, and they seem to have rejected, along with the father figure, all the "given" character of personal experience. *Everything*, they felt, could be changed. *Nothing* need be accepted as a necessary limitation. It is known that Shelley reread *Political Justice*, after meeting its author, in 1812, in 1814, in 1816, in 1817, and in 1820; its profound influence on him is one of the classic cases of how intellectual temperament can be inherited, and how it can overpower differences in natural endowment and experience. And insofar as Shelley's poetry reached the anthologies, Godwin's thought reached later readers, and lay latent in their minds.

But in the immediate time scale the radicals failed as writers. When one compares them with other groups of writers in other cities at the same time, one is struck by how much more time the conservatives of Weimar, for instance, could devote to their writing, how much more they produced of first quality, and how much more support and reward for their work they received. And this was not so importantly the external support and reward. It was what Goethe and Schiller and Herder did for each other as writers that is so impressive. No one was able to do anything comparable for Blake as a poet; no one seems to have effectively helped Paine with *The Rights of Man*; even between Godwin and Mary Wollstonecraft there is no evidence of any direct intellectual intercourse comparable with that between Coleridge and Wordsworth.

There is also a contrast to be drawn between London and Edinburgh, even though here the intellectual elite was hostile to the Tory government. One must except Scott and Mackenzie from that generalization, and the fact that they, although Tories, were an integral social part of that elite, marks the difference between the Edinburgh liberals and the London radicals. Nevertheless, men like Jeffrey, Horner, and Brougham *were* liberals, did suffer in their early careers from official disapproval, did have their names taken down by sheriff's men as present at suspect meetings. They did not meet each other, as the Weimar men did, in court dress and with court titles. They met, out-of-favor lawyers all, to gossip at their own end of the lawcourts. But this was equally far from meeting at the Revolution Society, and further yet from meeting at the Old Bailey on trial for treason.

If we date the era of these liberal writers from the founding of the *Edinburgh Review*, in 1802, they came on the scene ten years later than the London radicals, by which time the latter no longer existed, as a group or as an ideology. (And the liberals did not hold them in awe — an important difference from today's situation.) Success lay with the liberals. The *Edinburgh Review* (unlike the *Analytical Review*) was the model for a whole new breed of intellectual magazines. The Waverley novels (much more than the Gothic-social problem novels) were a financial and literary triumph. Those were the two master-formulas of the age, for intellectual and imaginative activity. And in practical matters, the pupils of Dugald Stewart ruled England for the next generation. Macaulay and Brougham set the tone for the Victorian age's *mind*, and Carlyle tutored its deeper and more poetic *soul*.

Nevertheless, with all the disadvantages of radicalism, the work of the London writers is more exciting to us today, in intellectual and imaginative terms, than the work of the Edinburgh men. Take for instance their work in the novel, the Gothic-cum-social problem novel, which began with *Caleb Williams*. Puzzling and clumsy though this book is, both intellectually and aesthetically, it is a fascinating experiment in consciousness. Godwin was plainly in touch with the workings of his own mind and personality, and although he made *eccentric* connections between his knowledge of that kind and his political theories (eccentric because of what I called his "repudiations" of personal experience) the former is still crucially connected to the latter. His knowledge of unconscious psychology, his speculations about his own "self," are at the source of his own philosophy and politics. His tone about himself is often pompous and unreal, because his mind was profoundly warped, but he was also capable of very acute self-analysis. Take this, from a fragment of 1800:

I am extremely modest. What is modesty? First, I am tormented about the opinions others may entertain of me; fearful of intruding myself, and of cooperating to my own humiliation. For this reason, I have been, in a certain measure, unfortunate through life, making few acquaintances, losing them *in limine*, and by my fear producing the thing I fear . . .

Perhaps one of the sources of my love of admiration and fame has been my timidity and embarrassment. I am unfit to be alone in a crowd, in a circle of strangers, in an inn, almost in a shop. I hate univer-

sally to speak to the man who is not previously desirous to hear me. I
carry feelers before me, and am often prevented from giving an opinion,
by the man who spoke before giving one wholly adverse to mind.

Again one thinks of Rousseau. This is the mind of an acute self-
analyst, of a novelist as well as of a political theorist. Paine could
never have written *Caleb Williams*. And neither could Scott. The
Gothic terror novel, of flight and pursuit, of suspense and revelation, linked with apocalyptic social analysis, this should have been
one of the great literary forms of this radicalism, if it had had full
development.

The contemporary scene includes a parallel literary phenomenon, the pornography-cum-social-problem novel, in which sexual
excitement takes the place held by terror in the Gothic form, and
— in the hands of some brilliant American writers — that crude
interest is allied with morally serious and sometimes apocalyptic
social criticism, without ceasing to be pornographic. I am thinking
of *An American Dream, Lolita, Portnoy's Complaint, Couples,
Giles Goat-Boy, Catch-22, Myra Breckenridge*. De Sade was formu-
lating the theory of such fiction in Godwin's time, and he of course
introduced into the form sexual material of the kind the modern
practitioners of the genre use, which Godwin could never have
handled. But even in revolutionary France that enterprise could
not prosper. Not until our own age of revolution had the radicali-
zation of the intellect and the imagination gone far enough to produce a series of books that actually exploit the possibilities of such
a theory. And there are also films in the same genre. But we can
recognize the first beginnings of our own enterprise if we look back
to Godwin.

Then the world of Doris Lessing's *The Golden Notebook* is very
like the world of Godwin and Mary Wollstonecraft, in the large
part played in the characters' lives by a similar enthusiasm for revolution, and by the threat of repression by the authorities, and by
the radicals' own gathering skepticism as time went by. Moreover,
Anna and Molly and their friends find many social and intellectual
parallels in the milieu of Mrs. Inchbald and Mrs. Robinson —
friends of Godwin — both of whom were successful as actresses
before they became novelists, both beautiful women with a succession of suitors, some rich and powerful, some men of ideas. Anna's

unhappy affairs with Paul/Michael and with Saul Green, follow the pattern of Mary's affairs with the American writer and adventurer Gilbert Imlay. Imlay had had an affair in Paris with Helen Maria Williams before he met Mary — Miss Williams was a novelist and poet of radical sympathies who made her home in Paris, after the Revolution, and wrote about it for British publications. She, after her affair with Imlay, formed a permanent union with John Hurd Stone, who left his wife for her. Imlay had other mistresses after Mary, and drove her to attempt suicide more than once. But he too was a novelist, an intellectual, a radical. His Don Juan career had its ideological glamour. He was a friend of Joel Barlow's, the American poet, diplomatist, and revolutionary, and actor of the same social role. They were both friends of Paine and of Jefferson. There was an international bohemia of the left wing then quite like the one portrayed in Doris Lessing's books. Mary Hays, another novelist, proposed marriage to Godwin herself, and then helped persuade Mary Wollstonecraft to marry him.

Another striking feature of the world of *The Golden Notebook* is the suicide attempt of Molly's son, Tommy. This expresses a concern which runs through all Doris Lessing's work, a concern for the children of the emancipated women and divorced radicals she describes, a guilt before their accusations and their mute maladjustments. The actual event finds a striking parallel in the suicides of Fanny Imlay, Mary Wollstonecraft's daughter by Imlay, and even more in Holcroft's son's death. Fanny took laudanum, believing herself to be of no use to anyone, after her two stepsisters, Mary Godwin and Claire Clairmont, had eloped with Shelley. (The genealogical jigsaw puzzle of the Godwin household is like that in *The Four-Gated City*.) The second case is an even more tragic story, for the boy, who was sixteen and trying to run away to sea, shot himself just when he heard his father's footsteps approach his hiding place on the ship. One could also cite the painful relations between Godwin and his protégé, Thomas Cooper. And the tangles of neurotic sexual involvement we can sum up in the names of Harriet Westbrook and Shelley and Claire Clairmont and Byron, are very like those of Anna and Molly and Richard and Marion and Tommy. In both cases, behind the private life stands the public, and the betrayed promise of Russia in the one parallels the betrayed promise of France in the other, and the land of hope — as a source of *men*, of individual life-styles — is still America.

It would be easy also to parallel the list of arrests and imprisonments of the 1790's among American radicals today, all the way from Dr. Spock and Norman Mailer to Eldridge Cleaver and Leroi Jones. And in London Paine's qualities, of thought and of language, are quite strikingly repeated in the work of the Catholic Marxists of *Slant*. Brian Wicker and Herbert McCabe are notable examples of Calvinist radicalism in our time. While some of the things we consider most modern, the idea of the free woman, for instance, were fully developed then. Mary Wollstonecraft's story of her life can sometimes sound like the missing link between *Pamela* and *Jane Eyre*, but she also leads on to women's liberation. Her letters to her sisters from Ireland, where she was a governess, are full of horror at the moral and intellectual crudity of her aristocratic employers. It was in the name of refinement and propriety she protested, as much as of freedom and self-fulfillment. The child of a drunken, shiftless father herself, she abducted her sister from a husband and child who were endangering her reason, and also rescued her friend Fanny Blood from equally bad predicaments with her father and later her husband. But despite the coarser vocabulary, the rhetoric of the attack on "male chauvinism" today really expresses very similar intentions.

But let us restrict ourselves to literary forms of expression. The Gothic novel, the ecstatic lyric (above all in the hands of Blake) and the philosophical drama or long-poem (Blake or Shelley); these are the major literary forms of this London radicalism, and these writers are the forerunners of the contemporary attempt at a radical literature. Especially in America, the years ahead are quite likely to bring conditions of political tension and/or repression very like those which Blake and his friends knew. Many of the same alternatives of response present themselves on our scene — antinomian mysticism, rigid, doctrinaire politics, experimentalism in behavior. There are a dozen powerful images in that London to which we are invited to affiliate our own fates.

4 — CONSERVATIVE WEIMAR: AN
APOLITICAL KULTURSTADT

"Let me tell you, Goethe; so perfectly at ease I did not feel in your presence, in your circle and your museum of a house. I was oppressed and fearful, I admit. It smells of sacrifice where you are. . . . These Riemers with their mutterings and grumblings and their manly honour floundering about in the bird-lime; and your poor son with his seventeen glasses of champagne, and this little person who will marry him at the New Year and fly into your upper rooms like a moth to the candle — . . . what are they all but sacrifices to your greatness? Ah, it is wonderful to make a sacrifice — but a bitter, bitter lot to be one!"

"The drawbacks and limitations of the place — ah well, Weimar has the lacks and failings of humankind, and provincial humankind in particular. It is borné, it is a hive of court gossip, its upper classes are arrogant and its lower stupid; an upright man has a hard time here as elsewhere — perhaps harder; the rascals and good-for-nothings are on top, as elsewhere — perhaps more than elsewhere. But, for all that, it is a stout, substantial little town; I would not know where else I ever would or could live or have lived." *

Goethe and Weimar

I have already mentioned some of the ways in which Goethe demands — as it seems to me — to be set beside Blake. The two men are alike in their bitter attacks on Newton and Newtonian science, and in their debts to Swedenborg and Boehme and the whole tra-

* The first speech is attributed to Lotte, the second to Riemer, in Thomas Mann's *Lotte in Weimar*, Penguin Modern Classics, pp. 51, 329–330.

dition of occult knowledge. They are most unlike, in their careers, in their production, in their poetic policies, in their worldly circumstances, and in their modes of belonging to their respective cities. Even in that last particular, if one compares them with Schiller or with Shelley, one realizes how much they do both belong to a city. But whereas Goethe dominated his in terms of position and power, and ignored it as a literary subject, Blake lived, as it were, under or at the foot of the mountain of London, and wrote about it assiduously. Weimar was a very different sort of city from London.

At the end of *Goethe the Alchemist,* Professor Gray says that Goethe, like Blake, had made a pact with the Devil, selling his soul for inward force, though believing, like Blake again, that the Devil was the true form of the Messiah. Occult knowledge was the legendary means by which such pacts were made, and no doubt both men's exceedings of normal bounds were fostered by their dealings in that knowledge. But unlike Blake, Goethe, says Professor Gray, remained aware of the dangers of that pact. He turned away from the Faust subject, for instance, he changed his Sturm und Drang friends for Wieland and Charlotte von Stein, and he repudiated *Werther.* In a word, he moved to Weimar.

In 1775, when Goethe went there, Weimar was a city of six or seven hundred houses, cobbled streets, a marketplace, two inns, and a Schloss. At night carriages were still preceded in the streets by a footman with a torch, and every hour a watchman called out the time. In 1785 the state consisted of seven hundred square miles, and contained 106,000 inhabitants. On the streets, high officials walked with special slowness and dignity, followed by a manservant, and were greeted deferentially by the public. One-third of the adult population were in domestic service or were casual laborers, and a quarter were either officials, of the state or of the town, or professional men. There was no mercantile middle class, such as was dominating the great progressive European countries of France and Great Britain. At court there was a strict distinction observed between those who might be presented to the reigning family — the Hoffähige — and the rest. There were receptions every Sunday, concerts every Wednesday, masked balls every week or fortnight. But this was only the raw material of the Weimar we are

"For time in this sense was life, was work, that through the decades had chiselled at the marble brow and so profoundly and movingly reshaped and graven the once smooth features. Time, age — here they were more than a loss, a liability, a natural decline, touching and even melancholy to reflect on; they were full of meaning, they were intellect, achievement, history; their effects, far from giving rise to pity, made the contemplative heart beat high with joyful amaze." — Thomas Mann, in *Lotte in Weimar*. (Portrait of Johann Wolfgang von Goethe, by Joseph Karl Stieler, 1828. Courtesy of Nationalen Forschungs- und Gedenkstatten der Klassischen deutschen Literatur in Weimar.)

interested in, which Goethe created for himself. This was a city of the mind, a collocation of intelligences brought into actual relationship by a city of fact which was quite laughably lighter weight than they, but whose exigencies those intelligences yet quite seriously observed and obeyed.

Even in *Werther* Goethe had shown himself sensitive to the counterclaims of Albert and the marriage — claims which are defined in very conservative terms, as moderation and productivity and reliability and sense of proportion. But in *Hermann und Dorothea* he gave prime importance to those values, and developed that theme in opposition to the stormy and rebellious music of the French Revolution. By then, as Goethe the minister of state, but also as Goethe the poet, he was a spokesman for conservatism, one who warned men against the dangers of radicalism and excess.

And clearly this awareness of the dangers of the diabolic pact, this hedging, in Weimar, of his bets, accounts for that part of Goethe's life so unlike Blake's, and for that part of his mind cultivated so assiduously in the second part of his life. His devotion to universal learning, to worldly wisdom, to pedantic exactness and impersonal clarity, to classicism as a life-style as well as a mode in art; this was all a pursuit of conservative values. These can be virtues of the Erasmian temperament, but in Weimar they were cultivated within a conservative life-style. Many of Goethe's enterprises were Erasmian and liberal, taken individually, but, conducted in a spirit of Faustian self-aggrandizement, they became parts of an aristocratic life-style. Classicism was the artistic and intellectual expression of that style. Weimar classicism is the imaginative mode which holds the two temperamental tendencies in balance, because of its exaltation of certain universal elements in experience, and, by implication, of certain universal individuals. Its cult of the timeless and recurring and universal, the serene and undisturbable, is intensely aristocratic. It parallels the social style of the city.

As the friend of the reigning duke, who was himself very impatient of social regulations, Goethe was personally free in Weimar. He and the duke at first flouted those conventions. But they did so as rebels rather than as revolutionaries, protesting against the laws instead of changing them, and soon coming to appreciate their value for other people. Goethe described the duke as "daimonic," a term he also applied to Napoleon and Byron, but Karl August gave expression to this quality only in private life. And, like many men with this temperament, he was conservative in other ways. There are conservative potentialities in all Faustians, even in Mailer. But it seems possible to use the word radical for him as a whole, and so to keep a contrast clear. Perhaps a crucial point is Mailer's hostility to Freud and to psychotherapy.

Psychoanalysis, particularly of the Freudian kind, has been America's major gymnasium for training in temperamental conservatism — for a muscularization of the individual personality, combined with cultural conservatism and domestic authoritarianism. Perhaps this is not incomparable with *Hermann und Dorothea* conservatism; which, if true, makes Mailer's rejection of it more symmetrical in our argument. But however that may be, small eighteenth-century dukedoms like Weimar offered the perfect setting for a conservative daimonic temperament to fulfill itself flamboyantly but undestructively. And what Karl August did, for himself, in the life of the court, Goethe did, for the world, in the life of the mind. He turned the tiny country town into a Kulturstadt. At his suggestion, Herder came to the town and was given an official position. Because of his example, Schiller moved there. Weimar became Germany's literary capital, in some sense Europe's capital city of culture, as the result of Goethe's work.

But his choosing to do that remains a psychological paradox, a reversal of psychic direction. Weimar was a notably small and old-fashioned place, and not where — in 1775 — one might have expected a hero of Sturm und Drang to settle. The Sturm und Drang writers had depicted above all conflicts between inner values and outer forms; and Weimar was a place where those outer forms were rigidly preserved. Moreover, though Goethe had by then *Werther* and *Goetz* in print, both extremely successful, and the Urfaust in manuscript, for twelve years after his arrival he published nothing new but poems and short pieces. Clearly the life he engaged in there was no continuation of his preceding pattern, but a radical experiment.

Politically, his experiment was to join an aristocracy, a governing class, and a government. It gave Goethe the experience of responsibility in politics and administration, an experience which he shows himself, in *Werther*, uneasy at lacking. When the peasant murders his successful rival, Werther insists that he must be found innocent because his suffering and his action both command our sympathy. The author asks us to share Werther's feeling, but to understand Albert's disagreement with it. In Weimar he learned to see such problems from Albert's and the judge's point of view. He rapidly acquired a wide experience of ruling. In 1776 — the year Herder came to Weimar as Generalsuperintendent, the head of clergy in the state — Goethe became Geheimer Legationsrat, a member of the Council of State. The Council met once or twice a week, and Goethe attended regularly. He joined the Mining Commission in 1777 and the Military and Roads Commission in 1779, and in 1781 took over many of the duties of head of the Treasury. He always corrected the elaborate titles and forms that had been miscopied or misapplied on the papers that came before him. It must not be Serenissimus Durchlaught Herrn Karl August, but Serenissimus Durchlaucht Herrn Herrn Karl August. "Anyone having to observe and deal in forms and ceremonies finds a degree of pedantry necessary," he said. But he insisted on both the thing and the word, imitating the hateful ambassador in *Werther* and not Werther himself. It was an experiment in temperament, too; the signing of a different temperamental contract.

It was for instance an experiment in cultural cooperation on an aristocratic level. The most obvious examples are his friendships with the other Weimar men of letters. He became friends with Wieland, whom he had attacked during his Sturm und Drang period, exactly in phase with his disengagement from Lenz and Stolberg. His renewed friendship with Herder, between 1783 and 1793, bore fruit in the latter's *Ideen zu Einer Philosophie*, and *Gott, Einige Gespräche*. His friendship with Schiller led to important modifications of both his own *Wilhelm Meister* and the other's *Wallenstein*, as well as influencing both men's development in general. But there were also several magazines produced in Weimar, which were important for the rest of Germany, and in which he cooperated to some degree; to mention only the most important, Wieland's *Der Teustche Merkur*, Schiller's *Die Horen*, and Bertuch's *Die Allgemeine Literatur–Zeitung*. And there were several clubs and societies, some seriously intellectual. To cite just one, the Friday Society, which met at the house of Anna Amalia from 1791 to 1795, and thereafter at Goethe's house. At one meeting of this society, Goethe talked on colors, Herder on cultural immortality, Voigt discussed a historical document, Batsch and Lenz read papers on natural history, Hufeland lectured on light and silhouettes, and Bertuch should have talked about Chinese colored inks. Serious popularization and mutual education — very Erasmian pursuits — were essential aspects of the Weimar enterprise.

The humbler side of that enterprise is well represented by the career of F. J. Bertuch (1747–1820). He settled in Weimar in 1773, did some translations, and became the duke's private secretary in 1775. Then he made himself into the city's first capitalist, building a paper mill and then a paint factory, and then an artificial flower factory. In 1784 he began the *Allgemeine Literatur–Zeitung*, which became one of the distinguished intellectual organs of Europe. Kant reviewed Herder's *Ideen* for it. But more typical of Bertuch was his *Journal des Luxus und der Moden*, which began to appear in 1786, and which made known the latest ideas in fashions, furniture, gardens, sculptures, etc. It was among other things a way of ordering luxury items from abroad. Finally, in 1791, he set up his Landesindustriecomptoir, to show off the work of Weimar craftsmen in luxury goods, and to be a clearing house for orders. By 1811 he employed over four hundred fifty people. He earned twice as much as Goethe did, and was in some ways a more important man for the town. A Kulturstadt must find a way to make its specialty economically viable. Bertuch did for Weimar in Zivilization what Goethe did for it in Kultur.

Zivilization and Kultur, both, turn away from politics. Just by cultivating them so intensely, Weimar may be said to have renounced liberalism. And in political matters per se, international as well as national, it was clearly a conservative city. Karl August, along with other German princes, led his troops against those of the infant French Republic; and after Napoleon had established himself as a fact of European life, Karl August attached himself to the conqueror and cooperated with him and frowned on the rebellious German liberals. And Goethe was in perfect accord with his master and friend in these matters. He was in camp with the duke at the battle of Valmy, and he responded with enthusiasm to Napoleon when they met. He became an open adherent of the French cause, thus isolating himself from all the generous-spirited liberals and patriots around him in the fervor of 1814. He wrote a good deal against the Revolution, most of it poor work, but including one of the great conservative poems of European literature, *Hermann und Dorothea*, marvelously moving praise of continuity and domesticity and apolitical pastorality. Seen politically, Goethe made himself the perfect propagandist for a small, antiquated German dukedom, where the old social distinctions were rigidly upheld, and political power was kept where it had always been. But seen in a larger context, he achieved something impressive even in relation to politics. Goethe, and the other Weimar writers, were studying the quality of life of a whole community in a way that has proved most fruitful for literature and politics ever since.

Herder and Weimar

In his travel diary for 1769, Herder more than once challenges himself by evoking the example of Calvin and what he did for Geneva. "Livonia . . . how much to do to destroy barbarism, to root out ignorance, to spread culture and freedom, to be a second Zwingli, Calvin, or Luther, to this province! Can I do this? Do I have the dispositions, the opportunity, the talents? What must I do to obtain this end? What must I destroy in myself? Do I need to ask?" And again later he compares himself with Calvin and exclaims, "How great if I can make Riga a happy city." But if this suggests a Calvinist enterprise, his immediate plans depended on his capturing the confidence of Catherine the Great, which suggests rather the liberal-historical model of Diderot at Petersburg and Voltaire at Potsdam.

In fact, however, Herder ended up in Weimar, and what he wrote, what he became, what he achieved for others, belongs to Weimar conservatism and not to Calvinist radicalism or to Voltairean liberalism. The 1769 diary shows us Herder at the intensest moment of his Sturm und Drang phase, against which he reacted in Weimar (as Goethe and Schiller did against their equivalent phases.) Sturm und Drang *was* the Faustian temperament as a literary movement — one sign of this is the number of times those writers treated the Faust story — and the conservatism of the three Weimar writers might be described as post-Faustian. (Conservatism is not always Faustian, of course. There are purely Erasmian conservatives, like Matthew Arnold, men whose temperamental aversion from ecstasy and power-politics and ideological excess leads them to a fear of all change. But Weimar conservatism, with its bias toward aristocracy and power, was *post*-Faustian.)

Herder's most striking contribution to Weimar seems to have been his cultural approach to both literature and politics, which was an approach from below, from the roots up, out of the darkness in which things grow. In literature he rejected the dominance of any single set of standards, and particularly the eighteenth-century standards of "high civilization," of clarity, glitter, and elegance. In politics he rejected the dominance of the state, and sovereignty, and power, and the ideology that goes with them. The image of the diamond, and the chandelier, and the mirror, the myth of Versailles and the Sun-King, all images of cruel brightness, symbolize much that Herder was against. He suffered from his eyes in literal fact, and emotionally as well as ideologically these images had great resonance of meaning for him. The Enlightenment was dominated by the image of light, and Herder rebelled against that. He prized the sense of touch, and all those more concrete, more emotional, more multidimensional meanings which derive from that. His rhetoric at its best, as in the essay on language, is visceral and titanic, and makes Rousseau, for instance, seem a cut-glass epigrammatist in contrast. Herder made his intellectual career out of renouncing the brightness of perfection above for the darkness of growth below. He had decided in France, at the end of his journey of 1769, that reform must come not from above, at the behest of an enlightened despot, but from below, as the result of the people's realizing its own Gestalt, developing its own Bildung.

The root idea in Herder's thought is *das Volk*; which means above all the common culture; which is in turn derived from the use of a common language. Both are *common*. Not of course vulgar, but even more not superior, polished, or elitist. It is to the use of the common language that he attributes the development of both individual and group identity. He differs from Rousseau in a way characteristic of his thought as a whole in thus replacing the metaphysical absolute of a General Will with this empirical fact of a common culture and language. He is also characteristic in insisting on the necessity for institutional pluralism and multiformity, something Rousseau wanted to eliminate from the state. Herder wanted no single monuments of power, topped with a single dome or tower, no monolith or pyramid. He distrusted even the Kantian ideal of a single world government; Humanität, the world consciousness which *he* wanted to develop, would have been in organizational terms only a loose linking of autonomous states. He was genuinely liberal in his feelings about particular political issues, in his insistence on freedom of thought and expression, and his indignation against imperialism and slavery. "The negro is as much entitled to think the white man degenerate as the white man to think of the negro as a black beast." But he put his faith in cultural and imaginative change as a whole, a slow, multiform process or tendency, rather than in any particular movement or machinery.

The state, he said, is a drug, by means of which men forget that they are men. And he saw cruel and sinister implications contained in any doctrine that subordinates the many individuals' interests to those of a vast abstraction. Germany's mission was to be a nation of thinkers and educators, for the benefit of the other European nations, not to compete against them, as he wrote in his verse epistle on German National Glory, in 1792. This idea was given a great many different meanings during the next hundred and fifty years, but essentially it is a Weimar idea. It both explains the Weimar enterprise and relates it to the largest ideals, like Herder's Humanität and Goethe's Weltliteratur.

In the last years of his life Herder differed from Goethe and Schiller over several matters. He charged their classicism with amounting to cultural idolatry of the Greeks, a fixing of the flow of life, and their idea of culture with being too formal, too aristocratic, too intellectual, too conservative. But he himself was equally conservative, in the eyes of the disciples of Kant and Fichte. He was not in sympathy with the new enthusiasm for either radical democracy or radical nationalism. He spoke of the French Revolution in the metaphors of myth — as an Apocalypse, or as a gigantic egg to be hatched by the World Spirit. He did not think of revolution as something men like him could intend, or bring about, or direct. Herder's view of history was essentially conservative in the value it assigned to the historical uniqueness of each people and culture. He insisted on interpreting and judging each period from inside, according to principles derived from its own unique experience and character, and excluding principles relevant to some other period or claiming to be relevant to all periods. Thus he excluded all radically moralizing, progressive, and revolutionary theories of history. Characteristically, it is the values of simple peoples, and often of primitive peoples, to which he responds most warmly; it is on their behalf that he writes, and their virtues he wants to preserve, to conserve, in periods when they tend to be corrupted or enfeebled by "civilization."

As much as Schiller, although he described the problem differently, he was conscious of divisions in his own sensibility, and invested much energy in a theory of wholeness, of "the naïve." As one would expect from Herder, his theory refers more than Schiller's to naïveté in a culture, and in an individual's relation *to* his culture. But like Schiller's, his theory calls on men to go *back*, emotionally, in order to reestablish that wholeness. However, there are radical differences between Herder and Schiller. As we have seen, Herder deplored the dominance of the visual sense, and of the printed words, and of conceptuality, in the educated culture of his time. Whereas Schiller, in *Aesthetic Education,* praises the eyes in particular as enabling us to exercise the aesthetic sense, to play with what we see as appearance, while the sense of touch chains us to the determined world of appetite and sensuality. Schiller was much more a man of the Enlightenment, and had little of Herder's imaginative response to cultural possibilities; either to radically different cultures from our own, or to the great variety of essentially similar cultures which he (Herder) had studied — each one grasped as a form characterizing a multitude of other forms contained within it, characterizing and interrelating everything, from riddles and eating regulations to sagas and political institutions. Schiller had something different to contribute to "Weimar." But this grasp of cultural form was a more significant contribution to the cooperative enterprise than may at first appear.

Isaiah Berlin credits Herder with fathering three ideas about culture important to subsequent thought, populism, expressionism, and pluralism, which are mutually supportive. The first is the theory of all the nourishment which a writer — which any man — receives from belonging to a cultural group; the last is the theory of how incommensurable — and equally valid — are different cultural standards; the second is the habit of seeing works of art not as objects but as voices, modes of self-expression, which express the individual artist, but equally the social-cultural group he belongs to. This last — but with the concurrence of the other two — amounts to Herder's theory of the naïve. The artist has to remain in touch with, and feel some sort of reverence and piety toward, the body of lived experience of the Volk he was born into. Separation from that is amputation and hemorrhage.

This group of ideas, and the moral-political attitude to art which they gave rise to, became very popular in Eastern Europe and Russia at the end of the nineteenth century, but also in England, where they formed the root, as I now see, of my education and my taste. That is why Leavis's radicalism has so little in common with any political or Calvinist radicalism, actual or imaginable; because it is in the Weimar sense conservative. The contemporary ecology movement is conservative in the same sense. Populism, says Berlin, believes in loose textures, voluntary associations, natural ties, and is opposed to armies, bureaucracies, and closed societies. It animates folk enthusiasts and culture fanatics, egalitarians and local-autonomists, champions of arts-and-crafts, and of the simple life. "Populism may have been in part responsible for isolationism, provincialism, suspicion of everything smooth, metropolitan, elegant, and socially superior, hatred of the *beau monde* in all its forms; but with this went hostility to centralization, dogmatism, militarism, and self-assertiveness . . . and with a hatred of violence and conquest as strong as any to be found among the other great Weimar humanists, Goethe, Wieland, and Schiller." This was the other side of Weimar culture from its aristocratic classicism, and this one must call a very liberal kind of conservatism.

Schiller and Weimar

Schiller is the best known of all the Weimar writers for his relation to politics, for being the poet as national culture hero. But to

approach him this way is not only to find him a brassy rhetorician
— *der Moraltrompeter von Säckingen* — but also not to find him
as the Weimar writer he was. The political poet was *Germany*'s
writer, though even that formula contains some falsification; it is
significant that his Freiheitsbegeisterung plays all deal with countries other than his own — with Swiss, French, or Dutch national
movements. His nationalism, like his liberalism, was idealistic.

What Weimar drew out of Schiller, and what is more rewarding
to study today, is rather his thinking about the nature of art, its
relation to culture, and its world-civilizing mission. His poem on
Germany's national destiny puts forward a theory very like Herder's. *"Deutsche Grösse,"* renouncing military and political triumph, declares:

> *Das ist nicht des Deutschen Grösse*
> *Obzusiegen mit dem Schwert.*

The Germans are *"das langsamste Volk,"* the last to appear in the
European community, and to them is reserved the special destiny
of conquering others by means of moral and aesthetic culture.

Schiller's ideas are set out in his letters to Goethe, in the essays
— *"Anmut und Würde," "Naive und Sentimentalische Dich-*
tung," in poems like *"Das Glück"* and *"Die Künstler,"* and above
all in *Aesthetic Education.* In their most developed and most interesting form, these ideas place the concept "aesthetic" within an
extremely wide perspective of meaning, and save it from that familiar opposition to "moral" and "political" which in English-
speaking usage is so enfeebling, while they keep it in referential
contact with the fine arts in general, and with quite specific features of art-work. The concept of appearance as that form of perceived reality which is free from the stresses of desire, fear, or
repulsion in the perceiver, and therefore free for disinterested contemplation; and of play as that self-delighting activity which proceeds from pure impulse, from spontaneous self-affirmation, joyful
creativity; these two together he traces as elements in every human activity, including the most morally serious and most intellectually complex. And the reader is convinced that if, in a living culture, the importance of this aesthetic element were recognized,
watched for, appreciated, there could indeed be an aesthetic educa-

tion which would amount to total education, to something which would healthily moderate, modify, modulate, both crudity of appetite and rigidity of moralism. The theory, and its application to, or derivation from, the particular cases of Goethe and Schiller, seems to me the real achievement of the Schiller of Weimar.

That application and derivation is very much a part of the achievement. Because Schiller is much more interesting on those subjects than on most others, Goethe alone had the power to fix his attention and trouble his equanimity long enough to win from him a complex relationship to a subject; and this is a moving spectacle, Schiller making himself accessible to experience. But also because this is how Weimar worked. People acted on each other by means of being so close to each other, and by the ordinary social machinery, but by nothing more bureaucratic.

A less satisfactory aspect of Schiller's Weimar work was his classicism, the enthusiasm for Greek art and life expressed in *"Die Götter Griechenlands,"* which merges into the idealism of *"Das Ideal und das Leben."* This is less satisfactory because one is not convinced that he cared that much about classical civilization — or cared that deeply, that authentically, that problematically. Indeed, Weimar classicism is a questionable achievement, even in Goethe, who certainly did care and who makes it interesting. But all Schiller's idealism bears the mark of that mechanical separation, opposition, and reconciliation of abstract entities, which seems so much a habit of his mind, and so much a manifestation of that mind's domination of his experience. It has something to do with what Mann calls Schiller's adolescent energy and grandiosity — *"dieser Lust am höheren Indianerspiel"* — which was expressed in his historical plays, his love of huge projects, his assault on Goethe's intimacy, his pleasure in titles and worldly success, his zest for and skill in all the mechanics of his career. It has often been pointed out how many of Schiller's protagonists are sincere usurpers, men living a lie but unable to unmask themselves for fear of injuring others. And there is perhaps a parallel to this dramatist's love of intrigues and subsequent explanations in his aesthetician's love of explaining his own techniques, tricks, effects. He was a man intoxicated with his own skills — a psychological character no doubt fostered and fixed by his early training as rhetorical Ganymede to Duke Karl

Eugen of Württemberg, when he learned (at the latter's military academy at Stuttgart) how to produce those glittering protestations of devotion while his mind gazed astonished, from a far psychological window, at his unfalteringly efficient pen.

But in his theories of popularization, as in his aesthetic theories, we find again that much more impressive Schiller, who was trying to repair that damage, to reunite what had been split apart in him, to achieve the kind of naïveté appropriate to him, by Weimar techniques. It seems clear that in the *Aesthetic Education* he was attempting something new in the way of form as well as of ideas; a form appropriate to what he thought of as a new way of thinking — *darstellend denken* — presentational thinking. He wrote to Fichte, "It is my constant endeavour, alongside the inquiry itself, to engage the whole ensemble of psychic forces, and as far as possible to work on all of them at once. I am not therefore content with just making my thoughts clear to the reader. I want at the same time to entrust my whole soul to him, and to work upon his powers of sense and feeling no less than upon those of mind and spirit." Herder had emphasized the impoverishment language had suffered both from the specialization of knowledge and from being translated into print; and the need for the writer to conduct a love affair with language to reenrich it, the need to engage his whole personality in words. Goethe too was very conscious of this problem of language, as a part of his general concern to reach a whole community. Schiller tried to get Körner, and others, to write on popularization for *Die Horen*, and finally himself produced the essay "On the Necessary Limits of the Beautiful." He was cooperating in all the Weimar enterprises.

Like Goethe and Herder, Schiller had had a Sturm und Drang phase before he came to Weimar. But his transformation was a more moving thing than theirs, because he came later, when they already *were* Weimar, and he had to come to them. He was accepting the world's discipline. The years after the wild success of *Die Räuber* were painful years for Schiller in many ways, when he was in effect taught by the world to lower his pretensions. When he fled Stuttgart to Mannheim, at the age of twenty-one, he was hoping to be acclaimed as the German Shakespeare; but in the next few years he in fact lost his health, contracted troublesome debts, and lost his self-confidence as a writer — as the kind of writer he had been. After hàving written three plays in three years, it took him another four years to complete *Don Carlos,* and during that time it became in some ways a more conventional play. He changed his position. He became conservative. His psychologism in *"Naive und Sentimentalische Dichtung,"* like Herder's culturism, was antipolitical and so potentially conservative (as is perhaps also *my* psychologism, my theory of temperaments) in that it attributed ultimate reality to metapolitical explanations of political phenomena.

In 1793 he wrote about the French Revolution:

If it were true that the extraordinary thing really had happened, that political legislation had been assigned to reason, that man was respected and treated as an end in himself, that law had been enthroned ånd true freedom made the keystone of the state, then I would say farewell to the muses forever and devote all my activity to the most glorious of all works of art, the monarchy of reason. But it is precisely this that I dare to doubt. I am very far from believing that a political regeneration has begun; indeed, present events rob me of all hope that this will ever come to pass for centuries.

That is a classic statement of Weimar apoliticism, or conservatism, and it led on naturally to the *Aesthetic Education.* But it is not mere conservatism. Schiller, accepting the world's discipline, also interpreted it. He disavowed his early total rebelliousness; he accepted the values of conservatism, but only in their most intellectually distinguished and exploratory form, as manifested in, glimpsed by, the Weimar enterprise. Together with the other Weimar writers he made out of that conservatism something intellectually and morally impressive.

A Visit to the City in 1969

Like most Englishmen, I took French, not German, as my foreign language in school. And like most literary people born around my time, 1927, I never felt German literature important enough to read for myself — at least, to read in the original. T. S. Eliot had dismissed Goethe for me, while D. H. Lawrence, my other mentor, dismissed "Literature." But over the last two years Goethe has become the most interesting of all authors for me. I learned German to read him. And in the summer of 1969 I went to Weimar to locate him. And this sudden interest seems all the more surprising because the pressures on me that I am conscious of, the pressures of the contemporary situation, were so inimical to Goethe. The revolt of the students, the disaffection within our society, the demands for radical political action, all that finds no responsive echo in his work, much less any solution. A dozen other authors would offer me more relevant subjects and forms, a more sympathetic temperament, more suggestive reflections. And yet there was, I felt, a connection.

I think I have worked out what it is. But I want to come at it indirectly, because it is an indirect connection, analogous, not causal, either historically or logically. It has a force, for me at least, this analogy, but it might not survive translation into strictly argumentative terms. I must first ask the reader's interest in Goethe, in the Goethe problem, and in Weimar.

Weimar, as everyone says, is a small place. When I set out with a map my first evening, several times I missed my way by going too far; every alley turned out to be one of the major turnings marked. Goethe and Schiller lived within a literal stone's throw of each other.

"In Weimar there are no distances. Our greatness is of the spirit alone," the waiter says in *Lotte in Weimar*. And it is significant that it should be a waiter who says it. Mann's novel is set in 1816, but a Weimar waiter might say it today, given the slightest taste for phrasemaking. It's *true*: and it's a trade-truth, a selling-slogan. I don't mean just that Weimar's cultural achievement has been commercialized. Of course busloads of tourists, many of them Russian, disembark in the town each day, several at a time. Every sign is in four languages: a fiesta of mistranslation. But this is different from the commercialization of, say, Stratford on Avon. Weimar is what it *was*; it was institutionalized, as a cultural Mecca, for at least twenty years of Goethe's life. And unlike Shakespeare, Goethe's personality can still be felt here, insofar as the most exhaustive documentation — *begun by himself* — can ever preserve a personality.

But of course it is a historical paradox that Weimar should be unchanged. It is nearly a hundred and fifty years since Goethe died, and those years were crammed with the most powerful changes in the conditions of human life ever known. Those changes are felt here, but by their absence, their ineffectiveness. Weimar *has* a non-Goethean atmosphere (as well as the Goethe-presence I spoke of), but it is the atmosphere of a sequestered small town, where nothing has the habit of happening. And it is Goethe who has prevented things from happening, in that the town — at his behest — dedicated itself to preserving him and his achievement. It made itself a city of education, of music, of art, a city of genteel retirement, a city of tourists. So that the non-Goethean atmosphere is also his work, or at least a predictable result of his work.

It is still strikingly old-fashioned. Country women come in with rectangular wicker baskets strapped to their backs, and with red-faced children who have leather purses and satchels slung round their necks. The chimney sweep wears a top hat. Old ladies wear lawn caps and fichus.

But these are quaint sights, exceptions. Most people dress as English people do, or did twenty years ago. And there are young men with long hair and blue jeans, carrying transistor radios. But the *forms* of life are old-fashioned and small-town. It is a town for going for walks. There are lots of little parks, and lots of benches to sit down on, every fifty yards or so. The typical form of transport is the bicycle and motor bicycle. The streets are still paved with what we call "sets." The typical figure is an old, or at least middle-aged, lady. In the Elephant Hotel, the best in town, such ladies on tours can be seen literally fifty at a time, listening to "Jealousy" or "Begin the Beguine" from a string trio.

Its economics, apart from tourism, are educational. There is a School of Music and a School of Architecture. The music students give very good free concerts all over town. The acoustics seem to be excellent everywhere, and the students are very highly trained. It is a pleasure to hear them. But at the same time it is disturbing, problematic, pathetic. Partly because the audiences are thin, the applause is loyal — from other students — the whole occasion is correct. The performers are very stiff and strained, solemn and red-faced. One wonders how they relate the music they play to the music from the transistors, which is after all today's Youth-music.

How do they relate their own rigid postures and gestures to the slouching animal grace of Youth today?

Youth in Weimar is — as Youth in Shrewsbury was when I was growing up — raw material being pressed into correct molds. They are not-yet-adults. This shows itself in a giggling, neoinfantile sexuality, which I remember well from my own adolescence but which I hadn't seen for many years. It is a kind of passive resistance to growing up. There is too sharp a dividing line, too tense a frontier, between those activities that are rewarded by one's elders and those that establish one's adult independence. So tense a frontier is costly to cross, and not to cross, particularly for boys. This accounts for the rather meltingly beautiful aspect of many sixteen-year-old boys in Weimar, and the perky, giggly aggressiveness of the girls, who visually — and jokingly — accost you at every corner. This is very much a small-town phenomenon. In a big city there are many routes round that frontier.

There is nothing for Youth to do. When you come out from the Wittumspalais, after all that Bach, there isn't a sound. Oh, the tender chill, the soft damp silence, of even ten o'clock, in even June, in Weimar. Only the grass is growing. And that neglected overgrowth of grass and trees gives you the feeling that Goethe is only just dead, that things have run down since then, as if that had been fifteen years ago, not a hundred and fifty.

In fact, world history affected Weimar very directly during those years, including art-history, culture-history, the sort that should have displaced Goethe. Franz Liszt lived here, under the grandson of Goethe's duke, most of his working life, 1848–86. He made a big figure in the town, and the present music school is called the Franz Liszt University. The Franz Liszt House is in its way a rather splendid piece of interior decoration, an exquisite jewel-case for The Artist: there is an argument for preferring it to the Goethe house. But of course no one in his senses would put Liszt in competition with Goethe, as a human phenomenon. That *he* should have lapsed out of the town's history, that *he* should not impose himself or his era upon us, calls for no explanation.

But there are human phenomena in Weimar not so easily drowned out. The town lies under the shadow of the Buchenwald memorial. The Buchenwald concentration camp, in which fifty-six thousand prisoners were murdered, was situated on the Ettersberg, a hill just outside the town on which the Weimar dukes used to have one of their pleasure palaces and on which, now, the Russian army has a camp. Buchenwald has a fully documented museum; schoolchildren visit in great numbers; because the D.D.R. makes much of the concentration camps and of the survival, in Western Germany, of the capitalist enterprises which profited from the camps' slave labor. The D.D.R. is a *Friedensstaat*, a peace-state; East Berlin is a center of the Communist peace offensive. And however cynical one may be about that, there is no need to doubt the sincerity (or the validity) of the regime's denunciation of West Germany. Incomparably smaller and poorer, more virtuous, more peasant, more *lumpen*, it exists in an ineffective antithesis to its sister state, which it showers with Lilliputian darts every day in its editorials.

Weimar has then a political significance, and one which is culti-vated by the regime. The tourists go up to Buchenwald too. Weimar was one of the Nazis' show-cities, and one of Hitler's va-cation cities. July 3, 1926, is the first date on which his name ap-pears in the guest-book of the Elephant (where everyone has stayed in Weimar since 1696). When he rose to power his room there had its walls specially strengthened. I met two or three people who could remember being on the Market Square when the crowd cheered for him to come to the window to show himself. Throughout his regime, the town was protected, given a special status. In 1945 the American general who captured the town made the citizens march through Buchenwald, to force them to face the facts they had ignored. After the war, the hotel was for a time a teachers' training college. Now, disinfected, it belongs to a big chain, and again strives to have the grandest guests it can get. And the talk is all of Goethe. There is not much one can say in a luxury hotel about Buchenwald.

There was another famous inhabitant of Weimar, who stands part-way between Goethe, on the one hand, and Hitler and Bu-chenwald on the other. Number 36 Humboldt Strasse used to be the Nietzsche archives, because there Nietzsche lived, after he lost his mind in 1891, under the care of his sister, Frau Elisabeth Fors-ter-Nietzsche, until 1901. She continued to live there till 1936, and

Hitler used to visit the archives and be photographed gazing at Nietzsche's bust. He was the official philosopher of Nazism. One can understand why, when the Russian troops reached Weimar in 1945, they closed the house immediately. It now stands empty, without a sign of any kind, occupied only by a janitor and his wife, who live in the basement. Kulturstadt or no, that boldness of thought, that heroism of the mind, is a little too much. Of course Nietzsche was never a citizen of Weimar in the sense that Goethe was. He was very absently present to the city. But those years of insanity in the upper stories while below visiting savants and ideologues concocted a political travesty of his ideas, in collaboration with that sinister sister — surely that is one of the most vivid modes of presence, of citizenship, that the history of philosophy has known.

The Nietzsche villa stands high on a hill on the opposite side of town from the Buchenwald Monument, and as I looked across, a series of detonations in the Russian camp formed an ironic refrain (a giant *Bejahung*) to the claims of *Friedensstaat*. And between Nietzsche and Buchenwald lie the town and its literary monuments: humanism, as they call it; and what else should they call it? It produces a kind of stupefaction, any attempt to hold together in one's mind both Buchenwald and Goethe. This stupefaction is, I take it, the heart of what George Steiner has called "silence." But I felt rather that the two things had no relation, not even the relation of contradiction. It was rather that any discourse, verbal or not, that attempted to bridge the abyss between the two, got nowhere, ended in meaningless elaborations, apologetics, abstractions.

Certainly Weimar offers no connections. The Memorial stands square and grim on the hill, its huge bell silent, its bunkers full of machine guns and bloodstained uniforms and instruments of torture. And the town is occupied in effect by Goethe. Not only are the streets filled with busloads of tourists, the commerce of the town, but the streets themselves, the very substance of the town, is dedicated to often trivial details of his life story. I thought it funny enough to come across Bettina von Arnim Strasse, but then Freiherr von Stein Strasse! The Freiherr's role in Weimar classicism, so far as I know, was to neglect his wife, that Charlotte von

Stein with whom Goethe had perhaps the most serious of his love affairs. But here again, what the town has done is to trivialize, but not entirely to betray, not to change the direction of, what Goethe wanted. He, of all writers, repudiated savagery, revolution, war, and politics on the giant scale. He took in only as much of life — but an enormous quantity it was — as he could bring into harmony with his own personality. The town institutionalizes that effort.

The central nervous system of this Goethe-Weimarism is the *Nationale Forschungs — und Gedenkstätten der Klassischen Deutschen Literatur in Weimar*. This employs about two hundred and fifty people, of whom twenty or thirty are trained researchers and the others guides, guardians, overseers, who often know a lot about the great men. They often stand in the same relation to Goethe as they would if he were alive. The lady at the Kirms-Cracow house, when the question came up of Goethe's attitude to smoking, was overcome with giggles at the thought of how strongly he disliked it, how he would rage against it. Her red-faced laughter was the succumbing of one personality to another stronger than itself. And the whole town echoes that nervous laughter.

Of course Goethe's personality was a very strong one. Not only in the sense that he made his will felt, but also in the quite extraordinary range of his abilities, aptitudes, energies. The collections of minerals, of plants, the historical tables, the electrical machines, the majolica, the busts, his own sketches . . . What did Goethe not try his hand at, assemble, create, control, construct, over eighty-three years? And all this serious productivity — we haven't mentioned the administration of the dukedom — went along with a quite frivolous worldliness, the participation in court life and picnics and masques and practical jokes. Not to mention the love affairs, the friendships, the discipleships, the collaborations, all the relationships to which the letters testify. No one has ever crammed so much into a human life-span.

But — Goethe is surely the most problematic of authors — but, among other things, he exacted a heavy price from the people he worked with. Perhaps the saddest sight in Weimar is the house whose plaque says that Eckermann lived there. Eckermann came to Weimar in 1823, an engaged man, but could marry only in 1832, the last year of Goethe's life. His own life was put in storage while he worked for the other man. Eckermann did a number of jobs for Goethe, like identifying early unsigned articles, and himself produced one real book, *The Conversations of Goethe with Eckermann.* His house is sad because it is so much humbler than Goethe's, and also because of an anecdote in Friedenthal's biography: On the hundredth anniversary of Goethe's birth, when every window in Weimar was lit in celebration, Eckermann's alone remained dark. And there was Reimer, long Goethe's secretary, who said "We" are working on *Dichtung und Wahrheit*, whose epistolary style became indistinguishable from his master's, who flirted with Goethe's women friends when Goethe was away, and who married Fraulein Ulrich, another minor figure in the Goethe household, who adoringly embroidered slippers and lampshades for the great man. There were valets, like Stadelmann, who did optical research himself in imitation of his master, and equally in imitation drank too much. In 1844, when he was living in a poorhouse, he was invited to the unveiling of the Goethe memorial in Frankfurt, and arrived wearing Goethe's old coat. He was promised an annuity by the Goethe admirers there assembled, to save him from the degrading life he had been reduced to since Goethe's death. But before the first installment arrived he got drunk again and hanged himself in the attic.

There were his friends, like Lenz, who followed Goethe as suitor to Frederika Brion, and then paid court to Cornelia Goethe, and finally, following him to Weimar, to the Duchess Luise. There were his protégés, like Fritz von Stein. In accordance with Goethe's educational theories, Fritz became as a boy his messenger, reader, copyist, and later his assistant and treasurer. He was, along with all the others, absorbed into Goethe's life. Later independence he naturally found difficult. He married twice unsuccessfully, and only found some stability after leaving Weimar for good.

There were above all Goethe's own family, from his tragically maladjusted sister to his son, whose entire life was lived in his father's shadow, and was psychologically mildewed in consequence. August Goethe, like Riemer, married a girl who was fascinated in fact by his father. His wife, Ottilie von Pugwisch-Goethe, herself came to a sad-shameful end, offering herself to the young men who visited the Frauenplan in homage to Goethe. And both her sons, the last of the Goethes, shy and friendless, died unmarried far from Weimar, on a journey like a flight from home. One of them described himself as a remnant of the house of Tantalus.

This is not to say that Goethe was simply an exhauster of other people. He gave as well as took a lot. Otherwise so many people would not have entered into and continued the exchange with him. But the balance of the exchanges does seem to have followed this pattern, which is the classic Faustian pattern. This is the problem Mann examined in *Lotte in Weimar*. And Mann himself is part of the dossier. He is perhaps the most important example of the obsessive interest Goethe and Weimar have had for German intellectuals ever since 1800.*

One is bound to be interested in Weimar if one is interested in Goethe, just as much as vice versa. Because Goethe planned his life, planned his career, planned his production. Every part promoted every other part. Not a plan like a blueprint; quite the opposite; a royally careless, largely ex-post-facto deliberateness, seeing what had helped and what hadn't, ruthlessly rejecting this and enthusiastically redoubling his efforts in that. If he lived in Weimar, if he knew these people, if he used them the way he did, he meant it — meant it as much as the forms of his writing. His was an exemplary life, much more than other writers'. The eyes of the world had been on him ever since he was twenty-five and wrote *Werther*.

In his work you can see him trying every kind of subject matter and every kind of form. *Werther, Goetz*, the lyrics, *Iphigenie*, the Roman elegies, *Wilhelm Meister, Faust* — well, the point is obvious. He turned from one thing to another; as soon as he had achieved something he lost interest and wanted to do something different. He also turned away from things when they were half done and returned to them as much as fifty years later; because he was continually testing the sincerity of his interest, the intensity of

* And his novel, *Doctor Faustus*, is only the most obvious example of his obsession with the themes of forbidden powers and forbidden knowledge. Mann was, like so many liberals, an anti-Faustian, a man directing most of his energies toward a self-image which he kept safely interdicted by a negative sign, a disapproving prohibition. Time and again he returned to one or other of these themes, Faust, Goethe, Weimar.

his inspiration, the purity of his mood. Every artist does something of this, but Goethe more than anyone. Schiller did perhaps less than anyone. His moods were all sincere, because in him will and disposition acknowledged no separations. That is why Schiller is always the more sympathetic writer to radicals, despite his conservatism in practical politics. But Goethe's head was ever bent, one ear cocked to catch the murmurs of his heart. This accounts for the ambiguity of his accounts of the poetic process; on the one hand he claimed to be the victim of inspirations that visited him from outside, on the other he was clearly the most self-conscious, self-planning, of all writers. Both are indeed true.

The same ambiguity is to be found in his love affairs. On the one hand he fell in love readily, and loved with all his heart. His case may be taken to define the phrase. Werther loves Lotte for her face, for her body, for her mind, for her tastes, for her virtues, for her limitations. He loves her for being everything she is, and the feeling seizes upon him, and its nonfulfillment drives him to despair. And this was true for Goethe himself again and again, from Frederika Brion, or at least from Charlotte Buff, to Ulrike von Leventzow. But at the same time he was always self-protective, never really carried away. He never married any of them. He made his life companion a woman with whom he did *not* fall in love with all his heart. We see the same principle at work: a man listening to his heart, enchanted by what he hears, but not inclined to translate the message into action — or only into artistic action.

Here again he is like other writers. Our three greatest celebrators of married love, domestic and family life, are surely Goethe, Tolstoy, and Lawrence.* But Lawrence never in fact lived a domestic and family life; he wandered the world with Frieda von Richthofen. While Tolstoy, typically, *lived* that life and then repudiated it, dying in flight from his family and home at the age of eighty-two. But Goethe is the most extreme case of the three. He embodies in its most disturbing form the problem of the man who establishes absolutes for others but eludes them himself; whose su-

* Rousseau illustrates the same pattern, and is closest to Goethe in his choice of wife. I named Lawrence and Tolstoy in preference because Rousseau is too palpably tricky, too ambiguous on the surface, to make the point challenging.

periority as a writer derives from a sincerity which, once seen from an unsympathetic point of view, provokes resentment, which becomes ambiguous the moment we get up off our knees.

And he chose to live in Weimar because in Weimar was the perfect apparatus for such a life. In Weimar he could do everything and not commit himself — not limit himself — to anything. He could be minister of state, army recruiter, court poet, theater director, library supervisor, masque arranger, as well as organize his literary and scientific pursuits. Of course in one sense he committed himself to these activities. He did them very thoroughly. He did them with all his heart, just as he fell in love. But he could always draw back. He could always take up something new.

He did not always do this very gracefully. Especially in the early part of his life he tended to panic and flee. Take his disappearance from Wetzlar, with just a note to explain to Lotte and Kestner. And the most dramatic example was his unannounced slipping away to Italy, away from Charlotte von Stein, and away from his official duties, in 1787. He soon felt trapped by any absorbing relationship or occupation, and his revulsion against feeling trapped was his absolute, his ultimate emotion.

In Weimar he was less trapped than anywhere, he could more easily draw back and change course. This was partly because he had the favor, the sympathetic understanding, the friendship, of the duke. And partly just because Weimar was such a small place. It had a little of everything, but nothing in such demanding dimensions that it could impose itself as an ineluctable life-task. Those dukedoms were all comically small places; and the Weimar Schloss was small by comparison with, say, the Würtzburg Residenz. Anna Amalia's income, for all purposes, was sixty thousand thalers, or nine thousand pounds. The city had six hundred to seven hundred houses when Geothe went there; under five thousand people in 1800. Philadelphia had then seventy thousand people and Berlin two hundred thousand, not to mention Paris or London. Goethe scarcely saw a big city in his life. The only one he lived in, Rome, was a culture city, not a metropolis. It did occur to him, in the last part of his life, to move to Paris, just as earlier he had considered going to America. He valued highly, after all, the concentration of brilliant minds, something he would have found in Paris. And he shared the Enlightenment idealism that took people to America. But in both cases these thoughts came to nothing. Weimar was his home. Because he could not have controlled all the elements of his experiences in those places; he would have lost some of his freedom, his variety, his fulfillment; they would have been bigger than he.

The smallness of Weimar was a matter not only of literal fact, but of consciousness. In Paris, in America, in London, the large political forces of the period were playing out a great drama. In Weimar everything was something of a game. It was a rococo-cum-Biedermeier place. It was Anna Amalia who had made it what it was, Anna Amalia and Wieland, and her little palaces, Tiefurt and the Wittumspalais, are perhaps still the most successful houses in Weimar. I know of nothing more charming than Tiefurt, and in the fullest, and the purest, senses of the word. But the charm is essentially rococo. It is a matter of playing games, of practical jokes, of conscious artifice. There are the usual paint-imitations of marble and of draperies, a set of papier-mâché fruits and meats which they served unwary guests, little theaters where they acted, exquisitely fitted-out cosmetic tables, and the famous door to Fräulein von Goechhausen's room (a door walled up and papered over one day by the duke and Goethe so that this lady-in-waiting to the duchess had to pass the night on the veranda — a famous Weimar joke).

Excluding the writers, the men of Goethe's own kind, whom he easily surpassed, what was there of larger dimensions than this in Weimar? The duke certainly was a remarkable man, and of an earthier, more masculine kind. He was a huntsman and a soldier, a man of great personal force, but very shrewd and free, very self-possessed, in his dealings with his intellectuals. But if one thinks of world-historical forces, Karl August was as rococo a figure as Anna Amalia. All his masculine forcefulness fulfilled itself on a stage three yards wide by two deep.

This rococo strain is there in Goethe himself. There is a case for saying that his *characteristic* artistic form was the *Maskenzug*, the Court Masque, of which he devised so many. This is what shapes *Faust II*. He loved practical jokes, he loved acting, he loved disguising himself. The keynote of his character is his strong sense of multiple possibilities, of many roles he could play in life, and his reluctance to renounce any of them. (Though the *need* to renounce them haunted him — hence his preoccupation with *"ent-sagen."*) In his early years he responded ardently to each new invitation, yielding himself very fully, very generously, to for instance Herder, and to Charlotte von Stein. In later years, perhaps in order not to be forever changing, he made himself stiff and unyielding and domineering. This is what made his stiffness so cold, so repugnant to many; that it was willed.

But of course his personality, in both its responsive and its assertive powers, was much too large to be circumscribed by the word rococo. Goethe was a great man, if the term has any meaning. He was a great writer. And Weimar is the great exemplar in world history of a literary society, or a culture city. Many of us — espe cially in my profession — are haunted by the dream of a society which would express the same values as get expressed in literature; in which the basic moral, economic, political questions would be taken care of without much fuss, and in which the greater part of men's intellectual and emotional energy would be put into the arts and the sciences, the creative games of life. But most of us believe that such a place could never exist, or if it did it would soon become morally decadent or intellectually and artistically sterile. But Weimar did exist, and did produce one of the world's great literatures, and there was Goethe.

And for us today — for me today — all this is particularly relevant. Because I think we have had a kind of equivalent to Weimar in America over the last twenty years, in certain American colleges, most typically the Ivy League schools. And the present ferment of discontent among both students and faculty is — among other things — putting this neo-Weimar classicism on trial. American universities as a whole seem to have been, at least since the war, rather like the German states during the eighteenth century in that they are all, despite their variousness, consciously small kingdoms, divorced from the major brutalities of the world and yet surprisingly complete. They are the structures in which the best minds and talents of today have come together, earned their livings, got their experience of life. And they often have a marked rococo atmosphere, with their green lawns, their white columns, their long summers, their crowds of handsome young people. (Pastoral communities where the shepherds are all, or some of them, aristocrats of the intellect.) Their Junior Years Abroad, their abbeys in England and villas in Italy, like Harvard's *I Tatti*, have an opulent and festive rhythm of life that can only be called aristocratic.

I'm seeing them primarily from under the aspect of the Faculty Club, and I'm suggesting that the mixture of talents and the mode of community there, at a good university, can be comparable to that of the court of a good German state. The similarity of the position of resident artist is obvious; but even in the quite different case of Goethe's ministerial career, the process of his being looked over (by other princes before Karl August) and the criteria by which he was judged (they wanted a bright young man, with all the new ideas, but if possible an amusing and civilized companion) make it sound very like hiring a dean.

These places have had their characteristic writers, from Robert Frost to John Barth; their distinguished foreigners, like Nabokov, writing *Lolita* at Cornell, and Mann, writing *Lotte in Weimar* at Princeton; their personalities, like Perry Miller and Galbraith at Harvard. The characteristic style of life is, unlike the popular myth of the academy, forceful, masculine, sardonic, skeptical, *grand seigneur*. And in their literature, too, there is a cultivated force of personality, controlled but intensified by the complicated forms which can even be called, loosely, neo-classic. (I am thinking of Frost and Lowell's poetry, of Barth and Nabokov's fiction, of Perry Miller and Edmund Wilson's essays.) It has been an antipolitical style of mind because it has been antienthusiastic. These men never got carried away, as Schiller complained about Goethe. It has been, I think, one of the richest and brightest phases of cultural history. But the present mood of radical puritanism, and the political crisis that engenders it, puts that style of life in jeopardy, and presumably, whatever the next ten years bring, there will be a difference. A diminution of self-confidence, at the least. It is ultimately this analogy, I think, which has led me to concern myself so much with Goethe and Weimar.*

* I realize that this academic environment has been the protective setting for a safe, controlled Faustianism of temperament and sensibility; has been the locus of a certain kind of conservatism.

Goethe himself had in due course to deal with student revolt: both in the literal sense, when the students at Jena University rebelled, and he was immediately responsible, and in the looser sense, when all generous and cultivated society in Weimar sympathized with the students. This was the period of German nationalism in revolt against Napoleon. Goethe put his faith in Napoleon, the daimonic personality, and was isolated in consequence as well as proved wrong. (Incidentally, one would expect Frost's attitude to the present troubles, if he were alive today, to be very like Goethe's.) Goethe seemed in those years, around 1815, an outdated phenomenon. Twenty years later it seemed rather that the rebels had been wrong.

History and its analogies provide no solutions, but they can clarify one's feelings. Present-day Weimar argued against conservatism in my mind by its self-subordination, its submission, on the part of all fifty thousand inhabitants, to that long-dead personality. There is a (quite recent) book on translators of *Faust* called *Half a Hundred Thralls to Faust* — perhaps even the miscalculated quaintness of the language is another human tax levied to support Goethe's greatness — and Weimar sometimes seemed like Half a Hundred Thousand Thralls. If it seems to have put Goethe in its pocket, the truth is equally the reverse. He has it in his pocket. He did so in his lifetime. Each incorporated the other and petrified itself. Both in cultural and in purely literary terms, this was too heavy a price to pay.

On the other hand, to come to political terms, it is an achievement, in the D.D.R., to have kept one city dedicated to humanism rather than to dialectical materialism. Weimar is Goethe's city and not Marx's. That force of willpower and self-assertion, which often feels so monstrous, has after all made literary values count, in political terms, even a hundred and fifty years later. It is when literature is *enforced* this way that it counts for something in the world. Something similar was true of America's neo-Weimarism. We cannot be without regret as we move — it seems inevitably — into another period.

Thomas Mann and Weimar and Faust

Mann has written often about Goethe from a point of view very like that of this book. His intellectual career revolved around the questions of daimonism, of culture in the Weimar sense, of German national destiny, and of the destiny of the modern man of letters. He began with a devotion to the daimonic, as found in the work of Schopenhauer, Nietzsche, and Wagner, and as late as 1918, in *Betrachtungen eines Unpolitischen,* he described it as being Germany's special destiny to realize herself in the darkly irrational and in music, not in the clear and comprehensible terms of liberal culture.

But by the time of the essay "Goethe and Tolstoy" (1922), Mann was turning his keenest attention to Goethe, and *Der Zauberberg* (1924) is full of allusions to *Faust. Lotte in Weimar* (1939) reveals an extraordinary imaginative absorption in Goethe and in Weimar, and though it stresses the daimonic element — the cost to others of the artist's greatness — it also stresses the contrary element. "Appeasement, compromise — are they not all my striving? To assent, to allow, to give both sides play, balance, harmony. The combination of all forces makes up the world." This idea, expressed by "Goethe" in one of his monologues, is perfectly Erasmian. While *Doctor Faustus* (1948), taking up the subject with which Goethe's name is virtually identified, explicitly condemns that enthusiasm for the irrational and for "music" which he had begun by endorsing as specially German. Mann's life was a journey to Weimar. He ended up in a position as close to Goethe's as his natural endowment would allow him to occupy.

The three quotations which follow indicate that position, the reconciliation — so reminiscent of Goethe's own — which Mann finally made between Erasmian and Faustian virtues of temperament. He is to be identified within the novel with Zeitblom, who is an Erasmus-figure, a humanist, a Catholic, a northerner, and sometimes explicitly linked with Erasmus and opposed to Luther. But Mann does not repudiate Leverkühn, the damned, doomed artist. Indeed, the identification with Zeitblom defines a mode of allegiance to the other man, as this first quotation makes clear.

Yes, that is how it was: this arrogance was the chief motive of the fearful love which all my life I cherished for him in my heart.

— Serenus Zeitblom, *Doctor Faustus*, p. 67

To use Goethe's phrase, Mann here acknowledges himself subject to the Daimonic, though it is no part of his own nature. (Of course the prime referents for Goethe's phrase are unlike those for Mann. The two men had different strengths and weaknesses. It is in the act of compromise that they become alike.)

I am by nature wholly moderate, of a temper, I may say, both healthy and humane, addressed to reason and harmony; a scholar and conjuratus of the "Latin host," not lacking all contact with the arts (I play the viola d'amore) but a son of the Muses in that academic sense which by preference regards itself as descended from the German humanists of the time of "Poets."

Heir of a Reuchlin, a Crotus of Dornheim, of Mutianus and Eoban of Hesse, the daemonic, little as I presume to deny its influence upon human life, I have at all times found utterly foreign to my nature. Instinctively I have rejected it from my picture of the cosmos and never felt the slightest inclination rashly to open the door to the powers of darkness; arrogantly to challenge, or if they of themselves ventured from their side, even to hold my little finger to them.

— Serenus Zeitblom, *Doctor Faustus*, p. 3

The artist is the brother of the criminal and the madman.

— The Devil, *Doctor Faustus*, p. 23

It was then to Weimar that Mann finally made his way, to the city of light, which always offers an *uneasy* hospitality to the Sons of the Morning, cherishes for them a *fearful* love in its heart. These next two quotations, taken from outside *Doctor Faustus* but referring to it, show Mann's Erasmianism.

All sheer personalities! I think I am none. I personally will be as little remembered as Proust! How much *Faustus* contains of the atmosphere of my life! A radical confession, at bottom. From the very beginning that has been the shattering thing about the book.

— Mann's diaries, quoted in *The Story of a Novel*, p. 154

Once again, I sympathized with Goethe's rejection of the "untamed human soul."

— Ibid., p. 216, after looking at, and disliking, facsimiles of some Beethoven letters

Mann uses terms so close to those of this book, and is fascinated by
so many of the same figures, because his fate was to represent all
writers whose endowment was characterized by the Erasmian type
of spiritual bargain. Though fascinated by the Faustian type, he
clearly could not and would not make that bargain himself, and so
remained hypersensitive to such things in other people.

And he uses our terms also because the city of Weimar as well as
the figure of Goethe crystallized the problem for him. As in the
case of Rousseau and Calvin, one great man can inherit another
great man's experience via his city, via the traces of his way of life
in institutions and anecdotes attached to particular streets and
houses. This can be mummy-seed as much as the books he wrote.
Lotte in Weimar is one of the world's finest examples of that.

One of Mann's most interesting pieces on this subject is the
quite early essay "Goethe and Tolstoy," published in *Bemühungen*
in 1922, which raises some problems for our interpretation of
Goethe. His main point is that these two great men were "godlike," whereas their contrast figures, Schiller and Dostoevski, were
"saints." The first pair spoke for nature, the second for culture; the
first for health, the second for sickness; the first for physicality, the
body, brutality, vitality, enduringness, nobility of natural life;
the second for the opposite qualities, for freedom, the spirit, and
the nobility of a revulsion away from nature and life and self.

His characterization of the second pair suits Mann's purposes
better than mine, and indeed does not seem entirely valid to me.
But he points to a series of striking similarities between Goethe
and Tolstoy (as men, not as writers) which illustrate the Faustian
idea vividly. Take the very epithets "godlike" or "divine" — which
were in fact applied to both men by their contemporaries — and
their derivation from the men's own consciousness of superior gifts
and assurance of superior fates. Among which gifts, Mann points
out, they particularly prized the animal ones; that is to say, those
that could not be earned or deserved, morally or intellectually, that
must be given, and used, amorally. Both loved blood-sports and
hunting; both were unusually agile and vigorous in old age; and
both insisted on these traits in themselves. And if they had often
an excess of animal spirits, these were recurrently replaced by not

just equanimity or depression, but by a tormented melancholy and total cynicism.

Gorky described Tolstoy as being on occasion "the apotheosis of negation, the deepest and most hideous nihilism, springing from a stratum of boundless and hopeless despair." This is the despair of a man who cannot be roused by any promised human experience or human value, because he knows how they are all created, having created them himself. Gorky called Tolstoy incomparable in this respect, but Mann asks us to compare the figure of Mephistopheles and his creator. And Goethe in the second half of his life also imposed an appalling cynicism and coldness on all kinds of people who came in contact with him, from Schiller himself to Riemer and Eckermann. Turgenev's explanation of this condition in Tolstoy was that "He has never managed to believe in the sincerity of mankind. Every expression of feeling seemed to him false; and he had the habit, due to his extraordinarily penetrating gaze, of boring through with his eye the man he considered insincere." Turgenev was himself one of those who suffered from that treatment by Tolstoy. He confessed that never in his life had he suffered from anything with such power to dishearten him as this same piercing gaze, which, accompanied with two or three biting remarks, could bring to madness anybody who did not possess particularly strong control.

Mann tells an anecdote of Tolstoy pursuing Turgenev, from one city to another, in order to inflict this gaze upon him, and to observe the result. Mutatis mutandis, there are perhaps similar episodes in the relationship of Lawrence to Middleton Murry, or of Goethe to some of his victims. Of course such episodes, if described by Tolstoy or Goethe or Lawrence, would have a quite different meaning. Turgenev might have gained from the experience if he had been able to face the sort of interrogation which Tolstoy was trying to force on him. The point for me is not the morality of the episode but its illustrativeness.

Turgenev is a good example of the Erasmian artist, and the incident is a good example of the confrontation between that type and the Faustian. From my point of view, Turgenev seems a better contrast figure to put beside Tolstoy than Dostoevski, and Wieland might be better than Schiller. Dostoevski was himself a man

of excess, of forbidden knowledge and evil powers, a highly dangerous man. He does not have the charm of the noble animal, but he
perhaps belongs to the same subcategory of the Faustian as Rousseau, which we might call the negative, the Faustian by natural
weakness as opposed to natural strength, the man who knows and
can do more than others because he has explored and exploited his
own shames and guilts and evils. (This group often coincides with
the literary-Faustian in part; Proust and Joyce belong to this subcategory too.)

Gorky also complained of Tolstoy's destructiveness in personal
relations, his disturbing interrogation — " 'Do you love your wife?
Do you like my wife?' — Disingenuous. The whole time, he is
making an experiment . . . He is the devil, and I am a babe in
arms beside him. He ought to leave me alone." But at the same
time Gorky says, "There is something about him which always
makes me want to shout: 'Behold what a marvellous man lives
upon this earth.' For he is, so to speak, in general and beyond everything else, a human being, a man." Mann then reminds us of Napoleon's famous comment on Goethe after their meeting, "Voilà
un homme." And there is plenty of testimony to Goethe's rousing
the same enthusiasm in even his victims. The locus classicus is perhaps Eckermann's description of Goethe's body after death, which
stresses so much its perfect fullness of manhood, its animal nobility. It seems, from the doctor's postmortem report, that Eckermann must have been deceiving himself, but if so that is further
testimony to the power with which Goethe gave out that impression. His and Tolstoy's frightening inhumanity was somehow
linked to their "human humanity," their more than normal normality.

Both Goethe and Tolstoy made their homes, Weimar and
Yasnaya Polyana, places of pilgrimage, to which men of all kinds
made their way. But it was equally notable that the visitors very
often drove away from both places chilled, disappointed, reproach-
ful. Having gone to meet an anarchist, one had been confronted by
a haughty prince; having gone to meet Werther, another had been
confronted by a stiff and meticulous official of the state of
Weimar. They were not to be relied on, to be taken for granted.
They imposed the terms of each encounter.

Mann points out that both men had like Rousseau a passion for educating others. But pedagogy, idealism, and moralism, like criticism and rhetoric, belong to the spirit, according to Mann, and he therefore calls Tolstoy and Goethe children of nature who yearned to be children of the spirit. I prefer to say that they deliberately cultivated Erasmian qualities which their Faustian temperaments caused them involuntarily to betray. But I would say also that those *temperaments* also were something that they cultivated, sometimes in just the same way, sometimes at a less conscious level of deliberateness. All these qualities are in the significant sense self-determined, the results of spiritual contracts.

Mann, an anti-Faustian, felt closer to Goethe at the time he was writing this essay, and shows himself nervous of Tolstoy. It is the latter he makes characterize the Faustian temperament most extremely. Tolstoy, he says, was interested in the body above all, and for that reason also in death and the dissolution of the body. Mann quoted from Tolstoy's *Recollections*, "However much I dislike to speak of it, I can still remember the characteristic sharp odour which was personal to my aunt, probably in consequence of some carelessness in dress." (From this kind of hint so much of modern writing has developed; and our whole civilization's mind has been sexualized because our artists have all acquired the Faustian sensibility.) But Goethe also was extremely sensitive and responsive to all natural and physical phenomena — for instance, to the weather. And like Tolstoy he was extremely sensitive and responsive sexually. Indeed, he too was preoccupied with death. He hated funerals, and forbade all mourning, all mention of death and sickness, in his house.

Finally, Mann quotes Gorky saying that Tolstoy seriously hoped to be immortal; an illuminating idea, and a plausible one, as attributed to Goethe as well as to Tolstoy. Both men had outlived so many others, in years but also in life, in achievements, in variety of being, in power of selfhood; they show that they felt they had done so much, had changed so much in themselves and in other people, that they must be different. They exceeded the limits that confined other people. They were more like creators than like the creatures they saw around them, who could so largely be defined by their limitations. (This limitedness is true of even brilliantly gifted men, if they are Erasmian by temperament.)

That syndrome is what we mean by the Faustian temperament. And its psychic cost, the guilt that goes with it, is nowhere more vividly illustrated than in that black destructive cynicism and nihilism the two men suffered from at times. As Gorky said of Tolstoy, "His superhumanly developed individuality is a monstrous phenomenon. . . ."

The position from which Tolstoy was *writing* during the years when Gorky knew him was of course radical; and his writing seems Calvinist in temperament; just as Goethe's writing position in his Eckermann years could be called liberal and Erasmian. Perhaps both men were in flight from the monstrousness of the selves they had developed, and which they saw reflected in the eyes of their friends. But they did not deceive anyone. Everybody remarked the contradiction between what they advocated and what they were. They remained Faustian personalities.

The problem Mann's theory raises for us is that this is the Goethe of Weimar, of the period when we described him as being conservative, and in some ways Erasmian. In using the word "contradiction" just now I indicated the kind of connection I want to claim. I want to claim that there was such a contradiction in Goethe's own life. And if I develop that idea, I can resolve the conflicting tendencies in my attitude to Weimar, and relate conservatism more fully to my general scheme of temperaments.

There can be no doubt, I think, that in his Sturm und Drang phase, and in his alchemical studies, Goethe did aim at acquiring more than normal powers of personality and of intuitive knowledge. The literary evidence is there in *Faust* and *Werther* — to some degree in *Goetz* — and in poems like "Prometheus." Before settling on Faust as his hero, he had tried Ahasuerus, Mohammed, Socrates, and Caesar. The theme of dangerous power was clearly what obsessed him, and in his life as well as in his writing. Traces come through even in *Dichtung und Wahrheit*, where he is much on guard against seeming to endorse that early ambitiousness. After describing the effectiveness of his oral telling of "The New Melusina" to his friends at Sesenheim, he adds:

If anyone should one day find the tale in print and read it and doubt that it could have such an effect, he should reflect that man is really only qualified to make an impression in the present. Writing is a misuse of language; reading alone quietly is a sad substitute for talk. A man makes every impression he possibly can on others through his personality — the young most powerfully on the young — and that is where the purest effects are achieved. It is the young who enliven the world and don't let it die, either morally or physically.

Implicitly — and just for a moment — he pays homage to power just as recklessly as he had done in the days he is writing about. One notes too that — just for a moment — in so doing he repudiates contemptuously the Erasmian disciplines of writing and being printed and published, to which he had submitted himself so laboriously in Weimar.

For there can be equally little doubt that once in Weimar Goethe aimed at something other than Faustian power; that his politics were conservative and his intellectual and imaginative enterprises were liberal — were aimed at virtues that go more naturally with the Erasmian temperament. In his discussion of the daimonic with Eckermann, on March 2, 1831, he insisted that the daimonic was not something in his own nature, but something to which he was subject. One does not believe everything Goethe said about himself to Eckermann, but there is much to support this idea, or at least the idea of a double contract, in Goethe's relations with others. He had that remarkable susceptibility to others — for instance, his self-yielding to Herder — and he had those periods of *Dumpfheit*, of feelinglessness, convictionlessness, when he was at best passive. He could indeed exert power over others, if they were expectant and receptive, but in the presence of powerful men, he was in danger of being himself the receptive one. He made increasing use, during his time at Weimar, of his privileged position there, in order to build up for himself artificial aids to, equivalents of, daimonic power. He erected for himself social and official barriers and formalities — daises and divans on which to appear — to put himself at an advantage with others. Thus even the daimonism of personality to which Mann points could be said to be a Weimar compromise; between residual Faustian ambitions — a determination not to sink into receptivity and two-dimensionality — and the Erasmian-impersonal qualities he was also cultivating. It is because of those residual ambitions that the Weimar temperament must be called conservative; the motive power was Faustian even while the directional control was not. And thus Weimar too has a double aspect, and as the personal kingdom of Goethe can repel even while as the city of light it attracts.

Finally, one must not assume that everything written by Goethe in Weimar expressed "Weimar" in the sense defined. *Faust* must of course *seem* the city's supreme literary production, finished as it was over such a long period there. But that fact is quite misleading, and not just in the sense that the label does not explain much, but in the sense that it is categorically wrong. Over the years quite contrary impulses were built into the Faust material — to damn the hero and to save him, to take evil seriously and to explain it away, the mood of the Gretchen tragedy and the mood of the Helena Act. There are several plays, several modes of art, juxtaposed within *Faust*, and the final character of the whole is not what we here have meant by "Weimar."

That character can be located in the prodigious efforts which Goethe made toward reconciling the different parts in the enormous, and rather abstract, overall form, as well as in the latest-written parts themselves. Of course, much of Goethe's work written after he came to Weimar had a rather abstract and encyclopedic form; the encyclopedia is an Erasmian form, as we shall see. But the form of *Faust* (particularly Part II) is not "encyclopedic" in that sense. It is an elaborate and ambitious gnostic masque. This is an Alexandrian, not a Weimar, form, and belongs to the gnostic-Faustian temperament, which I shall discuss more fully in Chapter 8.

What follows is as brief an explanation as possible of that phrase in its relation to *Faust*. It is no accident that Faust's relations with Helena in Goethe's play so exactly parallel those of Simon Magus (who was also called Faustus, the fortunate one) with his Helena, in the second century A.D. Simon Magus, the gnostic philosopher and magician, traveled with a whore called Helena, whom he alleged to be the reincarnation of Helen of Troy, who had herself been really the incarnation of Sophia, Divine Wisdom, the First Thought of God, trapped and errant in human flesh, and the cause of wars between nations. Goethe had inherited gnostic traditions of imaginative thought via his Renaissance masters, Pico, Bruno, Cusanus, etc. Thus *Faust*, in its final form, is a profoundly Renaissance-gnostic play. As Professor Jantz has shown, figures like Wagner and Mephistopheles have equivalents, real-life and literary, within the Renaissance, to recognize which is important. But this Renaissance-gnostic spirit was not something which Goethe derived from, or shared with, people at Weimar. (It is more closely related to, though quite different from, his Sturm und Drang daimonism.) It is in many ways antithetical to "Weimar."

The spirit of the encyclopedic learning displayed in *Faust* — like that in Joyce's *Ulysses*, unlike that in Schiller's *Wallenstein* — is not historical but gnostic. It has no more piety of feeling for the past as past than it has for human suffering, or moral greatness, or intellectual achievement. It *plays* with its material, intellectually and aesthetically; it combines powerful feelings like pathos (made real in realized situations) with ideas *about* feelings, like literary modes. It makes the Helena Act out of the mating of two ideas, classicism and romanticism. This is not the classical-conservative-humane spirit of Weimar. This part of the play (which characterizes the whole form) was written out of a despair over the classical enterprise, in the last few years of Goethe's life, long after the deaths of Schiller and Herder; written in the spirit of Alexandria, not of Weimar.

"Weimar" was then a phase in Goethe's life, though a longer, stabler, more total self-manifestation than most men achieve in all their lives. He began in Sturm und Drang Faustianism, and ended in the gnostic variety, and even during the time he was plying the Erasmian trades of learning and administration, he reserved part of himself in Faustian arrogance. That arrogance is what made the Weimar enterprise conservative; but that enterprise made his conservatism moderate and not extremist. And it is the Weimar enterprise we are concerned with, rather than Goethe himself.

From our point of view, the crucial thing is the modification imposed on the Faustian temperament in all these writers by the

Weimar enterprise; a modification which included intensification as well as deflection, but which resulted in conservatism. It can be seen at work in the careers of all of them. Herder, it seems clear, had already learned that he was no Faust, when he arrived in the town. His Travel Diary was certainly full of extraordinary ambition and lust for experience; but in practice Herder could exert his powers only over the world of knowledge, of books; in relation to men he could easily be intimidated, or dominated, if he stayed within their range. In Weimar therefore he constructed theories that justified him in staying away from centers of power like Paris. While Schiller, who was in no danger of being dominated by others, and felt for that reason no impulse to dabble in the forbidden or the excessive, had been led in Stuttgart and Mannheim into a falsification of temperament. His Sturm und Drang phase had been an exuberance of theoretical egotism. In Weimar he accepted the world's discipline, renounced rebellion, and constructed theories of how to regain lost naïveté. And he took his lessons from, as well as in, Weimar.

They had all had some personal brush with the self-exciting lust for power and for giant vitality and for the destruction of all traditional values. And consequently they all, in their Weimar period, laid a stress on traditional psychological and moral values; in the roles of husband and wife, for instance. Compared with their Romantic contemporaries, they were old-fashioned in such matters of cultural sympathies, just as they were in their political policies. The same is true of Mann. The shape of his career was the opposite of Goethe's — *his* late work, though called Faustus, was a Weimar document, and his more daimonic work came earlier in his life — but his Weimar work was the same sort of compromise, and done for the same reasons, as Goethe's was.

The Weimar enterprise should above all be evaluated by comparison with other quasi-political schemes for intellectuals, like Rananim and Pantisocracy. The big difference is that Weimar happened. Goethe accepted the limitations of a small German dukedom and a small country town, as the price of realizing his desire in a community of imagination and intelligence. That acceptance of limitations, plus Goethe's loyalty to his old ambitions, his latent Faustianism, turned into political conservatism. But the intellectual and imaginative richness of what came out of Weimar — during an age of revolution — surely makes it the most challenging of historical examples to us. It is the best justification of the city of light, and therefore of what the universities of today might aspire to be.

5 — LIBERAL EDINBURGH: A GOLDEN AGE OF CULTURE

Le Mondain

Regrettera qui veut le bon vieux temps   4 1-2
Et l'âge d'or et le règne d'Astrée
Et les beaux jours de Saturne et de Rhée
Et le jardin de nos premiers parents:
Moi, je rends grâce à la Nature sage
Qui pour mon bien m'a fait naitre en cet âge,
Tant décrié par nos pauvres docteurs.
Ce temps profane est tout fait pour mes moeurs.
J'Aime le luxe et même la mollesse,
Tous les plaisirs, les arts de toute espèce,
La propreté, le goût, les ornements:
Tout honnête homme a de tels sentiments . . .

C'est bien en vain que, par l'orgueil séduits,
Huet, Calmet, dans leur savante audace,
Du paradis ont recherché la place,
Le paradis terrestre est à Paris.

                             — Voltaire, 1736

This was followed by *"Défense du Mondain"* in 1737, and *"Sur l'Usage de la Vie; Pour repondre aux critiques qu'on avait fait du Mondain"* in 1770. For our purposes it is most interesting to read the poem as (and this aspect of it is even more striking when one reads the whole thing) a light comedy version of the liberal creed which Rousseau was recanting in his first *Discours* in 1749, with the aid of his radical Calvinist heritage.

A *Grammarian's Funeral*

"What's in the scroll," quoth he, "thou keepest furled?
  Show me their shaping,
Theirs who most studied man, the bard and sage
  Give!" So, he gowned him,
Straight got by heart that book to its last page:
  Learned we found him.
Yes, but we found him bald, too, eyes like lead,
  Accents uncertain . . .

He said, "What's time Leave Now for dogs and apes!
  Man has Forever. . . .

Was it not great? Did he not throw on God —
  (He loves the burthen) —
God's task to make the heavenly period
  Perfect the earthen?
Did he not magnify the mind, show clear
  Just what it all meant?
He would not discount life, as fools do here
  Paid by instalment.
He ventured neck or nothing — heaven's success
  Found, or earth's failure . . .

This man decided not to Live, but Know. . . .
                    — Browning, 1854

Erasmus, Voltaire, and the Enlightenment

Quite apart from the attitudes they express, the poems above differ widely in the men they describe. But those men are the opposite extremes of the temperamental type I am labeling "Erasmian," and indeed the real Erasmus is recognizable in both of them. The Enlightenment was his period even more than the Renaissance. His *"paradis terrestre,"* his *"âge d'or,"* was in the here and now, and in some center of civilization. The recoil of Voltaire's hero both from the dirt and the violence of the past, and from the austerities of moral idealism, are themes constantly developed in Erasmus's correspondence. He resented obsessively the addled eggs and the squalid bedrooms and the severities of discipline introduced by Standonck at the college of Montaigu at the Sorbonne, and im-

This is to me the most poignant of all paintings. (*Erasmus of Rotterdam*, by Quenten Metsys, c. 1517. Courtesy of Fratelli Alinari, Florence, Italy.)

posed on Erasmus while he was a student there. He always coddled his stomach and his nerves and his whole physical apparatus quite lovingly. In Browning's poem we recognize the Erasmus who retreated from so many challenges to action, to "life," behind his editorial apparatus of manuscripts and annotations, who lived for months on end in the offices of printing presses, first that of Aldus Manutius in Venice, and then that of Frobenius in Basle, the Erasmus who was the very emblem of bookman scholarship, the very prince of Gutenberg.

Erasmus was unwillingly ordained an Augustinian canon in 1492, when he was twenty-six. He disliked the life of the monastery, and got himself sent away to the university of Paris, to study. But he found there that he also disliked dogmatic preaching and theological controversy, while his health gave way under the austerities then being introduced there. He achieved fame for some educational treatises which derived from his work as tutor, and made a trip to England, where he became the friend of many scholars, notably John Colet and Thomas More. Thereafter his life was peripatetic, a moving away from disagreeables, rather than toward any holy land. But he never returned to his cloister, and maintained his freedom from all institutions, all compulsory cooperation, all subordination. He never accepted having power over others, and accepted much less being under their power.

He became the most famous intellectual in Europe. Though not a great philosopher any more than a great theologian, he gave currency to a humanist and pietist scheme of ideas which dominated the Northern Renaissance, and which might have influenced the course of intellectual history more importantly but for the Lutheran Reformation. He was trying to return the mind of Europe to Greek and Latin literature, and in combination with that, to revive a simpler, less dogmatic, Christian piety. "Wherever you encounter truth, look upon it as Christianity," he said, and *"Sancte Socrates, ora pro nobis."* His *Philosophia Christi* was a nondoctrinal religion, to be approached through the morality of the New Testament, and notably nonbelligerent.

That evangelical spirit of Christ has its own prudence, it has its own courtesy and gentleness. Thus even Christ accommodated himself to the temperaments of the Jews. He speaks one thing to the more uncultivated crowds, another to the disciples, and he gradually leads these very men, bearing with them for a long time, to an understanding of heavenly philosophy.

Erasmus conducted an enormous correspondence, like Voltaire, with almost every man of thought and learning in Europe. He was a man of many friendships and cooperations, and much concerned about social relations; he needed harmony and peace, kindly manners, cultured tastes around him. (Note the reference to temperaments in the quotation above; Erasmians are particularly aware of such questions.) The letter was appropriately therefore one of his best literary forms — and this is typical of intellectuals of the Erasmian temperament. His first compositions were of letters in Latin for the young men to whom he was tutor, and much of his later work is related. *De conscribendis epistolis* is about how to write such letters; *De Copia verborum ac rerum* is a collection of expressions and sayings to enrich them; and the famous *Adagiorum collectanea* is of sayings from Latin — and in later editions Greek literature — for use by those who aspired to an elegant style. In fact, though, these sayings and their elucidation amounted to an education in a much broader sense — an education in the spirit of antiquity. Here we glimpse other typically Erasmian forms; the educational treatise, and the encyclopedia.

Erasmus's intellectual virtues were clarity, exactness, hard work, and discrimination, combined with the graces of humor and liveliness and taste. Above all, perhaps, self-critical honesty; thus he said about Luther, before the challenge for him to declare himself publicly on the issue became inescapable,

But even if he had said what he has to say in polite and decorous language, I would not have deliberately placed my head in danger for truth's sake. Not everyone has the strength for martyrdom; and I am afraid I must sadly admit that, were a tumult to occur, I should act the part of Peter. I obey the decrees of popes and princes when I feel that they are just, and I tolerate their bad laws because such an attitude is safer.

He was of course a Latinist, and Huizinga says that he could not have written well in anything but Latin, because the vernacular names of things would have made them too real, too substantial, too three-dimensional for him. "At bottom the world of his mind is imaginary. It is a subdued and limited 16th century world which he reflects. Together with its coarseness he lacks all that is violent and direct in his times." Remember the accusation often leveled at the philosophes, by for instance Herder and de Maistre, that their language and their thought was purely conceptual and two-dimensional and only a shadow of reality, of life. Erasmus's greatest work, *Moriae Encomium*, expresses his own sense of this by identifying folly with gaiety and sensuality and love and self-love, with all the forces that make the world go round. Civilization, and wisdom, and sense, and virtue, all the things with which Erasmus identified himself, are restraints upon life. This was a serious paradox for Erasmus. That is why the humor with which he expresses it has value. Think again of Voltaire and Candide, and the philosophes' wit at its most serious. Humor is very much an Erasmian quality.

He satirized many things in the Church, and quite severely often, but he did not want change at the cost of destructive violence. He wanted reform, not revolution. Though he declined to live in or under an institution, and directed at all existing institutions a stream of bitter, and destructive, criticism, he still relied on their continuing to exist, and had no faith that they would be replaced by anything better as a result of revolution. When he was charged with having laid the egg that Luther hatched, he replied that he had expected a different bird to emerge from it. This answer has some of the lightweight sprightliness which made many Lutherans despise Erasmus, as someone who could not be serious, could not be passionate, could not be manly, in the face of life's tragic dilemmas. These were men who were Lutheran by temperament — which is to say Faustian by temperament — like Dürer and von Hutten and Luther himself. "God has not blessed you with strength sufficient to be of use to the cause, nor did He wish you to have such powers," said Luther to Erasmus; and later, "In my testament I mean to declare plainly that I hold Erasmus to be the greatest enemy of Christ, such an enemy as does not appear more than once in a thousand years." Whereas men like Melanchthon were Lutheran by position, but remained friends and admirers of Erasmus. (And men like Sadolet were conservative by position, but remained his friends.) They remained Erasmian by temperament. And this is a classic case of the clash of temperaments.

Whatever Erasmus's personal courage, his passivity in the struggle expresses more than cowardice. More did not lack personal courage, but confronted by the Lutheran unrest in the Church, he was ready to withdraw — to ban in England — both his own *Utopia* and Erasmus's books, because of their disturbing effect. Erasmus and More and the humanists of their kind believed in changing the Church by a different process.

They were sympathetic, as long as they could be, with the more violent approach. Erasmus avoided attacking Luther, which was a considerable service to the other man, until forced into it in 1524. Indeed, he defended him, in the *Axiomata*. But there could be no question of his joining him. For Erasmus, as he wrote to Luther, "I always freely submit my judgment to the decisions of the Church whether I grasp or not the reasons which she prescribes." This decision, and this parting of liberal from radical, was to be repeated down the centuries of church history — in for instance von Hügel's differing from Tyrrell in the Modernist crisis — and in the history of other orthodoxies.

It is with Luther that we must always contrast Erasmus; in use of the vernacular, in style, in theology, in rebelliousness, in force of personality, in everything. In the course of their theological quarrel, Erasmus defined human nature as being without — by Lutheran standards — any original sin. It was a free, unspoiled, rational human nature he believed in. He elided from it all sense of man's passion and power, all gross appetitive voraciousness, all mystery and sublimity. Erasmus disliked the spirit of the Old Testament as a whole, and reacted particularly against the Apocalypse, that favorite text of Faustian radicals, the book of revolutions, the book of mysteries. He had neither the mysticism nor the realism of Luther, about either individual or political behavior. Princes and war and the exercise of power were things he dealt with mainly by ridicule, by satire. When he tried to formulate what he wanted from a government, he spoke of bridge-building, street-cleaning, pool-draining, the reclaiming of moors and swamps. But he wrote five books attacking war, the first in 1504 and the last in 1517, and pacifism was his one political passion — just because it was not only political.

I cannot help it if I hate discord and division, while loving peace and mutual understanding, for I have long since realized how dark and complicated are all human affairs. I know how much easier it is to incite to disorder than to damp down such disorder once it is let loose. And since I do not trust my own reason in all things, I prefer to step aside and not force myself to agree or to disagree with another man's mode of thought.

This is the sort of passive pacifism which made Luther say, "He who crushes Erasmus crushes a bug which stinks even worse when dead than when alive." And again, "When I pray, 'Blessed be Thy holy name,' I curse Erasmus and his heretical congeners who revile and profane God." But Erasmus's reply, in *Hyperaspistes II*, has force as well as dignity; and we note here again how he translates other ideas into terms of "temperament," "kind of mentality."

I could have wished you to possess another kind of mentality than the one you possess, the one you admire so greatly. You may wish me anything you like with the exception of this mentality of yours. May the Lord intervene to change it.

Surprisingly, Erasmus had some political influence in later periods, although it was extensive rather than intensive, Huizinga says. William of Orange and the municipal magistrates of the Netherlands in the seventeenth century were Erasmian in their social policy. It is hard, of course, to distinguish the influence in the Netherlands of the Devotio Moderna in general, in which Erasmus was brought up, from the influence of Erasmus in particular. But Huizinga, who is not generous to Erasmus, yet ascribes to him the rarity there of witch-persecution, and a whole complex of cultural virtues promoted by those magistrates, prominently including social discipline and the avoidance of violence and general charity.

And when the reaction came against the Wars of Religion, Erasmus was a culture hero to men like Voltaire and Diderot. He was the one man in that welter of religious fanaticism and violence whom they could approve of. Indeed, the publication of the *Encyclopédie*, and Voltaire's great campaigns against injustice and oppression, are better examples of the cultural and political activity of Erasmian liberalism than anything of Erasmus's own. The diffusion of knowledge, thought the philosophes, in such a way as to foster habits of clarity, skepticism, tolerance, and judgment, would of itself lead to political and social progress. The heroes of the Enlightenment thought to see this principle in Erasmus's work, though they put it into practice themselves on a much larger scale, and allied it with real political agitation. And even during the French Revolution Erasmus was an inspiring emblem to a political party in the Convention Nationale — typically, it was a party without effective organization for action — the Marais. While in religion, a whole succession of nonparty Protestant theologians and mystics, known as the Spiritual Reformers, descend from Erasmus. Wherever liberality of spirit is an important ideal, his influence is liable to revive.

After a brief period of adulation, Erasmus came to seem religiously trivial. Luther made him so to Protestants, and when in 1542 the Roman Inquisition was established, he became out of date to his coreligionists too. In 1554 his former friend Cardinal Caraffa became Pope Paul IV, and put all Erasmus's books on the Index. Only Poland and Hungary remained lands of religious toleration on the Continent, and there the practice of the occult flourished as much as that of scholarship. But in one European country, Britain, Erasmus's influence took root. Thomas Cromwell had his works translated, in order to justify Henry VIII's divorce and the break with Rome. Then Edward VI had his paraphrases of the Gospels put in every parish church in the land; and the Elizabethan Settlement of the Anglican Church, and the work of Hooker, both show his influence. In the seventeenth century, his educational books were those most often translated into English; in the eighteenth his satires; in the nineteenth his pacifist treatises; but his ideas were always at work. And his temperament was a significant influence on other culture leaders in England and Scotland, as we shall see.

Physically, he was a good, if somewhat caricatural, emblem for this temperament. Despite his avowed taste for this-worldly pleasures, he was, like Voltaire and Pope, chaste by nervousness of stomach. Meagerly endowed for sensual rapture, his body seemed barely strong enough to support his head, with its enormously developed content of mentality. His physique was less melodramatically shriveled than that of Voltaire, whose image so haunted anti-Enlightenment prophets like Herder and de Maistre, but still his face and body spoke eloquently of the same psychophysical balance, the same temperamental contract. (Houdon's bust of Voltaire, and Roubilliac's *Pope*, are fine sculptural equivalents, for Erasmians, of Michelangelo's *Moses* and Rodin's *Balzac*, for Faustians.)

Stefan Zweig describes Erasmus thus.

Nature was not lavish with her bodily gifts when she fashioned this man whom she richly endowed with intellectual capacity; she was thrifty, too, in the matter of vitality and plenitude of life. His body was delicate, his head small instead of being solid, healthy, and resistant. He was emaciated, pale, and listless; no hot red blood coursed through his veins. Over his sensitive nerves was stretched a thin, sickly, skin, all the sallower because of his sedentary occupation within the four walls of stuffy rooms. As the years accumulated upon him, his skin grew ever more grey and brittle, so that it came to look like parchment, and was riddled with creases and wrinkles. What strikes the onlooker most is this constant repetition of a lack of vitality; hair sparse and not sufficiently pigmented, so that it lies in colourless blond wisps upon his temples; hands bloodless and transparent as alabaster; nose so pointed as to look like a bird's beak; lips too thin, too sybilline; voice toneless; eyes, in spite of their luminosity, too small, and veiled . . . No warmth or stream of energy radiates from this cool countenance; and, as a matter of fact, Erasmus was always cold, huddling himself in wide-sleeved, thick, fur-lined robes, cossetting himself against the slightest draught by wearing a velvet skull-cap upon his prematurely bald head.

Luther, contemplating a portrait of him, said, "This is the face of wily and malignant man who has made mock both of God and of religion."

But he was a favorite of the Enlightenment, in all the countries of Europe. Wherever the philosophes gathered, at Ferney, in Paris, or in Edinburgh, Erasmus's satires were appreciated and imitated. And his spirit, his temperament, as I am calling it, was reborn in the Scottish philosophes, Hume and Adam Smith, two close friends and leaders of Edinburgh intellectual society whose influence can be felt on Dugald Stewart, Sydney Smith, Horner, Jeffrey, etc. — the Edinburgh liberals of the age of the French Revolution.

They were good men, clever men, gentle men, single men, Erasmians.

The Dictionary of National Biography says of Sydney Smith that he had no sympathy for radicals or levelers of any description, nor for mysticism in either literature or religion. We may take that as defining the limitations of Smith's sympathies in particular, but also as suggesting the shape of the temperament we are attributing to the whole culture. Mysticism is likely to be the expression of a Faustian mind, and leveling radicalism of a Calvinist. The Edinburgh liberals had nothing to do with the radicals of their time — who did in fact hold Conventions near Edinburgh, both in 1793 and 1794. Some were arrested, tried, deported; some died martyrs to their beliefs. But though Jeffrey, Horner, Brougham, etc., were bitterly opposed to the Tory government that did these things, they were no allies of Muir and Skirving. They were liberals, and not radicals.

There are indeed limitations here, literary as well as political. As we turn away from Weimar and toward Edinburgh, we are bound to be conscious of a lack of great names and famous figures and flamboyant legends — and indeed simply of marvelous books.* We are entering a land of Erasmian temperaments, and Faustian fire is not to be expected. The Edinburgh style was formed by David Hume and Adam Smith, two friends of the French philosophes whom one can well imagine in company with Erasmus himself. Men of beautiful acuteness, exactness, subtleness of mind, humorous, gentle, generous, severe, temperate, but the least monstrous and godlike men that ever set pen to paper.

Liberalism and the Golden Age

Edinburgh at the end of the eighteenth century was a provincial capital which had made itself into a city of culture. Much more dramatically situated than Weimar, on its granite crags, much larger and more splendidly built (one of the model cities of neoclassical architecture) it was also much more significantly related to

* We must deal with this literature much more as a cultural product, in terms of supply and demand, financial incentive and circulation figures. It would be slightly inappropriate to ponder the form and content of these books as things-in-themselves. And although the main reason for that is the quality of the minds engaged, another is the type of their temperaments.

its history. It was much closer, in many ways, to the primitive fierceness of the clans and the rigorous moralism of the kirk on the one hand, and to the massively mercantile powers of Hanoverian England on the other. Comparatively speaking, Weimar culture was free from such outside pressures. Goethe and his friends were able to design a value complex there as free from such determinants as can ever be the case. In Edinburgh the culture had to be liberal, in reaction against the Philistine conservatism of co-operating with London, and the crude radicalism of kirk and clan.

The golden age was not therefore golden politically, but only in its high culture product, and primarily in its literature, philosophy, and science. Politically, indeed, Scotland at the end of the eighteenth century was dead, says Henry Cockburn, in his *Memorials of His Time*. It was not unlike a village at a great man's gate, the great man being England. "There was then in this country no popular representation, no emancipated burghs, no effective rival of the Established Church, no independent press, no free public meetings . . . Without a single free institution or habit, opposition was rebellion, submission probable success." Henry Dundas, the Lord Advocate, managed Scotland on behalf of Pitt and the Tory party in England. Whig lawyers therefore had small hope of professional advancement, a strong sense of grievance against the regime, and a great deal of leisure. Within the social center of the legal profession, the Outer House of the Court of Sessions, they formed a group of their own, meeting always at the north end. And they, the disgruntled critics of the status quo, the theorists of reform, played a key role in the culture of the city's golden age. "That the flag was kept flying, was owing almost entirely to the spirit of the Whig lawyers."

Cockburn was writing after the Reform Bill of 1832, which finally realized the Whigs' main demands, and proved them historically right. A meeting of protest against slavery in the West Indies was held in Edinburgh in 1814, and that was the first public meeting for twenty years, apart from those to celebrate victories and those to aid charities. But Edinburgh remained a brilliant city, and among the causes was "the extent, and the ease, with which literature and society embellished each other, without rivalry, and without pedantry." And of all social types, it was again the Whig lawyers in whom the two could be seen embellishing each other best. Cockburn himself was one of the shrewdest of these lawyers, and his *Memorials of His Time* and his *Life of Lord Jeffrey* are two of the finest manifestations of golden-age culture.

There were of course Tories in literary Edinburgh. Mackenzie wrote propaganda for Pitt. Later on, Lockhart and his father-in-law, Scott, worked out a cultural equivalent for Toryism, in reaction against the dominant Whiggery. They stood for Feeling, as opposed to Reason; for Humor, as opposed to Wit; for Romance, and Legend, and Personality. And because by then, by 1820, there were powerful similar forces abroad in international culture, in favor of such a change of sensibility, they made a difference, they qualified the Whig label one would attach to Edinburgh society. But still there were no *serious* Tories in literary Edinburgh, just because Edinburgh was Scottish. Even Scott had some grudge against the powers that were, just because they ruled from London. Equally, there were no radicals in literary Edinburgh, no one like Paine or Blake or Godwin.

All these people belonged to the same society — both literally, in that they were all members of the same city, the same profession, the same clubs; and also culturally, in most matters of taste and belief. There was a consensus, which one has to call predominantly liberal, because it wanted to change things in the direction of more justice and freedom, but with a Tory wing of rather whimsical protest against that consensus. Imaginatively speaking, Burke and Fox were everyone's heroes at Westminster; dashing figures who attracted an easy, nonpolitical enthusiasm; and it was Burke's Whig theory of history which provided the model for Scott's. That may seem to make the political antithesis unimportant. But to be a Whig in Edinburgh in the 1790's did cost something. At the annual banquet for Fox's birthday, sheriff's men came and took down the names of those present. The discipline of resisting that intimidation, and the professional penalties, braced the spirit of key figures of the golden age, and that is why we can call its consensus predominantly Whig, or liberal.

Of course, the Golden Age, like many important concepts, is ambiguous in even the simplest sense. There are at least two periods now given that title — the first in the middle of the eighteenth century, and associated with the names of Hume and Smith, and also of Adam Ferguson and William Robertson; the second, 1790–1820 (or 1826 or 1832), and associated with Scott and the *Edinburgh Review* and the *Encyclopaedia Britannica*, and in science with Playfair, Black, and Hutton. There are, moreover, subtler ambiguities, deriving from the differences between, for instance, the literary and the scientific aspects of so complex a phenomenon. I am looking at the second golden age, and primarily under its literary aspect, when I make these generalizations.

What makes an age golden is the number of important works it produces, but also — sometimes — the social intercourse of the men producing them. This second criterion — by which Edinburgh scores very high — accounts for some of the ambiguity about dates, because that intercourse was a prominent feature of society there through both periods of high productivity and through the gap between the two. Many visitors were impressed by how well the great men from different fields of knowledge got on together, how often they saw each other, how much society took from and gave to scholarship. There is a painting of Scott and his friends which illustrates this. Scott is shown reading a manuscript to Sir David Wilkie the artist and Sir Humphry Davy the scientist, Ballantyne and Constable the publishers, Jeffrey and Wilson from the great reviews, Ferguson from the university, Campbell and Mackenzie to represent Scottish poetry and fiction — not to mention Sassenachs like Wordsworth and Crabbe.

There was a fairly well-defined position of leader of literary society, and fairly general agreement as to its occupancy and succession. David Hume had held it till his death in 1776. His Sunday suppers had brought together the most distinguished people in the city. Adam Smith succeeded him and reigned till his death in 1790. After that Henry Mackenzie was the leading man of letters until Scott established himself; but things are not so clear-cut after 1800 or 1810, because Scott did not live in the city. But if there was uncertainty about the single central figure, there could be none about the central six or twelve.

The social-intellectual life of the city was also organized into clubs to an unusual degree. There was for instance the Select Society, founded in 1754 by Hume, Kames, Robertson, and Blair.

Hume had returned to Edinburgh from Paris in 1751, and in 1754 he published Volume I of his *History of England*. There was the Friday Club, founded in 1803 by Scott, Mackenzie, Playfair, and others. There was the Speculative Society at the university, which Francis Jeffrey said he owed all his education to. He joined it in 1792, when he was nineteen, and debated against Henry Brougham and Francis Horner, with whom he joined to found the *Edinburgh Review* later.

The Select and the Speculative were both designed to encourage philosophical inquiry and public speaking, and that tradition of formal debate had a visible effect on the aggressive argumentative style of all the great reviews; the *Edinburgh*, founded in 1802, the *Quarterly*, founded in 1809, and *Blackwoods*, founded in 1817. The membership of the clubs — and thus the editorial staff of the reviews — had anyway received a professional training in debate. By 1759 the Select had 133 members, the whole Edinburgh literati; and of the 110 whose professions can now be ascertained, 48 were lawyers. This is the other organizing factor in Edinburgh cultural life, behind the profusion of clubs, the predominance of lawyers. As Henry Cockburn says, Scotland differed from Italy and Holland in their cultural primes, in that the Scottish merchants counted for so little. Politically they were powerless, and culturally unambitious. The lairds, the lower aristocracy, patronized learning socially; but the participant role was taken by lawyers. It was a courtroom culture. All the great literary men had had that formation, even Scott and Boswell.

The city was perfectly conscious of this. Lockhart says, in his *Peter's Letters to His Kinsfolk* (1819), that lawyers are the source of all authority in Edinburgh, that they have kept the spirit of independence alive in Scotland since the Union with England of 1702, that they walk round the city in their legal robes like its rulers, that the language of polite society is peppered with legal expressions. Cockburn, as we have seen, credits particularly the Whig lawyers with creating the golden age.

And there was another ideological bias built into the structure of Edinburgh culture which made it in some sense liberal. After the union with England, Scotland had been left with no court or government, and with an aristocracy which gradually transferred their homes south of the border. It had three national institutions left, all of which became of great importance. There was the legal system, about which something has been said, the educational system, about which almost as much must be said, and the kirk. But this last played its most important part in golden-age culture as something against which writers reacted sharply, or else ignored, or at best palpably sentimentalized.

That is a simplification. Already by the mid-eighteenth century, the Moderate movement had triumphed in the upper levels of the Scottish church, and some ministers were among the makers of the golden age. The debates at the church General Assembly were brilliant affairs, oratorically and intellectually. Alexander Carlyle claimed that Scottish ministers had written the best histories, the best tragedies, the best mathematics, philosophy, and rhetoric, of modern times. But Alexander Carlyle, known as "Jupiter" Carlyle, is a good example of why we can't simply associate that achievement with the church, why we rather set that high culture in antithesis to what the Presbyterian kirk had meant in imaginative terms, and had been. Carlyle's very worldly *Memoirs* would have been anathema to the heroes of the faith of the preceding generation, and indeed of his own.

Some simplification is necessary because the church in eighteenth-century Scotland was a paradox, containing two opposites, which could not be described in a single statement that would do justice to both. In most of its parishes it was of a savage Puritanism, which was only subdued from outside, by the intellectuals, acting through the lairds' power of patronage. Ministers of milder opinions, imbued with Francis Hutcheson's ideas of virtue and the harmony of the passions, were imposed on elders against their wills. Before that, the church had been fiercely Calvinist, in temperament as well as in doctrine. John Knox was its great hero, and it is men like Samuel Rutherford, Hugh McKail, Donald Cargill, John Brown, James Renwick, Alexander Peden, whom we must associate with Scottish Presbyterianism, not "Jupiter" Carlyle.

The oversight of the kirk-session extended to every department of life. In some places the elders themselves patrolled the streets at night, searched the taverns for loiterers, entered homes looking for those who had cursed or worked on the Sabbath. For serious moral offenses, a man might have to stand in the pillory on Sundays (for ten, fifteen, or as many as twenty-six weeks) and be admonished by the ministers. (The rich could escape by paying a fine.) On the Sabbath there were no hot meals. One read the Scriptures, repeated the catechism, and went to the service. There the prayers were extempore, and the sermons were long. At the second service the minister preached from his "ordinary," a text which remained the same for many weeks. This drove him to ingenious feats of interpretation, to say something new. Hell was an important theme; "God shall not pity them but laugh at their calamity," said Thomas Boston.

The Lord's Supper was served only very occasionally, and for weeks before the occasion the ministers visited their flocks and catechized each member. Every rumor of scandal was searched to the bottom. Elders reconciled those at enmity. On the Thursday to Saturday preceding, there were two or three services a day, exhorting to penitence. On the Sunday the service was held out of doors, beginning at nine and often lasting all day. Each successive "table" (there might be as many as thirty) was admonished on the penalties for communicating unworthily; a "fencing address" specified the sins that disqualified and denounced the thoughtless. The day ended with a sermon; and on the Monday the communion season closed with a service of thanksgiving.

All this represented a cultural institutionalization of the Calvinist temperament against which the Erasmian liberals of the Scottish Enlightenment reacted very sharply.

John Knox is the villain of the drama of Scottish history, for commentators from David Hume to George Scott-Moncrieff. Religious stringency and moral severity have seemed antithetical to, or scarcely compatible with, the humane qualities which Scottish literature has promoted. Mary Stuart attacked by John Knox, Charles II reviled by the Covenanters, have been the heroes of the sharper minds, while milder temperaments have kept such a balanced balance between both contestants as to punish the moral aggressor. Scottish literature has no real equivalent to the great line of writers in England, starred by Bunyan, Blake, and Lawrence, which have combined moral and prophetic vehemence with the richest humanism and the most vivid art. The result has been to exclude from literary expression, from alliance with the aesthetic imagination, the severer strains of truth and passion. In our century two of the most persistent purveyors of light entertainment are professional Scotsmen, Eric Linklater and Compton Mackenzie. And I think one can detect as far back as Scott the influence of that split, in a resolve not to take things too seriously. What was skepticism in Hume became slackness of mind in Scott. Because in Hume's mind a living faith in reason replaced as well as displaced religion. Sir Walter put warmth of temperament in place of both. That is the corruption of liberalism, of course; its essence is merely the reaction against fanaticism. And that other strain in Scottish life, the morally severe, ran more or less separately from "culture." It can be seen in the missionary dynasties; Robert Moffat, for example, born 1795, died 1883, who spent fifty years in Africa, and who recruited Livingstone for his life work there in 1840, and whose daughter, Mary, married Livingstone in 1844.

There was of course one Scotsman who in some sense united both cultural strains — Thomas Carlyle. It was partly because he did unite them, did overcome that antithesis between "culture" and religion and moral severity, that he could make himself more important to the literary Britain of the nineteenth century than any other Scotsman — than almost any Englishman. Carlyle recognized the exhaustion of the liberal Enlightenment image by the time he came of age, and he made himself into a Faustian radical instead. It is a most deliberate self-formation which he describes in *Sartor Resartus*. And though he later recommended *native* sources of strength, it is clearly Goethe and other Sturm und Drang writers to whom he owes most. His radicalism was never Calvinist, despite the stress he put on his religious heritage. He was an admirer of heroes, of Faustian figures; in English puritanism he responded to Cromwell more than to anyone or anything else; and under his pen John Knox becomes a Faustian hero.

His own Faustianism was concentrated intensively in his manner, his style, as a declaration of intention. It is significant that *the* Goethe book for Carlyle was *Wilhelm Meister*; significant because there Goethe declares himself an ex-Faustian, a conservative. One feels that Carlyle needed the assurance that there was that way out before he signed the contract — that he was an ex-Faustian from

before he began. Carlyle was an intentional, in some sense an imitation, Faust, who had picked up the trick of it from others. (It is
true that real Faustians often want to *seem* Faustian, as we saw
discussing Mailer, Fiedler, and Bellow; and Carlyle reminds us
more than other nineteenth-century Britishers of such Jewish
psychopomps, for that reason. But an imitation Faust, a bogus, like
Gersbach, is detectable and rejectable. Carlyle is a nineteenth-
century Gersbach all too often.) But at the moment we must see
him as illustrating what happens at the end of a historical phase, at
the end of the dominance of a certain temperament. Carlyle was
the child of the exhausted loins of liberal Edinburgh. He saw that a
new temperament was necessary at any cost. He saw that the liberal literature of the golden age was no longer imaginatively valid,
and that the liberal Toryism which Scott was offering was no real
alternative.

Literature and the Golden Age

The leading figures of Edinburgh cultural life then, commentators agree, were two men of letters, Scott and Jeffrey. The culture's
two great achievements were thought to be *their* achievements, the
Waverley novels and the quarterly reviews, which all derived from
the *Edinburgh*. To these two I would add a third, the *Encyclopaedia Britannica*; and I will discuss that first, because it was the most
representative of the city as a whole, and the most expressive of the
liberal-enlightened mind. It was representative of the important
role played by publishers in the city's culture, and of the city's as-
semblage of trained minds in fruitful interaction. And it was expressive of the Edinburgh mind's aspiration to the useful rather
than the beautiful or brilliant; and of its cooperative, cumulative,
clarificatory mode of action.

The encyclopedia form is specially suited to the Erasmian temperament, like the letter, the Menippean satire, Bayle's dictionary,
and Erasmus's paraphrases. That form had just been brought to
life, by Diderot, d'Alembert, Condorcet, etc., with a gaiety, energy,
wit, and daring which made it transcend its seeming limitations. In
the salons and the political *causes célebres* of the French Enlightenment, the Erasmian temperament achieved its apotheosis, and
seemed — until the rebellion of Rousseau and the Sturm und

Drang — to have acquired its own equivalents for the splendors of the Faustian temperament and the rigors of the Calvinist. The Scottish encyclopedia began as in some sense an imitation of that great predecessor, but with a less decided ideological bias. At first, indeed, it professed a conservative purpose, of avoiding the excesses of the French in their attacks on religion and royal authority. But it was in those first days by no means so distinguished as either Diderot's creation or its own later editions. When it did acquire a higher intellectual quality, in the period we are dealing with, it was classically liberal.

The *Encyclopaedia* had first been the project of an engraver, Andrew Bell, and a printer, Colin Macfarquhar, and was brought out in sixpenny numbers, 1768–1771, edited by William Smellie. The fourth edition appeared in twenty volumes between 1800 and 1810, edited by James Millar; and this edition was reprinted twice with minor revisions, calling itself the fifth and sixth editions. But the great publisher Constable had bought the enterprise in 1809, and he determined to make it into something worthy of the city. Constable was a man of great commercial and indeed cultural enterprise. He responded imaginatively to the idea of the city of culture and the golden age, and tried several ways to translate them into larger effectiveness, by publishing ventures. He entrusted to Macvey Napier the editing of a supplement to that sixth edition which we may take as a high-water mark of Edinburgh culture. For it Playfair and Stewart wrote prefatory essays, on the Progress of Science in the Age, and the Progress of Philosophy in the Age, for which Constable paid them a thousand pounds each, an enormous sum. It appeared between 1816 and 1824, and was the first to include signed articles.

The signatures included those of Jeffrey, writing on Beauty, Leslie on Aeronautics, McCullough on Political Economy, Malthus on Population, Ricardo on the Funding System; and James Mill on Government, Education, and a number of other things. The supplement, like Edinburgh University, was particularly strong on the social sciences. Such studies were the natural training ground of the mind for reforming liberals then, and the articles just mentioned were a charter for reformers throughout nineteenth-century

Britain. In the essay on Government, Mill makes some remarks on "the Middle Classes" which indicate the lead that Edinburgh was already giving to what would become Victorian Britain.

He calls the middle classes "the most wise and virtuous part of the community," and is eloquent about the moral dependence on them of the working classes. "The opinions of the class below are formed by them — to whom they fly for advice and assistance in all their numerous difficulties . . . to whom their children look up as models for imitation." The middle class, he says, "gives to science, to arts, and to legislation itself their most distinguished ornaments, the chief source of all that has exalted and refined human nature." Its members have nothing to fear from representative democracy. "If the basis of representation were ever so far extended, their opinion would decide."

With such a combination of reform and respectability, it became a standard work of reference. But though the supplement, and the *Encyclopaedia* as a whole, were successes, they were not such brilliant successes as the Waverley novels and the reviews. Let us examine the *Edinburgh Review* and its editor, Francis Jeffrey.

He was born in 1773, two years after Scott, but was only a year behind him in Edinburgh High School, and only one year ahead of Henry Brougham; while Francis Horner and Henry Cockburn were in slightly lower forms of the same school. He went to Oxford and acquired an English accent, but without the intonation; this, and a shrillness in his voice, and a smallness of stature, were compensated for by a remarkable fluency of speech, clarity of argument, profuseness of example. In other words, he was something of a child prodigy even as a man, and could not appropriate the broad, warm, genial manliness which Scott offered — though Jeffrey was just as amiable a man at bottom. To put the same point a different way, Jeffrey's temperamental contract and balance of forces, his temperamental type, was that of Erasmus, Pope, and Voltaire, while Scott offered the conservative and "manly" alternative of Goethe and Karl August. An important influence on Jeffrey's political opinions and behavior, says Cockburn, was "the gloomy intolerance of his Tory father, contrasted with the open-hearted liberality of his Whig uncle of Herbertshire." Out of deference to his father,

Jeffrey abstained from voting on an important issue (another lawyer was being deprived of office because of his liberal opinions) and "thought the less of himself" thereafter.

Jeffrey became in later years a very successful lawyer, but his chief claim to importance is as founder and editor of the *Edinburgh Review*. Cockburn attributes the birth of the *Review* to the lively discussions provoked by the French Revolution, to the resentment felt against the governmental repression in Great Britain, and to the grouping of lively and idle young men (Whig lawyers) in Edinburgh then. The catalyst was Sydney Smith, a young Englishman of similar talents, opinions, and temperament, who brought a pupil to the city for the winter of 1798. In 1802 he, Horner, Brougham, and Jeffrey founded a Whig magazine which devoted long and authoritative articles to the questions of the day, and reviewed anonymously and aggressively the significant new publications. Constable was the publisher, but it was so successful that it was independent of booksellers from the beginning. The *Analytical Review* shows the disadvantages of — the tameness of tone that resulted from — being tied to a bookseller, even a radical like Joseph Johnson. The *Edinburgh's* steady circulation of twelve thousand represented a readership enormously larger. After the first two or three issues it paid contributors ten guineas a sheet, and later sixteen, and these were minima. Certain writers got twenty to twenty-five guineas. This professionalizing of magazine work was an important innovation: one not followed, to their disadvantage, by some would-be imitators, like the *North American Review*. Like *Waverley*, the *Edinburgh* had many imitators, because its formula was so clearly a success. The Boston magazine tried to maintain the old-fashioned, gentlemanly tradition of scholarly journalism, but the British epigoni more shrewdly realized that the new professionalism was a crucial part of the formula. The *Quarterly Review*, founded by Murray for Scott and others, was an ineffective rival, but *Blackwoods*, founded by Blackwood for Lockhart and Wilson, did manage to challenge its original in popularity. Lockhart and Wilson exaggerated the undergraduate insolence of Jeffrey, Brougham, and Smith, and passed off a lot of personal insult as Tory frankness. The "Noctes Ambrosianae" series had its own line of genial fantasy, but the magazine was never as intellectually serious as the *Edinburgh* had been.

Politically, the *Edinburgh* stood for reform, for social change, for criticism of the Tory government. That criticism was sharp enough to prove disturbing to patriots and conservatives like Scott. Britain was at war with Napoleon, and it was particularly patriots who were offended; the *Edinburgh* pushed its skepticism, its criticalness, its contempt for current pieties, to the point of disloyalty, as it seemed to Scott, disloyalty to British armies in the field, in the crucial case of the Peninsular War. The Erasmian temperament has never been very responsive to military glory.

Jeffrey was famous above all as a literary critic, and for the severity of his criticism. His piece on Wordsworth's *Excursion* began, "This will never do," and that catches the note of impudent pedagogy which, while not the most frequent, was in some sense the characterizing note of his critical voice. He was always very severe on Wordsworth and the Lake School, and yet he was, he claimed, particularly fond of their poems for private reading. He seems to have regarded this fondness as a personal vice, and to have blamed Wordsworth for making public what he should have kept private. He objected, in accordance with classic eighteenth-century taste, to the solemnity with which Wordsworth treated his village idiots, his leech-gatherers, his daffodils, etc. What he approved was Crabbe (who observed the traditional allotment of style and genre to subjects) and Thomas Campbell and Washington Irving. His taste, as one critic puts it, was for classicism in form, moralism in message, and sentimentality in sensibility.

He was not, then, a great critic. He did not allow himself to become engaged deeply enough by works of imagination. He wanted to keep on top of them. He held the emotionally disturbing at a distance. Moreover, there was an element of paradox and epigram in his literary opinions — the same was true in politics. He insisted, writing about Burns, on the dangerousness to a poet of having a literary education — of acquiring the qualities which Jeffrey himself represented. "Nor can we conceive any one less likely to be added to the short list of original poets, than a young man of fine fancy and delicate taste, who has acquired a high relish for poetry, by perusing the most celebrated writers, and conversing with the most intelligent judges." (In Weimar such a complacent culturicide would have met the obstacle of Goethe, and this explains one of the ways in which Weimar excelled Edinburgh.) But Jeffrey wrote lucidly, energetically, eloquently, about literature, and gave it an important place among the things serious men care about. Lockhart blamed the *Edinburgh Review* for its own and its readers' philistinism; for its habitual skepticism about the works it reviewed, and its hostility to "feeling." This "spirit of facetious and rejoicing ignorance," he said, had taught Edinburgh that it need not read Lamb, nor even Wordsworth. There is something to this charge, but we need only compare Jeffrey's criticism with Lockhart's own to realize how respectable Jeffrey is.

In Sir Walter Scott we find a case which calls for an adjustment in our general argument about Edinburgh. Scott was clearly conservative, in position and temperament, in politics and literature, and yet he just as clearly belonged to the heart of the Edinburgh culture, and bulked large in it. He is too large a fact to be called an exception to some general rule; he must be said to constitute a qualification to the definition offered — to the label liberal. Because of Scott, as personality and as writer, Edinburgh must be called to some degree conservative. Its enthusiasm for him and for the Waverley novels, the imaginative influence of those novels, infected the whole city with a conservative strain. With the aid of Weimar ideas, Scott was able to mobilize and energize the backward-looking and anti-Establishment elements in Scottish culture, which had before been dispersed and ineffectual in their conflict with Erasmian liberalism.

Scott's temperamental pattern, typical for a conservative in that age, may be compared with Goethe's, except that he was almost incomparably more limited in every direction. But he was still a powerful and complex figure. Scott was genuinely a genial man, generous with everyone, a great promoter of general enjoyment. But there was an underside to his good nature which we need to take account of, in order to see him in the right perspective. He was a man of uncomfortably shrewd perceptions about people, and a very hard worker; it was by force of intention that he made himself seem, made himself be, a kind of Tom Jones, all boisterousness and recklessness and boyishness. The long-sustained mystery of the

Author of Waverley is one example of the obstinacy, the secrecy, the slyness, beneath the surface. Another is the story of the school-fellow whose place in class he coveted, and whom he discomfited by cutting off that bottom waistcoat button with which the boy played when answering questions — so that the boy, unable to answer, was sent to a lower place. Another is his description of Burns's praises of another poet — "the caresses which a celebrated Beauty is often seen to bestow upon girls far inferior in beauty to herself, and whom she 'loves the better therefore.'" This is a mind too sharp, too skeptical, too ruthless, to be simply good-humored. Scott was resolved to be a success from early on, and seeing him play the lazy dog is rather like hearing Bing Crosby sing "Ho hum — ain't never gonna get rich, I guess."

He was a man of remarkable gifts, and he could direct them in the service of a remarkable shrewdness. Unsuccessful as a lawyer, he became a literary antiquarian, publishing *Minstrelsy of the Scottish Border* in 1802-1803, and going on to produce modern equivalents himself. In 1805 he brought out what became the best-selling poem "The Lay of the Last Minstrel," of which forty-four thousand copies were sold *before* the famous collected edition of his works began to appear. In 1808 Constable gave Scott a thousand guineas for "Marmion," the next of these long narrative poems; he also offered him fifteen hundred guineas for a collected edition of Swift. Publishers could make a lot of money out of the right ventures then, and Constable, Blackwood, and Scott himself in partnership with the Ballantynes, were an important factor in Scotland's golden age, as far as literature went. In 1810 came "The Lady of the Lake," another enormous success, selling twenty-five thousand copies in eight months. He was paid four thousand pounds for that, whereas Jane Austen's four novels published in her lifetime earned during that lifetime seven hundred pounds. Scott had found in the legends of Scotland, as later in her history, the perfect playground of the fancy for the middle class of a commercial civilization.

After that, the long narrative poem began to fail in Scott's hands — not that he found it any harder to write, but that he lost his market to Byron — and he turned to the prose romance. Byron was ready to mythify his own personality, his own life-story, in his poems, and so he could give his reader a satisfaction which Scott could not match. Their kind of romanticism dealt in damned, doomed Faustian heroes, the opposite of the Tom Jones figure. Scott produced "Rokeby" and "The Bridal of Triermain" in 1813, and the first sold 10,000, which would have been success for anyone else, but after one more try with "The Lord of the Isles" in 1815, he gave up. "Since one line has failed, we must stick to another," he said to his publisher. And there is less of metaphor in his use of such commercial language than in other writers'. Even Byron, who talked equally cynically about his literary product, was in fact working out his destiny in his poems.

The Waverley novels, 1814 to 1831, were one of the greatest success stories in all literary history. Scott had found the master formula of culture for his age: the long prose narrative, full of history and humor, solid fact and common sense, but also full of the new romanticism. That it was a formula is demonstrated by the ease with which other men made fortunes out of it — Cooper in the U.S.A., Ainsworth in England. It is demonstrated also by the novels' high foreign language reputation, which still to some degree survives. In translation the formula shines through and the commonplaceness of its realization, its rendering, the hastiness of execution, the artistic unscrupulousness, are less visible.

It gave the reader the luxury of identifying with rebellion, secure in a plot structure and a narrative presence which promised to resolve everything finally in favor of the status quo. Waverley needs to know the passionate and unreasonable values of Flora MacIver and the '45 and the Highland clansmen, but finally, of course, he returns to Rose and to England. He is enriched by the experience, his emotional life is refertilized, he is saved from realism's blight of spiritual aridity, but the determining powers of his life remain — become more — realistic. And this is what happens to the reader, too; much to the comfort of a middle-class generation bruised and disturbed by twenty years of radical enthusiasm and government repression and war. The Waverley novels were as much a response to the imaginative pressure of the French Revolution — of the age of revolution — as the *Edinburgh Review* was. That one was a conservative response and the other liberal did not matter very much. A reader could enjoy both with no sense of strain to his loyalties. The novels were for entertainment; Scott's conservatism had the absolutely minimal necessary strain of Faustianism. Both positions — at least by 1832 — expressed the same temperament, that of the nineteenth-century consensus.

Judgment on Edinburgh

The general financial failure in London in 1825 ruined both Scott and Constable. Constable's ruin might be almost comparable in importance as a determinant of the final date of the golden age, because it marked the end of the great era of Scottish publishers. They had secured extraordinary financial rewards for Scottish writers throughout the eighteenth century; Hume and Robertson's histories, for instance, earned a great deal of money. Hume got thirty-four hundred pounds for his *History of England*. Robertson got forty-five hundred for his Charles V. Scott owed seventy to eighty thousand pounds in 1826, and though he redoubled his literary efforts, he still owed twenty-two thousand when he died in 1832. But Cadell, Constable's successor, bought the copyright from the Scott family, and died worth a hundred thousand.

And if we take its two great cultural formulas, the historical romance and the quarterly review, as Edinburgh's achievement, we can measure its cultural success by comparing it with that of any American city of the period. The comparison is legitimized by the very similar status of Boston, Philadelphia, and New York as provincial capitals within the cultural area of which the metropolis was London. Their size was roughly similar; they were middle-class cities, without an aristocracy; lawyer-dominated; with a largely Whig ideology; and with all those problems of provinciality which focus in the question of language, the very sore point of correct accent and correct usage. (Adam Smith taught English pronunciation for a time after his return from Oxford; and there was an Edinburgh joke about Hume's having confessed his Scotticisms on his deathbed in place of sins.) And the comparison is invited by the cultural ambitions of the American cities in this period — their determination to excel decadent England and produce a new free literature commensurate with the new free nation. What they did produce was Washington Irving, a personal protégé of Scott and a critical protégé of Jeffrey; Cooper's Leatherstocking novels, an adaptation of Scott's formula; and the *North American Review,* an adaptation of the *Edinburgh*'s formula. What they did achieve was by grace of Edinburgh's achievement, as we shall see. They lit their torch from hers.

If, on the other hand, we compare Edinburgh with Weimar, everything takes on a different aspect. The two cities are alignable in certain ways. In fact, Goethe's Weimar had learned a great deal from the Edinburgh of the earlier eighteenth century. Francis Hutcheson (1694–1746) wrote in Edinburgh his *Inquiry into the Originals of Our Ideas of Beauty and Virtue,* 1724, which adapted Shaftesbury's theories about man's moral *sense,* his instinctive preference, as a matter of aesthetic taste, for virtue. Hutcheson's thought strongly influenced the Scotland of the first golden age — as we have seen in discussing the church — and his ideas were developed in Hume's *Treatise of Human Nature* of 1739, and Smith's *Theory of the Moral Sentiments* of 1759. And Hutcheson–Shaftesbury influenced Weimar via Wieland, whom Goethe described, in his funeral oration, as a twin soul to Shaftesbury. Moreover, the romantic side of Edinburgh, and Scotland, meant a lot to Herder.

Reciprocally, Edinburgh was the first British city to take note of the new German literature. In 1788 Henry Mackenzie delivered a lecture on German authors to the Royal Society in Edinburgh, following which six or seven young men, including Scott, learned the language and read the literature. Several translations resulted, including Scott's lively version of "Goetz von Berlichingen," which was a major source for his whole series of historical novels, and for features of several particular novels. By 1799 it was a natural thing for a young Scottish writer like Thomas Campbell to make a literary pilgrimage to Germany.

But Edinburgh produced no dramatist or aesthetician to compare with Schiller, no theorist of culture to compare with Herder, no writer to compare with Goethe. Scott was more than once confronted in literary society by Coleridge and his disciples. He maintained a wary silence, acknowledging an incommensurability. But Goethe had both Scott's and Coleridge's qualities. And he chose to aim at an audience like Coleridge's. He left to Kotzebue the best-selling success on which Scott depended. He wrote "Goetz von Berlichingen" *once*.

One is bound to ask why — why Edinburgh was scarcely even trying for the prizes which Weimar won. Scott's *Edinburgh Review* essay on Hoffmann shows how firmly he rejected the bolder German efforts of the imagination, and he carried his readers with him. He confirmed the conservative British interpretation of Romanticism, contrasting Hoffman's fever with Wordsworth's health. Now it happens that Goethe read that article, and commended it. This reminds us that Weimar had its own timidity, its own limitations, even in strictly literary matters. It conspicuously failed to do justice to Hoffman, to Hölderlin, to Kleist. But those failures cannot disallow Goethe's claim to be called a first-class literary intelligence, endlessly responsive to new ideas and new subjects and new writers, endlessly inventive in new forms and styles himself, taking literature with a seriousness, an intensity of mind, which has rarely been seen before or since.

Certainly it was not seen in Edinburgh. Scott and Jeffrey did not engage with literature or with the imagination at that depth, with that strength; and they were the models for their society. If we look at other big Edinburgh names on book covers, we see Macpherson of Ossian, Homer of "Douglas," Campbell of "The Pleasures of Hope," Mackenzie of *The Man of Feeling*. These are all books and authors who were overrated in their own time. So what we are most reminded of by the Hoffman essay, finally, is Edinburgh's inferiority to Weimar in sheer intellectual seriousness. It was too cozy.

And at the end of our period the fate that always hangs over cozy cultures like Edinburgh — over-humane, civilized, *liberal* cultures — fell upon it in the form of "Christopher North." This pen name at first belonged to Lockhart, James Hogg, and John Wilson, when writing as a group for *Blackwoods*; later it was appropriated by Wilson alone. The first issue of the magazine, which they wrote collaboratively over a bowl of punch one night, had three anonymous controversial articles. One was an attack on Coleridge, in the guise of a review of *Biographia Literaria*; the second an attack on Leigh Hunt's morals — the first of the famous series against the Cockney School; and the last a biblical allegory of the Whig-Tory literary conflict in Edinburgh, full of highly personal details, called the Chaldee Manuscript. This attack on the old Edinburgh values of gentlemanly discretion and politeness broke the spell of Whig culture in the city, according to Professor Daiches. But the "Christopher North" disaster grew even worse when the name referred to John Wilson alone. In 1825, just after staying at Rydal Mount, and protesting his admiration for Wordsworth — his friend of many years standing — Wilson wrote a typically contemptuous article on the poet. "Wordsworth often writes like an idiot. . . . He is, in all things, the reverse of Milton, a good man and a bad poet. . . ." Wilson regarded the violence, and the anonymity, of these attacks as a joke, but not one to be shared with the object of the attack, as we shall see. To continue, "Not one single character has he created — no one incident — not one tragical catastrophe. He has thrown light on no man's estate here below; and Crabbe, with all his defects, stands immeasurably above Wordsworth as the Poet of the Poor . . . I confess that the 'Excursion' is the worst poem, of any character, in the English language." When it seemed that his authorship of the article might have to be revealed, Wilson took to his bed in panic, and wrote to Blackwood, "I was seized with a trembling and shivering fit, and was deadly sick for some hours. . . . To own that article is for a thousand reasons impossible. It would involve me in lies abhorrent to my nature. I would rather die this evening." The whole phenomenon of *Blackwoods* distressed Scott, who could see Edinburgh culture deteriorating before his eyes.

In 1820 Wilson was elected to be Professor of Moral Philosophy at the university, even though he knew practically nothing of the subject, on the vote of the Tory town councillors. And for thirty-one years he gave lectures on philosophy, with immense gusto and to immense success, lectures composed out of letters written to him for the purpose by his friend Alexander Blair. Sometimes the letter only arrived on the day of the lecture, and Wilson had to read it on the way there. When a student raised an objection or a question, Wilson had him write it out, and he then forwarded it to Blair, who sent a reply which Wilson declaimed to the student. The classroom was always crowded with visitors and even with other professors on days when one of his big performances was due.

It was his oratorical technique that was most admired, though the content seems to have been swallowed without protest. He had an impressive physique and a big, booming voice, and he improvised with dramatic gestures.

This fraud happened in Edinburgh because the values of the intellectual and imaginative life had been so completely domesticated there, had lost that natural wildness which makes people respect and fear them. Faustian fire, like Calvinist rigor, had been exiled so long that no one could any longer tell the real thing from the fake. All the marks of intelligence and judgment and inspiration and learning had been translated into social gestures so completely — and with the assent of the whole society — that they were a constant temptation to the charlatan. Everyone had said so often that they could recognize a Hume or a Smith by his manner, had said that the best of him was in his conversation, that they no longer bothered to read.

The Legacy of the Golden Age

But though literature was what Edinburgh prided itself on, its true achievement in the second golden age lay perhaps elsewhere. It was perhaps a matter of the social sciences and the applied sciences rather than the aesthetic imagination, and to be located in the university rather than in highly individuated imaginations. Universities, as organized cooperative social bodies, and ones devoted to learning in many fields, are natural organs of the Erasmian temperament institutionalized. It was from the university that the influence of Edinburgh poured forth upon Victorian Britain in its most impressive form.

Edinburgh after the Union made itself an Enlightenment city, and its college was an Enlightenment academy. Scotland had suffered even worse than England from the religious civil wars of the seventeenth century, and beneath the urbane surface of Hume's thought runs a passionate current of determination to save men from a recurrence of such errors. Philosophy, which meant Enlightenment philosophy, was much more prominent in the Edinburgh University curriculum than in that of any English university. It had also more connections with the enlightened Continent. Scottish lawyers often went to Dutch or French universities,

Scottish clergy to Dutch or German, and the medical school inherited a great tradition from Leyden and passed it on to Philadelphia. Oxford and Cambridge were notoriously bad in the eighteenth century — Gibbon and Bentham have left us sharp accusations of the education they gave. Oxford offered the classics, but without taking note of German philology. Cambridge offered mathematics, but without taking note of any developments since Newton. They did not produce graduates capable of either the technological or the administrative innovations which the commercial and industrial revolutions required. The Dissenting Academies did something of that job, but between the middle and the end of the eighteenth century they gradually failed and closed down. The choice for an alert student then lay between Edinburgh and the Continent, and the Napoleonic Wars largely closed off the Continent. When Sydney Smith brought his pupil to Edinburgh in 1798, it was because he could not take him, as he had intended, to Weimar.

During the years 1785–90, the Physics Class at the University had an average attendance of 215, of whom only 91 were Scottish, 55 English, 35 Irish, 12 American, and 12 West Indian. Costs were low, and because professors' incomes derived directly from individual students' fees, they lectured on subjects of current interest, and made their presentation seem relevant.

The most popular of all professors in our period was Dugald Stewart, the professor of Moral Philosophy between 1785 and 1809. He was in matters of practical ethics a developer of Hume's line of thought, and recommended moral taste above all. He also lectured on political economy under the title of moral philosophy, and here too he developed the themes of Hume and Smith. Hume had thought that it was philosophy's function to establish the bases of the moral sciences of economics and history, and the Edinburgh tradition in teaching these subjects was broadly humanist. Stewart was a humanist; not an original thinker, but an eloquent speaker, and a versatile, brilliant man; he taught Greek on occasion, mathematics, and natural philosophy. He was the real thing, of which Wilson was the imitation. He was politically liberal, even when that was unpopular, visiting France in 1788 and 1789, and getting into trouble with the government in 1794 for published remarks attacking established institutions. But thereafter he was prudent in his utterances; his career was extremely successful in every way. He exemplifies the too-perfect adaptation to existing circumstances of the Edinburgh intellectual, but he also exemplifies the harmonious development which his moral theories recommended.

The main thing for us, however, is the audience Stewart reached, in his pupils, auditors, and social circles; particularly those later to be important in shaping Victorian Britain. Lord John Russell, for instance, was one of his pupils. Palmerston lived with him as a lodger. Lord Shelburne, the radical Whig, sent his son Henry Petty, later the Marquis of Landsdowne. There was James Kay-Shuttleworth, the founder of England's educational system, and the two Lord Mintos, one Governor-General of India, the other Lord Privy Seal. There was M'Cullough, who took the chair of Political Economy when the University of London was founded, and the two brothers Horner, Francis of the *Edinburgh Review*, and Henry of the School of Arts in Edinburgh. Both Horners, like most of his pupils, felt a personal devotion to Stewart. And many people not strictly his pupils attended his lectures; Playfair, Scott, and Sydney Smith, for instance. Oscar Browning says in his *Memoirs*, 1910, that he became a university tutor in the hope of becoming the Dugald Stewart of Cambridge. Browning had been reading the life of Francis Horner, and he wanted to be able to send out a succession of pupils like him, who would do as much for their country.

We might also mention briefly three institutions to which Stewart was important. First the *Edinburgh Review* itself, where his most important effect, achieved via Horner, was to make it give so much space to questions of political economy. Then the secular and modern university of London, which was the work of Edinburgh men, and together with that the voluntary education movement in England, centered in the Mechanics' Institutes. (Birkbeck was another of Stewart's pupils.) And finally Holland House, the social center of Whig reform in London, where Stewart's ex-pupils were usually to be found.

Other Edinburgh professors had a similar though not equal influence. In the sciences the most prominent example was John Playfair, who was politically liberal, and interested in the arts. (His

book on geology, in true Edinburgh style, was a classic of popularization as well as a help in establishing that science.) Then John
Robison, who helped James Watt with the steam engine, and was
a friend as well as teacher of John Rennie, the great designer of
London's bridges. And Leslie included among his pupils both
George Stephenson, the railway designer, and his two sons. The
medical school did pioneer work in public health and in mental
health, and the sciences of chemistry and botany and geology were
significantly advanced at Edinburgh at a time when Oxford and
Cambridge ignored them.

But in all this complex of achievement literature played a small
part — and overplayed it. The center of gravity of that complex
was in the social sciences. The passionate questioning and exploring of individual experience out of which literature grows, the imaginative playing with fire, was gradually subordinated in Edinburgh to other kinds of truth, was — by 1820 — substituted for
with sentimentalism, moralism, romanticism.

The literary equivalents in our own times of the Edinburgh
achievements seem likely to be what is being written in exactly the
same genres. The *New York Review of Books*, for instance, has
had a career, a style, and a function very like those of the *Edinburgh Review*. Those long, learned, lively articles have filled in a
very similar gap in the provision of intellectual fare for the public,
and a gap equally unsuspected before it was filled. It has more
radical articles than the earlier magazine, but that is because New
York is still a more radical city than Edinburgh was in 1802. The
relations of the two magazines to their cities are very similar. And
the equivalents of the Waverley novels are the novel sequences of
C. P. Snow and Anthony Powell and Simon Raven, and even of
Doris Lessing; there is something eternally and invincibly liberal,
not to say bourgeois, in the form of the novel sequence.

Edinburgh in the 1790's was not the best that Erasmian liberalism can do, but it was good enough for an Erasmian to be proud
of; it was good enough to deserve the admiration of everyone.

Goethe's Weimar was of course a more remarkable achievement,
but then it had something monstrous about it. It cost a great deal.
Jeffrey, Horner, Stewart, Scott, these were all men of human proportions, of humane virtues, who worked for the public weal, and

found their individual glory in being prominent within their community. They were a part of their culture. Admittedly that was a class culture, and their participation was highly privileged. But no more than was the norm then.

And if one compares them with the London radicals, one must remember a degree of ineffectiveness in Godwin, Mary Wollstonecraft, and Blake, or rather a superb effectiveness in the Edinburgh men. We admire people for what they achieve, and these people achieved something. The great imaginative writers of the Victorian age, Carlyle and George Eliot, for instance, owed more to liberal Edinburgh than they did to Blake's London. In politics, education, philosophy, government, engineering — in the whole texture of life examined in *Middlemarch* — these men's work played a big part. Literary men we associate with administration and legislation, Matthew Arnold and Mill, even more obviously came out of a world in which the best was the work of Stewart, Horner, Brougham, Jeffrey, and their disciples. Above all, Edinburgh was a concentration of cultural life which, without the presence of men of genius, created a fire at which other cities could light their torches. We shall see that the American cities of the period were able to do what they did by grace of Edinburgh. This phenomenon, of the mutual intensification of intelligences in a community to the point of incandescence, is of great importance in any argument for the value of culture. And that it can happen even to Erasmians, in a liberal city, is a sign of hope for the future.

6 — AMERICAN LITERATURE 1780–1820: THE GOD WHO NEGLECTED TO COME

Philadelphia in 1800 was still the intellectual center of the nation. For ten years the city had been the seat of national government, and at the close of that period had gathered a more agreeable society, fashionable, literary, and political, than could be found anywhere, except in a few capital cities of Europe.

*"In the society of Mr. Dennie and his friends in Philadelphia I passed the few agreeable moments which my tour through the States afforded me. If I did not hate as I ought the rabble to which they are opposed, I could not value as I do the spirit with which they defy it; and in learning from them what Americans can be, I but see with the more indignation what Americans are." ***

Symptoms and Complaints

Turning from Edinburgh and Weimar, to consider *this* group of writers and *their* patrons and public, one is reminded of Professor Godbole's song in *Passage to India*. It invites the god Shri Krishna to come to the singer, calling come, come, come, come, but the god refuses to come. "But he comes in some other song, I hope?" said Mrs. Moore gently. "Oh no, he refuses to come." And later Forster associates the false dawn seen and then not seen by Adela on the way to Marabar with a god coming and then not coming to inhabit the drab landscape, to give it meaning and splendor. The earth of

---

* Both quotations are from Henry Adams, *The History of the United States during the Jefferson and Madison Administrations*, Vol. I, 1889. The second quotation is spoken by Tom Moore, 1804.

India calls come, come, come, come, but the god "neglects to come."

American cities in this period were all calling come, come, come, come, to the god of literature. But anyone who reads what got written is bound to find it disappointing — as American cities themselves did. No matter which genre you are thinking of, for forty years (and think what those forty years produced in England, and in Germany) the harvest is very thin. And this phrasing ("disappointment" and "thin harvest") comes to mind because expectations were high for something better, and with reason. We now, it seems to me, must share that disappointment, when we think of what the eighteenth-century colonial writers had achieved, Franklin, Jefferson, Edwards, and of the enormous potency of the ideas of revolution, of nationhood, of independence, of nature, of reason, all of which *belonged* to Americans in this period. The generation of them who lived between 1750 and 1830 — it happens to be one clearly grouped by dates — included many who had set their hearts on being great American writers. We shall note how many of the men we mention planned, when they did not write, epic or prophetic poems on American subjects.

Hugh Henry Brackenridge wrote one, at the beginning of his career, and when he said, toward its end, that he had never "been a writer," for lack of "the garrets of London," that is, for lack of the right city, his case became a paradigm of many other American writers.

Nature intended me for a writer, and it has always been my ambition. How often have I sighed for the garrets of London; when I have read histories, manners, and anecdotes of Otway, Dryden, and others, who have lived in the upper stories of buildings, writing paragraphs, or essays in prose and verse, I have lamented my hard fate that I was not one of these.*

— *Modern Chivalry*

Why did American cities so fail their writers in this period?

There has never been, in all the revolutions of taste since, a school that discovered prime virtues in Brackenridge, Freneau,

* Brackenridge finally wrote to Scott and offered his *name* for a character in a Waverley novel. By then that seemed to him, I presume, the best chance he had left to inscribe himself on the honor roll of literature.

oth of these illustrations are from *Our Literary Heritage,* by Van
Vyck Brooks and Otto Bettman (New York, E. P. Dutton). This book
as published in 1956, and the text was written by a man who had
een, who on occasion still was, a fine critic. What a long, strong blight,
en, did Washington Irving cast over the life of letters in America,
hat a blight did Fiedler have to deliver us from. (*Washington Irving.*
liniature, oil on ivory, by William Henry Powell, 1855. Courtesy of
leepy Hollow Restorations, Tarrytown, New York. *Sunnyside.* Water-
olor by William R. Miller, 1852. Courtesy of Sleepy Hollow Restora-
ons, Tarrytown, New York.)

Brown, the Hartford Wits, etc. And in their own times there was
an acute feeling of failure among Americans, though disguised
sometimes as defensiveness. As late as 1889, Henry Adams's discussion of the problem in "American Ideals," Chapter Six of his *History of the United States*, is markedly defensive about the artistic
poverty of the country then. His rationalization is that Americans
were "living in a world of dream, and acting a drama more instinct
with poetry than . . ." They didn't need literature as Europeans
did. "The unconscious poet breathed an atmosphere which the
conscious poet could not penetrate." The problem was obviously
still a thorny one for Adams.

It had been, in earlier days, a favorite subject for the annual
orations to Phi Beta Kappa societies. The most famous of these
was Emerson's "The American Scholar," which ended — or has
been credited with ending — the impotence it diagnosed; but there
were many others.

Charles Jared Ingersoll gave some details of America's humiliat-
ing dependence on England in his well-documented address to the
American Philosophical Society for 1823, "A Discourse Concerning
the Influence of America on the Mind." He pointed out, as evidence of that continued dependence, that two hundred thousand
copies of the Waverley novels had poured from American presses
in the preceding nine years, and that the *Edinburgh Quarterly* and
the *Quarterly Review* were reprinted there and sold four thousand
copies each. (More modern figures say five hundred thousand
copies of the novels by then — and thirty-five towns were to be
named Waverley.)

George Tucker's essay "On American Literature," which appeared in the Philadelphia *Port-Folio* in 1813, compared America
with Scotland and Ireland. Ireland, so unfavorable an environment
for intellectual life according to the contemporary theory, had in
fact given Goldsmith, Berkeley, Sheridan, Moore, Swift, and Burke
to English literature. Scotland had given Smollett, Thomson, Boswell, Burns, Hume, Smith. (The two significant novelists in English seemed to the *North American Review* in 1815 to be Scott and
Maria Edgeworth, a Scotsman and an Irishwoman. And they were
so partly because they lived far from London, in places rich in local
color and legendary history.) Why then, Tucker asked, was Amer-

ica not producing more? Great Britain had eighteen million people and produced five hundred to one thousand new books a year. The U.S.A. had six million people, and produced twenty. His answer was that there were fewer college students in America, and they spent fewer years at their studies, and so on. But these were answers which could not satisfy.

There were those who felt that such debate only worsened the condition it promised to explain; that American writers should concentrate on being writers rather than American, or else that literature in a democracy was *bound* to decay. These tended to be disaffected minds, sardonic or embittered, New England Federalists uneasy with the new America, like Joseph Dennie or Fisher Ames. But they were not the least acute. Fisher Ames's essay, "The Mire of Democracy," has some impressive insights into what exciting literature-and-ideas are like, and makes some bold, quasi-Nietzschean contrasts between the culture of ancient Greece and that of his own America.

But the representative voices were rather those of the three Channing brothers of Boston, each of whom had something to say on this subject; William Ellery, the Unitarian leader, Edward Tyrrell, the Harvard professor of rhetoric, and Walter, the physician. They all hailed the coming of a great American literature, while admitting the poverty of what had so far been achieved. The third brother, in the *North American Review* in 1815, made a moral analysis of the problem, reproaching his countrymen for having lacked literary enterprise and intellectual courage. The only *American* literature so far has been that of the Indians. What white Americans have written has lacked national idiosyncrasy, and so has none of what dazzles us in recent German literature. (This shrewd thrust was as painful as the comparison with Scotland, for the Germans too seemed to have started from scratch in the eighteenth century, in literary matters.) In an article in the same magazine the next year, Edward Tyrrell Channing made similar points, exalting the sanctity of original genius, deploring the tyranny of the classics, using "Augustan" to label a mode of literature inferior to "Elizabethan"; in other words, invoking Romantic criteria. Bold, wild, free originality — who out of the nations of the world should produce that but democratic America? Where but in America was

Nature bold and wild and free — Niagara, the Mississippi, the prairies, the mountains — why then such dull and feeble poetry? Again the analysis was moral, the solution was an exhortation. And William Ellery Channing, in the *Christian Examiner* for January 1830, wrote "Remarks on National Literature," saying that a country's really important product is its men, and that this was America's destiny, to produce a superior race of men, and that the most powerful means to that end was a national literature. Modern conditions of life, which stress privacy, favor literature, where the conditions of ancient life favored politics. The new American literature we are waiting for will derive from this "religious" impulse and purpose. But that was 1830, and they were still waiting for it.

In the period immediately preceding ours, and to some extent in this one, the liveliest literary form had been the political pamphlet. Of nine thousand books and pamphlets published by American presses between 1763 and 1783, two thousand were political pamphlets, and *The Rights of Man* falls into our period. Paine himself lived on until 1809, even though — and this fact has a more than accidental parallelism with the facts of literary history we are dealing with — he ceased long before then to be a notable figure in American life. Having gone to England in 1787, taken part in the French Revolution, been imprisoned by the Jacobins, he returned to America in 1802, to find its Revolution, as he saw it, betrayed. He disapproved the Federal Constitution, he despised Washington, and he was in turn disapproved and despised by America, labeled an atheist and a drunkard. Hooted by a mob in Trenton, New Jersey, literally refused the right to vote at New Rochelle, he sank into extremest misery, both of inward and outward life, and died alone, rejected, in 1809.

His silent but spectral presence, both before and after his death, is an important fact about our period. And alongside Paine stand Franklin and Jefferson. Franklin clearly belongs to the earlier period, but Jefferson lived on till 1826, and many of his letters and speeches during our period are of the first quality and interest. But — and this is a striking fact about Jefferson — he remained very much an eighteenth-century man, as much so as Washington and Adams. He is a liberal and not a radical hero. That very liberality of

mind, that extraordinary range of interests and talents, that beautiful temperateness and health of temperament, prevented his making — in terms of a whole life — Paine's sort of unequivocal assertion. Not that Jefferson equivocates, but he balances, he combines.

In other words, Jefferson's temperament was, like that of the
whole group to which he belonged, Erasmian. The Enlightenment
as a whole was Erasmian; and so was the American Revolution,
that part of it which finally triumphed. Those revolutionaries who
did partake of the radical temperament were never effectively organized, and were edged out of those positions of power which
they had held as soon as the fighting was over. Early New England
culture had been Calvinist, of course, and Jonathan Edwards had
revived that imaginative temperament (given it intellectually serious expression) only shortly before the Revolution, but in our period the conflicts, in the realm of high culture, were all between
different versions of Erasmian liberalism. It was the reluctance of
this temperament to yield to the Romantic solicitations of the new
age, to explore the Faustian experience, which caused the artistic
poverty of America in the century just beginning. (I develop this
argument, as it applies to New England, fairly fully in *The Problem of Boston*.) This was an age of revolution in the world at large,
but in America the leading minds were determined to make it an
age of reform, and in the moral-imaginative sphere an age of con-
servation.

The literary forms in which earlier America had achieved distinction were, apart from the political pamphlets, the sermon and
the description. Of this last there is one example within our time
limits which demands some notice, Crèvecoeur's *Letters from an
American Farmer*. His is *the* Western — and therefore *the* American — myth, the WASP myth of re-creating civilization personally
from scratch, reconstituting order and cleanliness and industry and
productivity. Crèvecoeur's description of Nantucket, the Quaker
Paradise, where men, even when standing in the market chatting,
keep busy carving a piece of wood, is a minor classic in this line.

But *Letters from an American Farmer* clearly belongs to an earlier period than ours, in all but date. In our period the description,
the sermon, and the political pamphlet all yielded to the novel, the
short story, the play, the lyric, the epic, the essay, the satire. Amer-

ica was now an independent nation, and it was time to write an independent national literature, to attempt the great literary forms.

In Hartford

The first writers we must consider are a group very clearly associated with a particular city by their traditional label, the Hartford Wits, the Connecticut Wits. These men all knew each other at Yale in the 1770's, and afterwards either lived in or visited each other at Hartford, in the 1780's. But the label of the city and the state draws attention to more than geographical or social connections. It announces an ideological community and an agreement about literary standards, aims, and models, to the point of literal cooperation. Ideologically, Connecticut stood for the most conservative of all interpretations of Americanism, the most continuity with the pre-Revolutionary past compatible with uncompromising support of the Revolution. It was known as the land of steady habits, and it saw even Massachusetts as dangerously volatile, prone to anarchy and infidelism and worldliness. Steady habits meant primarily moral and social traditionalism, but they also involved economic principles, like a hatred of paper money and inflation and public debts; political policy, like a firm hand to put down such "democratic" uprisings as Shays's Rebellion in Massachusetts in 1786; and a religious policy of return to Jonathan Edwards's Congregationalism. They belonged, especially by virtue of their religion, to America's oldest elite, the New England Calvinist saints, though their literary ideas were liberal. Timothy Dwight, the political spokesman of the group, himself a clergyman, dated the decay of Connecticut back to the decade before the Revolution, when British officers had been the prime agents of moral and intellectual sophistication. The Revolution had removed that danger, but men like Paine and Jefferson, with their "French" ideas, were then revealed as a yet greater threat. One of the Wits themselves, Joel Barlow, became a renegade, going over to what was thought to be, quite literally, the Devil's party.

"Connecticut" was therefore a powerful political ideology, and the Connecticut Wits were prominent among the men who kept their state steady. Timothy Dwight, above all, dominated the Federalist Party there, and it was not until the year after his death,

1818, that that party ceased to dominate Connecticut. But he had ceased being a poet before 1800, and we are concerned with the years when he was one. For twenty-five years the Hartford Wits wanted to be great poets as well as wanting to promote a certain politics, and the two concerns affected each other.

Hartford was not a large or important city, even by American standards, and as soon as Yale was measured up against European universities, it looked a small affair. Hartford only became a city in 1784, and had no regular theater until 1794. Its population at the beginning of our period was about 5,500 people. New Haven had only 4,000 people in 1795, and no hard pavements or street lighting. Whereas Philadelphia was the second English-speaking city in the world, with a population of 70,000 in 1800, and New York then had 60,000, Boston 25,000, Charleston 18,000, and Baltimore 13,000. But Weimar, with *its* neighboring university town of Jena, was about the same size as Hartford, and in Weimar a group of poets with a reactionary political position were creating a great new literature. Like Goethe, the Hartford Wits were determined to guide the national literature against the current of the times, and into the paths they approved. They belonged to the oldest American elite, and they had the confidence too of what they thought were new ideas, literary as well as political.

Their training at Yale had centered around Locke and Edwards, but in ethics and aesthetics the urbane spirit of Edinburgh had prevailed. They did not read Hume, but they read the moderates' answers to him, like Beattie's *Essay on the Nature and Immutability of Truth* of 1770, and Kames's *Elements of Criticism* of 1762. Yale, like Edinburgh, believed in seeing "things as they are," which meant seeing them in *all* their relationships, and acting with the concurrence of the majority in anything important. This steady ethics allowed a greater function to aesthetic education — for the refining of human nature — than extremer doctrine would have. So that we find the Wits writing Masters' Dissertations asserting the value of literature. Trumbull's "Essay on the Uses and Advantages of the Fine Arts" advocated the study of literature (for its moral advantages) and even pleaded for the abandonment of the neo-classic Rules. (In those days, vernacular literature was not ordinarily a subject for university study. Mathematics, theology, and the classical languages were the "solid learning" Yale offered.) Dwight's "Dissertation on the History, Eloquence, and Poetry of the Bible" credited its authors with literary genius, and defended them against the charge of breaking the Rules. These were the marks of a certain faith in literature, and the Wits also set out to write great American poetry themselves.

Ignoring such minor figures as David Humphries and Lemuel Hopkins, we can mention three of them. John Trumbull (1750–1831) was very precocious as a boy, passed his entrance exams to Yale at the age of seven, and entered at thirteen. After graduating, he spent a year away and then returned for a year as tutor. During these years he wrote "The Progress of Dulness," a heroic couplet satire about fops and coquettes, much in the manner of Pope and Gay, and much praised at the time. He became a lawyer, serving for a time in John Adams's law office in Boston, and then moved back to Connecticut, where he was active in state politics. He wrote, on various occasions, some sharp personal satire, but always retreated before the protests this aroused. His whole career evokes the image of precocity, of a quick mind, skillful in mimicry, which finds itself armed by schooling with sharper weapons than it knows what to do with, and which therefore avoids the confrontations in which they might be used. He had practically given up his literary career by the time he was thirty-two, and had withdrawn his major energies from it by the time he was twenty-three.

This precocity was emblematic of the Wits, various as their personal temperaments were. They were all the late-born children of a culture about to decline, the carefully nurtured and acclaimed prodigies of a tradition still determined to preserve what it had, but not eager to expand; on the defensive against the new ideas of the time. In literature Trumbull disliked Wordsworth and Coleridge, Byron and Moore, even Crabbe and Southey. He was the Ronnie Knox of his day, and the other Wits were quite like Knox's group at early twentieth-century Oxford.

Trumbull's most famous poem was *M'Fingal*, which describes a conflict between loyalist and patriot at the outbreak of the Revolution, in Hudibrastic verse; and although the name M'Fingal is an allusion to "Ossian," the actual figure of the hero — an overweening loyalist — is closely related to that of Hudibras, another "great man" with a rusty sword, a quarrelsome disposition, and a love of tropes. There were three editions of this during the war, and in 1782 he recast the whole poem, and added two more cantos, and the whole thing was reprinted thirty times between 1782 and 1840. However, though it began as satire, it quickly became general literary parody, and Honorius, the patriot opponent of M'Fingal, is just as bombastic as he. And, ironically, after the war, M'Fingal was often quoted *seriously* in support of conservative policies — in the debate over the Federal Constitution, for instance — and Honorius was quoted seriously in Fourth of July orations. Trumbull's mockery was too delicate, his criticalness and detachment of mind were drowned out by the loud political themes he tried to make use of. The whole story is an ironic comment on the ways literature and politics can mismatch, and on the Wits' unavailing attempts to marry the two.

Of the group, the most assertive, dogmatic, and powerful, was Timothy Dwight, Jonathan Edwards's grandson, known as "Pope" Dwight. He too entered Yale when he was thirteen, having already done the work of the first two years, and he too bears some of the marks of precocity, or at least of a certain thinness of experience. It is typical of him that his first book, published in 1785, was a serious biblical epic about the Revolution, "The Conquest of Canaan," ten thousand lines of heroic couplets; presenting, as Leon Howard says, eighteenth-century Americans with Hebrew names, who talk like Milton's angels, and fight like Homer's Greeks. There is a great deal of high discourse and noble gesture in it, and — someone has counted — forty terrible storms. Trumbull said that one needed a lightning rod to read it with. Dwight was certainly talented, as indeed was Trumbull, and that is most evident in passages of description. But the poem is a demonstration that its author can do what real poets, in England, had done.

His next poem, "The Triumph of Infidelity," was dedicated to Voltaire, and attacks atheism, rationalism, horseracing, drinking, Sunday amusements, etc. It is an ironic narrative, with footnotes signed Scriblerus, much parody of other poets, and some harsh satire of living persons. The "hero" is Satan, and his victim-ally is

Charles Chauncy, a liberal theologian in Boston. Satan's greatest enemy is Jonathan Edwards, "that moral Newton, and that second Paul."

Dwight was headmaster of Greenfield Academy between 1783 and 1795, and in 1794 he published "Greenfield Hill," a long, rambling, pleasant account of the countryside, of local history, of Connecticut institutions, etc. In Part I he imitates Thomson, in Part II Goldsmith, in Part IV Beattie, and so on. Like Trumbull's, Dwight's love of literature never included a taste for lively *new* writing.

He became president of Yale in 1795, and continued in the office until his death; he was a great success, much admired and loved by his students. Of his voluminous other writings we need mention only *Travels in New England*, published in 1821–22. This too has a good deal of ambling interest and charm, as he defends America against the sneers of British travelers, then attacks the British quarterlies, then expounds the virtues of owning property and of steady habits, then disapproves of frontiersmen. But we are a long way from the great poetry he set out to write. He became perhaps a Quiller-Couch or a George Saintsbury to Trumbull's Ronnie Knox.

The last of the three, Joel Barlow, was the most unlike Dwight, in opinions and in temperament. Dwight was always a father (he had looked after ten younger brothers and sisters during his teens) and Barlow was always in some respects a son. This led to his being the most interesting case or career of them all, though not the most talented. For, leaving Connecticut in 1787, when he was twenty-four, he met with new figures of authority, in fact with Jefferson and Paine, and changed his opinions radically. The change did not help his poetry, however, because he did not change his imaginative temperament.

He studied at Yale from 1774 to 1778, and he had settled on the subject of *his* epic poem by 1779. He worked on it while he was an usher in Dwight's Academy, and as a chaplain in the Revolutionary army. The poem, called "The Vision of Columbus," came out in 1782, dedicated to Louis XVI. It is a description of America's history and geography and future, told in the form of a vision. He took the history and geography pretty directly from *The History of America*, by William Robertson of Edinburgh. Barlow's friends had helped and encouraged him in many ways. He was personally popular, and his undergraduate poetry had been highly thought of. For instance, David Humphrey helped him get subscriptions for copies from army officers, and Barlow grossed fifteen hundred guineas from the publication, with another edition issued five months later. Louis XVI took twenty-five copies, Washington twenty, Lafayette ten, Franklin six; there were twelve generals and fifty-two captains, plus Hamilton, Paine, and Aaron Burr, on the list.

Barlow then became an agent selling Ohio land for the Ohio Company, and later for the Scioto Company, a shadier organization. (This story, a fascinating example of American speculation, connects Barlow with Gilbert Imlay.) On the company's behalf he went to France, survived the collapse of the enterprise, and stayed to take part in English and French radical politics. In London, through Paine's introductions, and perhaps Imlay's, he moved in the circle of Blake, Godwin, Mary Wollstonecraft, and the Society for Constitutional Information. This was a logical enough development of certain tenets in the early creed of the Wits; the Rights of Man was a slogan of theirs in their War of Independence writings; but as applied by Paine and the Jacobins, it was anathema to them. Barlow was soon severing all his old connections. Like Paine and Mary Wollstonecraft, he composed an answer to Burke, called *Advice to the Privileged Orders of Europe*, and a satiric poem, *The Conspiracy of Kings*, which together got him into trouble in England. In Paris, he was made a citizen of the Republic, and he got *The Rights of Man* published when Paine was put in prison.

After a varied and successful career — he made a fortune importing American and Scandinavian goods into France — he returned to America in 1802. Like Paine, he was out of sympathy with the country he found, and his old friends were alienated. He left New England to live in Washington, near Jefferson. Jefferson and Fulton, the inventor of the steamboat, were his main companions. (It is interesting to note how a certain life-style characterized all these philosophe-radicals. Jefferson, Barlow, Fulton, Paine, Franklin, all were inventors, all amateur scientists and gadget-makers, whose houses were full of ingenious devices.) He revised "The Vision of Columbus" and reissued it as "The Columbiad" in 1808. The most speculative book, the eighth, he revised in the light of more modern science, using the geology of James Hutton, the Edinburgh scientist. It was very sumptuously printed and illustrated, but got badly reviewed in America, being accused often of atheism. (This version everyone agrees is worse, the diction artificially elevated and pedantic.)*

And why, with such high ambitions and energies, and with such favorable circumstances, of mutual encouragement and external applause,† was so little achieved? The short-term answer obviously involves their imitativeness. They failed to reach the degree of originality appropriate to their talents. But why had they to be so merely imitative? The case of Pope and Swift, the case of Goethe, shows us that conservative politics need not produce dreary writing, as long as the *literary* intelligence is alert. (Reverting to the comparison with Ronnie Knox and his friends, one can point to the brilliant work of Evelyn Waugh.) The Wits' work does not suggest that they could have been poets of the first rank, but it does suggest that they could have written better than they did. Their conservatism was imaginatively blighted.

In Philadelphia

The next group of writers belong to Philadelphia, and though they are much less of a group, belong to each other and to their city in much more tenuous and tortuous ways. Yet Philadelphia was so complex and powerful a phenomenon, so much more of a city than

---

*(As has been seen, the form most practiced by these writers was the epic poem, and it may well cause surprise that they should be known as the Hartford Wits. The label refers to a brief episode in their lives, in the 1780's, when they were involved in political controversies over the sales of public lands, and over the growth of the public debt and the debtor class. They expressed this concern by writing, collaboratively, a poem called "The Anarchiad: A Poem on the Restoration of Chaos and Substantial Night." This was published serially in the *New Haven Gazette*, and was more exactly a series of papers about, including extracts from, an alleged ancient prophetic manuscript in twenty-four books. This, like "The Triumph of Infidelity," had footnotes signed Scriblerus, and like that poem ended with the defeat of Anarch/Satan, who is shown threatening Massachusetts with his ally Daniel Shays. Barlow contributed to this poem, though it was written immediately before his departure for Europe and opposite opinions. The poem had little effect politically, and it cannot be said to be successful in literary terms.)

† The first anthology of American poetry, *The Columbian Muse*, published in New York in 1794, gave over half its pages to the Wits' work.

Hartford, that once we grasp all the different things it stood for, we can almost talk of its writers as Philadelphia Wits. But in politics it stood for mutually opposed ideas, and when its writers espoused those ideas they opposed each other, instead of joining forces like Dwight and Trumbull. Sometimes they espoused more than one idea, and made their own minds an ideological battlefield, like the city.

Philadelphia was America's city of painters (Benjamin West, Thomas Sully, Charles Willson Peale and his sons); America's city of theaters (at one time about twenty theaters operated there); America's city of science (Franklin's Philosophical Society, founded in 1742, and men like David Rittenhouse and Benjamin Rush). Above all, it was an international city. The most important linguistic minorities were the Germans and the French, of whom there were ten thousand there in our period, refugees from France or from Saint Domingue. German contributions to Philadelphia culture can be seen in names like Rittenhouse and Caspar Wistar, professor of chemistry at "the College"; French contributions in the names of Audubon, the naturalist, and Charles Lucien Bonaparte; while Paine and Cobbett and Joseph Priestley left England to settle there.

But most significant, in their immediate effects on the climate of ideas, were the Irish and Scottish immigrants. In the world of publishing, for instance, Mathew Carey, an Irishman, ran the most successful American magazine between 1787 and 1792, and became America's leading book publisher; while another Irishman, William Duane, edited the *Aurora*, a radical newspaper, for which Freneau wrote; and George Bryan was one of the political leaders of the radical party defeated by the Federal Constitution. The Irish were mostly radical. The Scottish influence was more evident in the world of learning and education. After Franklin, the two most powerful men of learning in the city were probably the Scottish-born Provost William Smith of the College, and Dr. Witherspoon of what was to be called Princeton. The Medical School was founded (in 1765) by a group of young doctors, all of whom had got their M.D.'s in Edinburgh. It had a thistle carved over its door, and Benjamin Rush said he wanted to make Philadelphia into another Edinburgh. The leading printers (after Franklin and Bradford) were the Scottish-born Robert Bell, Andrew Steuart, and Robert Aitken, and what they published were often Scottish books; Robertson's *History of America* and *History of Charles* V; Ferguson's *Essay on the History of Civil Society*; Kames; Beattie; etc. But the Edinburgh seed could blossom only when planted in eighteenth-century soil and climate. As first the age of revolution and then the nineteenth century made their pressures felt on Philadelphia, its seed was killed, that cultural embryo was aborted.

There are four Philadelphia writers worth discussing; Joseph Dennie, Philip Freneau, Hugh Henry Brackenridge, and Charles Brockden Brown; that is, one Tory, one radical, and two with elements of both extremes combined. Brackenridge (1748–1816) may not seem much of a Philadelphia writer, being both brought up on the frontier and a later exile there. But his education, both in the ordinary sense and his literary training, was got in Philadelphia, and it is a Philadelphia audience he aims to please in his novel, *Modern Chivalry*. He tried his hand at many forms of literature; a heroic poem, "The Rising Glory of America," written in collaboration with Freneau; two patriotic plays, in neo-classic blank verse; eighty-eight sermons and six political discourses; a literary journal, *The United States Magazine*, that ran for twelve months in 1779. But in that year he turned to the law as a way to earn his living, was admitted to the bar, and went to Pittsburgh, then a frontier town, to practice. He was thenceforth a lawyer with political interests; and his literary efforts were largely confined to his serial novel, which appeared in six parts between 1792 and 1815, and which has something of the character of a private journal and eccentric's monologue.

It began as yet another Hudibrastic poem, "The Modern Chevalier," at the expense of a political opponent of Brackenridge's. The scheme was to tell the travels of Captain Farrago, a man of education and leisure, who rides about America observing, with his Irish servant, Teague; Teague, like Brackenridge's enemy, is a complete ignoramus, but he keeps being elected to public office. They are modeled on Don Quixote and Sancho Panza, and Cervantes's influence luckily induced Brackenridge to revert to prose. Chapters of narrative are followed by chapters of comment, in rather a heavy-footed way. Thus Chapter 2 of Volume I is headed "Containing

Some General Reflections" and begins "The first reflection that arises is. . . ." Long essays on law and constitution-making are interpolated into the narrative, and there is much talk addressed directly to the reader. Particularly in his Postscripts, and more and more as the book proceeds, Brackenridge talks about himself, about the book, about the sales prospects, about what he has written so far. At the beginning of Volume III he quotes the critics' comments on the first two volumes.

The main themes of his satire are the excesses of democratic behavior, the inordinate ambition of the unqualified, and the unintelligent choice the voters usually make. The Irish servant is always the butt; awkward, illiterate, a liar, a coward, a boaster, a sensualist, helplessly dependent on Farrago, he is yet constantly being elected by popular vote, while the captain, the clear-headed, thoughtful man of principle, remains ignored, and often resented. Yet Brackenridge's attitude is not simply conservative. He believes in democratic institutions as opposed to aristocratic, he is very hostile to Britain, and his imagination is plainly engaged by the life of the frontier. He is perhaps closest to Cooper in attitude, and indeed in temperament; a dry, detached, idiosyncratic mind, simply and rigidly masculine, judicial as well as judicious, and yet democratic by conviction. "There is a natural alliance between liberty and letters. Men of letters are seldom men of wealth, and these naturally ally themselves with the democratic interest in a community." Literature, learning, and the law are very close to each other for him; all are defenders of *real* liberty. In nineteenth-century America it proved very hard to believe this, and the temperament of men like Brackenridge and Cooper was forced into imaginative retreat, with only oblique and tangential sallies. It made its mark in Southwestern humor, and one catches echoes of Brackenridge in Twain and the Gavin Stephens side of Faulkner, though also in Cozzens and Auchincloss and Marquand. One gets no strong sense of failure from *Modern Chivalry*, because it offers no intimations of striking talents to be wasted, but one does feel the nation's very limited range of aspiration and sophistication to be symbolized by it.

Brackenridge was a conservative member of the democratic party in American politics. Philip Freneau (1752–1832) was a radical member of that party. Both were involved at different times in newspaper battles against Cobbett, then quite reactionary, but for Freneau such warfare was a much larger part of his life. He was much shriller and harsher in his invective than Brackenridge.

His career was an alternation of political-literary journalism with commercial seagoing, editorships following on captaincies. The most famous of the newspapers he ran was *The National Gazette*, which he edited from 1791 to 1793 in the interests of Jefferson and France, and very much against the interests of Adams and England. It ran a campaign against Hamilton and the Bank of America, the political agents of the upper class, and printed extracts from Paine's *Rights of Man*, Part II. (Part I he had serialized in another paper he had edited.) He was the enemy of the Hartford Wits, and his poetry as well as his politics were often attacked in the Hartford *Daily Mercury*, which Barlow had founded in his conservative days.

Jefferson credited *The National Gazette* with having averted the threat of a revival of monarchy in America. Whether or not that would have come, politics then were very bitter in Philadelphia. John Adams wrote of 1793 that there were ten thousand people in the streets daily, clamoring to drag Washington from his house (Freneau had intimated in his paper that Washington wanted to be made king) and that only the yellow fever epidemic of that year saved the city from bloody revolution. Later in life, when the political excitement had died down, and the balance had settled against his party, Freneau continued his journalism, but it was more literary, and he invested more hopes in his poetry.

As a poet, Freneau clearly had talent, and the group of his poems always anthologized do stand out from the mass of what was being published then. But it is striking that they are so unlike each other. He never found his own voice, and he was not the sort of virtuoso who could make a considerable contribution by sheer technique. He wrote every kind of piece, humorous, satiric, invective, epic, lyric, but he is at his best in the last, when he is most quiet and reflective. In polemic, or any situation of direct comment, his tone is habitually violent and unmeasured. In part he was a simple victim of circumstances, of the contemporary maelstrom of angers. But Paine survived that without losing his individuality. It was harder for a primarily literary man, especially one with radical opinions. Freneau's temperament was evidently not in accord with his opinions; indeed, he had no temperament that was ever nourished to full growth. Even his letters give the sense mostly of a bundle of opinions, and of ambitions to get into print. His biography by Lewis Leary is subtitled "A Study in Literary Failure." That should perhaps be a subheading under Philadelphia (or indeed America): "A Study in Cultural Failure."

Joseph Dennie (1768–1812) stood on the opposite side from Freneau and Brackenridge politically. He was a firm Federalist, so firm in his contempt for democracy that he was indicted by a Philadelphia grand jury for a paragraph deemed actually treasonable. He was a New Englander by birth and training, but his major work was done in Philadelphia, and is Philadelphian in style. His migration thither, in 1799, is a good example of the magnetism then of Philadelphia as the literary capital, though that position, which it had held for thirty or forty years, was soon to be lost, never to be recovered.* In the next period it was to Boston that literary aspirants came. Boston was already reading the new and dangerous books, the German books, which Philadelphia never accepted.

Dennie was an essayist, a critic, and above all an editor. The essay was a very popular form in this period. Between 1785 and 1800 a hundred brief series of light periodical essays appeared in New England journals alone, not counting those reprinted in larger papers. Dwight and Freneau both wrote several such series, which were usually given some pseudonymous signature; Freneau made use of forty-four such pseudonyms at one time or another. It was not a form at the service of the big new ideas and experiences of the period. Its model was Addison, or — for the daring — Sterne. Dennie's famous series, *The Lay-Preacher*, claimed to combine "The familiarity of Franklin's manner and the simplicity of Sterne's." Sterne was morally disapproved by the Hartford Wits, but Dennie used Sterne's sermons when he read in church, and it was this ability of his to appreciate and respond to some of the liveliest writing of his time that enabled him to make a significant

* Royall Tyler, 1757–1826, is another New Englander who made the same migration. A friend and collaborator of Dennie's, he is most famous for his play *The Contrast*, of 1787, the first Sheridanesque American comedy.

contribution to American literary life. His essays have some stylistic life, of a very elaborate kind, and curiously resemble passages of Emerson at times.

As a critic, Dennie did useful work, of a kind then rare in America. He reviewed *Lyrical Ballads* with understanding, and praised Wordsworth's later work. He was a friend of Tom Moore and Leigh Hunt, and gave his readers a sense of equality with British literary amateurs. And he would copy, for example, a paragraph of high-flown American rhetoric from the New York *Advertizer*, describing the launching of the frigate *President*, and follow it by a mockery and a criticism. He trusted his own sensibility as an organ of knowledge.

He went to Philadelphia to become editor of the *Gazette of the United States*, a Federalist journal, but in 1801 he founded the *Port-Folio*, America's first successful literary magazine, which ran until 1827 and achieved a circulation of two thousand, largely because of his editing. Since most magazines derived from clubs of men with literary interests, of the city's lawyers and doctors, editing required a talent for social organization, which Dennie evidently had. But he had also a real interest in literature, and the *Port-Folio* printed, for instance, hitherto unpublished letters written by Smollett, and others by Boswell. But Dennie's taste, though in some valuable sense authentic, was also narrow. He disbelieved in American writing, and though this could be in some cases a reasonable position then, it plainly derived in his case from an unhappy relation to his culture, just as his shrill politics did. He was a self-caricaturing man, a dandy both in dress and opinions, who declared himself that he could never be profound, that his talents were superficial but showy. His pseudonym was Oliver Oldschool, and the primness, the perverseness, the poutingness, which the signature suggests are there in the writing too. He showed what could be done for letters in America — and something *could* be done — by impudently following an antidemocratic line. But this line, of course, allied literature with the feebler or the perverser forces in the national life. He as much as anyone made hard the way of Whitman and Twain, heralded the coming of Irving and Longfellow.

Charles Brockden Brown (1771–1810) was probably the most

talented of these Philadelphia men; one cannot be sure because his opinions were rather ambiguous, his temperament rather muddy, his career rather irresolute, rather full of changes of direction, rather lacking in continued effort. Born of Quaker parents who read French philosophy, he entered a law office at the age of sixteen, but was already then planning epic poems on subjects out of American history. At eighteen he had a contribution to the *Columbian Magazine* printed, and in 1793 he left the law to devote himself to literature. He wrote for the magazines with some success, and in 1798 moved to New York, became a member of the Friendly Club (men with mostly conservative opinions, who read the Hartford Wits with enthusiasm) and edited their *Monthly Magazine*. That year and the next he published five books: *Alcuin, Wieland, Ormond, Arthur Mervyn,* and *Edgar Huntley.* Two later novels were published in 1801, less melodramatic in style, and less interesting. The rest of his life he spent as an editor, with an occasional political pamphlet.

His novels are worthy of being compared with Godwin's. He is noted, and justly, for having adapted the Gothic form to the life-conditions of democratic America, away from those of feudal Europe, which until then seemed inseparable from that form. Instead of Gothic castles, ruined abbeys, wicked barons, mad monks, torture cells, ancient manuscripts, he dealt in cruel Indians and savage panthers and the yellow fever, ventriloquism and somnambulism and spontaneous combustion, and men driven out of their senses, their moral senses, by too much speculative philosophy. He used the form, as the liveliest European practitioners did, to dramatize or mythify unconscious conflicts deriving from a man's committing himself to a radical creed, to a Faustian or a Calvinist temperament.

Brown's opinions, or at least his tastes, when he began to write, were aesthetically radical even by European standards, and he is the only American writer of whom this was true. His early Journal contains notes on a Utopian Commonwealth, a new religion, a new alphabet, and thirty-two pages of architectural drawings and designs. Though it is not certain how much German literature he had read, he wanted his readers to think he was familiar with it; he recommended Kotzebue, Schiller, and Goethe; he made use of

Tschink's *Geisterseher*; and he offered the "German" kind of experience — headlong passions portrayed in wild numbers with terrific energy. And an early essay series for a magazine, called "The Rhapsodist," defines the author thus: "The life of the rhapsodist is literally a dream. Love and friendship, and all the social passions are excluded from his bosom. Nature is the mistress of his affections, in the contemplation of whose charms he is never wearied." The man who writes this in 1798 was as in tune with the imagination of his age as the Hartford Wits were out of tune with it. He was ready to read Godwin's *Political Justice* and *Caleb Williams*, both of which had a great effect on him.

But by the time Brown became an editor, which was almost immediately afterwards, he was avoiding politics and fostering history, declaring himself the ally of Christian morals, praising Hamilton and attacking the French Revolution. The editor's policy shall be such, he wrote, that "His poetical pieces may be dull, but they shall, at least, be free from voluptuousness or sensuality, and his prose, whether seconded or not by genius and knowledge, shall scrupulously aim at the promotion of public and private morals." What had happened? Plainly something sinister for American literature. Brown was not a thinker, or a fighter; the literary men he knew in New York were Federalists; and after all one may say that the whole world had changed its mind about politics and morality. But whereas Wordsworth made great poetry out of his change of mind, Brown was never able to write any lively fiction in the conservative mode. (It was, more exactly, a change of temperament that Wordsworth made into the subject of his great poem, and Brown never achieved a new temperament, though he lost faith in the old one.) Perhaps the experience of being turned back, turned around, ideologically, was too discouraging; perhaps his talents were irredeemably oriented toward radical fiction; perhaps he had never had real confidence in those talents — it seems clear that he never *employed* them confidently, always hurriedly and amateurishly. Whichever of those is true, one must also say that America did not help him.

It is surely an exaggeration to talk of Brown as a significant novelist. There is only a promise that he might have become one. But one sees why he was a favorite author of Shelley's (Constantia

Dudley of *Ormond* was Shelley's idea of the perfect woman) and had he lived in Godwin's circle in London, had he exchanged ideas and manuscripts with Holcroft, Shelley, Godwin, Mary Wollstonecraft, Brown might have written more and better. In Philadelphia, however, he had to fail.

In New York

In New York in our period one writer overshadowed all others, Washington Irving. He made over $200,000 from writing, and had hotels, steamboats, squares, cigars, and wagons named after him during his life. When he died, New York closed down to honor him. The funeral procession had one hundred fifty carriages, and a thousand people waited outside the church. He showed how the American writer could be a national hero. But he showed even more vividly how he could also be an imaginative failure, an intellectual fraud.

(James Fenimore Cooper lies slightly outside this period, by virtue of his publishing dates, but a few sentences can make clear his relevance to the argument. In his novels he applied to American material the cultural formula devised by Scott. He gave his countrymen the national myths they thought they wanted, and was rewarded with popularity for doing so. But because his temperament belonged, much more purely than Scott's, to the Enlightenment, there is no imaginative intensity in these works. His essays, particularly his culture-criticism of America, expressed his temperament much more successfully, and are very interesting even today. But they made him very unpopular. So he too was made to fail by his situation, in the sense that his talent was misdirected, that he did not achieve his full potential, and was involved in endless feuds with people who thought they represented "America" against him.)

Irving was born in 1783, the youngest son of a large family, and his elder brothers protected him, first against his severely religious father, and later against the world at large. Until he was forty-five they planned his life for him in important ways. They were merchants and quite important figures in the commercial life of New York, and through them Irving remained a citizen of that city even while he wandered in Europe. He remained a citizen of the fastest-growing city in America, with the greatest mercantile and fashionable contact with Europe, and the least intellectually serious establishment for its size.

He was never strong, either physically or nervously. He began publishing with essays over the name of Jonathan Oldstyle in the *Morning Chronicle* in 1802–1803, and five years later cooperated with his brother and his friend, J. K. Paulding, in another such series called *Salmagundi*, which commented on contemporary phenomena like waltzing, tea-drinking, and feminine fashions. In 1809 he produced *Diedrich Knickerbocker's History of New York*, a parody history of the Dutch colony, a whimsical combination of true history (much of the mock research is genuine) and outrageous falsification, with a good deal of reference to contemporary events and personalities, particularly political, and always from a Federalist standpoint. Wilhelm Kieft in Book IV, for instance, is a satiric portrait of Jefferson. This very New Yorkish book about New York is Irving's liveliest work, at least as originally written. It was an enormous and lasting success, and he revised it twice (the second time, forty years after it was written) making it tamer each time.

After this success he was editor of *The Analectic Magazine* for a year, and then in 1815 went to Europe for the family firm. In 1819–20 he produced *The Sketch-Book of Geoffrey Crayon*, which established his reputation for good on both sides of the Atlantic. This contains a number of famous stories like "Rip Van Winkle" and "The Legend of Sleepy Hollow," plus essays like "Westminster Abbey," meditations on mortality, descriptions of an English Christmas, humorous character sketches, etc. Geoffrey Crayon is an elaborately worked out persona; an avuncular bachelor, a sentimentalist, a traveler, an observer, prone to foolish mistakes, irritabilities, rashnesses of heart, but growing more human with each stroke, gaining more of the reader's affections with each line. Irving made use of the great eighteenth-century tradition of foolish, sentimental, flute-playing strollers and loungers across Europe — Goldsmith, Sterne, Rousseau. But one feels as one reads — as was the fact in life — that he was farther from that persona than they; a very circumspect person. Goldsmith *was* foolish and rash; Irving only pretended to be so for literary purposes.

The two stories mentioned had German originals — are in fact to some degree translations — and this represents the more nine-teenth-century side of his offering. Scott, whom Irving much ad-mired, had pointed out to him the importance of German litera-ture as a source of fictional material. Typically it was through Scott, and Scotland, that he came to Germany — and then to *Undine* and *Der Freischütz* and the *Dresdener Liederkreis*. Irving's parents were Scottish. One of his brothers was born in Scotland. Like Brackenridge (who was born in Scotland) Irving was another exiled Scot; but New York was a different environment from Phila-delphia — politics mattered less, manners mattered more.

His taste was essentially conservative. His essay on Thomas Campbell, of 1810, praised him for obeying the "established laws of criticism" even then, in an age when "we are confounded by a host of poets of vitiated tastes and frantic fancies." He had no liking for Wordsworth or Coleridge, even declaring that Leigh Hunt was a nobler poet than the first, and Scott a profounder intel-lect than the second. He admired Byron, was a friend of Moore and of Rogers, and preferred the aristocratic London of Holland House to that of Hazlitt and Lamb, or that of Dickens, whom he found "outrageously vulgar, in dress, manners, and mind."

His work for American literature was to find the formula that combined as much as possible of what was harmless in the new Romanticism with an essentially conservative sensibility, and to serve up the result with such obtrusive grace and suavity that the American reader would feel culturally flattered. Though a bad writer, he was a phenomenon of the first order in the history of American literature. So many later American writers, such as Long-fellow and Hawthorne, imitated him, just as he had imitated Scott and Moore. They had done the same thing for England, serving up mildly exotic confections in the new style with — in Scott's case — plenty of hearty substantial common sense in the old style, like fruit cake, underneath. But in England alternative voices, like Coleridge and Carlyle, were also listened to by men of letters. In America, Irving's popular success was inadequately counterbal-anced because the centers of culture had not built up courts of strictly literary judgment; at least not of a sort that dealt seriously with life as a whole.

In Boston

As for New England, the years 1790–1820 there were singularly barren and dark, said Emerson, looking back; there was not a book or a speech or a thought in Massachusetts. He first broached this idea in a letter to his brother William in 1850, when it was proposed to do something to honor their father's literary achievement, and he incorporated the phrase into his "Historic Notes of Life and Letters in New England." The men of letters then were small figures, and it is probably fair to take Robert Treat Paine (1773–1811) as the emblematic poet for Boston. His real name was Thomas Paine, but he changed it to remedy the cruel coincidence. He was a friend of Dennie and Tyler's, another firm Federalist (he got physically attacked in the streets for his saucy opinions), and a favorite of the Federalist gentry. He was rather like Dennie in stature and temperament, small, dainty, and shrill, and one can see that precocity — of a different kind from the Hartford Wits' kind — would be likely to characterize the spokesmen for the Bostonian class in possession of the culture of the past and on the defensive against an insurgent Demos.

Massachusetts in 1800 had twenty thousand Republican voters and twenty-five thousand Federalists, and the latter included all the wealth, social position, and education in the state. Passions ran high; men were murdered in the streets for their opinions; and even the Reverend Joseph Buckminster, a man of literary tastes and liberal opinions, preached that Jefferson's presidency would bring down the vengeance of God on the country.

Boston was the most homogeneous, in terms of national origins of the population, and the most conservative, of all the large cities. But its conservatism was not the effect of unbroken continuity. Its rulers in our period were not the rulers of pre-Revolutionary Boston. Those men had been driven out with the British, and had been replaced by merchants who had made fortunes privateering during the war, and who came predominantly from outside the city, from Essex County (Salem, Marblehead, Beverly, Newburyport) and hence were known as the Essex Junto or the Country Party. Leading figures were Timothy Pickering (who brought Dennie to Philadelphia when he was secretary of state), Fisher

Ames, and George Cabot. And in New England, unlike the rest of the country, the end of the war did not bring the disestablishment of the clergy. The New England Congregational clergy had been leaders in the Revolution. They were still leaders of their people in the Federal period, and the alliance between them and the other ruling classes was unbreakable. And so, of all big cities, Boston was the most averse from new ideas.

The Essex Junto effectively silenced the radicals among the revolutionary leaders, for instance, James Otis and Samuel Adams. They allied themselves rather with men of the old Province House set — which had centered round the Province House, the Colonial Governor's mansion — those of them who had, usually because of patriots in the family, been allowed to stay in the country. These included Harrison Grey Otis, Charles Bulfinch, William Tudor, and Josiah Quincy. This alliance proved a saving grace to the arts in Boston, for these "intermediary families" preserved the cultural interests of the old ruling class much more than the new men. In one area, architecture, Boston flourished during our period, and Bulfinch, who invented the Federalist style of building, an adaptation of Robert Adams's Neo-Classicism, is the artistic center of the times much more than any Bostonian writer. (It is interesting to note yet another fruitful affiliation of the arts in America to the arts in Scotland.) But, new men or old, Boston connoisseurs took a conservative position, on the defensive against all dangerous new ideas.

But signs were not lacking that even in literature Boston had a remarkable future ahead of it. William Tudor, another member of the intermediary families, began the *North American Review* in 1815, which, though always ponderous, was also lively in its first few years, and championed the milder romantic fiction and poetry. In this were published several of the really interesting essays on the plight of American literature. And before that there was the *Monthly Anthology*, which had pieces by Tudor and Ames and Josiah Quincy, and poems by John Quincy Adams and Washington Allston. As Emerson said, his father's real services to literature were that he helped run the *Monthly Anthology*, not what he himself wrote.

But the real omens of the future are the essays by the Channing brothers cited before; not only because of their intrinsic intelligence and literary skill, but because of the way they foretell Emerson. It was Emerson, after all, who brought American literature finally out of its doldrums; and stylistically, in Edward Tyrrell Channing's essay, and ideologically, in William Ellery Channing's, Emerson is already there, potentially. And how was Boston, through these two, able to produce the writer America was waiting for? The answer must be because Boston was reading German literature. The escape from the constrictions of both the Federalist and the anti-Federalist sensibilities did not come by means of political change but by means of literature itself.

That is perhaps the main point of this case-study, taken as a part of the book's total argument. American literature in this period is a "case" because in it we are able to survey nearly all the writers and writings of any significant talent in a whole nation; our scrutiny is not dazzled by meeting any really great books or great minds — which are always to some degree incalculable — and there are vivid contrasts to the actual work done, available both in the expectations of the Americans, and in the achievements of foreign writers. It is therefore much more diagnosable as a case than most seeming equivalents. And the diagnosis must be that in American cities literary values — meaning most importantly a responsiveness to the boldest new writing and thinking of the age — were allowed to decay. In an age of cultural revolution, this could only lead to intellectual and imaginative stagnation. Neither moral seriousness nor political radicalism are any substitute, if they are combined with literary insensitivity or ignorance, or even mere orthodoxy in literary matters. Until American writers began to read and respond to the German writers who had met and mastered the new experience, they were doomed to decade after decade of imaginative stagnation and cultural frustration.

In the American educated consciousness, Germany had scarcely existed before Mme de Stael's *De l'Allemagne* came out in 1814. Everyone had read *Werther*, but no one had taken Germany seriously, so that when Ticknor decided to go to a German university, he had difficulty finding a German grammar book in Boston. He and Edward Everett and Joseph Cogswell and George Bancroft brought back to Harvard in the twenties the benefits of the new

German university world, long before the rest of America received them.

But his was philological Germany. Many Germanies were important for nineteeth-century America, some of them in deleterious ways, like the Dresden pseudo-Romanticism of Irving and Longfellow, and the terror novels Brown used. But the most important was the Germany of Weimar, of Goethe, Schiller, and Herder. This was William Ellery Channing's Germany. It was a Weimar idea we saw him putting forward on National Literature; that under modern conditions of life, because they intensify privacy, literature will have the function which politics had in ancient times, of creating a national identity, a national soul. In England in 1819 he had spent time with Wordsworth and Coleridge, discussing the new ideas, and back in Boston he read Schiller and *Wilhelm Meister* with his disciples, along with Plato and Shelley. He said, "We want great minds to be formed among us. We want the human intellect to do its utmost here"; that is, in Boston; and as the means to that end, he wanted music and dancing taught in the schools, picture galleries and halls of sculpture opened, festivals fostered. He wanted the arts to educate mankind, in just the ways that Weimar proposed.

Weimar was to be also the Transcendentalists' Germany. Goethe's life as well as his work were of the first importance to Emerson and to Margaret Fuller. And when we read F. H. Hedge in *The Dial* in 1840 saying, "The work of life, so far as the individual is concerned, and that to which the scholar is particularly called, is self-culture"; or when we read his title, "The Art of Life — the Scholar's Calling"; we remember both Fichte's "*Über das Wesen des Gelehrten*" and Emerson's "The American Scholar." The declaration of America's literary independence itself owes something to Germany.

But Weimar's achievements became relevant to American writing only in the latter's next period. What actually got written at this time invites us to compare the American cities with Edinburgh. Both are crucial criteria for this cultural diagnosis. Goethe and Scott both died in 1832. So did Freneau, and Trumbull the year before. Goethe was born in 1749, and if we take the five years before and after 1750, we find that Dwight and Barlow and

Humphrey and Brackenridge and Freneau and Trumbull were all born then; were all in their twenties during the American Revolution, and their forties during the French Revolution. Dennie and Brown also were born and died between those dates. They all formed a generation, one which has to stand beside Scott and Goethe, has to be measured by the standard of their splendid productivity. And measured by that standard, their work clearly reveals a deterrent to creativity, an aborti-facient, a blighting influence, the nature of which this essay has tried to define.

Diagnosis

In summary, the trouble seems to have been that a provincial culture, hitherto quite flourishing in literary matters, was blighted by the destructive strains of revolution. It had been a consensus culture, of the eighteenth-century kind, expressing an Erasmian temperament, and hostile to both Calvinist and Faustian cultural images. The revolution should perhaps be defined as threefold, the American, the French, and the literary revolutions, all interrelated. The American Revolution brought with it the strain of needing an American style, a non-British and therefore non-Erasmian image, and the strain of popular violence directed against men of culture. America's first professional architect, Peter Harrison, had his house sacked and his library destroyed in 1775, and in the nineteenth century Cooper, an aristocrat by temperament, was the object of vicious attack. Most artists felt to some degree uneasy in America. The French Revolution brought a strain to liberal and progressive opinion all over the world. It acted as a huge object lesson in the dangers of enthusiastic radicalism, for all but the most committed. It separated the Tom Paines from the Charles Brockden Browns. And the literary revolution brought the strain of new genres and modes of feeling for which there were neither safe exemplars nor audiences. No audiences because of the association of the new Romantic genres with the dangerous opinions and events of the other two revolutions. One value of our categorization lies in its distinction of one kind of Romanticism from another — the Faustian temperament's Romanticism being most often the significant kind, and the non-Faustians merely decorative. America could swallow only the latter. As Van Wyck Brooks says, "The freedom of mind of such good readers as Jefferson, Hamilton and Aaron Burr had all but disappeared by 1830, when the very names of Rousseau and Voltaire, so admired in former days, had become, as an observer said, mere 'naughty words.' " Alongside Rousseau and Voltaire you might put Tom Paine, Godwin, Byron, and Shelley. When Adams and Jefferson died, in 1826, they were succeeded by Webster, Clay, and Calhoun, who were far from comparable in liberality of mind.

The social and intellectual bases of literature suffered badly under these strains; the public became genteel, responding only to consolation and entertainment; and the writers became too confused to constitute themselves each other's discriminating audience. To describe the same thing from the point of view of the individual talent, the strains of the age of revolution prevented the American writers from achieving any temperament. Brown and Freneau, as we have seen, never became themselves, never achieved a tone or a style which could give expression to any significant proportion of their new experience or their adventurous intentions. They tried a series of different voices and forms, some quite promising, but all abandoned before appropriated. They were both, in different ways, bewildered by the course of events, bewildered by the mutual contradiction of authoritative voices round them, made uncertain of their experience, however certain they tried to sound of their position. Robert Treat Paine and Joseph Dennie took another way out of the same dilemma, the way of dandyism. They betrayed their serious intentions by a self-caricaturing posture, flouting reproaches they could not refute; they paraded an overtly false temperament. And the precocity of the Hartford Wits was the subtler self-betrayal of the covertly false. They armored themselves into a judicious weightiness and a severe authoritativeness which they could not justify in terms of experience and imagination. Solemn conservatives, as opposed to the impudent conservatives from Boston, they too turned their backs on the new experience and new ideas of their time, because they trusted no one who might have interpreted it for them. The times were too much in crisis, they felt, to experiment, to run risks. All rebels were rebels against the truth. While Washington Irving is the incarnation of false temperament. He presents himself most insistently as the performer of a personality with which his observed behavior — literary behavior — does not accord. He is playing a part, his sense for which derives much more from his observation of successful models and his expectation of applause — from his purpose to be the part — than from anything more unconscious and profound.

Of course false temperament and blind conservatism occur in all periods; but so many cases occur in this period because the new ideas and new experience seemed dangerous and bewildering; because this was an age of revolution, and because the American cities' avant-garde of cultural idea-men did not successfully mediate these things to their men of imagination.

One can throw some light on this by pointing out how little of the Faustian temperament — so important to the new Romanticism — got expressed in American conservatism. These were all constrained personalities, compared with their equivalents in Europe. They were Erasmians. It was hard for a man of education and reflection to be Faustian, or even temperamentally large, in America. The one figure of those times who seemed to his contemporaries to have something of that dimension was Daniel Webster. He was made the subject of many legends (including the Faustian story of the Devil and Daniel Webster) but he did not, like Goethe or Byron, combine those powers of personality with literary and speculative talents, did not have that *imaginative* temperament. American conservatism remained either prim and principled or fanciful and phony.

Among American radicals there were to be some Faustian figures. In nineteenth-century literature, it is clear, the American imagination identified the Faustian temperament with the working-class outsider, in opposition to the genteel and Erasmian man of education and reflection. We see that very clearly in Mark Twain and Whitman, but also in Captain Ahab. Poe is the only one who attributes Faustian intensities to the educated man, just as he is the only one to constitute a strictly literary court of judgment on cultural problems. But this was not yet. In our period radicalism seemed on the retreat politically, and culturally too much the enemy to be responded to by men of imagination. There had been a strain of radical *Calvinism* in the forms of the Revolutionary period, but in our period only Freneau shows any direct effect of that.

Meanwhile the dominant Erasmian temperament was exhausted as a mode of the imagination. It was identified with certain eighteenth-century Enlightenment forms and styles and positions, some of which were under suspicion for having led to revolutionary excesses, and all of which were being replaced all over the world. The men who wrote out of that temperament, Cooper and Brackenridge, reveal that exhaustion, even though they remain, to my Erasmian taste, at least, the most likable of all the writers of the period. They wrote at their best when farthest from the act of pure imagination — when writing essays; for instance, Cooper's culture criticism. This could not take the place of the great Romantic works being written in Europe.

The most interesting case, for this book's theory, is Barlow's revision of "The Vision of Columbus," after his change of opinion, into a still more neo-classic *Columbiad*. He had made plans, just before that revision, for a new original poem, which was to have been on canals ("A poem on the Application of Physical Science to Political Economy in Four Books"), after the manner of Erasmus Darwin. In other words, it would have been yet another Enlightenment poem.* Barlow did not know, we must realize, any model for a Romantic radical poem. He had met Blake in London, but he was not ready to understand Blake's poetry; or *Prometheus Unbound*; or Goethe's "Prometheus." Hartford had not trained him to do so, and neither would have Boston, or New York, or Philadelphia. These were difficult times for literary men, being an age of revolution, but also times of wonderful opportunity. In Weimar, where literature treated on equal terms with ideas, the living ideas of politics, religion, and science, writers found it a golden age. But American cities did not give their writers the best chance.

Prognosis

An Englishman today, thinking over this period, is bound to draw some depressing parallels between the cultural plight of

---

* Coleridge, in *Biographia Literaria*, describes Darwin's "Botanic Garden" as "one of those painted mists that occasionally rise from the marshes at the foot of Parnassus," and as "a Russian palace of ice, glittering, cold, and transitory"; it was, for the Romantics, a classic example of the kind of poetry whose inauthenticity time had revealed.

America then and that of Britain now. London, Cambridge, Birmingham, Liverpool, all the British cities which have to my imagination some high-cultural identity, seem to be stunting their children's growth in one or another of the ways of Philadelphia, Hartford, New York, or Boston. There are new modes of art at large in the world now, and new modes of experience, just as there were in the 1790's, and England has a strong temptation to retreat from them, to turn her back, to turn an age of revolution into one of reform by decree. These new modes have a lot to be said against them. They work largely in the service of moral disintegration, individual and social. And England now, like America then, has some right to feel that it stands for moral integrity; in matters of high-cultural policy, that is. But now, as then, the smaller country is very viscerally connected with, hypersensitively alerted to, the larger, booming, crashing, self-convulsing country across the Atlantic. What Byron was to America then, Mailer is to England now. And the cultivation of moral superiority is now as then an ineffective defense against imaginative domination.

Of course there is an immense difference between the two cases, in the levels of high-cultural development attained in, say, 1950 in England, and 1780 in America. English literature had been, still in the twentieth century, one of the world's great literatures. But if one measures the tendency of the last twenty years, and then extrapolates, then it is perhaps not exaggerated to compare the two, to draw the parallel with America.

On the whole, as has often been remarked, contemporary British novelists and poets decline to experiment with the large new forms and themes and modes of sensibility which their American equivalents have explored with such remarkable results. Such British counterparts as exist to *Armies of the Night*, or *Giles Goat-Boy*, or *Lolita*, or *Love and Death in the American Novel*, are enormously smaller, and look enormously diminished yet again by being brought into such a comparison. (The one exception to the rule I can think of is theater production.) This seems to be the result of, the expression of, a conservatism which is equally moral, emotional, artistic, and intellectual, and which can lead to complete stagnation.

Particular comparisons must be hit-or-miss, but one might say that John Osborne is to the play what Charles Brockden Brown was to the novel, and one might align the orthodox Leavisites with the Hartford Wits, for their moral conservatism, and their highly established position in the university world, as well as because of their sterility of ideas. The Marxist Leavisites, like Raymond Williams and Edward Thomson (and I would associate Doris Lessing with them) might be compared with Cooper and Brackenridge, writers one *approves* of. The equivalents for Joseph Dennie and Robert Treat Paine were more prominent a few years ago — the sort of writer I discuss in *Mirror for Anglo-Saxons*. (The only British writer who seems to have guided his development by any significant — any risk-taking — concern to be true to his own temperament, is Kingsley Amis. That policy has not so far guided him to any Himalayan heights, but it has resulted in a body of work more eccentrically and idiosyncratically authentic, more artistically alive, more lasting, than anyone else's.) And I have already pointed out the likeness of our novel-sequences to the low-pressure pastimes retailed by Scott in the Edinburgh twilight.

But the particular parallels are neither so valid nor so useful as the general likeness between the two periods. And what use *can* one make of that? My reading of that likeness is that we should constitute courts of strictly literary judgment, holding in suspense our more moralistic evaluations; and respond enthusiastically to all those writers who explore the new experience by the criterion of temperamental authenticity.

7 — OTHER CITIES, OTHER AGES, OTHER REVOLUTIONS

The cultural era is past . . . The city, which was the birth-place of civilization, such as we know it to be, will exist no more. There will be fixed nuclei of course, but they will be mobile and fluid . . . There will be no fixed constellations of human aggregates . . . The politician will become as superannuated as the dodo bird . . . Man will be forced to realize that power must be kept open, fluid and free. His aim will be not to possess but to radiate it.*

Sexual Revolutionaries, Etc.

Naturally, in the course of writing on this subject, I to some degree thought about, to some extent investigated, other cities and other revolutions. As a result, I realized that I needed a chapter — which turned into two chapters — of more general theory. My exempla so far had all been picked and scrutinized for their bearing on my own dilemma. I needed something more like a theory of history in general to see the pattern even they formed in themselves. Seen from the point of view so far adopted, my examples suggest that the energies of art, of the imagination in general, all derive from the city, are all culturally constructive; or, at the very least, that any other energies must be changed, in more than just direction or position, before they can be made to do cultural work. Of my three temperamental types, only the Faustian is not a man of the city, and he only when he is a radical, and even then only when he refuses the kind of accommodation to his culture which Mailer accepts. But suppose we look at other types, not of the city, and yet heroes of imaginative energy? Put beside such cases, and seen from

* Henry Miller, *Sunday After the War*, New York, 1944, p. 154.

a point of view more wide-ranging in time and sympathy, my examples suggest other generalizations. In particular they suggest that if one source of such energy is the well-ordered city, then another is the opposite of that — the city torn apart by conflict, or the revolt against the institution of cities, or the destruction of all existent order in the name of some quite hypothetical improvement. The orderliness of the city may imprison energy, not train and strengthen it. Familiar enough, and surely undeniable, this idea yet needed more acknowledgment and more function with my theory.

The Autobiography of Malcolm X gives us a vivid example of a life split in two by a conversion, a reversal of temperament, from one kind of revolutionariness to another, opposite kind, from the rebellion against all cities to the building of a (rebellious) city of his own. In the first half of his life Malcolm was a culture hero of that black anti-culture which Mailer describes in "The White Negro"; an embodiment of all the powerful anarchy of that world of immediate and violent gratification of appetite, in total rebellion against the internal as well as external structures of "decent" society; a hero of the anti-city temperament. In the second half of his life he became in our terms a Calvinist; and it is worth noting that his conversion began, not with new ideas or feelings, but with an unreasoning act of bodily asceticism, the renunciation of pork and cigarettes; and developed by a process of total self-subjection to the "social" disciplines of reading and writing. Having almost lost both those skills during his life on the street he wrote, he calculated later, a million words while in prison, mostly by copying them from a dictionary. He then acquired, thanks to the Black Muslim organization, a reputation as a revolutionary; but he was, in terms of allegiance to the culture, just becoming a loyal citizen.

In the course of developing that theory, I found that I wanted more examples, more material, more subject matter. I found a fruitful contrast to the cities of culture in one or two cases where the spirit of the city was in some sense anticultural; cities dominated by revolutionaries in revolt against so much of their past that they built for their future what might be called an anti-city. I found an interesting parallel to the age of the French Revolution, and to our own, in the 1640's and 1650's in England, the time of the Puritan Revolution. Many things are prominent in such periods which disappear as if forever in the periods in between, and then reappear as if unprecedented when revolution is again in the air. And I found it even more fruitful to study the periods between two revolutions, to see what happens to the revolutionary energies, and what relation they bear to the artistic energies which replace them. Finally, though it comes first in the chapter, I looked at a neat example of the city of culture attempted, which reminds us how often this can be the tomb of imaginative energy.

My theory is not much more than that it illuminates intellectual and imaginative history to look at cultural history as an alternation of ages of revolution with ages of prosperity and peace, ages of consensus. An age of revolution is one in which the fact of revolution is so present to everyone's mind that men of imagination and reflection feel called on to participate, for or against it. An age of consensus is one in which it seems clear that the days of heroic commitment and idealistic struggle belong irrevocably to the past, and men of imagination and reflection feel called on to labor in their respective fields for the repair and rehabilitation of the existent social structure. (In such an age even a radical — unless he has become a nonparticipant — will be able to imagine only minor changes in society.) I hope to show that to trace the connection of what gets written in one kind of age with what gets written in the other — via the careers and opinions of men who lived in both, for instance — will illuminate even works that seem to relate entirely to the conditions of their own times, and will illuminate not only their character, the category they belong to, but their nature, their success or failure as literary works.

For a piece of verse to be a poem, as for a city to have a culture, and for an individual to have a temperament, is an achievement, deriving from the skillful efforts of always fallible individuals, or forces within an individual, operating under always difficult conditions. But the achievement of one possibility nearly always means the sacrifice or the neglect of another. The piece of verse may become a successful poem by eliminating very lively content of self-projection, or of verbal anarchy. Those three words, poem, culture, and temperament, imply judgments and values, imply certain kinds of purposive organization, imply the city. Though we remain men of the city, we must be able, without abandoning our values, to enter imaginatively into others. Particularly when those values are the skeleton of an imaginatively vivid body of experience. It is instructive therefore to look at some "failures," cultural sins and sinners; to see what in some cases derived from an attempt at another life-option, a fundamentally different temperamental structure or social grouping; though in other cases the option was our option and the failure was simply failure.

There were other cities in Britain in the period of the French Revolution which tried to become cultural centers, besides London and Edinburgh. There was for instance the Liverpool of William Roscoe, an example interesting to us because it is like the case of the American cities (the promoters of American culture were great admirers of Roscoe's efforts) and because his Liverpool plays a part in Part II of this book.

William Roscoe (1753–1831) was born poor but rose to become the local Maecenas. He made his money as banking partner of Thomas Leyland, twice Mayor of Liverpool, whose fortunes, originally established by a lottery prize, were greatly augmented by slave-trading — a trade vitally important to that city's economy. Roscoe, however, was a liberal, even a radical, in politics. He campaigned against the slave trade in company with the Quakers, and voted against it in Parliament when he became an M.P. in 1807. The seamen of Liverpool rioted against him, and he was attacked in the street. He was moreover a despiser of royalty, and an opponent of the war against France. He wrote on "The Wrongs of Africa" and "An Ode to the People of France" in 1789. And in 1791 he published another of the many answers to Burke's *Reflections*. He was a friend of Mary Wollstonecraft, and a great friend of Fuseli.

However, his work in the area of high culture — both what he himself wrote and what he patronized — characterizes him as that common phenomenon of revolutionary times, the Erasmian temperament with a radical position. His own literary work featured a very successful children's poem, "The Butterfly's Ball," an edition and biography of Pope, and above all his biographies of the Medi-

cis, which are said to have "carried the cultural reputation of Liverpool across the whole world." He published the biography of Lorenzo in 1795, and that of Pope Leo X in 1805; the Medicis sent
him thirty-eight paintings from the Pitti in gratitude. To choose
the Medicis to write about was a gesture of historical affiliation, a
declaration of cultural intent, an appropriation of a precedent, a
parallel, and a sponsor for the future. The Medicis had made their
fortune out of banking, too, and had presided over a great trading
city, and had made it a center of artistic achievement. But Roscoe
meant to be a *Unitarian* Lorenzo, a *moderate* Medici.

He became indeed Liverpool's patron of culture, and he did a
great deal for the city in terms of cultural institutions. He helped
found the Society for the Encouragement of Drawing in 1774, and
was a great patron of Fuseli; he himself painted. In 1802 he
founded the Liverpool Botanic Garden, which in 1811 sent John
Bradbury sixteen hundred miles up the Missouri. Roscoe himself
wrote on the Scitamineous order of plants, and had a genus named
after him by Sir James Edward Smith. Audubon visited him and
named a bird after him. In 1807 he founded the Liverpool Athenaeum, and in 1817 the Royal Institution for adult education.

But both in terms of artistic achievement, and as a center of
taste and ideas, Liverpool's record was very disappointing. Roscoe
was considerably less successful as a patron than Joseph Johnson,
who was a much poorer and obscurer man, but whose radical bookshop was more of a center than all Roscoe's institutions. (The two
men had connections, being both Liverpudlians and friends of
Fuseli.) Liverpool's artists are the poet Mrs. Hemans, the sculptor
John Gibson, and the painter George Stubbs. Roscoe's heart was in
the right place, culturally as well as politically, but his taste was
fatally drab. He had no temperament worth the name, in his creative designs or in his critical taste; he had no discriminating ear
even for "the best that was being thought and said." He disliked
the *Lyrical Ballads,* and though he was an early patron of Hazlitt
and de Quincey, the latter says of him, "there was the feebleness of
a mere belles-lettrist, a mere man of virtue, in the style of his sentiments on most subjects." Crabb Robinson called him "a common
man in his small talk and bulky volumes." The one positive tribute
is from Washington Irving, who visited the Liverpool Athenaeum,

and "drew back with an involuntary feeling of veneration" when he first cast eyes on the man.

He had, and still has, his reward from his city. In 1953 the City Council of Liverpool brought out a handsome memorial volume, *William Roscoe of Liverpool*, edited by the City Librarian, and with an introduction by Sir Alfred Sherman, the Chairman of the Finance Committee, which says, "There was about his outlook something universal and godlike. Nothing humane, enlightened, tasteful and tolerant appealed in vain for his fearless support." One can honor the intention of that, and yet say that those words are not meant for the likes of Willlam Roscoe. They are meant for the likes of Goethe. The commercial and administrative city is not the best judge of its artistic counterpart. The Beatles, after all, were around in Liverpool in 1953; and even if they hadn't been, Sherman's idea of what culture is (like Roscoe's idea) was a deadening one. Even Goethe's idea, as we have seen, was far from enlivening when institutionalized. The city of light, even when built with the best directions, can easily be a whited sepulchre, a gallery of plaster-cast classical statues, with guardians to keep your voice down.

However, the conditions that promote the life of the imagination, even the more easily defined life of art, are not so easy to prescribe that one should condemn Sherman, or Roscoe, unsympathetically. If it should seem that Liverpool's external situation was obviously too dull, too lacking in stimulus, for the city to become a center of art or ideas, consider Paris, in the very center of the Revolution, and yet unproductive in those years. The major achievement in poetry was the *Elégies* and the *Idylles* of André Chénier; but they were written before 1789 and not published till 1819, in between which dates the author was guillotined. Such conditions are not favorable to literature. The genres that were productive were political oratory and political pamphleteering, as is usual in ages of revolution. Apart from those, the record names the sexologues, de Sade and Restif de la Bretonne, and the ideological exiles, Joubert, de Stael, and Châteaubriand. It was by action at a distance, either of space or time, that the Revolution promoted literature — that is, in the major genres. But the energies out of which the most imaginative literature comes, out of which all imagination comes, were of course everywhere and immediately stimulated by the revolution far more than by the cultural conscientiousness of Sir William Roscoe.

For instance, the sexually libertarian writers are typical of such periods, as we see in our own times. Revolutionaries are often said to be sexually puritan, but that is the temperament of one group of radicals, the politically serious ones, the Calvinists. To some extent even their puritanism is a reaction against dangerous allies. They see the energies of the revolution being dissipated, and try to protect it. But in early phases of a revolution, there is often a different relation between the various advocates of freedom, however hostile their temperaments may implicitly be. Early on, every kind of experiment stimulates every other; practice stimulates theory and theory stimulates practice.

There are some interesting parallels in the English Revolution of the seventeenth century. There we find the Ranters asserting that the flesh *cannot* defile the spirit. Lawrence Clarkson, in his autobiography, *The Lost Sheep Found*, of 1660, confesses that as a Ranter he had believed that no man could be freed from a sin till he had acted it out, and enacted it *as no sin*. "Till you can lie with all women as one woman, and not judge it sin, you can do nothing but sin." Clarkson had been successively a Presbyterian, an Antinomian, a Seeker, a Ranter, and the leader of his own sect, My One Flesh. Later he became an astrologer, and then a Muggletonian — an emblematic career for an age of revolution. (It is not entirely a trivial coincidence that so many contemporary "groups" take their names from seventeenth-century sects, like the Seekers and the Diggers.) It seems likely that Clarkson was not piously falsifying his former doctrine, for in *A Single Eye*, 1650, he had written that sin exists only in our imagination. Drunkenness, theft, swearing, all are in themselves nothing distinct from "Prayer and Prayses." Moreover, to be saved you must make the flesh and the spirit one, and that is done by the sexual act. You must, he says, change your five senses for one — "that lovely pure one who beholds nothing but purity, wheresover it goeth, and whatsoever it doth, all is sweet and lovely." Such teaching makes an odd bedfellow with Cromwell's kind of Puritanism, but bedfellows they were.

You can find analogous teaching, even more poetically expressed, in Joseph Salmon and Jacob Bauthumley's pamphlets. Abiezer Coppe deserves a quotation, because of his stylistic animation, which is typical of the Ranters in general:

. . . yes, give, give, give up, give up your houses, horses, goods, gold, lands, give up, account nothing your own, have All Things common, or els the plague of God will rot and consume all that you have.

This comes from his "A Fiery Flying Roll," in which he declares that he came to God "through baseness," and seems to mean through fornication in a brothel. He exults in his breaking of the moral law.

I am confounding, plaguing, tormenting, nice, demure, barren Mical, with David's unseemly carriage, by skipping, leaping, dancing, like one of the fools, vile, base fellowes, shamelessly, basely, and uncovered too, before handmaids. . . . It's meat and drink to an Angel (who knows none evil, no sin) to sweare a full-mouth'd oath, Rev. 10.6. It's joy to Nehemiah to come in like a madman, and pluck folkes haire off their heads, and curse like the devil. . . .

The message is clearly an attack on all the values of the city, and it reminds us of many messages today.

Indeed the Ranters' ideas include a very modern awareness of the need not to grow up, not to become a mature human being, not to become a member of the city — or the need to reverse that process — in order to be a Ranter, or, to use their term for themselves, an Angel.

Give over, give over, or if nothing els will do it, I'l at a time, when thou least of all thinkest of it, make thine own child, the fruit of thy loines, in whom thy soul delighted, lie with a whore before thine eyes: That that plaguy holinesse and righteousness of thine might be confounded by that base thing. And thou be plagued back again into thy mothers womb, the womb of eternity: That thou maist become a little child, and let the mother *Eternity*, *Almightinesse*, who is universall love, and whose service is perfect freedome, dresse thee, undresse thee, swadle, unswadle, bind, loose, lay thee down, take thee up, &c.

And to such a little child, undressing is as good as dressing, foul cloaths, as good as fair cloaths — he knows no evill &c — And shall see evill no more, — but he must first lose all his righteousnesse, every bit of his holinesse, and every crum of Religion, and be plagued, and confounded (by base things) into nothing.

Clearly the Angels were what I have called elsewhere post-Freudian revolutionaries.

The writing there is full of interest and vitality, just as writing; and the pamphlets of the Levellers, in quite a different way from the Ranters', are also important to the lover of language, of literature. The imagination was powerfully stimulated by the Revolution, not to create in the major forms, but to intensities which later found expression in the major forms.

The Ranters' style of thought must also remind us of Norman Brown, Timothy Leary, Ken Kesey, and even more of the less academic among our current enthusiasts and irrationalists, like Jerry Rubin and Abbie Hoffman. We have today plenty of such manifestations of the spirit of revolution. They are often the gentlest, the sweetest, the sincerest of people, though there are pockets of violence, depravity, and evil among them. And they are among the most imaginative and creative, there in their no-man's-land (as it seems to the city) between life and art. Even when there is no violence, however, and even when they are brilliantly imaginative, these cults must be alien to the Erasmian temperament. And of course to the Calvinist, not to mention the conservative Faustian. Because we are all city types — it is we who have drawn the lines of life and art and say what shall be no man's land between them. They are the opposite of everything an Erasmian means by civilization even when they are people he has to admit to be more loving and perhaps more intelligent than himself. He feels with them uncomfortably like Pilate with Christ, because even while yielding them a moral superiority, sometimes in some sentimental way yielding them his heart, he turns away, washes his hands, a pacific Grand Inquisitor. It is a scene out of a thousand movies, and a thousand lives, where the temperament one has chosen involves one in an action one would not have chosen. In these enthusiastic sects the group temperament is a version of the inverted Faustian, exceeding all limits in the abandonment of aggression and self-preservation. Of my categories, only the Faustian radical comes anywhere near either this, or the other anti-city types and behavior I shall discuss. But though I shall apply that term as their label, it must be taken as a much looser categorization than my terms usually are.

There were some extreme examples of the religious-sexual revolutionary among the Taborites of Prague at the beginning of the fifteenth century. More exactly, it was among the Pikardi and Adamite sects within the Taborites that the most extravagant behavior occurred. The Taborites were the radicals among Hus's followers, and predominantly poor, though organized as a social force by the artisan guilds of skilled workers. "Cast down Nimrod and his tower," was their cry, for Nimrod, who built the Tower of Babel (identified with Babylon) was the first builder of cities, and the originator of private property and class distinctions. They were so called after Tabor, the town they built near Usti for their anarcho-communist experiment, and which they named after the Mount of Olives. The town was built on a promontory jutting out into a river, which they renamed the Jordan. They hated Prague, their metropolis, which they identified with the Babylon denounced in *Revelation*, the birthplace of Antichrist, the embodiment of *Avaritia* and *Luxuria*. *Revelation*, the one book of the New Testament which Erasmus disliked, is the only one which revolutionaries always quote. The great families and upper clergy of Bohemia then were mostly German as well as Catholic, so the rising had a nationalistic as well as religious character. All the kinds of revolution went hand in hand at first, and the institution of the city itself, of Western culture itself, was the enemy.

But the Taborites were soon separated in sympathy from the moderate Utraquists, or Calixtines, who took their names from their demand to receive the Communion sacrament in both kinds. This was one of a series of religious changes which they and the Taborites demanded. The four Articles of Prague, drawn up perhaps in 1417, and promulgated in 1420, constituted the general program of the Husites. These demanded freedom for the priests of Bohemia to preach the word of God; expropriation for the Church; poverty for all priests; and the punishment of all offenses like simony. The Taborites also rejected the idea of purgatory, prayers for the dead, the use of images and relics, and the practice of several rites. They relied heavily on the direct reading of, and inspiration by, the Scriptures. The Utraquists were much more moderate in both social and religious philosophy, and soon separated themselves from, and in time became the enemies of, their former allies.

The Taborites were crushed militarily by the Utraquists at the battle of Lipan in 1434, though Tabor itself was not taken until 1452. Thereafter they survived as the Moravian Brethren, pacifist, apolitical, unrevolutionary. But in the 1420's they were the reverse. They abolished rents, taxes, feudal dues, etc.; they declared a policy, in some cases, of killing the rich and privileged and Catholic; they threatened the cities — their leader Martinek Hauska, an ex-priest like many of their leaders, prophesied that every town in the area should be burned to the ground during the four days of February 10–14, 1420.

The Taborites planned to establish a worldwide anarcho-communist order. Early in 1420 communal chests were set up, controlled by Taborite priests, to begin the revolution. Thousands of peasants and artisans of Bohemia and Moravia sold all their belongings and paid the proceeds into these chests. Sometimes they burned their homesteads to the ground, in sign of their break with their former settled, property-owning lives. Many joined the Taborite armies and lived always on the move, like the *plebs pauperum* of the Crusades. Others joined the Taborite communities, where owning private property was made a sin.

Dissension arose among them partly because their theoretical egalitarianism was never practiced in their armies. Their military commander, Zizka, was hostile to the ideological extremists, and in 1421 he drove Martinek Hauska and three hundred Pikardi out of Tabor. The Pikardi had, as their name implies, connections with the *Homines Intelligentiae* of Flanders, who had been a powerful underground movement both there and in France, preaching mystical and libertarian doctrines. They believed that Heaven and Hell were states of the soul in this world, and that at death each soul melts back into its Divine Origin. They themselves were "the subtle in spirit," and they could melt back even in this world. The only sin was to be ignorant of one's divine origins. They made credal statements like "I *am* eternal life and wisdom." They cultivated absolute passivity and indifference (sometimes by means of accustoming themselves to torture) and were dishonest on principle in their dealings with the outside world. The sexual act they called the acclivity, the ascent to sexual ecstasy, and adultery an affirmation of emancipation from the world.

Zizka hunted them down and burned fifty of them. To the orthodox Taborites their religious, social, and political heresies all
blended together. Zizka carried the eucharistic chalice on a pole
into battle as a banner, whereas the Pikardi rejected Transubstan-
tiation, and therefore disdained the Eucharist. And among the
Pikardi were a smaller group of Adamites, who believed that they
were the Saints of the Last Days, in whom God dwelled, and that
they would live forever, whereas Christ had been only mortal.
They dispensed with both Bible and Creed, keeping only the
Lord's Prayer: "Our Father who art in us, illumine us, thy will be
done. . . ." Their first leader was probably an ex-priest called Peter
Kanisch, under whom they held out against Zizka by establishing
their camp on an island in the river. On his death a peasant called
"Moses" or "Adam" inherited his command, "the government of
the world." Under his orders, they made nocturnal sorties against
neighboring villages, killing, burning, and looting, we are told.
Promiscuity was obligatory in their community, and they danced
naked round the fire, singing hymns. (Adamite cults elsewhere had
held sacramental banquets with people dressed in shining robes, á
Virgin Mary figure, and a naked preacher exhorting them all to
practice nakedness.) The Bohemian Adamites were exterminated
October 21, 1421. The Taborites had no mercy on them; their
creed, which was the anti-city temperament made into a policy,
was destructive of all civilization. All across Europe for a century
the Bohemians were feared as a threat to the social order, and were
such a threat. There were often risings of the guilds, or the peasants, in fifteenth-century Germany, which were inspired by the
teachings of the Husites.

The most famous case of revolutionary antinomianism is the
Anabaptist regime of Jan of Leyden in Munster in 1535 and 1536.
Jan Bockelson, only twenty-five when he came to power, was a man
of great good looks and personal magnetism, illegitimate by birth
and unsuccessful in ordinary life, prone to visions and ecstasies,
and an enthusiastic writer, actor, and producer of plays. The Munster regime was genuinely communist for a time, and the poor
people under oppressive rule in the districts around looked to the
city as an inspiration and a source of hope. Money was abolished,
workers were paid in kind and only by the government, and people

addressed each other as Brother and Sister. Goods were available to all who needed them in communal stores. It was a religious revolution as much as social, for the former ruler of Munster had been a bishop, and Bockelson was overthrowing the corruptions of the Catholic Church, and leading his people toward a renewal of the religion of the Old Testament. He, and even more the earlier Anabaptist leaders of Munster, Jan Matthys and Bernt Rothmann, were possessed by a vision of a genuinely new society. And it was an anti-intellectual revolution; all books except the Bible were publicly burned in the Cathedral Square, along with other artworks.

The city was soon besieged by the forces of the bishop, and food and other supplies gradually grew scarce. The police powers exerted by the rulers became very severe, and monarchical display was cultivated — Jan and his consort appeared seated on golden thrones in the Cathedral Square, wearing crowns, and surrounded by their court. Although there had been a severely puritan code of morals, imposing the death penalty for all offenses, even for lying, slandering, or merely quarreling, at a certain point he introduced polygamy, and made divorce easily available. All women in the city under a certain age were forced to marry, including those already married, if their husbands belonged among the ungodly. Jan himself took fifteen wives. He had himself proclaimed King of the World, and Messiah of the last days. It seems clear (though of course few accounts can be entirely trusted) that before the bishop's forces captured Munster, it had lost not only material wellbeing, but also all civil and religious liberty, all freedom of behavior and expression. At the end Bockelson was conducting a reign of terror. But it also seems clear that earlier on the Munster movement, like the Bohemian movement, was an extraordinary adventure of the spirit. Calvin, Erasmus, Luther — Calvinist, Erasmian, Faustian conservative — all recognized it as anathema.

Sexual revolution, religious, and political, the three are often intricately involved together, and often frustrate each other's aims. The political radicals oppress their earlier allies because they see, or think they see, that if the revolution is to establish itself it must be by their taking control. "To establish itself" means of course to constitute itself a city.

In *Major Trends in Jewish Mysticism*, Gershem Sholem points out some strange connections between Jewish revolutionaries of very different temperaments. In the excitement of revolutionary action Calvinists and Faustian radicals are to be found together and almost indistinguishable. (Those are not his terms, of course, but he is contrasting rationalist and rabbinical reformers against antirational religious revolutionaries; his categories are like enough to mine for him to feel this cross-connection to be a riddle.) He points out that many of the Jewish reformers of the nineteenth century came from among the sects, or from families that belonged to the sects, of Sabbatai Zevi and Jakob Frank, two of the corrupt messiahs and black Faustians. Sabbatai Zevi, like Simon Magus before him, credited his ex-prostitute consort with divine powers; and like Jakob Frank after him he apostatized, taking with him out of Judaism a large body of followers. Yet the man who should have succeeded Frank as leader of the community at Offenbach became a political leader in France, under the name of Junius Frey, and was sent to the guillotine in 1794. Aron Chorin, the pioneer of reformed Jewry in Hungary in the middle of the nineteenth century, had been a member of the Sabbatai Zevi sect. The Frankists of Prague were the leaders of the 1832 reform organization there; one of their leaders quotes mystics like Zevi and Isaac Luria alternately with rationalists like Kant and Moses Mendelssohn as authorities.

Reformers of this kind are good examples of the Calvinist temperament, intellectuals cooperating in committees for the legislation of radical change. While Sabbatai Zevi was a man of no intellectual discipline and small intellectual vitality. He was a manic depressive with powerful charisma who was driven in moods of exaltation to forbidden acts of an erotic and daimonic character. In other words, he was a religious Faust; more specifically, a holy sinner of the kind Dostoevski has made familiar to the Western imagination, and his apostasy was a natural climax to his religious career. This climax his more intellectual disciple, Nathan of Gaza, theologized, giving a sacramental character to his apostasy, and also to all his antinomianism; and thereby giving a Faustian cast to the whole religious movement which grew up round his legend.

Jakob Frank's religion, which also reached a natural climax in apostasy, was even more morally nihilistic; he taught the holiness

of sin and the necessity of hypocrisy and apostasy. Yet their followers became rationalists, reformers, and political revolutionaries.
The riddle is partly solved as soon as we remember the difference
between leaders and disciples within any movement. A powerful
organization needs men both of Faustian temperament, to lead,
and Calvinist temperament, to organize. It can even happen that
as a disciple inherits his leader's position, he changes temperament.
The radical position, like other positions, brings together men of
very different temperamental types. But the deeper riddle of how
we should feel, as men of the city, toward such cesspool plungings
of the spirit, such mephitic flights and flounderings of the imagination, is not so easily solved.

Seventeenth-Century Revolution

Let us concentrate on the English revolution and its likeness to
the French, looking alternately at some of its political features, and
at some of its intellectual and imaginative expressions. It is agreed
that 1648 saw at least six revolutions — as many as 1848 did; revolutions in England, in France, in Catalonia, in Portugal, in Naples,
and in the Netherlands. Christopher Hill would add two more, one
in Sicily in 1647 and one in the Ukraine in 1648. This was then
an age of revolutions, and there were interactions between them,
just as in other such ages. For example, the Scottish Army of the
Covenant was officered almost entirely by men who had served in
the Swedish Protestant armies of Gustavus Adolphus; the Fronde
in France was much influenced and inspired by the example of the
English Revolution; and the Dutch officially approved the execution of Charles I, which every other government condemned.
The Dutch revolt meant as much to its times as the Spanish Civil
War did to the 1930's. A regiment of English Roman Catholics
was raised and sent over, all the chaplains Jesuits, to fight for the
Spanish royalists. Then five thousand Protestants volunteered to
fight for the other side, and the merchants of London sent five
hundred thousand pounds to help the Dutch rebels. The world
was in revolt, as it was again in the 1790's, and may be in the
1970's.

And if 1648 was the year of revolutions, 1644 was called by Milton the year of sects and schisms, which may serve to remind us of

the antinomian side of the revolution. George Fox's Journal gives many accounts of his conflicts with Ranters, and Richard Baxter called the same sect a warning to Professors to be humble, fearful, cautelous, and watchful. The Professors were becoming much more disturbed by antinomianism than were the men on the Establishment side.

We may take as an example of such religious extravagance the Muggletonians, a sect founded in the 1650's by John Reeve (1608–1658) and his cousin Lodowicke Muggleton (1609–1698), who were also called the London prophets. Muggleton received a revelation in 1651, and the next year Reeve declared himself the messenger of the third and final dispensation, Muggleton being his mouth. In that year, 1652, they produced A *Transcendent Spiritual Treatise*, declaring that the apostolic succession had lapsed for thirteen hundred years, and now resumed again with them; and they cursed their opponents by name. Though imprisoned for blasphemy, they produced next year *The Divine Looking Glass or the Third and Last Testament*, which they had published in the style and print of the first and second testaments in the Authorized Version. They took up many of the themes of Joachim of Fiore's Everlasting Gospel, which had circulated widely and clandestinely in medieval Europe, and was often invoked by religious revolutionaries, including the Taborites and the Anabaptists. The Everlasting Gospel prophesied an age of God the Holy Ghost, to be to the age of God the Father and that of God the Son (both of which we have known, the second being Christendom) as broad daylight is to starlight and dawn, as high summer is to winter and spring. There would be no wealth, no work, no property, no authority. Both church and state would disappear. Norman Cohn describes this as the most powerful revolutionary myth Europe knew before the Marxist. The Muggletonians are particularly interesting because they survived into the London of Blake's time, as a religious body with chapels and services. In fact they had a revival after 1756, because of Swedenborg's proposing a somewhat similar religious system. Several of the founders' works were reprinted then, and may have come into Blake's hands.

The political revolutionaries also included some bold imaginations. The Diggers, for instance, George Woodcock considers to have been the first anarchists in history. Reason was their guiding principle, but Reason divinized. John Everard described God as "the incomprehensible spirit, Reason . . . Where does that Reason dwell? He dwells in every creature, according to the nature and being of the creature, but supremely in man. . . . This is the kingdom of God within man. . . . Let reason rule the man and he dare not trespass against his fellow creatures, but will do as he would be done unto. For Reason tells him is thy neighbour hungry and naked today, do thou feed him and clothe him, it may be thy case tomorrow and then he will be ready to help thee." This is from *Truth Lifting up its Head above Scandals*. In *The New Law of Righteousness*, he equates Christ himself with "the universal liberty," and attacks all authority as corrupting, even the economic power of master over servant, and the familial power of father over child and husband over wife. He condemns the principles of both authority and property. Everyone should work with his hands, and everyone should share equally in the products of work. There should be no buying and selling, but storehouses open to all to take what they need.

In the age of the French Revolution ideas very like these were worked out again by Godwin, under the pressure of the spirit of change. Woodcock also considers the Enragés, a group who emerged in France in 1793, to defend the cause of the poor in Paris and Lyons, to be in the line of anarchist thought. They were a loosely organized group, united in rebellion against Jacobin authority, and demanding direct popular action, and communistic economic measures. They were led by Jacques Roux, a priest, who was later joined by Jean Varlet and Théophile Leclerc; and they were supported by a women's movement, La Société des Républicaines Révolutionnaires, led by a beautiful actress, Claire Lacombe. (We are familiar with the same thing today, political rallies or marches led by Vanessa Redgrave, Melina Mercouri, or Jane Fonda.) Robespierre and the Jacobins repressed the movement early, but Varlet later published the first anarchist manifesto, *Explosion*.

If Godwin was the heir of the Diggers, Paine was the heir of the Levellers, who insisted that the laws of the land must be rewritten so that everyone can understand them, and reformed so that they

are equally just to everyone. *The Agreement of the People* demanded manhood suffrage, annual parliaments, the abolition of
feudal privileges, the reform of the legal system, and guarantees of
civil and religious liberties. The Levellers were the party of the
independent peasantry, and of the ranks in the New Model Army,
and above all of the smaller tradesmen, journeymen, and artisans
of the City of London. Their pamphlets, particularly those by Lilburne, Overton, and Walwyn, have won them the title of the fathers of plain English — that is, of controversial prose. But the
Calvinist temperament is carried further — perhaps to the point of
union with the Faustian radical — in the Fifth Monarchy men.
They could acknowledge no king but Jesus. None but godly men
should be in power; and the laws of the land should be replaced by
the laws of God.

In 1653 Cromwell drove out the Long Parliament and convened
the Little Assembly, which was to be a government of the saints.
Only sixty out of the hundred and forty M.P.s were radicals, but
because they were so zealous in their participation they impressed
their character on the whole. The Fifth Monarchy men hailed
Cromwell as Moses, but they soon quarreled with him and with
the other sects and parties. This was the Parliament that imprisoned Lilburne the Leveller; for the Fifth Monarchists had no sympathy, once they were in power, with either Levellers or Commonwealth men. Both the latter wanted government by the people, and
a full and free parliament, whereas the former wanted government
by the elect and a dispensation from Heaven. At the end of the
year Cromwell imposed the Protectorate, and those radical M.P.s
who refused to leave the chamber were driven out by his soldiers.
Cromwell was now compared by Fifth Monarchists with the little
horn of the beast described in Daniel. Some historians believe that
the intransigence of these men caused first the imposition of the
Protectorate, and then its increasingly repressive character. By forcing Cromwell to institute an organized church and a regulated
ministry, they turned the Baptists against him; and this is why the
Protectorate was overthrown after Cromwell's death, and the Long
Parliament restored, who predictably invited back Charles II. If
this analysis is correct, the whole story is a vivid example of the way
revolutions can end, in a conflict between centrifugal radicals and a

strong man, culminating in a return to the authority first rebelled against. Something roughly parallel can be seen in the course of events in the French Revolution, and could be seen again today. The men of the city, whatever their position originally, whichever their temperamental type, ultimately join in supporting Authority against the enemies of the city.

The Levellers were suppressed by Cromwell's Instrument of Government of 1653, and the Ranters were punished by numerous Acts of Parliament. The Puritan intelligentsia as well as those in power became more conservative. Milton in the 1640's had assented to the widespread radical theory that the Norman Conquest was at the origin of all the social inequities in England; but by the time he wrote his *History of England* he was taking a hostile tone toward the Anglo-Saxons, the heroes and victims of that theory, because by then he saw the danger as coming more from the radicals than from the conservatives. And it was after he had been convinced that the kingdom of God would not come into being as a political entity in seventeenth-century England that he began to write his great epics. It was when he believed that the Promise referred to the spiritual salvation of individuals that he turned to a literary career. Just so Bunyan thought the Holy War he described was something in the soul of the individual, not a social crusade, which was what Thomas Fuller had thought it a generation before. In somewhat similar fashion George Fox organized the Quaker sect once he was convinced that Christ's kingdom was not of this world. But it is significant that Bunyan, the writer, found Quakerism too radical. His earliest religious quarrels were with the Quakers, and his arguments against them show a distrust of enthusiasm and mysticism, a need to believe in the objective character of revelation. Fox, the man of action, organized the Quakers and saved them from Ranterism; Bunyan, the man of letters, was more conservative yet. As long as a radical temperament is dominant the enterprises of high culture are likely to be put off; and to be resumed when the state of affairs, however disappointing, is assumed to be stable, and when common sense, however low-pitched, can be listened to.

Eighteenth-Century Consensus

The great literary form of revolutionary London was the pamphlet, as it was to be in revolutionary Paris. There are fifteen thousand pamphlets listed in the British Museum's incomplete catalogue of the Thomason Tracts as printed between 1640 and 1666. This is the collection which Thomas Hollis persuaded George III and Lord Bute to buy and give to the British Museum, and which he persuaded Catherine Macaulay to read while she was writing her radical *History of England* (1763–1781) which brought their ideas back into circulation just when the next age of revolution was preparing itself.

But even more interesting, as one speculates on the succession of periods of revolution through history, are the alternating periods of consensus, the periods of seeming peace and prosperity. Because city men, of one type or another, are in control then, it is in these alternating periods that the major works of intellect and imagination are undertaken. Let us take as our example the period in England between the Puritan Revolution and the French, and try to understand how the intellectual and imaginative energies which had been aroused and directed by the revolution adapted themselves to new tasks. In particular we want to know what the energies that went into literature then have to do with those that had gone into revolution before. We have had one model of how that happened, in the case of Milton and Bunyan. But Milton and Bunyan are very unlike Defoe and Richardson, who were yet in some sense Puritans, and so related to radicalism. Has the energy of their work anything to do with revolution?

In 1660, it seems clear, there was a remarkable unanimity of weariness in England, and a determination, which bore remarkable fruit, to express and strengthen and give stability to that unanimity; by finding forms and ideas as well as institutions to embody it. It was a weariness of war, of conflict, of experiment, of upheaval, of theory, of enthusiasm. But England was, as a legacy of the Civil War, a deeply divided country; and, despite the plurality of sects and jealousies on the surface, a country divided into two. On the one side stood the Puritans, if we can use that name for all the groups descended from the groups that supported Parliament. On the other side, King and court, archbishops and generals and dukes and poets, the Establishment; I use that label because I want to keep the same pair of terms at work in analyzing the cultural history of the whole period between the two revolutions.

It is possible, therefore, to compile a list of opposite pairs, which will suggest the representative figures on each side of this great division of 1660. On the Establishment side, the memory of the martyred Charles I; on the Puritan side, that of Cromwell. On the Establishment side, Anglican theology; on the Puritan side, Puritan theology — either Calvinist or antinomian. On the Establishment side, high church ritual and decorum; on the Puritan side, the Quakers. On the Establishment side, the great landed proprietors; on the Puritan side, small craftsmen and journeymen. On the Establishment side, Cavaliers; on the Puritan side, Roundheads. On the Establishment side, country estates and the court; on the Puritan side, the city of London. On the Establishment side, playwrights and poets; on the Puritan side, pamphleteers and spiritual autobiographers. Obviously, such a list does not imply that any single man on either side (particularly on the Puritan, which included more extremists) would approve all the items said to characterize it. What it implies is that he would most often acknowledge a kinship to the men who approved the items he disapproved, while in the case of items on the other list he would feel less kinship with — perhaps also less anger against — those he disagreed with.

But men on both sides were determined to avoid in the future everything that would intensify their dividedness to the point of war, everything tainted with enthusiasm. They wanted to be *Englishmen*, whether conservative, liberal, or radical; whether Faustian, Erasmian, or Calvinist, *Englishmen*; temperamental differences were of course acknowledged, but only as making the consensus colorful. Anything that might lead to conflict was to be given strictly limited scope of action. One of the striking things about the period is the antienthusiastic character of the Dissenting, ex-Puritan sects. It was a reversal of tendency as sudden and complete as that of the Taborites after the loss of Tabor. They had a distinguished future ahead of them, but as educational and philanthropic institutions; to some extent they carried the seed of political radicalism within them throughout the eighteenth century, but always in a dry, theoretical, decorous way. They were primarily intellectual institutions, insofar as they were not primarily pious. Isaac Watts represents them, as human types.

The exceptions to this rule, the sects that remained enthusiastic, seem to prove the point, in one way or another. The Camisards, the French prophets, made their mark mostly by provoking Shaftesbury to write his *Letter Concerning Enthusiasm,* one of the classic statements of the Erasmian attitude. (In an age of consensus, the Erasmian temperament is likely to establish a certain hegemony.) The Glasites, who had their distinguished members, or ex-members, at the end of the century, in Godwin, Faraday, and Thomas Spence, the radical, were the epitome of obscurity during the years between the Revolutions. While the great propagator of enthusiasm during those years was Wesleyanism, so much a product of the Established Church and the upper class, so politically and culturally conservative. Like Evangelicalism, it was — from a social point of view — a religious movement run by the upper classes for the lower. Ronald Knox's analysis of Wesley was that he was a man incapable of religious enthusiasm himself, but fascinated by the spectacle of it in others, which meant in the lower classes. As for any other kind of enthusiasm, either political or intellectual-imaginative, no one could have been farther from it than either him or his movement.

Enthusiasm outside such limits was the great enemy of all, because it was to blame for the Civil War and the subsequent troubles. What was to be cultivated in its place, to unify and pacify? First of all common sense and skepticism and the social source of these qualities, the society of educated gentlemen, the coffee house. We see that recommended by Dryden and Swift and Addison and Steele — the writers of the beginning of the period. The advancement of science, exemplified by Newton and the Royal Society; clarity and impersonality of mind, proceeding step by step, from one demonstrable truth to the next. The pursuit of wealth, exemplified in literary form by Defoe; hard work, typically in trade, sobriety, discipline, method, honesty, with the reward a move up the social scale. The exaltation of England, exemplified by Fielding and Brooke in their novels; the Englishman who was worth ten Frenchmen in a fight, for example. The refinement of manners, advocated first by Addison and Steele, and then, more imaginatively, by Richardson, in whose hands manners, morality, and sensibility become the same thing. Piety and morality in religion, recommended by all shades of Christianity, from Bishop Butler to Isaac Watts. Materialism and skepticism in philosophy, as exemplified by Locke. All of these served the dual purpose of combating enthusiasm and of promoting unanimity. The word Enlightenment is not quite so applicable to the English eighteenth century as to the French, and Erasmus himself does not seem so appropriate a figurehead. But in fact these qualities, with the exception of patriotism, are all Erasmian qualities. The influence of Erasmus had penetrated deep into various forms of moderate English culture at the time of the Reformation, and after the Calvinist and Faustian eruptions of the seventeenth century, it reemerged.

This consensus was not established immediately, of course. In the government, Clarendon, until he was driven out in 1667, was pursuing a policy of repression. And in literature, Restoration comedy expresses a similar partisan triumphing over the defeated Puritans, the London citizens, by Cavalier courtiers. Something similar in tone, an aggressive insolence, can still be found in Pope and Swift, under the last of the Stuarts. It was not until the Hanoverian line was established on the throne that the Dissenters became really loyal to the crown, and we can perhaps date from then also the real hegemony of the idea of balance, of the Erasmian temperament. The Monmouth rebellion of 1685 was the last flicker of the old popular radicalism, the last armed revolt of the common people, as Christopher Hill calls it. He calls Monmouth the last Sleeping Hero in English history.

It is an interesting coincidence for literary history that that rebellion and the earlier conspiracy, which provoked Dryden's establishment poem, "Absalom and Achitophel," was also the one political event which links Defoe with Richardson and both to seventeenth-century Puritanism. Defoe, and his fellow students from the Dissenting Academy at Newington Green, fought for Monmouth at Sedgemoor — some of them died there. (Hazlitt and his friends at the Dissenting Academy at Hackney, at the other end of our period, gave a breakfast for Tom Paine, and sang the *Marseil-*

laise. In between, the academies' interest in politics was less activist.) And Richardson's father fought for Monmouth too, which is almost the only way in which politics touches Richardson's life. In both authors' lives the collapse of the rebellion marked the end of all interest in revolution.

For a striking thing about the novels of both men is the completeness with which divisive politics are absent, even from Defoe's, who had been a controversial pamphleteer. What both men's imaginative works express are ideas which unite the nation. Though Richardson's novels are partisanly Puritan, they show the Puritan party overcoming the Establishment party by sheer passive merit and loveliness — Pamela and Clarissa vanquishing Mr. B. and Lovelace by making them love and value their Puritanism. In *Pamela*, Part II, she and Mr. B. refuse a title on the grounds that it would involve them in party politics, in dirty dealing, in the sordid and divisive intrigues of the great world of Westminster. Their perfect life is essentially quietist and pastoral. They move outside their house only to perform acts of charity.

But Richardson's novels *are* Puritan. The antagonists in *Pamela* and *Clarissa* clearly belong to opposite classes, indeed to the opposite halves of England, and the writer's sympathies are all with the Puritan heroines and all against the Establishment rakes. The earnest sensibility of those heroines, their capacity for greater seriousness and intensity and purity than other people, is a secularized version of Puritan piety. Fielding's novels, moreover, are Establishmentarian, and answer Richardson's dialectically. *Tom Jones* answers *Clarissa* as much as, though better than, *Joseph Andrews* answers *Pamela*. In Fielding's novels, earnestness and seriousness are the marks of hypocrisy, to be associated with Blifil. Tom's qualities, of thoughtless good nature, of the right animal instincts, are closer to Lovelace than to Clarissa. And one interesting thing in this dialectic is that the Puritan has the first word; the Establishment answers — usually with satire. Defoe's *Robinson Crusoe* is answered — on several levels — by Swift's *Gulliver's Travels*. In the case of Fielding, the Puritan may be said to have the last word too, for, as Ian Watt points out, *Amelia* is something of a capitulation to Richardsonian sensibility.

Perhaps one can say, very roughly, that beneath the surface of, or

within, the eighteenth-century consensus, a dialectic was pursued
in which the Puritan party had the initiative in the moralization of
the stage; in the novel; in science; in political radicalism; and in the
refinement of manners — though of course Addison and Steele belong to the Establishment more than to the Puritans. But the
Establishment took the initiative in promoting skepticism about
religion; in neo-classic poetry; in classical scholarship; in the Ital-
ianate fine arts; and in satire. If these lists do not deceive us, we
must again say that the initiative lay more with the Puritans. One
neat example of their power is the career of a minor novelist, Eliza
Haywood. Her short light novels, *Lasselia* (1724), and *The Unequal Conflict* (1725), are cavalier in sensibility, the heroine taking
a light attitude toward her own chastity. "Such a ruin (as by the
nicely virtuous the sacrifice she made him of her honour could be
called no other) was too pleasing to permit her to repent it." But
in 1751 her *History of Miss Betsy Thoughtless* is a Puritan work
in four volumes, and the heroine suffers seriously as a punishment
for being flighty. "The honour of a young maid like you, is a flower
of so tender and delicate a nature, that the least breath of scandal
withers and destroys it." And the case of Sterne surely suggests that
the Establishment sensibility could only triumph over the Puritan
by corrupting it from within, by in some treacherous sense accepting it. The noisier satire of Fielding and Smollett betrays their feeling on the defensive and on the retreat.

But by the last quarter of the eighteenth century, the memory of
revolution's horrors was dim, and the propaganda had worn thin
that exalted the advantages of unanimity, of common sense, and of
balance. Literature was in the Age of Sensibility, described by
Northrop Frye, the age of Ossian and Chatterton, of Smart and
Collins and Blake. In politics the prospect of violent change
evoked hope rather than fear. Puritan radical ideas woke to life
again. Major Cartwright demanded literal manhood suffrage, equal
electoral districts, the payment of M.P.s. He borrowed from James
Burgh, who taught at the Dissenting School at Newington Green,
the idea of a national association or convention, which would act
when Parliament failed to do so. In 1779 Dr. Jebb, another Dissenter, demanded a convention composed of delegates from standing committees in all the counties, whose decisions would become

law, as soon as approved by the Lords and the King. The Society for Constitutional Information was formed in 1780. In 1789 Dr. Price preached his Discourse on the Revolution in France, warning the rulers of Europe to change their ways, and proclaiming the people's right to resist. These were days of intense excitement, under the impulse of which Paine and Blake, Godwin and Mary Wollstonecraft recaptured the spirit of the earlier revolution. The temperamental ideal of the eighteenth-century consensus was shattered.

Men were again compelled to declare themselves for or against revolution. The radical strain in their temperaments was intensified — as before and after it was muffled. And a man's temperamental type, which in the age of consensus seemed politically just a donnée, about which nothing could be done, for which no one could be blamed, from which everything starts, now became of crucial importance. In some cases (radicals like Paine) the power of the temperament — its effectiveness in the world — increased immensely. In others (Erasmians like Godwin) the temperament changed; he tells us for instance that he talked much more, and much more frankly, during these years. "But, in pursuing this scheme of practice, I was acting a part somewhat foreign to my constitution. I was by nature more a speculative than an active character, more inclined to reason within myself upon what I heard and saw, than to declaim concerning it. I loved to sit by unobserved, and to meditate upon the panorama before me . . ." Clearly, by the time of writing he had changed back again. But *then*, briefly, he was a different man. Then, as now, men were called on to consider who they were, and how to change; how to become, in the world of politics, Calvinist radicals; in the world of literature, Faustians.

Even then, individual writers held by the old ideal, and taught the old lessons with undiminished vigor. *Sense and Sensibility* (1811) is a novel about choice of temperament, its main alternatives are those of our argument, and its teaching is wholeheartedly Erasmian. A Romantic Byron-figure, Willoughby, is given every advantage of glamour over the very Erasmian Edward Ferrars, only to be revealed as inferior in every important way. And as we participate in the development of the girls' feelings about the two men, we see the moral and psychological consequences of *their* choices of temperament worked out. Jane Austen insists that Marianne *makes* herself into a heroine of sensibility, a Faustian figure all fire, impatience, and superiority; and in Willoughby's own life, one of rebellions against all restraint, and in Marianne's unhappy passion for him, the novel shows the deplorable consequences of that self-making, that choice. In *Northanger Abbey* (1818) a Romantic literary form, the Gothic novel, is considered, and condemned insofar as it gets taken seriously — insofar as it influences the heroine's attitude to life. "Remember the country and the age in which we live. Remember that we are English: that we are Christians. Consult your own understanding, your own sense of the probable, your own observation of what is passing around you . . . Dearest Miss Morland, what ideas have you been admitting?" As pastimes, Henry Tilney says, as holidays from the serious eighteenth-century meanings, such romances are delightful. But as serious myths of the spiritual life — once Montoni becomes Byron, once the Faustian temperament becomes incarnate in serious, passionate Romanticism — they cannot be tolerated. And in fact they never did win as many serious readers and writers in England as in nineteenth- and twentieth-century America. Catherine reflects on how far she had been led astray, how corrupted her sensibility had become, in these terms.

But in the central part of England there was surely some security for the existence even of a wife not beloved, in the laws of the land, and the manners of the age. Murder was not tolerated, servants were not slaves, and neither poison nor sleeping-potions to be procured, like rhubarb, from every druggist. Among the Alps and Pyrenees, perhaps, there were no mixed characters. There, such as were not as spotless as an angel, might have the dispositions of a fiend. But in England it was not so: among the English, she believed, in their hearts and habits, there was a general though unequal mixture of good and bad.

The vocabulary, of centrality, of mixedness, of probability, of Englishness, of England's modern safeguards, sums up the eighteenth-century compromise. But vigorous though Jane Austen was as an artist, she worked on two-inch pieces of ivory. Ideologically, even imaginatively, she could not command the tides of change. The eighteenth-century pattern was broken forever.

But the future did not lie with radicals, either. The London radicals were quickly dispersed and silenced, and while Hazlitt and Shelley kept something of their message alive, it did not amount to much of a force, either in individual works of imagination, or in impact on other people. The writers who were forceful were those who regretted the Revolution and the fervor of the nineties, like Wordsworth and Scott. In them, and even more in Carlyle, was born Victorianism.

Nineteenth-Century Consensus and Its Antithesis

Carlyle conducted his personal crisis and self-salvation (on behalf of his readers) in terms of revolution. He was providing a model for a new consensus, and he dignified it by the not unprecedented tactic of making it seem a continuation of the revolutions it displaced.

In *On Heroes, Hero-Worship, and the Heroic in History*, he talks about the rapid decay of Luther's heritage in Germany, the rapid loss of all that that great revolutionary had achieved, and then:

But in our Island there arose a Puritanism which even got itself established as a Presbyterianism and National Church among the Scotch; which came forth as a real business of the heart; and has produced in the world very notable fruit.

Among this fruit he counts everything serious in British culture between then and his own times; talking of civil wars in Britain, he says,

But that war of the Puritans has a significance which belongs to no one of the others. Trusting to your candour. . . . I will call it a section once more of that great universal war which alone makes-up the true History of the World, — the war of Belief against Unbelief! The struggle of men intent on the real essence of things, against men intent on the semblance and forms of things.

Laud and the king were such form-worshippers. "Charles Second and his Rochesters" were poor stuff, and so was the unserious age they ushered in. Carlyle caricatured that age as one of superficiality, by which he meant much of what we mean by consensus, but distorted so that his readers could despise it with no uncomfortable feelings of self-criticism.

This view of Cromwell seems to me the not unnatural product of a century like the 18th. As we said of the Valet, so of the Sceptic; he does not know a Hero when he sees him!

Carlyle of course staked everything on being able, and his culture's being able, to know a Hero when it saw one; and he particularly admired Cromwell. He clearly saw himself as similar.

Poor Cromwell, — great Cromwell! The inarticulate Prophet; Prophet who could not *speak*. Rude, confused, struggling to utter himself, with his savage depth, with his wild sincerity; and he looked so strange, among the elegant Euphemisms, dainty little Falklands, didactic Chillingworths, diplomatic Clarendons! Consider him. An outer hull of chaotic confusion, visions of the Devil, nervous dreams, almost semimadness; and yet such a clear determinate man's-energy working in the heart of that.

He describes him as a Faustian hero; defines him by his lack of all Erasmian qualities; and his own style is an incessant description of himself as the same. Carlyle thought his age needed a Faustian hero, and he was willing to play the part himself.

The revolution against which his own age was reacting he managed to assimilate to Cromwell's, and yet to make the reaction seem like a continuation by peaceful means.

Precisely a century and year after this of Puritanism had got itself hushed up into decent composure, and its results made smooth, in 1688, there broke-out a far deeper explosion, much more difficult to hush-up, known to all mortals, and like to be long known, by the name of French Revolution. It is properly the third and final act of Protestantism; the explosive confused return of mankind to Reality and Fact, now that they were perishing of Semblance and Sham.

The Victorian consensus was thus enabled to see itself as radically unlike preceding consensuses, because it set itself in antithesis to the Augustan age, and affiliated itself to the great revolutions in the name of Reality. Like the seventeenth-century Puritans, it recognized its Hero, Cromwell/Carlyle. But Protestant revolution, as interpreted by Carlyle, turned out to mean above all duty and work and obedience to great men, and individual moral strenuousness;

so there was nothing politically dangerous about it; nor about foreign revolutions that were really confused final acts of Protestantism. The consensus could safely invoke these heroic precedents. And other writers helped to complete the picture. Ivanhoe had included a rousing song against the Norman Yoke, and the next sixty years, up to 1880, were, as Christopher Hill points out, the hey-day of Saxon democracy as a middle-class decorative motif — Tennyson's *Harold*, Bulwer-Lytton's *Harold*, Kingsley's *Hereward the Wake*. In 1830 appeared the first edition of *Pilgrim's Progress* for literary readers, with a long introduction by Southey, acclaiming Bunyan as a "natural" genius.

The Victorian "Puritans," and particularly Carlyle, minimized the culturally dangerous character of the seventeenth-century revolution. He also minimized the dialectic struggle within the eighteenth-century consensus, and identified that consensus with one of the dialectic's two forces, that Establishment skepticism which was in fact only the antithesis. He needed to do this in order to construct his model for a consensus with glamour in his own day. He constructed for himself a temperament which was first Faustian radical, and later Faustian conservative. And it is just insofar as the Victorian mind at large took over from him the Faustian posture and gestures that it is unattractive to us today. (All those Mosaic beards and Ahaban scars, storm-tossed locks and cloud-wreathed brows, in the group portraits of provincial aldermen.) George Eliot, for instance, is attractive just because she avoided that posture.

But that Faustianism or daimonism, however neutralized by being combined with its contraries, remained dangerous to the nineteenth-century consensus, an active virus in its bloodstream, its antithesis. Carlyle himself, the "British Fichte," was the inspirer of revolutionary movements of national liberation, while the personal example of Byron and the fictional exempla of the Sturm und Drang Goethe sounded like clarion calls all down the nineteenth century.

Byron was all Europe's great poet of national revolt. His championship of the Carbonari inspired Mazzini; his death at Missolonghi aroused the French romantic poets to political action — Châteaubriand, Lamartine, de Vigny, Hugo. In Poland Mickiewicz wrote his "Konrad Wallenrod" in imitation of Byron, and that poem was a great symbol for the insurrection of 1830–31. In the 1840's he formed a Polish legion, like Byron's Greek army. In Germany Byron was a hero to Heine and Lenau, in Russia to Pushkin and Lermontov.

The case of Goethe as an inspirer to revolution is very ironic, because he was so long so eager to repudiate *Werther* and to modify *Faust*. But for many writers — and men of action — Goethe continued to be the creator of those figures of rebellion, those ideals of self-liberation. Napoleon himself is said to have read and reread *Werther* seven times, from the days of his earliest youth, when he wrote similar stories himself, to the days of his final exile, on Saint Helena. And Wertherian ideas were kept alive in nineteenth-century Europe by Romantic literature, particularly by novels. *René, Obermann, Lélia, Adolphe, Le Peintre de Salzbourg* (by Charles Nodier), all were epigoni of *Werther*. Mme de Stael sent Goethe a copy of *Delphine* with the message, "*La lecture de* Werther *a fait époque dans ma vie comme un événement personnel.*" George Sand's *Lélia*, which has a preface discussing *Werther*'s influence, is also about a passionate *woman*'s revolt against society, and in *Adolphe* again Werther's part is played by a woman. This is no doubt because the freedom the novel images is more personal than political, though still ideological.

Faust had more impact on men writers. Byron, Shelley, and Scott all urged Coleridge to make an English translation of Part I, but he refused for conservative reasons; he declared it an immoral and pagan work. Indeed, he considered writing an Anti-Faust, around the figure of Michael Scott, to counteract its influence. (*Werther* too was unpopular in conservative England; *The Anti-Jacobin Review* attacked it as yet another portent of the French Revolution, and no English writer of talent seemed able to learn from it what so many French writers had.) But Shelley was profoundly impressed and excited by *Faust*; and Monk Lewis read his translation of it to Byron just before the latter wrote *Manfred*, which obviously owes much to it.

Reciprocally, Goethe was influenced by Byron in his later years, and influenced in the same direction, toward making more heroic, or daimonic, demands on life, toward acting out the Faustian antithesis to the Erasmian consensus. Byron appears in *Faust*, Part II, as Euphorion, the son of Faust by Helena. Part II was begun in 1824, the year Byron died in Greece, and in the play the death of Euphorion is what awakens Faust from his dream of the classical past, what separates him from Helena, and what sends him on to his destiny of more strenuous and tragically heroic achievements. The illusion of classical serenity has gone, the Weimar illusion, and with it Faust/Goethe's stable enjoyment of a static life.

Byron's last letter to Goethe, written just before he sailed for Greece, reached him during his love affair with Ulrike von Leventzow. The first part of the great *Trilogie der Leidenschaft*, inspired by that affair, is entitled "To the Shade of Werther," but was in fact inspired by Byron. The biographies suggest that Byron inspired in fact the passionateness with which Goethe pursued this last great love affair. He once again demanded, under the inspiration of that example, perfect fulfillment from life, demanded the love of a nineteen-year-old girl for a seventy-four-year-old man.

And on March 11, 1826, Goethe began to talk with Eckermann about daimonism. He associated Byron with Napoleon, Cagliostro, and Karl August under this heading. Such men cut across the moral order of the universe; they form a warp to the moral woof of life; to use *our* terms, they enact the antithesis. But whereas political men (Frederick the Great and Peter the Great are other examples) express this power in their personalities, poets express it in their work. Thus Goethe himself could "escape" daimonism by "taking refuge in a symbol." But Byron was an exception to this rule. He had the power in his personality, too.

This idea of the daimonic was taken up by Nietzsche in *The Birth of Tragedy*. He actually quotes Goethe's remarks, from the *Conversations with Eckermann*, in defining his own concept.* And the daimonic Faust story was taken up again and again in nineteenth-century Germany, most often to be developed to a tragic conclusion. Goethe himself — and several other Sturm und Drang writers attempted the theme — was at work on the subject between 1775 and 1832; and since the latter date, when Part II was published, there have been over fifty more poems and plays, culmi-

* So that what Nietzsche has stood for in German culture is a result of this same antithesis to the nineteenth-century consensus.

nating in Thomas Mann's novel in 1947. Especially in Germany, then, the Faustian subject, the daimonic theme, remained dangerous even through a period of consensus. It became entwined in the national consciousness with the national destiny.

Mann said quite seriously in one of his wartime essays that Germany had made a pact with the Devil, and Jung, also in an essay of 1945, described Faust as the symbol of a hysterical split in the German soul, and gave Wagner and Nietzsche as real-life examples. Other people made the same connections. Mann said, "Hitler embodies to the letter the unpleasant side of Wagner, though only that much"; and his Faust novel is the culmination of a long tendency in his thinking to sum up all of German history in terms of that myth. He sometimes associated Hitler with Luther, for instance, who had also separated Germany from the European community, and taught her to separate the feeling of nationalism from the idea of political freedom; who had created the German language at the expense of German political self-respect. On occasion, Dürer too is made to stand for the same kind of German-ness — to which, in the novel, Mann opposes Erasmus and Riemenschneider. As we have said, he identifies himself with Erasmus, via the Zeitblom figure.

Sometimes he puts Luther, Nietzsche, and Hitler all together; ". . . the tumultuous and bloody role of Lutheranism is now being recreated by nationalism, with its anti-rational and inhumane tendencies, its obsession with blood and tragedy." *Deutsche Hörer*, the radio addresses of 1940–1945, from London and New York, were highly emotional and unironical. He repeated as a motif Voltaire's slogan, "*Écrasez l' infâme*"; we see Mann for once acting out the liberal's most active role in politics; a thing normally very difficult for him to do. "Churchill spoke with polish and Stalin crudely; neither, I felt, was altogether wrong. This is generally my reaction, and there is only one instance in my life — and this is significant — when I have not had it. Hitler had the great merit of producing a simplification of the emotions."

An age of consensus brings special temptations to try Faustianism, especially to the ironic artist, the Erasmian, who always feels threatened by sterility. In some sense, this seems to have been true of German literature as a whole during the century after Goethe's death. Especially as his greatness became established, such writers as Keller and Stifter seem to have been circumscribed and hamstrung by that great example. An ambitious writer, contemplating them as they contemplated Goethe (the Goethe of Weimar), might well feel compelled to attempt some new temperamental contract, in order to escape the limitations of rational consciousness and two-dimensionality. For to escape that Goethe was to escape the destiny he had assigned Germans, of greatness through culture and the pen, rather than through passion and the sword. Mann is a vivid case of the artist who did make that attempt and repented.

He had an essentially Erasmian endowment, in which he finally came to establish his identity, but he was born into a nation and a vocation where the only option of vitality seemed to be purchasable only by making the Faustian bargain. Marx had shown how, in another vocation of the intellectual life, making the Calvinist contract could lead one out of the Erasmian shallows. But even in that vocation the Faustian style was the one followed by Ferdinand Lassalle, who was the only nineteenth-century revolutionary to challenge Marx for the leadership of international communism, and who did so by sheer power of personality. Always engaged in amorous adventures, blatantly extravagant in his style of life and dandified in his manner, Lassalle dominated his proletarian followers by "personality" in the most Byronic sense. He was essentially a figure of excess. Exuberant enthusiasm, flamboyance, aggressive egotism, these were his characteristics. He offers a vivid contrast of temperament with Marx's systematic thought, self-dedication, quietness of life, rigidity of organization, in every way. It is an emblematic fact that he should have fallen mortally wounded in a duel with the fiancé of a girl he had seduced, in 1864.

Mann began by trying to make himself an intellectual temperament comparable with Lassalle's personality. He espoused irrationalism, intoxication, madness, in the works of Schopenhauer, Nietzsche, Wagner. And in *Betrachtungen* he still declared that the contradictions of European culture were not to be worked out rationally, but to be fought out as a tragedy inside the German soul, with its ethos of the cross, the tomb, and death. Even after he had declared against Nazism, and left Germany, he still wrote about

Hitler as an artist, in an essay entitled "A Brother." And yet all the time he knew himself to be profoundly Erasmian by temperament. "I sensed early and felt deeply what was coming. I suffered from it and opposed the conscienceless, spreading mischief; I incurred, as I expected, the reproach that I incline to sterile rationalism." His positions were in defiance of the core of his temperament, and in parallel with the amoralism of the Nazis. It is no wonder that *Doctor Faustus* is so personal a book. ("How much *Faustus* contains of the atmosphere of my life! A radical confession, at bottom.") When Leverkuhn confesses, at the end, he speaks for Germany, but he also speaks for Mann.

> "Know then," said he, at the table, "ye good and godly folk" (he said "god and goodly"), "with your modest sins and resting in Goodes godness, for I have suppressed it so long in me but will no longer hide it, that already since my twenty-first year I am wedded to Satan and with due knowing of peril, out of well-considered courage, pride, and presumption because I would win glory in this world, I made with him a bond and vow, so that all which during the term of four-and-twenty years I brought forth, and which mankind justly regarded with mistrust, is only with his help come to pass and is the divel's work, infused by the angel of death . . .
>
> — *Doctor Faustus*, p. 497

But with this example we are entering upon the subject matter of the next chapter, the nonpolitical Faustian bargain. This is combined with the political theme in the novel — not altogether successfully. We must return to the idea of an age of consensus.

What of our own such age, the consensus of the fifties? Its prominent aspects were the proliferating corporations, universities, and churches, all seeming destined to go on expanding and imposing themselves forever, all of them crudely solid and dully smooth. The Ph.D. programs expanded endlessly and there was no questioning the law that if you wanted to teach, or if you wanted the life of the mind, you had to submit to their requirements. The institutions were immutable. In literary terms its prominent features were the poetry of writers between Frost and Wilbur and Lowell, and the Ivy League novels of Barth and Nabokov, and so on. That was the America I accepted and flourished in.

Some striking cases of this feeling of immutability occur even in the scholarly books I have consulted in writing this chapter, books that seem to themselves to be stating merely the objective truth. For instance, in Jacob Sloan's introduction to his translation of I. B. Singer's *Satan in Goray*, a novel about a passage of political, sexual, and religious revolution in seventeenth-century Poland. (A real-life episode, caused by the teachings of Sabbatai Zevi.) Singer himself is clearly on the side of the rabbi of the community, who is driven out of Goray by the new movement; and Sloan draws an explicit parallel with his own times, commenting on the end of the story, in which misery, sin, and tragic disappointment accumulate in the town as a direct result of listening to the false prophets. "Like the people of Goray, we too have found that the end cannot be forced, ends and means are inseparable, there are no simple and complete solutions to the tragic complications of being fallible human beings in an incomprehensible universe." Revolution, in other words, is always wrong. That was written in 1955. And Norman Cohn's *Pursuit of the Millennium*, published two years later, is a history of religious revolutionary movements, like Tabor, confidently implying condemnation of what it describes. It emphasizes overwhelmingly the grotesque and fearful aspects of those movements; one of which was, since these were Christian movements, the murder of Jews. But the author's attitude derives less, one guesses, from racial or credal identification than from the rabbinical tradition within Judaism, with its conservative-moralist-rationalist temperament. These are men of established institutions, men of the city.

That tradition could not receive such blandly confident expression nowadays, only ten years later. It belongs essentially to an age of consensus, and not to an age of revolution. The rabbinical tradition has been overthrown — in part by wild Cabbalists like Mailer and Fiedler, who are rather like the cabbalists in Singer's novel — and the world lives in expectation of its end, as Goray did. There is no reason — even for Erasmians — to regret that past consensus, now that its sordid aspects are so prominent to us. But there is every reason — for Erasmians — to work toward the next consensus, to make it less sordid.

8 — AN ALTERNATIVE FOR INTELLECTUALS

There is no better means of intensifying the treasured feeling of individuality than the possession of a secret which the individual is pledged to guard. The very beginnings of societal structures reveal the craving for secret organizations. When no valid secrets really exist, mysteries are invented or contrived to which privileged initiates are admitted. Such was the case with the Rosicrucians and many other societies. Among these pseudo-secrets there are — ironically — real secrets of which the initiates are entirely unaware — as, for example, in those societies which borrowed their "secret" primarily from the alchemical tradition.*

The Cultural Function of the Occult

But there is another tradition of creative heresy in Western thought, unlike that which leads to revolutions, a tradition which eludes, or tries to, the cyclical alternation of ages just discussed; which saves society, or tries to, from the bitter dissensions of orthodox politics; and which saves art and thought from creative impotence, though at a price traditionally symbolized by the Faustian bargain.

So, courteous and beloved brothers and sisters, have I borne me, and let nigromantia, carmina, incantantio, veneficium, and what names so ever be all my sin and striving. And I soon came to the speech of that one, the make-bate, the losel, in the Italian room, have held much parley with him, and he had much to tell of the quality, fundament, and substance of hell. Sold me time, too, four and twenty years,

* C. G. Jung, *Memories, Dreams, Reflections*, tr. Jaffe, New York, 1965, p. 342.

boundless to the eye, and promised too great things and much fire under the cauldron, to the end that notwithstanding I should be capable of the work although it were too hard and my head too shrewd and mocking thereto.

— *Doctor Faustus*, p. 500

This is the tradition of secret knowledge, and the secret society. Some examples, among knowledge systems, are astrology and alchemy, magic and mysticism; and among societies that transmit that knowledge, the Renaissance neo-Platonic academies, the Rosicrucians, the Theosophists, the Freemasons. These are the social forms by which the Faustian temperament has been fostered and transmitted, among minds in rebellion (rather than revolution) against the city, against the public forms of life and modes of thought; wanting something different for themselves rather than for all the world, and so potentially conservative as well as radical.

Faustians are usually men of the city, most often of the great wicked metropoles. At the same time, they are rebels against the limits imposed on them by the status of being just citizens. They are self-aggrandizers, rebels against the diminishment imposed by growing up, by the loss of the pleasure principle in exchange for the reality principle. Their cultural nurture must be a stream of ideas, images, social forms, behavioral modes, which provoke and intensify that rebellion. There are several such streams in Western culture — adventure stories form one of them — but for intellectuals the most important, at least in certain periods, seems to be the occult.

We are, then, interested in this tradition mainly because of the opportunity it provides for men to make the Faustian bargain for forbidden powers. That has always been only an opportunity, only one option among many opened up by such study; for instance, the gnostic and neo-Platonic kinds of occult knowledge have often been notably "civilized," city-oriented, anti-Faustian in tendency, promoting the *refinement* of experience, intellectually and morally, the etherialization of meanings, not their incorporation. (Though, as we shall see, gnosticism can remain Faustian in a different sense of the word.) And the whole tradition could of course be studied under other aspects; as a chapter in the history of ideas, for instance; or as an achievement of intellectual ingenuity. It was a manifold phenomenon. Indeed, there is a paradox in looking at it as we shall. Insofar as knowledge of the occult forms a tradition and insofar as it is transmitted in societies, it must be less appropriate to the diabolic contract, which is a rebellion against social contracts. But neither this "tradition" nor these "societies" have quite the normal meanings of the words. The tradition of alchemy, for instance, is hectically disorganized; it is very unlike its public equivalent, the science of chemistry. Each new operator can decide how much of previous work he wants to accept, and what construction to put upon it, so enigmatic is everything concerned. All he takes over is the form, the artistic form, of certain experiments, which are really quests, like the quest for the philosophers' stone. And along with the self-expressive, aesthetic forms goes an equally aesthetic, or poetic, language. The *Dictionnaire Mytho-Hermetique* of A. J. Pernety, first published in 1758, lists six hundred names for the *Lapis Philosophorum*, and its materials, moving alphabetically from Absemir to Zumelazuli. One man, Basil Valentine, or the book published over his name in 1599, itself used sixty different hieroglyphs to represent gold. Such books used in addition acrostics and anagrams and secret alphabets and cyphers. Half of the point of alchemical directions was to keep the secrets of the art secret; the books are full of exhortations not to let the profane enter the mystery; as a science, naturally, it stagnated. The elaborate directions for experiments are half spiritual or allegorical, and the other half is a ritual that could not by itself produce the results promised. Alchemical books were written out and painted in longhand even after printing was well established; partly because they needed colors to represent their emblems, but partly because they were private and not public, not two-dimensional, not linear. The importance of emblems in itself illustrates the same thing, that this is anti-Gutenberg science, that Giordano Bruno hated Ramus, that this is *magical* knowledge.

And secret societies never have the solidity and compelling power of ordinary ones, because it is of their essence that they are not organs of the Great Society. There is something essentially willful and whimsical about them. They may on occasion terrify their members into obedience, but it is always by a nightmarish and unreal fear. And they may, alternatively, become so rational and pru-

The twelve masters of alchemy. Notice particularly Hermes, the original psychopomp, and Jung's prime "symbol of transcendence"; a symbol that does not integrate the initiate with any doctrine or group consciousness, Jung explains, but liberates him from all too-fixed patterns of existence. Hermes is therefore the supreme emblem of the Gnostic Faustian. The shaky drawing and shady character of the face (in most representations much more marked than here) is typical of Gnostic symbolic art, as we see in contemporary advertisements for Swamis and Maharishis. (Courtesy of Harvard University Library.)

dential that they cease to be secret in any significant sense, like the Freemasons; and then they cease to be an arena for the Faustian bargain.

But "unreal" or "real" — and just because of the blurring together of the two alternatives — the secret society and the occult tradition have provided many scenarios for Western intellectuals to play Faust in. The role has sometimes been defined according to the Marlowe-Byron-Mann reading of the story, which makes Faust conjure up Satan, and sell his soul once for all to radical evil. More often it has been defined according to the Goethean reading, which makes Faust bargain with spirits of the air, figures like Shakespeare's Ariel, who are mischievous and dangerous, but not Satanic. The second reading, obviously, offers more scope for modulations of tone. Only a self-tragedian could see himself in the first role. But both definitions of Faust have led to his making a psychic contract which resulted in major works of mind.

I shall say something about the three great periods of the occult in the West, its Alexandrian origins, its Renaissance rebirth, and its study by writers in English from 1900 on. I want to describe some of the personalities fostered by the tradition, particularly Bruno in the Renaissance, Goethe again, and Yeats in the modern period. And then I want to consider a somewhat different version of the tradition, a use of occult knowledge which gives a somewhat different meaning to the title of this chapter, arousing even the connotations of escapism that lie couched in "alternative." This mode of thought I associate with a line of men that runs from Marsilio Ficino to Northrop Frye; it is not Faustian as I have so far used the term, but it does belong, in a safe way, to the tradition of secret (esoteric) knowledge, and secret (graduate-school seminar) societies. Goethe's *Faust II* will provide a link between the two.

These knowledges and institutions are often hated by both the rulers and the ruled among whom they exist, but usually more by Puritans than by the Establishment. It has been suggested that the sixteenth-century introduction of magic into Christianity by the Neo-Platonists and Hermeticists may have helped provoke the Protestant schism. Certainly the English Puritans were always severe on alchemists and astrologers. John Dee was arrested and tried for treason under Queen Mary like other Protestants, and so like them was named in Foxe's *Book of Martyrs;* but in all editions after 1555, after his magical activities became known, his name was suppressed. They wanted no magicians among their Protestant heroes.

Whereas among the Establishment, certain groups have often dabbled in the occult, and one in particular is the intellectuals. Goethe is one example whom we have already discussed. Shakespeare, according to Frances Yates, is presenting Giordano Bruno as Berowne in *Love's Labour Lost,* and himself as a magus in *The Tempest.* (Prospero, whose name means Faustus, may be an answer to Marlowe's interpretation of Faust as a Satanist — he may also be a partial portrait of John Dee.) Newton left alchemical and numerological manuscripts amounting to 650,000 words, and his successor in the chair of mathematics at Cambridge, William Whiston, was involved in similar speculations and held chiliastic conversations with the English Philadelphians. Leibnitz studied Bruno and the Rosicrucians, perhaps was a Rosicrucian himself.

In some of such cases, there is a clear connection between the work done in the occult, and the pursuit of personal power, the Faustian bargain. In other cases, that connection, if it exists at all, is not clear. The acquisition of power is an ultimate aim, after all, of all knowledge study, and sometimes that aim, even in the study of the occult, is nothing but ultimate. My proposition is that the occult tradition has been used for the pursuit of personal power as an immediate aim, and used often enough to make us say that that use has been one of its cultural functions.

In our own day, because of the crisis of faith in public values, there is a revival of interest in the occult. The literary effect of its study is seen in the genre of science fiction, where certain books, like Heinlein's *Stranger in a Strange Land,* are an immense popular success, but also in the work of serious writers. Mailer is clearly something of an alchemist and a magician, offering an explanation of scientific and medical phenomena like cancer which runs counter to the methods of orthodox science, and claiming powers to know things and to affect people which defy rational explanation. John Fowles's novel *The Magus* is strikingly like *Wilhelm Meister,* because he is as interested as Goethe was in secret knowledges and societies. Both authors are fascinated by the idea of a secret society which exerts power over the whole life and consciousness of a young man, and educates him for life, by means of brutally bewildering him. And in Doris Lessing's last novel, *The Four-Gated City*, the central character acquires secret knowledge, and realizes that she has not been able, until she acquired it, to understand her own experience. She finds it in the library of a writer of science fiction, who uses it to give him ideas for his stories.

There were books on Rosicrucianism and the old alchemists; Buddhist books and the dozen or so varieties of Yoga; here were Zoroastrianism and esoteric Christianity; tracts on the I Ching; Zen, witchcraft, magic, astrology and vampirism; scholarly treatises on Sufism; the works of the Christian mystics. Here, in short, was a kind of potted library representing everything rejected by official culture and scholarship.

It may seem undiscriminating to run together all the different varieties of occult knowledge, as Doris Lessing does, but that is what this chapter will do too. There are important differences between these branches of knowledge — and we need not include minor skills like geomancy and chiromancy, because from our point of view these things become interesting only where they achieve some scope of intellectual or spiritual meaning. And clearly a man can easily be interested in one of them and not in another; can disapprove one while investing large efforts and faith in the other. But they all belong together, constitute together a spiritual continent. Any man who goes far in the study of one of these subjects is *likely* to study or practice the others to some degree. The frontiers between them are not so clearly marked or firmly fixed as the frontiers between the subjects of orthodox knowledge. Moreover, they are not to be studied with the coolness of purpose, the impersonality, possible in orthodox subjects. The student is hurried on feverishly, and obscurely, toward the hidden secrets of the universe. From whatever point he enters into, descends into, this land of knowledge, he advances toward the same center. In most cases he is greedy for the most personal of rewards, the empowering of his own personality.

The mistiness and imprecision of the knowledge is part of its cultural function. It enables the adept to exercise his willpower, his personality, even in the act of knowing, to compose, to create a knowledge, in a way forbidden to the student of public truths, who must submit to the discipline of fact and method and verifiability. And the secrecy, the scientific and moral disreputableness of the tradition, makes the process of learning also a subversive activity, an act of defiance. That is why the occult is always so attractive to great egotists, whether they are men of creative imagination or men of destructive fantasies.

A Historical Scheme

There is too a historical connection between these subjects. Most of them seem to have come to life in the same time and place, in the Alexandrian era in the eastern Mediterranean; most narrowly defined, A.D. 150–250 in Greek-speaking cities of Egypt and Syria. This seems to be the period of the flourishing of alchemy, and gnosticism, and freemasonry, and the origin of the Hermes Trismegistus manuscripts, and of the pseudo-Dionysus, and so on. They all bear the mark of a common cultural origin, a sharply characterized moral-intellectual milieu, which historians symbolize as the metropolis of Alexandria, the city of technology-and-the-occult.

Alexandria was from the beginning a modern and rational city, being founded and planned deliberately by Alexander the Great, and designed on the gridiron plan by Dinocrates. It reminds us of New York again and again. It soon developed an enormous activity, and enormous wealth, as a center of trade. By the first century A.D. it had three hundred thousand citizens and a multitude of slaves. But, Greek science and rationalism ceasing to be fruitful, the Alexandrians, particularly the Jews, turned to cultivating the Nous, the intuitive faculty. They taught that one reaches ecstasy by contemplating the world as reflected in one's own Nous or Mens, which gives one spiritual mastery over the world, because it reflects the world's divine meaning. And they were prepared to pursue that end by the most eclectic means. They revered Persian magi, Chaldean astrologers, Indian gymnosophists, Egyptian priests, all that was remote and mysterious in religion. Thus Alexandria became the great city of irrationalism (in the world of intellect) as well as of rationalism (in the world of commerce). It became the source of religions and magic and alchemies, and secret societies and secret practices, for all subsequent Western history.

It has been one of the type-cities of Western civilization, contrasting with its two more approved, more recommended models, Jerusalem and Athens. Out of Alexandria came imperial Rome, Elizabethan London, the Paris of Cagliostro, the New York of Timothy Leary and Norman Mailer. Out of Jerusalem, the city of faith, came Geneva under Calvin, Leningrad under Lenin, Havana under Castro. Out of Athens, the city of culture, came Weimar, Edinburgh, modern Academia. (We note that in this alignment Edinburgh and Weimar come together, despite one being liberal and the other conservative. This categorization crosses political lines at a broad angle.) The culture of a given period is characterized by whichever of these mutually hostile cities is dominant. Perhaps Western culture as a whole is irrevocably Alexandrian, but high culture can on occasion be significantly influenced by the city of culture or the city of faith. (Western high culture has very rarely and partially been occult, even when it has been Alexandrian in other ways. Habitually it has spoken the language of Athens and Jerusalem, despite what it was actually doing.) But the present moment, in America, does not seem to be one of those occasions.

As we saw in the case of Mailer and New York, the metropoles are often imaginative homes for men of the Faustian temperament; the brawling confusion and conflicts of streets and theaters and Times Squares and Bowerys and Greenwich Villages reinforces their sense of themselves, reenacts their sense of reality. The other intellectual temperaments are not often at home there. The philosophes loved the salons of Paris and Edinburgh and other centers of civilization, but equally or more purely Erasmian is the fear of the metropoles expressed in Jane Austen's novels. The discerning characters in *Mansfield Park* and *Persuasion* regard London and Bath life as the source of all evil, a round of heartless excitements and incitements to vanity, vulgarity, and frivolousness. It is in the villages that England is held together, that society is symbolically renewed, by the rituals of responsibility. England acquires a substance by the performance of those rituals which it continually dissipates in the effervescence of London-type parties and the mudbubblings of London-type intrigues. The responsibility is primarily that of the rich families in the village for the poor; but also that of the serious for the light-minded, the clever for the stupid, the educated for the ignorant. A responsibility discharged by, say, Anne Elliot in a calm, quiet, rational, though heartfelt manner which itself gives as much dignity as the matter of the action to all concerned. Weimar itself was such a village; so was Ticknor's Boston; so is Academia today. A certain amount of quietude, privacy, and routine is necessary to the Erasmian; conditions to which the crowded streets and theaters of a metropolis are in antithesis. (The construction of the private theater in Mansfield Park brings the fevers of London falsity into the very heart of England.) Metropolitan streets are a recognizable recrudescence of the high-school playgrounds and vacant lots of adolescence, where everyone is continually challenged for his manhood by everyone else. While for the Calvinist the imaginative locus is a mansion, or a street of mansions, in a *former* metropolis, now transformed into offices and committee rooms and filled all through the night with tense discussion and decision-taking, deputation-receiving, propaganda-making. Revolutionary Moscow and Havana, Calvinist Geneva, were such loci, as their literatures bear witness. These are the three kinds of city, each belonging to a different country of the imagination.

It seems that beside the two sacred countries of Western civilization, Greece and Israel, we must set a third, Egypt; *al Khem*, the land of dark soil, the home of alchemy. Like Greece and Israel, Egypt was the home of a body of theory and practice associated with it, as much in myth as in fact. Egypt is the country mythified in the Freemasons' lore (the builders of the pyramids), in the Hermetic legends (the temples with animated statues), in Bruno's teaching (the "ancient Egyptian religion"), etc. But unlike Greece and Israel, Egypt is the land of *dark* knowledge, truths known by a process in some ways antithetical to ordinary knowing, and its myths are intellectually suspect in a way that theirs are not. Frances Yates points out that of the three Golden Ages yearned back to by Renaissance intellectuals, the Classical, the Christian, and the Hermetic, the last was different because it had never occurred. The ancient Egypt of the Hermetic manuscripts was a literary convention, mistakenly believed in as historical fact. There was a high proportion of pseudepigraphy, misattribution, misdating, trickery, and plain lies among the truths of Egypt. The documents of the Rosicrucians and the Zohar are prime examples of pseudepigraphy; the pseudo-Dionysus and Hermes Trismegistus of misattribution and misdating; Basil Valentine and the pseudo-Lullian magic books are close to plain fraud. All these offer occult wisdom, allegedly handed down by oral tradition as too powerful for public dissemination. And whenever the occult revives, trickery seems inseparable from it, as we see in the case of Madame Blavatsky, and indeed of Yeats himself, in A Vision. Its cultural function is further defined by the disturbance we all feel to find a love of half-truth, of mystification, of untruth, in the life of the mind. Not to mention the associated love of the amoral and immoral. The occult is a province of highly sophisticated minds, which must be suspect to other minds, must be called, categorically, corrupt.

After the Alexandrian period, there seems to have been less activity of first-class minds in the occult — though of course magic continued to be practiced — until the Renaissance. Gemistos Pletho, the Byzantine Platonist, urged Cosimo de Medici in 1439 to found an Athenian Academy in Florence. That same year, according to the legend Ficino told, Cosimo chose Marsilio Ficino to be its head — he being then six years old — and to be educated as a Platonist. In 1456 he began to study Greek; his great task was to be to translate Plato. But in 1462 Cosimo sent him the manuscript of Hermes Trismegistus, which had just reached Florence, and asked him to work on that first.

The work he did on Hermes profoundly affected Marsilio's Platonism, and that of the Academy he created. Indeed, by Frances Yates's account, it gave an occultist tendency to much of the Renaissance's Platonism. This was partly because of the misdating of the manuscript. Hermes was thought to have been contemporary with or earlier than Moses, to have foretold the coming of Christ, (because he spoke of God uttering himself as the Word) and to have taught Orpheus, who taught Pythagoras, who taught Plato. All these later wisdoms therefore tended to be regarded — though orthodox Christians guarded themselves against saying as much — as being corruptions of the original Hermetic teachings, or the religion of Egypt. Ficino affiliated himself to Pletho by legend, D. P.

Walker suggests, because of the Orphic hymns, to the sun and the planets, and to the pagan gods, attributed to the latter, and which must have been occultist and pagan. Ficino composed similar hymns himself, which Walker considers to have been a form of astral magic, and, in concealed form, of daimonic incantation.

From 1462 to 1614 this Hermetic neo-Platonism was an important strain in the intellectual life of Europe. Its importance was ended or undermined in 1614 by the correct redating of the manuscripts. In that year Isaac Casaubon proved by internal evidence, by a stylistic and grammatical study of the manuscript, that it originated in the centuries after Christ. Casaubon was a Genevan Protestant scholar who had come to England in 1610, and was in the process of attacking Baronius's Counter-Reformation *History of the Church* when he examined Hermes. This is a symbolic fact in several ways; that it should be a Protestant, that it should take place in England, that he was attacking Catholicism in conjunction with Hermeticism, and above all that it was a scholar who destroyed this prime resource of the occult tradition. Scholarship (just the sort Erasmus himself practiced) also doubted the magic properties of the esoteric memory-systems so valued by Renaissance magi, and was suspicious of the pseudo-Dionysus. Erasmianism was the enemy of Faustianism by virtue of its intellectual methods as well as by its moral and spiritual beliefs.

But in the sixteenth century Hermeticism was a powerful influence on thought in general in Europe, and particularly among those interested in the occult. Pico della Mirandola married it with Cabbalism, Giordano Bruno with magic and with Lullism. Almost openly, the occult was claiming parity of esteem with orthodox knowledge. Magic was taught at the University of Cracow, and at Salamanca, and Toledo. The Faustian temperament was making its bid for power as it saw the Calvinist moralism of the church seeming to weaken. The Renaissance was Faust's epoch as much as the Enlightenment was Erasmus's.

But as well as being disreputable in the eyes of scholars like Erasmus and Melanchthon, the occult was dangerous in the eyes of civic and religious authorities. Even the cosmopolitan humanism of the age was suspect, insofar as it became a rhetoric of self-intoxication and an ideology of self-intensification, which legitimized individuals in casting off the restraints and limits of their condition as Christians and Westerners and clerics and citizens, and so on. Pico della Mirandola was condemned by the Church for thirteen out of his nine hundred theses of 1486, and though he fled to France he was arrested. Giordano Bruno spent eight years in jails in Venice and Rome, and was finally burned at the stake in 1600. The beginning of the seventeenth century marked the end of the great period of the magi. In the eyes of the world, the occult became even more mysterious and disreputable and dangerous: 1614 was not only the year of Casaubon's redating of Hermes; it was also the year of *Fama Fraternitatis*, the first publication about or by the Rosicrucians. The era of secret societies had begun. There had been such societies before, of course, but as long as there were great magi, the societies counted for less. But the magi were disappearing; some were put to death literally, and many more were assassinated morally and intellectually.

The Faustbook and Marlowe introduced more Satanism into the legends about men like Dr. Faust, legends which until then had been sometimes simply magical. If devils were raised by magi, they were not always worshiped; sometimes angels rather than devils were raised, and most typically it was spirits of the air, elementals. Luther's Satan-oriented Christianity changed all that. Much that had seemed harmlessly exotic became sinister. Men were forced to choose; either they held by their church and renounced the dangerous playing with forbidden ideas; or they continued to play and knew themselves to be enemies of the church and the state.

In the metropolis of Elizabethan England there had been private groups like the School of Night, which included Raleigh. Marlowe, Chapman, Hariot the mathematician, and the earl of Derby and the wizard earl of Northumberland — the last two known to be alchemists. They studied, and speculated about, subjects from the occult, themes from neo-Platonism, and various theistical and atheistical cosmologies. In literature *Dr. Faustus* and *Tamburlaine* are the school's most important representatives. But in life Raleigh was the most vivid figure, with his fantastical dress and the haughtiness of personal bearing for which he was known and hated in London. Such a Faustian was naturally, or at least appropriately, hated by the large Puritan element in the city.

Hare Krishna dancers performing as they do every day outside Park Street Station, Boston, on the edge of the Common. The really moving thing is the Western-adolescent-pimples above those Eastern robes, and the broad accents and thick diction of those high-school lips, which we could not get on the photographs. But we got instead the almost equally heartbreaking confrontation — appeal and gesture, stare and snigger — between them and the crowd. (Photograph by Carol Green.)

Shakespeare belonged to a different literary set, centered round Essex and Southampton; but his eyes must have been on Marlowe, and for different reasons on Raleigh and Dee.

By the time of James I the secrecy around the occult was redoubled, and the secret societies proper began to flourish. The brethren of the Rosy Cross began to meet at the Apple Tree Tavern in the early years of the century. They reunited the magic, mystery, and ritual which in the Protestant churches had been separated off from, purified away from, Christianity. Mystery is a key concept. The Freemasons' articles say that, "the royal art has, like the ancient mysteries, no other aim than the knowledge of nature, where all are born, live, and regenerate themselves." They associated themselves with Nimrod, the builder of the Tower of Babel and Babylon, and with Hiram, the architect of Solomon's temple — murdered by rivals seeking to know the *secrets* of his art — and with the mysterious Knights Templar.

Along with mystery went muddle, moral as well as intellectual. The disreputableness of the occult is shown in the fact that it is still not known whether or not such a body of people as the Rosicrucians ever existed; or what it means to say they existed, that they "believed" this or "practiced" that. Johann Valentin Andreae has been cited as one of the real-life predecessors for Goethe's Faust. But no one yet knows with what kind or degree of seriousness he wanted his readers to take his account of the life and teachings of Christian Rosenkreutz. Some of those who wrote about the Rosicrucians almost certainly held the beliefs described, and some of them certainly participated in the rites, but it is not clear what their manner of participation and of belief was; how cynical, theatrical, or experimental they were being. The *Fama* itself was first published in conjunction with an overtly cynical satire, and was taken to have the character of a spoof itself. But it was not long before people began seriously to study the ideas put forward in the book, and to claim that they knew members and branches of the society. Some claimed to be Rosicrucians themselves; Robert Fludd, for instance, the English magus, whose book of emblems may have inspired the first scene of Goethe's *Faust*; also Elias Ashmole and the man who inducted him into the Society, Master Backhouse, who also taught him the alchemical secret of the philosophers' stone; and Leibnitz was elected secretary of his local branch — whether or not it ever existed.

The first mention of the Freemasons as the kind of society we know today is the election of Elias Ashmole to the Warrington lodge in 1646. In the earliest surviving manuscript of the Constitutions of Masonry the craft is traced back to Euclid — to Alexandria. The pyramids and the Tower of Babel are claimed as early masonic achievements, which makes a neat contrast with the anti-Babelism of the Taborites. Puritans have usually made Babylon the symbol of everything they hate, as we see as late as Blake. It is the metropolis, the city of this world, which must be destroyed, in order that it may be replaced by the city of faith, the city of God, the new Jerusalem. This is natural for those who draw their inspiration from the Bible, and ultimately from Israel. Those who belong to Egypt, to Alexandria and its occult scriptures, do not hate this world, or want to tear down its metropoles. They want to take them over from the inside, by infiltrating the corridors of power, by fogging those corridors with the fumes of slow-burning incense, the clang of mysterious gongs, the echoes of distant incantations, the inscription of inscrutable signs; and then (often) they impart to the minds thus made malleable with awe such secret truths as that all men are brothers and we must love one another or die. In the eighteenth century, when the high officials of the Freemasons' lodges in England were members of the aristocracy, the climate of ideas inside was notably superior to the divisive prejudices current in the outside world. Though atheists were excluded from membership in theory, many deists belonged, and after 1723 Jews could become members. The Freemasons' lodges were the homes of the enlightened part of the establishment, and in some European countries worked actively against obscurantist forces like the Catholic church. *Die Zauberflöte* is a Freemason opera; Zarastro (Zoroastro) is a magus. *Wilhelm Meister* is a Freemason novel. Goethe and Wieland belonged to the Weimar lodge, as did the duke himself.

Goethe

The Enlightenment was not, of course, a great period in the history of the occult: light is by its nature hostile to what is hidden.

But there were several eighteenth-century men of mystery who made themselves careers partly by means of dealing in the occult, and partly by means of seeming to do so. There was for instance the man who called himself Saint-Germain (?1710–?1784), and who became the friend of Louis XV and Madame de Pompadour, and was entrusted by them with secret diplomatic missions. He was understood to be a Freemason of high rank, and also to possess the elixir of youth. Clearly, he had mastered various alchemical techniques for refining oil and manufacturing cosmetics, for dyeing and tanning skins. There was Casanova (1725–1798), who was believed to be a Rosicrucian and did finally become a Mason, and indeed a Master Mason. He made use of the occult in a number of ways; he had a numerical "cabbala" (a cipher or cryptogram for foretelling the future) and carried around the Black Books of magic; and was finally imprisoned by the Inquisition as a magician. But most important in relation to Goethe was Cagliostro, the Grand Copht (1743–1795). Having been admitted to a Masonic Lodge in London in 1777, he started founding lodges of his own — pure, "Egyptian" masonry, all over Europe — in Brussels, Milan, Dantzig, Konigsberg, the Hague. He became the Grand Copht of this rite, and was worshipped by his disciples as a being of divine powers. He had healing gifts, some kind of animal magnetism. He was reputed to be able to rejuvenate others, and also to transmute metals into gold.

Because of his involvement in the affair of the Queen's Necklace, Cagliostro was credited with having brought on the French Revolution. Goethe believed this, though he believed at the same time that Cagliostro was a fraud. Goethe was so fascinated by the man that he wrote a play about him, *Der Grosse Kopht*, and on his journey to Italy he visited Cagliostro's parental home to inquire about him. Cagliostro was, like Saint-Germain and Casanova, a man of very powerful personality, who bewildered most people he met and hypnotized many. This power was such men's stock in trade, and this is what fascinated Goethe.

He was interested in all sides of the occult, and the work he put in translating Cellini's *Memoirs* was inspired in part by Cellini's description of the magical invocation in the Colosseum in 1533.

Had Goethe been alive to see her, he would have been fascinated by Madame Blavatsky, and for the same reason. Because she too, like most of these masters of the occult, was a daimonic personality, a Faust of personal relations. This is why Yeats was fascinated by her. Goethe named Cagliostro with Napoleon, Byron, and Karl August, as his representatives of the daimonic. To be a great writer, it is necessary to be Faustian — or so Goethe and Yeats, and other writers thought.

It is not without significance that Madame de Warens was an alchemist. It is true that Rousseau represents himself as having been indifferent to this side of her activities. But one must remember that in Paris he produced a work of popularization called *Institutions Chimiques*, which employed Becher's alchemical idea of man's original transparency, both as a fact and as an ideal to work toward. This work, done in collaboration with Francueil, amounted to 1,206 manuscript pages. But in any case, the very atmosphere of Madame de Warens's establishment tended toward the occult. Everyone was living "outside the law," in hopes to outwit either the laws of nature or those of society, in hopes to pull off a big coup of one kind or another; at the same time full of fine religious sentiment. That ceaselessly speculative, mildly fantastic, slightly shady atmosphere is another side to alchemy. But to return to Goethe.

He began studying alchemy in 1768, when he was nineteen, with his mother's friend, and his, Fräulein von Klettenberg. (He later used her life-story for the "Confessions of a Beautiful Soul" volume of *Wilhelm Meisters Lehrjahre*.) Together they read certainly Georg von Welling and the *Aurea Catena*, an alchemical treatise with some Cabbalistic influence; and probably also Paracelsus, Basil Valentine, van Helmont, and Starkey. (Complete certainty is difficult because Goethe later tried to cover his tracks in this area, but we know that alchemy was a major interest of his for two or three years following 1768.) Certainly by 1770 he had read the Smaragdine Table of Hermes Trismegistus, the alchemists' creed. He had also experimented himself. As he tells us in *Dichtung und Wahrheit*, he had been cured of a serious illness by alchemy, by Dr. Metz's Universal Medicine. He experimented to produce that medicine himself, and also the Liquor Silicum, the Virgin Earth, and the *Luftsalz* — a salt that would melt away on exposure to air.

Alchemy was closely related in Germany then to a certain strain of Protestant piety — an exception to the rule I suggested, of hostility between Puritans and occultists. Boehme's disciple, Gottfrid Arnold, quoted extensively from alchemists, occultists, and mystics of all sorts, in his *History of the Church and of Heretics.* This showed how the indwelling God was born witness to by the Rosicrucians, the English Philadelphians, Paracelsian alchemists, etc., as well as by the orthodox. It was a book which Goethe had read by the time of his studies at Strasburg, and he says that his attitudes to such subjects then were very like Arnold's. There is no proof that Goethe ever read Boehme himself, but every likelihood. In any case, Boehme's work, in systematizing alchemy and allying it to his religious and metaphysical schemes, was available to Goethe via other people. Fräulein von Klettenberg, for instance, described Christ as he appeared to her in a vision as *Aurum Potabile*, one of the alchemical terms for the philosophers' stone.

It is clear that the subject of *Faust* — more strictly, of the Urfaust — derived much of its significance for Goethe from his own alchemical experimenting and speculating of those years. Goethe *was* Faust, in the sense that Marlowe was. Both writers aspired to powers of personality and knowledge forbidden by society. Goethe also *was* Werther; all his self-representative characters then were figures of excess and self-destruction. Moreover, at some time during this period of his life, Goethe read Giordano Bruno, whose mind and fate present the most challenging of all images of the Renaissance magus, to which we must return. Ronald Gray says that there is more of Bruno than of Shaftesbury in Goethe's neo-Platonism. (I am relying on Professor Gray for most of these facts.)

It was Herder's arrival in Strasburg in 1770 which brought this period of Goethe's life to an end. Herder was the most impressive mind Goethe had up to then met, and he apprenticed himself to him eagerly and humbly. By the force of his personality, and also by the example of his encyclopedic learning, Herder effectively daunted Goethe's adolescent self-confidence. The older man accepted the invitation to be masterful, and caused the younger one great pain by the sarcasm he lavished on many of his enthusiasms, including his alchemy. Probably never again did Goethe spend much time on what can be called pure alchemy. But he did study Swedenborg, and probably Boehme, over the next four years. It was not until after his establishment at Weimar that he became a collector of scientific facts, and a scientific worker of something like an orthodox kind. This was in part the result of his State duties, which involved him in the ordered collection of data, as Keeper of Parks and Gardens, for instance, and as in charge of the mines at Ilmenau. Weimar was a manifold agent of Erasmianism. But only of a compromise Erasmianism; even then his work in optics, particularly his campaign against Newton, shows that he was determined to create a new science, in the image of Paracelsus rather than of Newton. He still hankered after a world of innate energies and giant forces, conflicting or harmonizing with each other, in place of the static and rectangular scheme which Newtonian physics offered. And in botany his diagram of the seven stages of the Urpflanze is strikingly like Boehme's diagram of the seven Divine Qualities. Diagrams are of crucial importance in thinking of this kind, and these two diagrams are fundamental to elaborate schemes in the two men's work.

Alchemical motifs run through all Goethe's literary work. "Die Geheimnisse," which he worked on between 1784 and 1786, would have been a Rosicrucian poem if it had been completed, and "Das Märchen" probably owes something to The Chymical Wedding of Christian Rosenkreutz, one of the Rosicrucian texts. In Faust itself dozens of alchemical motifs are employed; perhaps the most striking, the most fully developed, is the Homunculus. Moreover, alchemical "ideas" occur in seemingly realistic works. For instance, the hermaphrodite figure turns up often in alchemical myth; an image of the human condition which arouses strong and conflicting feelings in the adept who contemplates it. And in Goethe's fiction and drama there is a rather striking occurrence of man-woman figures and brother-sister confusions. It seems that alchemical myth supplied Goethe with a way of dealing with "problematic" sexual themes. It is also clear in Wilhelm Meister how fascinated he was with the whole idea of a secret society and secret knowledge, and

290 CITIES OF LIGHT AND SONS OF THE MORNING

with the apprenticing of a young man to the masters of such lore. Indeed, the novel itself takes on an analogous aesthetic character, becomes a body of doctrine and a myth, alternately rationalist and mystic; first he puzzles the reader, then he rather overexplains, and then he puzzles him again. These are some of the aspects of Goethe most off-putting when one first approaches him, and they derive from his use of the occult.

But the Enlightenment was not a period when the alchemical side to the occult seems to have been taken seriously by the intelligentsia — even in Germany, despite some colorful exceptions to that rule. Goethe inherited Renaissance traditions of the imagination which the new rationalism was soon to make inaccessible to alert minds. It was "like Marlowe" that he *was* Faust in his youth. The books of art and iconography, and the polyhistorical works, collected by his father, opened up to the boy Goethe that gorgeously mythical Renaissance vision of the world which went so well with Doctor Metz's alchemy, but which did not long thereafter remain available to men interested in the best that was being thought and said. A figure like Kepler, whose combination of science, poetry, and mystical religion was condemned as "against Nature" by the Enlightenment, represents the Renaissance synthetic mind to which Goethe himself remained loyal.

The occult seems to become widely and dangerously popular at periods of religious change and renewal, when the established churches are in a state of upheaval, and faith is on the one hand lapsing, on the other intensifying — periods like our own, that is, and the Renaissance-Reformation, and the early centuries A.D. In the Enlightenment, the occult does not seem to have been, even for Goethe, the crucial arena for the psychic bargain we have called Faustian. In the Renaissance, that does seem to have been the case.

Bruno

There were many men in the Renaissance who pursued personal power by trafficking in the occult. We shall say something about Agrippa, Paracelsus, Campanella and one or two others. But the most striking of all the magi was Giordano Bruno. He is striking for his fate — burned at the stake for heresy — for his speculative and literary achievement, and for his attempts, made in the magus style, to apply his insights in practical politics.

Bruno was born in 1548 near Naples, and became a Dominican in a monastery there. But he left the order and went to France, and England, and Germany, playing a prominently mysterious role on the edge of court and academic circles in several places. As is natural in an occultist, prominence and mystery were the keynotes of his life and even of his personality; though he projected himself with great intensity, that self remains hidden, unclear, unrealized, uncommunicated. We don't know much about him. But he does give us, in his comedy *Il Candelaio*, a strongly satiric picture of monastic life as he had known it, and for a man of his ambition that life — well suited to the Calvinist temperament — must indeed have been intolerable.

Bruno advanced many heretical propositions at one time or another, including that "scientific" one of the existence of an infinite number of worlds, but he was probably condemned by the church rather for being an "Egyptian"; that is, for founding a movement which taught adepts a return to the magical religion of Egypt as the only cure for the wars, persecutions, and miseries caused by contemporary sectarian Christianity. And there are some grounds, we read, for supposing that he did found a secret society in Germany, the Giordanisti, and that that society was at the origin of Rosicrucianism.

In any case, he participated in every branch of the occult of his time. He was the archetypal magus. He was an operator in, and teacher of, magic, and this was transitive as well as subjective magic, to follow D. P. Walker's distinction. Transitive magic is much more likely to be demonically performed, and in a way unperceived by the "patient," so it was much more feared and hated. Like Campanella, Bruno aimed to alter and control people's emotions and imaginations for his own ends in the realms of politics and religion. In the realm of science, he was a hylozoist, as alchemists in general were; he believed in a living earth which moved around a divine sun, and in innumerable worlds moving like great animals in courses of their own through an infinite universe. He thought Nature full of a divine life which an operator in magic could make contact with, could benefit from, could to some extent direct and dominate. Thus though he used Copernicus's formulas in his cosmology, he despised Copernicus as a mere mathematician. Bruno himself practiced mathesis, the magical use of numbers, rather than mathematics. And Aristotelianism was for him the epitome of everything dead and dry in both philosophy and religion.

He was also a cultivator of the art of memory, an art by which the mind can be made to reflect the divine mind which is behind the universe, and can itself become divine— divine in fact, as it is already divine in potential and origin. *De umbris idearum*, for instance, is a book which describes a device he was recommending to the king of France. He had 150 magic images of the stars inscribed in the 30 sections of a wheel; 49 images of the planets; 28 stations of the moon, 36 decans of the zodiac, and 36 houses of the zodiac. Concentric with this star wheel are other wheels, one with 150 animal, vegetable, and mineral names inscribed, one with 150 adjectives describing qualities, and an outermost one with 150 names of the inventors of skills and crafts. By revolving the wheels, a man may conjure with this device. He may bring a star into conjunction with a given plant, quality, and craft. The stars are the shadows of the divine ideas, and each one has its influence on the sublunary world, via those of the world's objects which are vitally linked with it. We may influence the stars by manipulating the sensory objects that belong to it. And also by understanding those connections we understand the universe and understand ourselves. We mirror it all correctly in our minds. In the primordial chaos of a man's unregenerate mind the archetypal images exist in a confused ineffectuality; conjuring, magic memory, restores their order. You repossess the universe, and your own divinity. This is Hermetic philosophy as much as magical.

The magus acquired great powers for his personality as he reorganized it by means of the art of memory. In Bruno's later book, called *Thirty Statues*, he describes images you can construct in your imagination, by means of which you can capture daimonic powers. The construction of mental images is recommended in all arts of memory, some of which date from as early as classical times and are written by minds as unmysterious as Quintilian. In such cases, the images seem to be only mnemonic devices. But in other cases they seem to have other functions, of intensifying the mental powers, by means of intellectual incantation. This is the tradition which Bruno was developing; and in this book he allied it to Hermes's divine statues. These statues — brought to life by incantations, music, inscribed signs, burned herbs, etc. — haunted the minds of Renaissance Hermeticists, and Bruno adapted them to the art of memory. The thirty statues he prescribes basically represent the classical gods and the zodiacal signs, but the individual is to associate many other things with them, and to concentrate great imaginative intensity on them. And by doing so he will become not only more wise, more knowledgeable, more insightful, but also more strong, more commanding, more terrible to his enemies.

Bruno's own personality, in his books, is overbearing, quarrelsome, threatening, and mysterious. It is sometimes hard to understand what he is talking *about*, or whom *to*, but the ego talking is projected with great force. He makes a good deal of his powers, and of his contempt for, and superiority to, his enemies. He often appropriated other people's ideas, without acknowledgment, or with the most condescending kind — as with Copernicus — because he felt himself wiser than they about the real significance of their discoveries. He was, it seems, humiliated in a debate at Oxford, because it was publicly demonstrated that he had been using Ficino's arguments and learning as his own, and something similar occurred in a debate in Paris. It seems clear that he was brilliant; but that his policy of self-aggrandizement and mystification led him to break the rules of the life of the mind.

Coleridge, who read Bruno assiduously, mentioned him in his essay called "Egotism," together with Paracelsus and Cardan, two other brilliant Renaissance egotists, whom Goethe also studied. This is not just egotism in its meaning of moral meanness, but as a synonym for daimonism. Coleridge also compared Bruno with Heraclitus, as a philosopher of polarity and conflict. Heraclitus (who was the subject of Lassalle's first major work, and a major influence on his thought) was the philosopher of fire as well as of conflict; so that from him it is only a step to Prometheus, with whom Napoleon often identified himself, and who was the subject of so many Romantic poems, by Blake, Shelley, Goethe, Hölderlin,

Byron, Rimbaud. Bruno, Heraclitus, Prometheus, a man, a manuscript, a myth, these are other fragments — besides the occult
proper — out of which the Faustian idea and soul-nurture are put
together whenever people need them again.

There are some grounds, too, for associating Bruno, like modern
Faustians, specially with the body and with sexuality. D. P. Walker
says of his *De vinculis in genere.* "Treatises on witchcraft came
near to being a pornographic *genre*, and Bruno made a remarkable
attempt to outline a technique for controlling all emotions which is
explicitly based on sexual attraction." Transitive magic tended to
concentrate on sexual feelings in the patient, because they are the
most susceptible imaginatively. And Faustians themselves are usually profoundly sensual, as we have seen. They try to escape the
Erasmian bargain of exchanging body for mind.

It is interesting to note a conscious hostility on Bruno's part toward Erasmus. Erasmus belonged to the earlier, Latin, Renaissance, which was interested primarily in Latin literature and in
Christian piety, and which invested most intellectual energy in exactness and correctness of knowledge, balance and moderation of
temperament, elegance and subtlety of style. Bruno belonged to
that later Renaissance which turned more to Greek antiquity, and
was more magical, mystical, and religio-speculative. Erasmus belongs with Casaubon; he was what Bruno called a pedant, and
pedants were Bruno's abomination. He hated exact knowledge and
its corollaries of personal limits and impersonal structures. He
meant to blow up the city of light. In his dialogues the figure that
represents himself, usually called something like Philothemus, is
always attacked by pedants, called something like Logifer, who
often quote Erasmus. In *Il Candelaio* the pedant is said to represent Erasmus himself.

Bruno had a position of some privilege at the court of Henri III
in Paris, and when he went from there to London he lived in the
house of the French ambassador to England. Frances Yates believes that he was entrusted — to some degree — by the king of
France with a mission to the court of England. (Faustian types are
often sent on secret diplomatic missions, because of their powers of
personality; for instance, Saint-Germain, and Madame de
Warens.) This mission seems to have related to the cause of peace

and religious toleration. Henri III was trying to pursue such a policy against the pressures of the Catholic Ligue for a fiercer (more Calvinist) religious politics. The Medicis in France were interested in Hermeticism, and in magic, and in peace. His policy bore fruit in the setting up of a religiously free state in the Netherlands in 1582 when François d'Anjou was installed by William of Orange as Prince of Antwerp; this was the state, and the ideal, for which Sir Philip Sidney was fighting when he was killed at Zutphen in 1586. Bruno, in his dialogues written in England, represented Sidney as his friend and pupil, and dedicated a series of poems to him. Later, after the death of Henri III, he seems to have concentrated his efforts on securing the patronage of Henri de Navarre, who was no religious fanatic. And he was tempted into Italy, and thus into imprisonment and ultimate execution, by the hope of winning over to his views the Pope of the time. Bruno's politics were thus typical of the occultists; in their means, secret missions and private conversations and the great magus's induction into the mysteries of certain key men — Campanella also tried to convert a Pope; and in their aims, peace and toleration and alliance between sovereigns in transcendence of sectarian hostilities. At the same time, it is probably significant that, according to Melvin Lasky, Bruno was one of the first people to use the word revolution in its modern sense. He has an important place in the history of the word's use in English, via his pupils like Fulke Greville, and his friends like John Florio, whose word-books introduced many new words from the Italian — new words for new concepts — to Elizabethan London. Bruno was no Erasmian, no philosopher of peace; he was a philosopher of conflict, of revolution, but his revolutions were Faustian in style, not Calvinist; mental wars, as Blake would say, not military or political.

It is worth our glancing at one or two more of the Renaissance magi, because it is part of our point that this temperament was not an individual but a cultural phenomenon, a life-option of the times. Jung quotes Cornelius Agrippa — the magician and owner of a Mephistophelean black poodle.

> Agrippa spares no man.
> He contemns, knows, knows not, weeps, laughs, waxes wroth,
> reviles, carps at all things;

being himself philosopher, demon, hero, God,
and all things.

Agrippa flaunted the fact that the aggrandizement of his own personality was an aim in his studies. The same thing seems to have been true of Paracelsus, who said, "I under the Lord, the Lord under me, I under him outside my office, he under me outside his office." With his tiny and feminine body, his violent language, his extravagant quarrelsomeness and boastfulness, Paracelsus is a vivid case of a man buying personality power at all costs. The world has taken the word "bombast" from his name Bombastus; and he gave himself the name Paracelsus in order to proclaim his equality with Celsus. Jung describes the neologisms of Paracelsus's literary style as power-words, which he compares with similar phenomena in the vocabulary of the clinically sick. (Jung says that the line of stylistic heritage runs direct from Paracelsus to Nietzsche. English readers will think of Carlyle.)

In 1525 Paracelsus burned the books of Galen and Avicenna, the fathers and lawgivers of his profession of medicine, in public, before the burghers of Basel; just as Luther had five years before burned the Papal Bull at Wittenberg. It is no wonder that their contemporaries compared him with the real Faust, who was a magician. Paracelsus declared that a doctor must know all alchemy, all astrology, and all theology. His death came as a result of either a drunken debauch, or of being thrown down a steep incline by emissaries of jealous rival physicians. The double image is a good example of the ambiguity of such figures in the eyes of those who know them. Such men live and die mythically; they transcend facts.

Tommaso Campanella, the author of *La Citta del Sole*, published in 1623, followed the outlines of Bruno's career twenty years later. He too first became a Dominican in a convent near Naples, where they were both born. But Campanella was involved in the Calabrian revolt of 1599, predicting the establishment in 1600 of a new Christian cult with Christ as magus, within a new Calabrian republic. The revolt was not professionally or carefully organized; Campanella relied on the power and attraction of his own personality to give a focus and an inspiration to everyone's individual efforts. (This exemplifies the Faustian style of insurrection). He spent twenty-seven years in prison, and while there composed his famous Utopia. Its central conception owes a lot to Adocentyn, a city mentioned in the Hermetic and pseudo-Hermetic treatises. Adocentyn was a city of the sun, too, built in Egypt, ruled by means of magic, and with animated statues in its temples. Campanella's city is divided into seven concentric circles, each dedicated to one of the planets. In its center is a round temple of the sun, with a mappemonde on the altar, and on the dome all the stars represented. The ruler of the city is a Sun Priest, assisted by ministers called Power, Wisdom, and Love. Every action is astrologically determined. The powerful influence of this book can be traced in the Rosicrucian legends. Campanella's sonnets, too, express an excited intellectual hunger and ambition which have caused him to be cited as one of the prototypes of Goethe's Faust. He spent the last years of his life in France, where he wrote an ode for the birth of Louis XIV, the Sun King, and in 1637 dedicated a book to Cardinal Richelieu, asking him to build a City of the Sun. (The ascription to the sun of divine status, and the primal antithesis of light and darkness, are common to nearly all forms of the occult. The great addresses to the sun of Goethe's Faust belong to a Faustian tradition.)

As has become clear, many lines of Renaissance thought, not only the neo-Platonic and the Hermeticist, fostered spiritual ambition. We see this even in Cardinal Nicholas of Cusa, who condemned both the humanist and the scholastic forms of intellectuality, in favor of a more practical engagement with reality, in an effort to change it; and even better in Pico della Mirandola, who explained that man's special status as made "in the image of God" lay in his self-determinability, his calling to make himself. The acting out in practical terms of these ideas, by Michelangelo and by Leonardo da Vinci, makes them prototypes of Goethe's Faust, particularly the second, with his work in hydraulics and in the reclamation of land from the sea.

Bruno went to Prague to seek the Emperor's patronage, as did John Dee, and Goethe's Faust. The magi were always looking for royal protection. Campanella as well as Bruno tried to win over a Pope, and he was actually commissioned to perform spells in the Vatican, to draw down astral magic in protection of Urban VIII's health during an eclipse of the sun. He hoped to use the structure and power of the Catholic church to disseminate his own (significantly different) religion; early in his career he hoped to enlist the patronage of Spain also; later that of France.

This search for a patron was of course a necessity for most special groups within the state. The Puritans in England for a time angled for the Duke of Buckingham's protection, alien as he was to them temperamentally. But the basic political strength of the Puritans lay elsewhere, lay among themselves, in their own organization, and ultimately in the compact of the saints. The magi never had significant numbers or organization or social faith. Their strength lay in ideas which had to be occult, hidden, private, which resisted presentation in public preaching or public debate. This is one reason why their position tended to be conservative politically. They allied themselves always with individuals in power. This habit was followed by the secret societies, like the Freemasons; and it is because the Jesuits did the same thing that the personalities of the two societies, doctrinally hostile though they were, blurred into each other. Their intellectual temperaments were similar, though their positions were opposed. All these societies were regarded with suspicion by the world outside, particularly by the poor and fervent. Yeats dramatizes this in the destruction of the secret Rosicrucian temple by the Catholic Irish peasantry in the story "Rosa Alchemica."

Modern Occultists

In our own century, the major new form of the occult — which has had the same effect on its practitioners of breeding political Pyrrhonism — has been psychoanalysis. Both the structure of its theory, and the analyses of individual patients, have amounted to a strenuous engagement with those hidden and forbidden truths which undermine public decorum, morally and intellectually. Particularly after its first thirty years or so, the movement certainly has had its own kind of scientific and cultural respectability. But it also was, and is, essentially a trafficking in the occult. It is no accident that Freud and Jung both drew on the traditions of such knowledge in the West; Freud particularly on those of Jewish mysticism, perhaps unconsciously imbibed via his circle of Jewish friends, and Jung on Christian gnosticism and alchemy. Both men, in their own lives and in those of their patients, transacted a Faustian bargain, acquiring personality power and intuitive knowledge by the sacrifice of ordinary self-respect. But it is no accident also that both men were Goetheans, and each took in Goethe the kind of personally engaged and dialectic interest which is always a means of self-definition. Both were profoundly *conservative* Faustians. But Freud forced his patients to make the descent into their own hells, to deal with their own nightmare desires and hatreds, the monsters of their own unconsciouses. Whereas Jung, a gnostic Faustian, rather assimilated their problems to noble myths, the best heritage of human culture, and taught them to dream a splendid tapestry of myths and rituals — to become creative artists in fantasy.

Freud's scorn for the Swiss heresy is expressed at its mildest in this passage of a letter to Pfister.

Your analysis suffers from the hereditary weakness of virtue. It is the work of an over-decent man who feels himself obliged to be discreet. Now these psychoanalytical matters need a full exposition to make them comprehensible, just as an actual analysis can proceed only when one descends to the small details from the abstractions that cover them. Discretion is thus incompatible with a good presentation of psychoanalysis. One has to become a bad fellow, transcend the rules, sacrifice oneself, betray, and behave like the artist who buys paints with his wife's household money, or burns the furniture to warm the room for his model. Without some such criminality there is no real achievement.

Jung's use of alchemy is a conscious and explicit confirmation of our proposition about the function of the occult, but Freud is an even more interesting example of our theories as a whole.

He felt himself to be — and others felt him to be — destined to a conquering and triumphant style of success in earliest childhood. He said of himself, "A man who has been the indisputable favorite of his mother keeps for life the feeling of a conqueror, that confidence of his success that often induces real success." But he grew up into very stern conditions of life, domestic and political and intellectual, and he internalized them into a very stern sense of duty and decency and demonstration in argument. He lost his sense of himself as genius and hero, as his twenties and thirties went by, and began to talk and think of himself as a mere work-horse. He signed, in other words, a very far-reaching temperamental contract of the Erasmian kind. He saw himself as plodding along and achieving by force of virtue what others were granted by grace of fortune — by innate ability. But all his remarks of that kind were filled with resentment and unrest, and as he approached forty he made a heroic act of adventure which was in effect a renewal of his first temperamental enterprise, to be a conqueror. He risked everything, in intellectual and moral as well as practical terms, on the sexual etiology of neuroses, and it cost him a great deal. As Ernest Jones says,

Evidently there was something in leaving the safe, if rather tedious, field of neurology for the unexplored one of psychology which had some supreme inner meaning for Freud. It certainly signified satisfying the deepest wish in his nature, the one that drove him ever farther onward. But it must also have been accompanied by some profound sense of forbiddenness which evoked anxiety and the other distressing and paralysing moods. It is as if he divined all along that the path he was treading would sooner or later lead to terrible secrets, the revealing of which he dreaded but on which he was nevertheless as determined as Oedipus himself.

Jones's vocabulary is of course that of Freud himself, but what he is describing here is the Faustian contract. He insists that in the 1890's Freud suffered from a very considerable psychoneurosis, and that it was just in the years when the neurosis was at its height, 1897–1900, that he did his most original work. With this he regained his Faustian dynamism. In 1900 he described himself thus: "For I am not really a man of science, not an observer, not an experimenter, and not a thinker. I am nothing but by temperament a *conquistador* — an adventurer, if you want to translate the word — with the curiosity, the boldness, and the tenacity that belong to that type of being."

The *most* interesting thing for us is that he achieved this rebirth by apprenticing himself temperamentally to a practitioner in the occult, from the age of thirty-one to forty-six. Wilhelm Fliess, though in practical life a successful (Jewish) physician, was in the world of the mind something of a Bruno figure, intellectually showy but shady, with his universal bisexuality and his numerology; and yet Freud made himself dependent on him, emotionally and mentally, in a way unparalleled in the rest of his life-story. A brilliant personality, Fliess was, as Jones says, "extremely self-confident, outspoken, unhesitantly gave the most daring sweep to his generalizations, and swam in the empyrean of his ideas with ease, grace, and infectious felicity." And the empyrean of his ideas, it is quite clear, was Jewish-occultist; the bisexuality, the numerology, and the "portions of life" theory, which enables one to predict the date of a man's death, are all Cabbalist. But we find Freud the workhorse, the patient practitioner of logic and accumulator of evidence, adopting these ideas himself and writing to Fliess, "For your revelations in sexual physiology I can only bring breathless attention and critical admiration. I am too circumscribed in my knowledge to be able to discuss them." But he was learning from Fliess how to transcend this and other circumscriptions, how to set free in himself what Jones calls his creative side; "the original love of mastery that had got so completely transformed into the passionate desire to discover the secrets of human life, one so urgent at times that it treacherously beckoned to the short cuts of philosophical speculation." Jones himself easily resisted the "temptation" to take such "short cuts" because his temperament was more limitedly Erasmian than Freud's. Freud's work, as analyst, as theorist, as organizer of the movement, was a compromise of equally well-marked Erasmian and Faustian virtues (which perhaps accounts for that specially strong sense of concrete fact, which distinguishes him from both Jones on the one hand and Jung on the other). And those latter virtues — this is our main point — were made available to him at nearly forty by his adventure into occult fields of knowledge, that is by an intellectual and conscious bargain, even though by the sexual or Freudian bargain he had been endowed with them from earliest infancy.

But we are above all interested in the relation between Faustianism and the occult in the world of literature.

The Faustian temperament remained a latent force in nineteenth-century culture, in literature as well as politics; it remained the antithesis of the nineteenth-century consensus. But it was not, it seems, until the turn of the century that the study of the occult revived among literary men, and then as a part of Symbolism. Among writers in English the great example is W. B. Yeats. In his case it seems clear that the occult provided the arena for a Faustian bargain for forbidden powers of personality and of intuitive knowledge. In other cases, of great writers acquiring such powers, it does not seem that the occult had anything to do with it; for instance, D. H. Lawrence. Perhaps the occult is likely to be the means employed by those people who feel themselves farther away from the end they want to achieve, in whom the ambition to become brilliant and dominating personalities is more deliberate and theoretical.

Yeats classified himself as only a lunar poet, while Blake, his hero, was solar. He put himself into Phase 17, Blake into Phase 18, of his great cycle. Yeats had become determined in early manhood to make himself by imagination into something he was not "by nature," in order to escape the limitations of the Erasmian temperament, which much oppressed him. George Eliot was his bête noire, and he repudiated every manifestation of Victorian liberalism. "I hated and still hate with an ever-growing hatred the literature of the point of view."

He often described the type he feared to become, and we immediately recognize it as what we have named the Erasmian.

Those learned men who are a terror to children and an ignominious sight in lovers' eyes, all those butts of a traditional humour where there is something of the wisdom of peasants, are mathematicians, theologians, lawyers, men of science of various kinds. They have followed some abstract reverie, which stirs the brain only and needs that only, and have therefore stood before the looking glass without pleasure and never known those thoughts that shape the lines of the body for beauty or animation, and wake a desire for praise or for display.

He was perfectly clear about the connection between the imaginative virtues he sought for his poetry, and his "desire for praise or for display." And he was just as clear about where he would find the means to both these ends: in the practices of the occult and in the theories of Renaissance neo-Platonists.

[Art] approved before all men those that talked or wrestled or tilted under the walls of Urbino, or sat in those great window-seats discuss-

ing all things, with love ever in their thought, when the wise duchess
ordered all, and the Lady Emilia gave the theme.

Perhaps more clearly than anyone else, Yeats shows us how a man's
temperament can be changed by means of the Faustian bargain in
our time. He did capture forces of personality for himself as he
studied the occult arts. He also tried to escape liberal feebleness by
the other route, by taking part in active politics, and participating
in the action of a group, the power of a party member. In other
words, he tried to conclude a version of the saints' compact, the
Calvinist bargain. But he soon came to feel that that was a mistake,
whereas the Faustian strategy was largely successful for him.

Yeats's A Vision is another memory system, very like those of
the Renaissance (which it imitates), another way of mastering all
human knowledge, all history, in a series of images, so as to bring
increased powers to the soul of him who contemplates it with intensity. A somewhat similar book is Robert Graves's *The White
Goddess*, a historical grammar of poetic myth, and Graves can perhaps be associated with Yeats as a deliberate and intentional Faustian.

The Renaissance memory artists were all comparative religionists
and speculative mythologists in a style which Graves follows. He
tells us that the poetic myth languages of the Mediterranean and
Northern Europe were all part of a magical language bound up
with popular religious ceremonies in honor of the Moon-goddess of
Muse, and this remains the true language of poetry. (The high style
of Graves's assertions is also Faustian, as we have defined the
term.) This language was tampered with in late Minoan times,
when invaders from Central Asia introduced patrilinear institutions, and remodeled myths to justify social changes. Luckily, mystery cults and witch covens have preserved for us some traces of
the Moon-goddess's language, which was driven out of circulation
by the Greek philosophers with their religion of logic, and with the
rational poetic language they called classical. (Simon Magus's
Helena was also known as Selene, and he had disciples of the lunar
number of thirty.)

Graves's dedicatory poem, to the Goddess, neatly sets out the
triangular conflict between her devotees (the men of Faustian

temperament) the Calvinists or saints, and the Erasmians or Apollonians.

> *All saints revile her, and all sober men*
> *Ruled by the God Apollo's golden mean . . .*

Like Bruno, Graves resents prophetic Israel as much as classical Greece. He blames Ezekiel for instituting a religion of pure meditation, of Absolute Mind, which was taken up by the Greek-speaking Jews of Egypt, and taken up from them by the Pythagoreans. This led finally to impoverishing changes in the very alphabets of Greece and Britain. Which reminds us again of Bruno, who called the Jews the excrements of Egypt, because the Hebrew alphabet had only numerological values, whereas the Egyptian hieroglyphs were all sacred signs. This is an idea that many modern poets besides Graves would join Bruno in; for instance, Pound; and the coincidence is not trivial, because it derives from the effort of all modernist art to rival magic, to subvert Gutenberg. The last two lines of Graves's poem remind us of that connection between the Goddess and pure or impure illusion.

> *Whom I desired above all things to know*
> *Sister of the mirage and echo.*

Yeats and Graves seem to be, like Mann, significantly different from the naturally Faustian temperament we find in Tolstoy and Lawrence, and perhaps in Blake. At least in England, such a temperament seems often to have recoiled from the occult. (I shall discuss some possible reasons for this in the last chapter.) Lawrence was distrustful of the Apocalypse even while fascinated by certain imaginative possibilities in it. He tells us to see the sun *as if* it were a god, and *in that sense* believe in it. That is as far as he will go, which is not to let go with one hand of common sense. He disliked the Apocalypse because it expressed a hatred of power; but also because the "splendiferousness" of the images was "unnatural." "Phrases like the wrath of the Lamb are ridiculous on the face of it." This demand for the natural, and keen sense of the ridiculous, are exactly what one must lay aside if one is to enter the darkened temple of the occult. Yeats would make that sacrifice; Lawrence would not. It is no accidental coincidence that he objects to Poe's descriptions of people and things on the same grounds that they are "unnatural"; it is no accident because Poe is a writer of the occult.

Lawrence does say that there is a connection between the occult content of the Apocalypse and the acquisition of personal power by those whose imaginative life is fed by the book. He says that the Primitive Methodist colliers he knew as a child, whose religion was based on that book, possessed a kind of power (in their dealings with their wives, and with their children, and with people generally) which men who went to his mother's Congregational chapel could not have. But he elsewhere declares his own lifelong dislike of the book, and in general it seems clear that he continued to belong rather to the Congregational side of that antithesis. This is typical of the many traits in him which we call collectively his "Englishness."

But "natural" Faustians make their bargain without needing the apparatus of the occult; they acquire their personal power by such means as we have seen Mailer describe in *The Armies of the Night*. To others, however, the occult can be such an aid, such an apparatus, because it enables men to boldly deny the truths and the forms of life by which all their friends and neighbors live. It enables them to speculate about scientific and religious matters according to their own "method"; their own both as not being the general one, and as bearing a marked character of voluntariness, even of arbitrariness and fancifulness. The occult is a hidden, underground world of adepts living, at their most serious, in a conscientious contradiction of, a religious blasphemy against, the world above. It makes all its devotees priests, who can move about the world above in hidden pride, bearing the symbols with a hieratic stiffness, however invisibly. It gives them what Stephen Dedalus thought to get from becoming a Roman Catholic priest, without the cost to their sensual pride which he would have had to pay. For them there is no poverty, chastity, or obedience, no wearing of a uniform or observing of uniform rules. The whole personality is expanded, not just the priestly part.

Of course Catholicism itself has seemed in modern times, especially to men who were not born into it, an occult area, full of secret knowledge and secret power. It has played in some men's imaginative lives in this century much the same role as alchemy and Hermeticism did in the lives of Renaissance magi. British converts like Evelyn Waugh, Frederick Rolfe (Baron Corvo), and Graham Greene, have been particularly responsive to that; but the phenomenon has its parallels in American and French and German literature. These writers attribute to the Church all kinds of unspoken and unspeakable wisdom and wealth, and inscrutable irrational powers (Baron Corvo). Or they attribute to individual Catholics the possibility of special spiritual bargains with God and the devil (Waugh). Or like the alchemists they insist that the mystery of grace, of sanctity, is to be found in the humanly least appealing of hiding places (Greene). *Lapis philosophorum in stercore invenitur* is a recurrent motif of alchemical myth.

In Erasmus's time Catholicism seemed like the main road of mankind, and it was other branches of knowledge that ran invitingly off and down into the darkness. And even in this century Catholicism has fed other temperaments besides the Faustian — indeed, neither Greene nor Waugh is simply that, but there is an important strain of romantic blackness in their Catholicism. T. S. Eliot, though strongly attracted to the conservative possibilities in Anglicanism, was in matters of personal temperament an Erasmian, and made his religious faith feed a Weimar kind of compromise. Whilst Brian Wicker, Father Herbert McCabe, and others of the New Left Catholics have developed a radicalism with a potential of Calvinism. Essentially this is true of the Berrigans, too, though intellectually their style has not so marked a character. The British writers' brilliantly clear, firm, rapid, impersonal style is one of the most attractive and authoritative expressions of that Calvinism, and very like Tom Paine's, for example. A huge body of knowledge, practice, and faith, like Catholicism, even one as large as alchemy, can be put to a great number of cultural functions.

Gnostic Faustianism

Besides the two just discussed, the "natural" and the "occultist" Faustian, there are other varieties of that temperament, or other types to be associated with them. For instance, what I have called the negative or black Faustian, which has acquired power through the magnification of psychic weaknesses, through intensified ignobility, instead of nobility, shame instead of pride, feebleness instead of strength, narrowness instead of breadth and variety of powers; but weaknesses exploited and explored, failures insisted on and capitalized on. I cited Dostoevski and Joyce as examples of the black Faustian, Proust and Rousseau of the negative.

The very practice of art itself, and particularly of modernist art, is a field that invites this version of the Faustian bargain. Rousseau's *Confessions* offer a vivid description of how this can happen to a literary man. He emphasizes often how stupid and inept he was in social and personal relations, how tongue-tied and tactless and humilated, in a word, how deprived of power. Even in his writing, he says, every personal reference went wrong. He only spoke with power when he spoke as The Writer, dealing as a superior with kings and courts and society at large. So he concentrated his sensibility in the network of his relations with his writing. He read from his books to Madame de Luxembourg instead of talking to her. He gave manuscript copies to friends. He copied out extracts to other friends. He gave others passages that had never appeared in print — for instance, "Lord Edward's Adventures," which might have gone into *Julie*. And he became endlessly involved in matters of publication, censorship, reputation. Other parts of his life were anesthetized. Sensitivity was withdrawn from them — his relations with Maman after leaving her, his relations with Thérèse, his children. Above all, he built up a network of conspiracy among his literary enemies. He spun, in fact, out of his literary entrails, a new world in which he *was* the center of everything, and which replaced the old world in which he counted for so little. The *Confessions* create that world by describing it. Creative writing is always an activity which invites a man to do that, whether or not he can also assert himself in social-personal terms. But when he cannot, in extreme cases it assimilates itself to that sinister model of the same activity, the daydreams in which the psychotic isolates himself.

But there is also another way of dealing with the occult, and of transacting even a version of the Faustian bargain, which avoids paying the usual price. That price can be described as the guilt and shame which go with forcing oneself into acts which all one's inhibitions forbid — and the black cynicism and misogyny which result from having broken the human compact. But it is of course possible to experience forbidden things without doing them; by following others' doing of them in one's imagination. This is particularly attractive to the literary-academic mind. We might call it gnostic or rosewater Faustianism, to oppose it to the sulphurous Faustianism of the men of smells. (The two are not mutually exclusive; we can see Yeats, for instance, employing both to intensify each other; but they are different.)

I am using gnosticism (following Professor Jonas) to mean a whole range of syncretistic manifestations of religion and philosophy, all to be associated with Alexandria; Babylonian astrology and magic, Eastern mystery cults, neo-Platonism, neo-Pythagoreanism, Syrian-Egyptian gnosticism proper, Alexandrian Christianity, Alexandrian Jewish philosophy. These were all reemergences of the East in Hellenistic thought in the first two or three centuries A.D., and belong to the Hellenistic city then; most typically, therefore, to the great metropolis.

A gnosis is a revelation of the meaning of the world, and there are many prophets offering them in such phases of culture. These were characteristically roads to salvation through the land of the *mind* — though using the imagination as well as the intellect, and so involving spiritual effort — rather than through the land of *behavior*, which would involve the ethical faculties and the practical will. We might cite the Valentinians as being purely gnostic thinkers in the sense we are giving the word. Valentinus was an Egyptian "Christian" who was educated in Alexandria and taught in Rome between A.D. 133 and 160. He had many disciples, each of whom was called on to develop his own ingenious variation, his own interpretive version, of the basic doctrine. For the Valentinians, the Divine degraded itself in a series of emanations, without any external intervention — such as other gnostics predicated — and without any internal stress or tragic self-conflict. Christ revealed; he did not need to atone. The world and its history are not substantial manifestations of the Divine. The real is always spiritual. Even matter is a natural, though degraded, manifestation of spirit. Theirs was a philosophy for an intellectual elite. They divided mankind up into qualitatively different classes, with different spiritual destinies. At the same time, their philosophy had religious or mythical features, like the lunar number thirty which they assigned to their Aeons. They were essentially speculative, but carried their speculation to the verge of becoming a religion. This was Alexandrian gnosticism.

I will associate Renaissance gnosticism with the figure of Marsilio Ficino and with his academy in Florence. In philosophical position, Ficino was a Platonist; I use the term gnostic to describe the moral-spiritual character, or temperament, of his teaching. Ficino was a physician as well as a priest, and his *Libri de Vita* of 1489 are full of advice about how to care for one's health which is in effect white magic, astral magic. It is composed mainly for the benefit of scholars, who are liable by their pursuit of knowledge to melancholy, to the saturnine temper, the atrabilious humor, the undue influence of Saturn. We today might put it that their professional temperament is Erasmian, and involves a great deal of repression. It is particularly in the activity of his thought on these problems that we feel ourselves in contact with an authentic temperament in Ficino, and with a gnostic temperament. He tells scholars how to surround themselves with the stones, the plants, the perfumes, the colors, etc., that belong to Jupiter, Venus, and Mercury; how to make themselves jovial, mercurial, aphrodisiac, and above all, solarian, for Ficino was devoted to the sun. He revived the Orphic hymns (another product of the second and third centuries A.D.) and composed hymns of his own, to the sun, and to Venus, etc., that would produce the same effect. This was a kind of dealing in magic, and with forbidden powers, however astral. It was a transcendence, in the name of scholars, of the moral, spiritual, imaginative limits imposed by Authority.

To some extent, the ethereality and aestheticism in Ficino's spiritual-moral world may be deliberate ambiguity, because of his dangerous attraction to daimonic magic, his brand of which had to be disguised as natural or spiritual magic. But beyond that, he seems to partake of an intellectual temperament one can recognize in other times and places, which is never very incisive, earthy, or vigorous in such matters. His academy was a loosely organized spiritual and intellectual community of friends, meeting in the villa given him by Lorenzo de Medici in Careggi outside Florence, to discuss ideas and celebrate the intellectual life together; holding philosophical banquets, for example, on Plato's birthday, November 7, each year. There were edifying orations before small audiences; informal discussions, private readings, public lectures on Plato and Plotinus. Botticelli's *Primavera* hung on the walls of the villa, and Ficino would expound its hidden meanings to his young disciples. He had an elaborate theory of friendship, which he identified with Platonic love. "Divine" friendship links men with a common concern for contemplation and spiritual ascent, those who "take refuge in the Citadel of the Soul." So that even secular love-poetry has a place in his scheme of spiritual training.

This scheme of ideas reminds one of many another image of the refined and poetical life; it has been the dream of many an academic poet (like Walter Pater) throughout the history of literature. It is what Oxford has stood for in British imaginative life; while Cambridge stood for something much more earnest and engaged and untranscendent. And if we add to Ficino's social organization the idea of an organization of knowledge like the Memory Theatre of Giulio Camillo, we shall be reminded of a specifically contemporary phenomenon in the life of the mind.

Giulio Camillo Delminio (1480–1544) was very famous in his day, and so was his theater. It was very like the memory systems we have already discussed, but somewhat more similar than the rest, in some of its features, to what I am going on to. It was a wooden construct, imitating a Renaissance theater, and big enough for people to enter into. He had one built in Venice, and another one later in Paris. But it was, like other such systems, a mystery to the uninitiated eye, which needed to be explained. He made a journey to Paris to reveal its secret to the King of France, and he intended to write a book about it for the benefit of the whole world; but that never got written, and all posterity has is an account by other people composed after his death and published in Venice, called *L'Idea del Teatro*. From this we gather that it was a comparative mythology encyclopedia, but with the spiritual intention of Hermetic neo-Platonism built into it, having the function of drawing down favorable astral influences upon the man who made the proper imaginative use of it. Such a man stood upon the stage, looking up into the auditorium, which rose up away from him in seven grades, divided up by seven gangways, representing the seven planets, and with a gateway on each grade of each gangway. These gateways were memory-places, covered with images like Bruno's, that acted as psychic talismans when intensely contemplated. They had this effect partly because of their aesthetic perfection, being created in accordance with the much-prized laws of visual harmony. But more because of the archetypal power of the emblems themselves. And there were also drawers in these gateways, in which papers were kept, on which, presumably, knowledge was also preserved in more orthodox fashion, so that the theater was also an elaborate filing system, mythologically organized.

One might describe this as an elaborate and ceremonial union of the arts and exact knowledge in the service of education, an education in the appreciation of high culture in many different civilizations, of different periods and different countries. If that sounds like the description also of a liberal arts program at a wealthy and ambitious college, the similarity seems to me appropriate. Even the magical ambition in Giulio Delminio's scheme is not without its parallel in our own curricula.

But even more than a college catalogue, it is books like *A Vision* and *The White Goddess* and *The Anatomy of Criticism* and Jung's cultural schemata which the Memory Theatre reminds one of. And it is of course no surprise that it should remind us of those works, when their authors have declared their debt to the Renaissance humanists and alchemists of this kind, and their intention to carry on their work, to reconstitute their tradition. Frye, for instance, at the end of *Fearful Symmetry*, says that we today must complete the humanist revolution, and build an iconography of the imagination. This would deliver the artist from bondage to a "dingy and nervous naturalism." While Yeats's theory of poetry is drawn from those same writers.

It is only by ancient symbols, by symbols that have numberless meanings besides the one or two the writer lays an emphasis upon, or the half-score he knows of, that any highly subjective art can escape from the barrenness and shallowness of a too conscious arrangement, into the abundance and depth of Nature.

It must be this theory of knowledge which lies behind the Memory Theatre, as well as behind *A Vision*.

All sounds, all colours, all forms, either because of their preordained energies or because of long association, evoke indefinable and yet precise emotions, or, as I prefer to think, call down among us certain disembodied powers, whose footsteps over our hearts we call emotion; but when sound, and colour, and form are in a musical relation, a beautiful relation to one another. . . .

This is characteristically gnostic thinking, of the Syrian-Egyptian gnosis, to be identified with Alexandria. (There was an Iranian-Manichaean gnosis that was more religious.) Jung says that he found alchemy the bridge he had needed to lead him to and fro between this gnosis and psychoanalysis.

Of the three it is Frye who most concerns me, because he is probably the major literary force in Academia today. As Geoffrey Hartman says, Frye is the mystique man who is replacing Leavis; the mystique of myth replacing the mystique of judgment. He is for literature what Malraux is for art and Eliade for religion; he is creating a criticism without walls. He is also in effective alliance with Norman Brown and Marshall McLuhan in some things. They are all three great Blake men, great opponents of point-of-view culture, and you find them using the same quotations to give authority to their speculations.

Frye asks us to see literature (myth) as a language like mathematics. For Plato, he tells us, the ultimate acts of apprehension were either mathematical or mythical. To see the total form of an art — to see literature as a whole — is the only proper way to pass from the aesthetic to the ethical. For there are no external goals to literature; we must enter a self-contained literary universe, or rather verbal universe, for it includes all language. The literary critic can pass judgment on all rhetoric, and the only road from grammar to logic runs through rhetoric; *ratio* is part of *oratio*.

Approaching him from this angle, I see Frye offering us something very similar to what Ficino and Giulio Camillo offered — an elegant academic gnosticism. It is Faustian in that it enables us to transcend normal limits, to understand everything, and to love everything. But by the same token, it avoids all the fire and the explosion, the thunder and fearful sulphurous exhalations, which Faust himself went through, and which, in his way, Mailer went through; and, among critics, Leavis and Fiedler both.

One might contrast the college-catalogue effect in Giuilio Camillo and Frye with the same motif in *Giles Goat-Boy*, the Revised
New Syllabus. The title reminds us of how much the two have in
common. Barth too is an academic mind, and he too is discussing,
in anatomy fashion, education, the modern syntheses of knowledge, and the modern university. But his imaginative terms bear
some mark of the sulphurous-Faustian temperamental bargain, and
remind us of how different this rosewater Faustianism is. Fiedler
and Mailer and Barth have some things in common with Frye,
but the differences between the two minds is still one of the significant ones in modern literature. It is dramatized by the public feud
which Irving Layton, Canada's leading poet and leading Faustian,
runs with Frye. Layton is another example of the mind we discussed in Chapter 2, a phallic narcissist Jewish aggressor, who feels
it is his duty to warn the literary world against Frye's arid gnosticism.

From Ficino and Bruno to Yeats and Frye, the road seems to
pass by way of Elias Ashmole, Sir Thomas Browne, and Robert
Burton; all those royalist and Oxonian antiquarians, much concerned with curious knowledge, elegantly systematized, and all
much concerned to fight off the scholar's disease of melancholy.
They too were academic types, and in alliance with the king. Then
came Jacob Bryant's *New System of Ancient Mythology* (1774–
76), which probably influenced Blake, and Edmund Davies's *Cel-
tic Researches*, which possibly did. Bryant proved that Noah,
Dionysos, and Prometheus were different versions of the same
figure, for instance. Frye commends them as the Frazers of their
time, who created a morphology of symbolism. There is, too, the
tradition of Platonic scholarship and speculation, often verging on
neo-Platonism, running through the Cambridge Platonists, and
Thomas Taylor, the friend of Flaxman. And at the end of the
nineteenth century, Madame Blavatsky, so important to Yeats; and
Frazer, so important to Frye.

Nowadays it is Renaissance studies that are the liveliest everywhere in literature. It is the great system-makers that arouse enthusiasm from our scholars; Plato, Dante, Spenser, Blake, Yeats; how
often nowadays we hear these names recited in the attempt to
make a tradition out of list, just as we used to recite Jane Austen,

George Eliot, Henry James, Joseph Conrad, D. H. Lawrence. And how different the effects of the two incantations are. As Murray Krieger says, Frye liberates the poet from bondage to sublunary language, and the critic from the stringent procedures of critical discourse. He is charting the galaxies dreamed of by human desires, not realities. Our realistic, our existential sense is related to our concern for tragedy and irony, the major forms of literary feeling before Frye. But his taste centers on comedy and romance, the forms of spring and summer. And when Krieger says that the literary work is now to be seen in relation to the whole world of literature, of culture, of dream, the perspectives opened are not only exhilarating but vertiginous.

Frye's disciples have produced a book, *Northrop Frye in Modern Criticism*, which is full of such provocative and useful formulations. Angus Fletcher says that a critic like Frye introduces sacred time into linear history, and so accepts everything that can be regular, recurrent, traditional, and inherited. His criticism therefore tends to become periodic, festive, memorial, and dancelike.

This is essentially scholarship, learning, as criticism; most elegantly and ingeniously systematic of scholarly knowledge. But it derives its persuasiveness from something else, from its gnostic spirit, its rosewater Faustianism. Frye is in position socially progressive, Utopian, and even, in his gnostic way, revolutionary. He is concerned for the city. His is literary criticism in the name of social change, as much as Leavis's was. But the intellectual temperament of the two is quite different. Frye's criticism is in implicit alliance with all the apolitical formalism that is on the scene now; Susan Sontag's aesthetic criticism; Jungian archetypes; Eliade and Malraux; Norman Brown and Protestant mysticism; McLuhan and the anti-Gutenbergs. This is the strongest tide of tendency in literary studies today, and all the socially and politically progressive aspirations to be associated with it cannot make it seem — in one sense of the word — *serious* about culture. I mean, of course, that it cannot seem so to an Erasmian.

I at least am still glad to find that Erasmus and Melanchthon were suspicious of memory systems; and that Marin Mersennes and Descartes and Gassendi attacked Robert Fludd, and disapproved of Campanella; that all across the map of Europe in the seventeenth century rationalism and realism triumphed over the forces of the occult and the gnostic. I don't think they were warring against that part of the imaginative life which I — as an Erasmian liberal — most value. If poets are encouraged to invent huge schemes of "ideas," as Frye encourages them to, they are likely to lose that fruitful struggle with the facts of life, which gives rise to what I read them for. Just as Frye loses what I read criticism for — the fruitful struggle with particular poems, issuing in particular judgments. That struggle is always, in tendency, a struggle with one's moral past and future. Of course Frye is a man of fine taste, and evaluative as well as interpretive, but he puts his energy into something else. He puts our energy into that, insofar as his critical style prevails; and of course it easily may prevail. Rationalism and realism did not triumph completely, thank God; the forces of the occult and the gnostic are there inside us, and are genuinely there in much of our literary heritage. It is all a debate over which element has the hegemony. No one can deny that our poets meant what Frye says they meant, however much we may prefer other parts of their meaning. So it is perfectly possible to imagine the literary mind of our civilization becoming subject to their dominion.

I don't like to imagine that because I think that Frye is soaring above the battlefield and the workshop, that the critics who follow him will inevitably become too lightweight, too smooth, too elegant, too clever. As Geoffrey Hartman says, in Frye's literary universe everything is equally an element of a liberal education, and Jane Austen and de Sade have kissed. The sternest realities are transmuted at his touch.

This sort of rosewater Faustianism is a natural way for academics to react against their fate, though as long as our culture remains what it is, it can only be a reaction. They are bound by their vocation, as guardians of knowledge, to practice the Erasmian virtues of clarity, patience, impersonality, exactness, accumulation, categorization, more than anyone else. At the same time they are brought into imaginative contact and confrontation with great minds, minds that have scorned those virtues, minds with a Faustian temperament. This is particularly true, perhaps, of professors of the humanities. They therefore invent a scheme of ideas, a pseudo-temperament, which lifts them above the Erasmian limits without their needing to make the Faustian passage of fire. But the devil will not be cheated. Their handling of the experience of the great Faustians is palpably not only different but inferior. The objects in their hands have lost their weight.

Since we are called to the liberal position, the Erasmian temperament, by the necessities of our vocation, let us cultivate the virtues that go with that — they are all we *will* acquire, if those. And one of them is the recognition of limits, of the difference between the man who looks and the man who is looked at, between the man who describes and the man who acts. Not that the critic does not act, in describing; but when one man cuts down a tree, and another draws a picture of the event, we say that the first one acts. Not that the critic cannot have Faustian virtues — I have said that both Leavis and Fiedler have them — but he can have them only by breaking powerful laws, by making the passage of fire, by flying into the sun. Systematized transcendence of the Erasmian limitations, rosewater Faustianism, leads one only into the lunar world of gnosticism, where one leaps and soars without knotting a muscle or sweating a drop, and the hugest objects sail on in the direction you intended them to forever. It is a nice world to visit but one wouldn't want to live there.

Perhaps Goethe's *Faust* is an artistic equivalent. If the Urfaust treated its subject in some sympathy with the Lutheran treatment of the Faustbook, nearly all the work Goethe did on the subject thereafter was quite different. The Faustbook, and Marlowe's play, were Lutheran in the sense that they took the possibility of Faust's damnation very seriously, and took Mephistopheles as Satan, and consequently made drama out of the subject. But the Renaissance-gnostic way of treating the subject dismissed damnation and diabolism, turned Mephistopheles into a spirit of the air, and everything into a shape of Faust's imagination; and produced not drama but a masque. Goethe was indeed a Renaissance-gnostic humanist, in the same sense as our contemporary scholars are, and his *Faust II* is an extraordinary re-creation of Rennaissance gnosticism. It even includes tragedy within it, in the story of Gretchen, but tragedy alongside allegories, operettas, animated ideas, literary categories, all etherealized by the larger form to the same ontological status of semibeing. Just like *The Anatomy of Criticism*. As I said, it is a nice world to visit, but one wouldn't want to live there.

9 — RADICAL HAVANA

The ship came in the night to Cuba, to Havana . . . Many Americans were wandering around, and nearly all wore badges of some sort. The city seemed, on the surface at least, very American. And underneath, it did not seem to have any very deep character of its own left. . . .

"Ah, Señor," said the driver, with a Cuban grin. "You know they all come here to drink. They drink so much that they all get lost at night, so they all wear a badge: name, name of hotel, place where it is. Then our policemen find them in the night, turn them over as they lie on the pavement, read name, name of hotel, and place, and so they are put on a cart and carted to home. Ah, the season is only just beginning. Wait a week or two, and they will lie in the streets at night like a battle, and the police doing Red Cross work, carting them to their hotels. Ah, los americanos! They are so good. You know they own us now. Yes, they own us. They own Havana. We are a Republic owned by the Americans. Muy bien, we give them drink, they give us money. Bah!"

And he grinned with a kind of acrid indifference. He sneered at the whole show, but he wasn't going to do anything about it.*

Havana and Geneva

In a revolutionary society like Cuba, what I had to expect to meet was the triumph of the Calvinist temperament, the triumph of Party. And that is indeed to be met there, that is manifest in Havana. The severe and hollow-cheeked faces of people in authority, the pistols on the hip of olive-green uniforms, the uniform physique of the militiamen, the taken-over buildings, the Sierra

* D. H. Lawrence, *The Flying Fish.*

Maestra style in the innermost corridors of power; all this announces a rule of the saints; of men who have come down from the
hills into the city, into the corrupt city in bondage to worldly corruption, into Babylon, and have taken it over, determined to enforce the rule of righteousness, of justice and honesty and efficiency
and the new faith; determined to rule as a Party and to level all
class, creed, and race distinctions between citizens. Every few
blocks you see the headquarters of the area C.D.R., the *Comité de
la Defensa de la Revolución*, and there are stories about the operations of some of them which remind you of the kirk-sessions of the
Presbyterian Church in Scotland, or of the *Grabeau*, the regular
meetings for mutual criticism of the elders in Geneva. In Cuba,
too, the elders sometimes pry into people's private affairs, and insist on judging intimate matters by a rigid public ideology.

But if I found that, I found also that these signs of the triumph
of Party were, often, the signs of national health, too; that these
two things, Calvinism and national health, were in that time and
place very closely related. Whereas in East Germany the repetitive
orthodoxy of the newspapers was to seem to me in four days repel-
lent and even nauseating, in Cuba the newspapers, all the voices of
authority, said the same one thing, *porro unum necessarium*, and
yet that one thing was alive and meaningful. And perhaps that was
true also of some parishes in seventeenth-century Scotland, and of
Calvin's Geneva.

The city of Geneva won its political independence from the
dukes of Savoy and the bishops of Geneva — bishops who were
habitually cadets of the House of Savoy — by a long struggle that
went on from 1500 to 1531. And religious change, religious liberation, went hand in hand with political. In 1535, under the leadership of Guillaume Farel, Geneva chose Reformed Protestant
Christianity as its faith. Farel had spread that faith in Basel and
Bern before he came to Geneva. It was a time when many cities
were attempting self-determination, in rebellion against their ruling bishops. This was the year of Munster's attempt at Anabaptist
communism. But Geneva's destiny was to be nothing like Munster's, because Farel prevailed upon Jean Calvin — by means of a
religious appeal to his sense of duty — to take over the direction of
the city's religious and moral life in 1536. That life had become

corrupt under the rule of the foreign power and of Renaissance Catholicism. The hiring of mercenary soldiers, in the various Swiss cities, for the armed bands of men like Cesare Borgia, brought into circulation there quantities of money which were spent, or thought to be spent, in the purchase of luxuries and vices. (As American money was spent in Cuba.) As well as injuring national pride, and diminishing the proportion of men in the cities, it introduced the lax morals of condottieri in a foreign land. For instance, the *étuves*, the public baths, became in Geneva centers of sexual immorality. Immorality and irreligion were felt to be rife in the city, and a firm hand was felt to be needed to deal with them.

Calvin was then twenty-seven, had been trained as a lawyer, and had published his first book, a commentary on Seneca, in 1532. But having been converted to the Reformed religion, he fled Paris in 1533, and published in Basel his great work, *Institutio Christianae Religionis*, in 1536. This had five editions in his lifetime, and gradually grew from six chapters to eighty. It followed a traditional catechetical pattern, of a commentary on the Commandments, the Creed, the Lord's Prayer, and the Sacraments, but it became both a revolutionary and an authoritative document. He had been a precocious boy, intellectually and morally, with an austere conscience about his own and others' behavior, and he acquired the humanist skills of rhetoric and dialectic very perfectly. He was a born leader, or rather lawgiver. There was a polish and precision to both his Latin style and his logic which distinguished him from the other radical reformers, and which corresponds to a certain aristocracy of personal style. He never described the emotional aspects of his conversion, or gave any accounts of his private life, as Luther so richly did. Calvin's private life was kept private; and an unusually large proportion of his energies went into his public activities. The religion he devised for his followers was highly suspicious of emotion, even religious emotion, and put all its stress on actual behavior, and self-disciplining acts of will. Though his own aesthetic sense was keen, he distrusted it, and the arts in general. (His and Rabelais's comments on each other sum up the general hostility between the Calvinist temperament and the literary Faustian.)

He began immediately, in 1536, to draw up Articles of Church Government for the city. With the adoption of the Reformed religion the Roman Catholic monasteries had of course been closed and the churches seized, and there had been some attempt to stamp out the contagion of idleness and vice, the decay of morals and manners. (As in Cuba after the Revolution.) Calvin systematized that attempt to save the city simultaneously from the Devil and from its this-worldly enemies, who still hoped to recapture their property. He divided the city of thirteen thousand people up into three parishes, and provided that in each church there should be two services each Sunday, and one each weekday. And he provided for lay inspectors, to help the clergy watch over the people's morals. Gambling and the singing of frivolous songs were forbidden, and absence from sermon was punishable with a fine, and a 9:00 P.M. curfew was imposed. Elaborate clothing and hair styles and bodily self-display were repressed by decrees backed up with penalties. In 1537 he tried to impose a Confession of Faith on everyone, and when this failed, and when he was denied the power he had demanded, to excommunicate the unworthy, his relations with the Council grew so bad that he and Farel had to leave the city.

But it was not long before he was summoned back. It was clear to the magistrates that no one else had so good a chance of imposing a discipline on the unruly people and making an independent and self-respecting community out of their city. He returned, and drew up Articles of Government, which were as political as the title sounds. The function of a church for him was to govern men, to drive them up the hill to God. This conception was shared by other radical Christians then (and now), but Calvin was their supreme representative. The English Puritan community at Frankfurt (exiles from the Catholic England of Bloody Mary) produced a new "discipline," or church government, for themselves. The old one had twelve articles and provided for eight church officers; the new one had seventy-three articles and provided for sixteen officers — out of a congregation of sixty-two. The extremists among these Puritans had to leave Frankfurt soon after, and they went naturally to Geneva, the city of God, where they played an important part in Calvin's administration. Committees, constitutions, the delimitation of powers, these were of the essence of a church, for radicals.

Calvin's *Ordonnances* of 1541 established a Consistory of

If Mailer is a saving clause, a bright imaginative parenthesis within Manhattan, Fidel rises like a tower above Havana, subsuming all below, continuing it upward. (Wide World Photos.)

twelve elders, laymen, to represent the Church as a body, and to watch over the lives of Church members. Like Zwingli and Knox, Calvin insisted on involving the laity in the government of the Church. This was one of the several ways in which he tried to reintroduce the practices of the early Church (just as contemporary radicals want to do). Calvin's system was both representative-participatory and at the same time authoritarian. The elders compelled church attendance — people's houses could be searched at sermon time to see if they were there — and initiated new sumptuary legislation. Men could be punished for playing cards on Sunday, for cursing, for consulting gypsies, for saying there was no Devil, for singing songs against Calvin. In 1546 he closed down all the taverns, and opened five "abbayes" in their place, where men could drink in a moral and religious atmosphere until 9:00 P.M. and the general curfew. There was a regular meeting of mutual criticism for the elders, the *Grabeau,* and later also for the Council, communal examinations of the community conscience. But this discipline was a means to community self-respect and efficiency, and ultimately to freedom — freedom from the foreign yoke, cultural as well as political. Hooker said that the Genevans often longed to be rid of Calvin, but always in the end "they preferred to be somewhat hardly yoked at home than to be abroad for ever discredited."

It was to some extent an intellectuals' and enthusiasts' regime. Between 1549 and 1559 five thousand immigrants arrived in Geneva. This naturally provoked resentment from the original inhabitants, especially because so many of the immigrants were Puritan idealists. Calvin, an immigrant himself, met opposition from some of the old-established families; the party known later as the Libertines. They had been crushed by 1555, but Calvin continued to find his most faithful followers and helpers among refugee intellectuals and idealists from England, France, Scotland, Italy. He was himself, like them, an international revolutionary, an ideologist, with the temperament of mind that goes with that. These were men who had been driven from their native cities, by their enemies' power or by their own disgust, and had come to Geneva as to the one place where a community could live the way they believed men should live, the only way that did not breed evil among them.

Knox described the city as the most perfect school of Christ that ever was on earth since the days of the Apostles. Calvin made tiny Geneva the international center of militant evangelism in sixteenth-century Europe just as Cuba has sent out its emissaries to the other Caribbean islands, to South America, and beyond.

Calvin attacked those he called Nicodemites, his equivalent of "liberals," people who stayed within the Catholic Church even though their religious and moral sympathies were with Reform. But he himself did not exhort citizens of other nations to rebel politically, being concerned rather with how to run one's own community once one had power. Among the refugees at Geneva, however, that next step toward international revolution was taken. The Marian exiles from England and Scotland, of whom the most famous was John Knox, exhorted the faithful to rebel against any king or queen who prevented them from worshipping God properly. That is they preached revolution. And the French Huguenots developed a new political ideology around the figure of the conscientious magistrate, the governor who made his social function a kind of lay priesthood. These quite technical theories formed the two halves of the political mixture which exploded in the English Revolution of the seventeenth century and the righteous execution of the king. The figure of the Duke of Buckingham, and the act of his assassination, can be taken as representative of Renaissance (or Faustian) politics, in which the values of personality were supreme — the values of personal beauty, manners, style, wit, even costume. Calvinist politics were a totally different genre, with covenants, sermons, committees, resolutions, trained political bands.

But among the émigré intellectuals who flocked to Geneva to participate in the new and holy life there, there were those with whom Calvin quarreled bitterly, because they were a danger to the strict discipline of the city and the faith. And it happens that the two most famous of those quarrels were with men who strikingly represented the Erasmian and the Faustian temperaments of mind. Sebastian Castellio (1515–1563) came to Geneva in 1542, and was made rector of the academy. He had been Calvin's chief assistant at Strasburg, during his brief exile there. Having quarreled with Calvin theologically, Castellio was driven out of Geneva and settled in Basel, where he translated the Bible into Latin and French, and engaged in pamphlet controversy with Calvin over the latter's disciplinary policies. Between 1542 and 1546, fifty-eight people were condemned to death in Geneva, and seventy-six to banishment. Castellio did not rule a city. He was essentially a man of letters, a scholar and a humanist, a great admirer of Erasmus, in spirituality one of the line of Spiritual Reformers, which ran from Hans Denck to Boehme, all of whom owed something important to Erasmus. He was above all the apostle of tolerance in religion and in politics; he was an Erasmian.

Michael Servetus (1511–1555) was a Faustian, both in boldness of speculation and in arrogance of behavior. He was a neo-Platonist, had read Ficino, and was something of a pantheist. He denied the orthodox doctrine of the Trinity and the pre-existence of Christ. Christ was for him an emanation of God — a gnostic doctrine. He taught that the period of 1,260 years of false theology foretold in the Apocalypse was about to end, and he, Michael Servetus, was to be the foretold archangel Michael who would lead the battle against the Antichrist and revive the Church. A man of brilliant intellect as well as of almost incredible recklessness, he was an astrologer and a scientist, who established the theory of the pulmonary circulation of the blood. But he put himself in Calvin's power by coming to Geneva after contradicting him on points of doctrine. On Calvin's order, he was tried for heresy, condemned, and burned at the stake in Geneva.

In 1559 Calvin established the Academy of Geneva, under the direction of Theodore Beza, the most famous of his immigrant disciples. The instruction was free, and it drew students from all over Europe. It became the model for imitation by both the Huguenot schools in France and the Jesuit colleges. The instruction in secular learning was as good as that in the Scriptures and the faith — Calvin remained always a humanist — though the second of the two was clearly the more important. But ordinarily the two harmonized together, for the faith was essentially a rational and conscious thing. Literacy campaigns, and more broadly educational enthusiasm, have been a regular feature of the first years of Calvinist regimes everywhere — in Cuba and in Russia, for instance. "A boy of Geneva could give a more rational account of his faith than a doctor of the Sorbonne." And his faith was manifested in, as well as supported by, the whole way of life of the city of Geneva.

Calvin lived and died a poor man, with few external honors. He worked extraordinarily hard, preaching every day of the week, alternate weeks, and also lecturing three times a week. It is calculated that he gave 286 sermons and 180 lectures in a year. The key word for his personality as for his doctrine is "discipline"; the ruthless subordination of both id and ego — his and other people's — to a superego of a very partisan kind, the Party or the Church. This did not prevent his being recognizably both an irritable, imperious man, and, in some company, a gay, pleasant one. But his personality was not the point, was not even a point, of his life, and was never particularly stressed. Consequently, Beza never felt Calvin's presence to be as burdensome as Melanchthon came to feel Luther's. Indeed, though by the end of his life Calvin had become virtually civil dictator of Geneva, he did not intend to set up an autocracy, or even a theocracy. The church was not supposed to subsume the civil magistracy, but to exist alongside it, like the party and the state. It is typical of him that he was buried anonymously in the common graveyard of Geneva, with no stone to mark the place.

But of course Geneva *was* a very authoritarian, a very disciplined, city. And it derived from that discipline a pride which preserved its identity for centuries afterwards. Once a city has achieved a form, a culture of its own, it can transmit its faith across seas and across centuries. In seventeenth-century England, a king was executed, a church abolished, a devout commonwealth set up, on the model of Geneva. And in eighteenth-century France a series of books full of Genevan ideas had a powerful effect on leaders of the next great revolution.

Rousseau was born into a commercially flourishing Geneva, a center of clock-making and banking, nearly 150 years after Calvin's death; but it was still full of proud civic patriotism and of mutual moral surveillance. Once a year the citizens all assembled in the cathedral to choose their magistrates, still. Less than half of the then twenty-five thousand inhabitants were of the citizen class, it is true; the rest were called Natives, though theoretically there were three subclasses of them, Subjects, Inhabitants, and Natives proper. These were all barred from the professions, discriminatorily taxed, and limited in their commercial activities. Geneva was an oligarchy; in the Council of the Two Hundred and the Council of the Twenty-five a few leading families were dominant. But it still thought of itself as free, and virtuous, by comparison with, say, the Bourbon kingdoms of Spain and France — the France of Louis XV and the royal mistresses.

When Rousseau discovered his new identity, his new temperament, in 1749, it was in terms of that city, the city of faith. In the *Discours sur les Sciences et les Arts*, he praised Geneva's sumptuary laws and military exercises, and declared that luxury and good morals were hostile to each other. He equated virtue with a quite military discipline, and said that culture must be made to serve virtue — that is, to serve political ends. A strict self-subordination to the collective will of the community is the only mechanism for a virtuous society, because it is the only way to abolish competition, self-consciousness, self-display, domination by others' opinions. The luxuriant overgrowth of the arts and the sciences means that nowadays we have painters, poets, and philosophers, but no citizens. He himself set out to become a citizen again, leaving Paris, and intending to settle in Geneva. In much the same way did writers like Desnoes return from New York to Havana.

Getting the Dijon Academy's Prize for the *Discours* "awakened all the ideas that had dictated it and completed the fermentation in my heart of that first germ of heroism and virtue that my father, my country, and Plutarch had sowed in my childhood. I thought nothing was greater and more beautiful than to be free, above fortune and opinion, and to be self-sufficient." This is what Geneva meant to him, and he made it mean that to half of Europe. The idea of the small, virtuous, republican city — Sparta and early Rome as well as Geneva — dominated the imagination of radicals then just as Havana dominates our imagination now.

The anarchy of inequality and mutual corruption which we see everywhere in modern society, says Rousseau, can only be abolished by establishing the equal dependence of all on the collective whole. Man's nature, as we encounter it now, is all culture — his original nature can only be taken into account as a theoretical standard by which to condemn the present condition of his soul. (This idea, which is very like Calvin, is Rousseau's doctrine most of the time.) So man can only be redeemed by a total discipline, a total control of his environment; citizens must be *formed*; education is the prime responsibility of the state. Though originally and theoretically good, man is practically and in modern society evil. His breath is poisonous to his fellowman. Man is alienated from himself because he judges himself according to others' opinions of him, and this is to be blamed on the main features of liberal, lax, worldly, bourgeois culture — free competition, free inequality, free rights of private ownership. To save him from his individually free corruption, the general interest must be *made into* a social force as powerful as self-interest. The community must be *made into* the highest moral value, and the highest moral agent.

From Plato to Rousseau, from Sparta to Geneva, and on to Communist Moscow and Havana, this has been one of the great determining dreams of Western man. Depending so much on obedience and self-subordination, it has affinities with the military mind and even with war which often become explicit. This is one of the features of contemporary Cuba which disconcerts visiting sympathizers from a different radical tradition. It was the Protestant national armies of the seventeenth century (the Dutch, the Huguenot, the Swedish) who created a highly trained, highly mobile force, capable of rapid movement. They revived the cavalry charge, got rid of ornamental weaponry, and fought throughout the winter. Modeling themselves on the Roman armies, they introduced uniforms and marching in step. (Military drill even in peacetime was a recommended moral discipline in Puritan England.) Feudal loyalty and mercenary calculation were replaced by spiritual dedication and self-discipline. Cromwell asked Baxter to organize the East Anglican cavalry into a church. There was prayer and preaching before battle, the enemy being described in Satanic terms, and the war in Apocalyptic.

Every highly disciplined and idealistic Western institution carries the seed of that dream, the seed of the Calvinist temperament. For instance, the monastic orders of the Roman Catholic Church. But that temperament has rarely allied itself fruitfully with the aesthetic imagination, especially with the imperially, the hubristically, autonomous imagination so characteristic of modern art. One expects to find Joyce disapproved in Russia, and Rabelais and Calvin hating each other. I arrived in Havana expecting to find such a contradiction there too.

Meeting in Havana

My first morning in Havana I woke to loudspeaker announcements from a car, and found posters freshly slapped on to every wall and window, TODOS CON FIDEL EN LA PLAZA A LAS 6. But I got off my bus there alone. The sound-relay system all around was blaring out the battle hymns — the new music of the Revolution, a few voices in shrill unison singing militant hymn tunes. But there were no people in the whole rainy Plaza, except the giant ice-cream statue of José Martí and a young soldier on guard near the bus stop. He told me the meeting had been put off till 8:30. Everyone in the city had somehow known. It was then 5:30, so the only thing to do was to go back to my hotel. In another city I might have gone to a restaurant to wait, but in Havana there are lines in front of eating places before they open. You eat in your hotel and think yourself lucky. Unfortunately I had used my last five centavo piece, which is the only coin bus drivers will accept, and cabs are not to be found, so I trudged over to the bus terminal to get some change. That, however, had been taken over by the army, and there were clusters of frustrated travelers buzzing round the doors like angry bees. Absolutely no one might enter. The two soldiers at my door were very alike, although one was Negro and the other wasn't; both young, crew-cut, dark-skinned, with prominent cheekbones and dark glasses. Gaunt, above all, thin. Batista's police were always, it seems, fat. These men looked strained, as if each individually felt the responsibilities of the Revolution, and absolutely honest.

Still looking for change, I found a coffee counter nearby. Four men immediately formed a line behind me, but the lady (black) refused to serve me, because I was not at one of the appointed spots along the counter. Silently our little queue dissolved and was accepted into other queues. Later I noticed that at sit-down counters people waiting their turn stood back a few yards, giving the others breathing room while they ate. Everywhere the same social discipline, which in the setting of Havana still has the air of a miracle.

By the time I got my bus money it was 6:30, and I couldn't find my bus stop. I decided to pass the time in the José Martí National Library, but that too had been taken over by men in fatigues; there were many radio and TV cables trailing through the entrance hall. The same dark, muscular faces above the olive-green — the new faces of the Caribbean — the same pistols. The pistols are not just decorative, but neither are they factually murderous, as American policemen's pistols are. They are symbolic, symbolic of the Sierra Maestra.

By now the sky was clearing, the enormous Havana sky, which is more changeable, more dramatic, more inhabited, than any other sky in the world, a meteorologist's safari-land. Over the Plaza you got a good sweep of it, with huge forms moistly gliding away.

I knew that the meeting was to be an act of solidarity with South Vietnam, with the new Provisional Government the F.L.N. was forming. When I flew into Havana the day before, the airport had signs welcoming Tran Buu Kiem, and Che's giant poster was flanked by two Vietnamese faces. Most striking were the banners and newspaper slogans, written in South Vietnamese. Havana really does feel, or try to feel, that the bombs falling in Southeast Asia might have, in some sense *should* have, fallen on them. It is an international city, though the other countries it is conscious of are not large on our maps. Algeria, the Congo, Bolivia, South Vietnam, these are the centers of the world for Cuba.

People were arriving in the Plaza, in groups more than individually. Some represented trades, some individual factories or schools, some districts of Havana, some villages outside. All the lorries in the province had been used to bring them in. Some schoolchildren came in marching, but most came in groups, not even in columns, and few commands were given. None were barked. There was practically no marching in step, practically no bands. Lots of people carried banners or wore buttons, but the only music, I think, came from a group with bongos, from Rancho Boyero, a suburb, whose banner declared that "Los Boyeros" supported the F.L.N. They snaked their way through the crowd, dancing and laughing, and whoever they came near started dancing and laughing too, and stopped when they moved away. This was the old Caribbean music, the old Caribbean personality, feckless, nonserious. Not that there was any hostility between them and the battle hymns still blaring out. But the bongo-dancing was now confined to a minor function of the personality instead of being dominant or characterizing.

Men were setting up hollow squares of counters and started selling puff pastry and cartons of tamarind juice. There were trucks with water pipes emerging, and a number of taps. And a Red Cross tent. Meanwhile a few of the official guests had begun to appear on the lower ranks of seats on the rostrum.

The Plaza, which can hold hundreds of thousands, slopes gently down and away from the José Martí statue, and the ugly monument behind him. There is a concrete structure there to make speeches from, but (did Batista perhaps speak from there?) Castro had the crowd facing the other way, and a wooden platform was set up on the opposite side of the square. All around stand the huge, nondescript buildings occupied by d'fferent government agencies. And a few giant posters of Che and slogans.

By now it was eight o'clock and the light was beginning to fade. There was a Russian standing near me, a camera on his shoulder, someone who had not spoken for a long time; his Arctic-blue-eyed profile and blondness an alibi. That is how the Russians are in Cuba, foreignness embodied. Though their support alone keeps the country in existence, they are not to be noticed. And this alone, it seems clear, lets the alliance work. It is other countries, even the U.S.A., you will hear Cubans talk about with affection, not Russia.

The lower half of the rostrum was filled with visiting notables, South Vietnamese scholarship students, capitalist student radicals — their shirts much gaudier than the Cubans', their hair longer, barefoot, semi-bare-bosomed, to show off their costume jewelry. The lights were now on, the radio commentators had begun, and the foreign guests, feeling themselves on TV, began waving to each other, exchanging places, etc. The crowd was packed quite tightly together, and geological faults opened up in it, zigzag lanes along which people moved in conga-line when they wanted to get nearer or get away. Even during the speeches people do not stand still all the time. They listen, move away and talk together, return again.

When it passed nine o'clock and grew dark, people started to cheer as the really distinguished people began to dribble in, on the

top half of the rostrum. Olive-green fatigues became more prominent up there. These uniforms give the whole government, though
so stable, a curious air of an occupying force. And of course half the
big buildings of Havana are in fact occupied — their original purpose and function perverted.

Finally, to a great roar, Fidel appeared. There was lots of sustained applause, and there could be no doubt of his place in their
hearts, but I was struck by a kind of coolness — an opposite to
hysteria. It seemed the expression of a very secure relationship.
There is no official personality cult in Cuba. Or only of Che, and
that since his death. Fidel's picture is not often seen, and then it is
(unlike Che's) quite impersonal, simply energetic. His manner, too,
was very secure and simple, but that perhaps could be taken for
granted in an accomplished public figure. Their response to him
seemed more significant.

The speech itself (we had to hear Tran first, partly in South
Vietnamese) was a fine one. But I got most of it from reading
Granma next morning. I left before he ended. It took me a good
ten minutes to get to the nearest edge of the Plaza and tolerably
free movement, and there I found in effect another assembly. Not
so densely packed as the crowd behind me, not so attentive, but
still present, sitting down or strolling or chatting in the velvety
darkness, for a couple of hundred yards up the broad boulevard. As
I walked home the voice echoed at me out of loudspeakers, radios,
TV sets, all along the way. The first streets were lined with parked
lorries, and then along the long yellow arcades, it came at me from
open windows, cafes, and transistor radios. The night was warm
and the whole city was out, sitting on doorsteps. Not all were listening, and I didn't see anyone reacting. Several couples were holding hands, or were off in shadowy corners. It was a popular fiesta.
But it was also a great political occasion.

I knew it was easy for Cuba to have enchanted me by its politics,
and I took small stock in my enchantment. First of all because the
first ten years of such a regime have often proved its best. Secondly
because there are causes for alarm in the state of affairs there —
but this is not the place to discuss them. Thirdly because I am not
the person publicly to discuss such things or even privately to de-

cide on them with any authority. Taking only the most reluctant and conscience-driven interest in politics, I am perfectly suited to a Party regime, any regime in which I am asked to hand over the running of affairs to a dedicated group, a group whose dedication I can trust, however formal that trust may in certain matters be. I would be a perfectly happy citizen of any Communist regime which did not sin too grossly against common decency. The anti-political man is the most loyal member of the radical state, once it is set up. Both Calvin and Rousseau recommended to their readers acceptance of the political status quo, abstinence from political activity. One might, with some exaggeration, say that it is the *liberal* state which demands constant political activity as a duty from all its citizens. Calvin called the Utopian Anabaptists "foolish Jewish fanatics." He meant what we have called Faustian radicals. "That is a Jewish vanitie, to seek and inclose the kingdome of Christ under the elements of the world . . ." He saw the social experiment of Munster in terms of the heretical sects of fifteenth-century Tabor and earlier, people he called "Spirituels and Libertines." Discipline was for him the better half of religious and political valor. I feel that way myself. What I want is the chance to concentrate my mind with a quiet conscience on the arts and sciences and their environs in general culture. It would be when I looked at the state of literature in Cuba, and its relations to the state, that I might make more meaningful judgments. My temperament is mildly Calvinist in politics — mildly because I have so little temperament there, so little force and clarity of reaction. But in cultural matters it is quite clearly and energetically Erasmian. So I turned to the writers of Cuba with anticipation.

Notes after Conversations with Cuban Writers

June 4.

Eliseo Diego* belongs to the older generation that was established before the Revolution. He published his poetry in *Orígenes*, José Lezama Lima's literary magazine, in the forties. Nowadays most of that group, the Catholic poets of Cuba, work in the Bibli-

* Author of several volumes of verse, including *En la Calzada de Jesús del Monte*.

oteca Nacional. Eliseo works in the Children's Department; Octavio Smith, Roberto Friol, Cintio Vitier, and his wife, Fina Garcia Marruz, all poets, work in the same building. They are the most unequivocally nice people I have met here, with an old-fashioned niceness, not specifically of the Revolution. (The Director of the Library wears army fatigues, and is specifically of the Revolution. But his poets seem to like and admire him and to have the feelings returned. Of course, they all *believe* in the Revolution.) They are serious, gentle, polite, good. Eliseo, whom many consider the best poet in the country, is the mildest *hidalgo* type, his courtesy never infringing on your liberty in the slightest, never asserting itself. The strong black brows, the steady voice, the slow walk, the inclining of the head — a confessiorial presence. Even his sadness, which in his poetry makes itself felt powerfully, does not assert itself. What he offers you is steadiness, stillness, self-sustenance. He acted recently in a dramatization of *The Christmas Carol*, and he reads Chesterton and Belloc still. English literature is for him still British rather than American.

At his suggestion I went today to see Padre Gaztelu's church of the Holy Spirit, the oldest in Havana, in the old quarter of the city. Padre Gaztelu "converted" Lezama Lima at the beginning of his literary career, and so in a sense inspired the whole *Orígenes* movement. The church has more appearance of wealth about it than any other I've seen, with saints' statues in gaudy satin and gorgeous velvet, under glass cases. There is a rather lurid Crucifixion, and a Virgin with her heart pierced by seven swords. And some of the square pillars are painted to simulate draped curtains. It is a glimpse of the old baroque colonialist culture, which Eliseo does in some sense derive from. When we went to the very elaborate 1830 restaurant, I discovered that as a young man he had visited the house when it still belonged to the Minister of Transport, who built it for himself — as a by-product of building a highway for the state. Eliseo had actually seen the bear and the peacocks kept in the Japanese garden, then complete with Japanese gardener, which stretched its grottoes out into the water behind the house. Not that there is anything baroque, much less anything corrupt, about Eliseo. Even his poetry is full of silences and solitudes, the white light of noon in dusty courtyards, memory, regret. But those images are heavy with the awareness of brutality and crude splendor elsewhere. Revolutionary hope is not in his line.

June 5.

Edmundo Desnoes* begins "taking a position" in the first five minutes he is with you. "Norman Mailer is the court jester of Washington, D.C. . . . Socialist countries at least take writers seriously enough to send them to jail." And you know — even before you actually see them in print — that these are sentences he has prepared, things he has said before, public utterances. But the effect is not to alienate; rather the reverse. So uneven a style, offering public utterances in private places, is very self-exposing. He is an abrupt, disjointed personality, the masculine, purposeful elements establishing a lead over the feminine, receptive elements, only with a palpable effort, and minute by minute. He talks loudly, holds his head erect, avoids your eye. And he has made himself Cuba's most interesting writer by interrelating this personal conflict with the cultural revolution. The triumph of the Revolution in Cuba is (will be, would be) the triumph of those elements in him I've called masculine and purposeful. (They are also the public as opposed to the private elements, which is why he converses in headlines.) Its failure would mean the reestablishing of the old coalition of masculine and feminine in pessimistic, inert, rentier dilettantism; the style of the Batista bourgeois intellectual. That interrelationship is what all his books are about. And in that context his whole physique takes on a very dramatic meaning. He's unusually tall, broad-shouldered, healthy-looking. And such large blue eyes, such a pink-and-white baby skin, such silky blond hair, such large perfect teeth, in Cuba these things look paid for. They are the rewards of the rich, the preserve of privilege, the *anglosajón* imitated to perfection even in terms of flesh and blood, skin and bone. And of course he has appropriated these features. They make him a handsome man. (Just as — appropriating his educational advantages as bourgeois — he speaks a fluent and idiomatic and off-putting American.) But at the same time it's a countenance full of

---

* Author of *Inconsolable Memories*, New York, 1967, and two other novels in Spanish, plus a book of essays, *Punto de Vista*.

conflict — not at all handsome. The eyes roll like those of a nervous horse, and the mouth has a triangular pout, the base corners pulled down in defiance of the impulse to charm or conciliate. Altogether the most likable, the most *understandable*, man I've met in Cuba.

June 13.

Pablo Armando Fernandez* invited us to his house this evening. It is the first Havana home we've gone into. The other writers all came to my hotel, or else saw us at their place of work. This is explained by the rationing — making it difficult for them to offer hospitality — but it exists as a style. Pablo lives in Miramar, a suburb of beautiful avenues and expensive houses, now mostly occupied by schools and scholarship students' housing, etc., though next door to Pablo still lives the pre-Revolutionary owner of that house. And Pablo has Tiffany lamps, modernist paintings, folklore curiosities, on his marble floors.

Pablo is the hardest of them all for me to get on terms with. We talked about the Padilla scandal (Heberto Padilla, one of Cuba's leading poets, has suffered a series of marks of official disfavor) and Pablo took the "official" line — that the case is not really political, that personal factors played a large part, that indignation about it abroad would do Heberto harm. But what is characteristic of Pablo is the wild inconsistency of his arguments. On the one hand, the case is not political at all. On the other, a whole series of the details he offered only made sense as proof that it *was* political, in cause, career, and consequence. On the one hand, Heberto has not suffered — "no more than everyone in Cuba suffers; we all suffer." On the other hand, since Heberto has no job and no income, he, Pablo, and other friends, keep him alive.

And this intellectual kaleidoscope — each new sentence a new shake of the box — comes at you so unabashed, so complacent, so intended. Pablo is, I was told before I came, "What everyone thinks a Cuban poet should be — impulsive, talkative, mystical." I didn't think anybody "should be" all that, and I decided that the

---

* Best known as a poet, but recently won a prize with his novel, *Los Niños se Despiden*.

genre "Cuban poet" was highly suspect. But the description is true enough of Pablo; and he's not as overbearing as that might suggest; quite a mild presence. He is no Faust. More of an Aziz, or one of Forster's Italian Pans. He represents the Pan contract. We were also told before we came that "Everyone loves Pablo." And indeed I saw everyone loving him — people laid hands on him in the street. And his conversation is a card-file of all the hearts that he has won, his friends all over the world, and the presents they have given him.

Well, I'm the last person in the world to be fair to someone whom "everyone loves." But beyond these personal problems I think I see a question of Cubanism. Pablo *is* something Cuban, certainly, and very persuasively so. He, unlike Edmundo, is un-equivocally — unobtrusively — handsome; short, broad-shouldered, curly-haired, curly-bearded, smiling, easy; eminently caressable Pan. And he can feel he has done his duty by being human — can sit back and collect prizes for it — when he has been charming, spontaneous, warm, and sensual. He doesn't have to be, for instance, consistent in argument.

This *is*, of course, very Latin, very Caribbean — very Cuban. But isn't that a Cubanism which (as well as *my* not being at ease with it) the Revolution is ultimately against? Isn't the Latin role, after all, something that leading nations assign to secondary nations? Castro's Cuba doesn't intend to be secondary.

June 14.

Miguel Barnet,* very American-looking in a maroon T-shirt, is a cross between Edmundo and Pablo in these ways. Also "being Latin" a lot of the time, his performance is yet disturbed by an intelligence (as well as a nervous intensity) not perfectly integrated into that role. He would fit better into New York. Much more than the other two, his temperamental rhythm is very like that of young Americans today. But he believes — as Pablo believes — in the Revolution. They are committed to Cuba, and to the isolation and insularity of its great experiment, even to its — they hope temporary — provinciality and puritanism.

---

* A poet, youngest of the well-established Cuban writers, and author of the translated *Autobiography of a Runaway Slave*.

What most concerned me, of course, was the relation to these writers of their city, that legend, that mirage, the radical city, so rarely to be actually encountered, either on a visit or in reliable reportage. I wanted to estimate its pressure, and the results for their imaginative life.

But I took the writers' accounts of such things wherever what I saw of the city could confirm what they said; even when it was clear that another account of the matter was possible. They were all honorable men — that is why I could honorably believe them — but they were all justifying themselves and their city and their revolution. But I did not pursue hints that could have led me to really opposite interpretations, partly because there was no chance of reaching certainty in them.

For instance, certainty about the short-term aspects of the Padilla case is possible. He has been done an injustice, and of a kind which is a serious matter for Cuban writers in general as well as himself. But an "interpretation" would have to balance against that, the fact that he does live and write freely, and moves about Havana a symbol of opposition to official policy; and the facts of the other writers' lives. I did not form an interpretation which I could recommend as authoritative.

I looked for, that is to say, I allowed myself to be shown, what could confirm my favorable impression, and allotted to my skepticism an external function. I set it on guard of my faith, to incorporate in advance all that might be said against Cuba. It armored rather than muscularized my mind, that part I had consecrated to the idea of Cuba, in defense against possible shocks of revelation later.

And even in discussing the literature I found my mind divide itself into internal and external, faith and skepticism, emotional and intellectual, in a way that made the two halves hard to recombine. I had allowed myself to sound, to be, quite softly enthusiastic about political things, because, although I had some other impressions, I had no way of combining them with the first ones, no properly muscular process for digesting the whole. I must either be naïvely and breathlessly affirmative, or carpingly and cautiously reserved, and of the two it seemed more honorable to be affirmative. About literature I expected myself to be more judicious, but I still decided to avoid the Scylla of self-preservation more vigorously than the Charybdis of reckless recommendation. I did not know as much about Cuban literature — not to mention Cuban society — as was quite proper, but I was ready to recommend certain things in it to anyone who would trust my recommendation. My sense both of myself and of my audience was that prudence was more our enemy in this matter than our friend. So this account of Cuban literature also leans toward the naïvely assenting, I'm afraid.

Literature and the Revolution in Havana

I want a drink, Harry was thinking. What the hell do I care about his revolution? F— his revolution. To help the working man he robs a bank and kills a fellow works with him and then kills that poor damned Albert that never did any harm. That's a working man he kills. He never thinks of that. With a family. It's the Cubans run Cuba. They all double-cross each other. They sell each other out. They get what they deserve. The hell with their revolutions. All I got to do is make a living for my family and I can't do that. Then he tells me about his revolution. The hell with his revolution.

> — Ernest Hemingway, "A Boatload for Cuba,"
> *To Have and Have Not*, 1937

Hemingway is for Cubans the archetypal American writer, the archetypal capitalist writer, perhaps the archetypal writer. So this paragraph rings in their ears with very brazen resonances. So it does in ours, as a reechoing. We hear how it sounds in their ears. The initiative, the advantage, is theirs. In literary matters, as in others, Cuba seems specially well placed to confront the West; it has, it is, the record of our dealings with the Third World.

Take for instance Graham Greene's novel, and the film made from it, *Our Man in Havana*. That title has, I take it, two points of irony, two points at which it creaks under any stress of pronunciation: "our man," which mocks the British Secret Service, and "Havana," which mocks Cuba. But the bitingness, the bitterness, is all in the first one. The joke against Havana is an obvious and also a gentle one; the novel is really in sympathy with what Havana — its Havana — stands for. And the plot, the substance, of the novel, has the same double-acting irony which really sharpens its edge only in one direction — against serious Whitehall politics — which isn't really aware that there is anything to bruise or to be cut in the other direction. Havana represents, and is loved for doing so, all the cities in the world where corruption is contentedly rife, where idealism is known to be impracticable, where serious politics is out of the question. The rebels in Oriente get mentioned, but only as a part of the landscape, or a habit of the weather. And the point of view of the novel as a whole is "Cuban" in that sense. Wormold wins the prize — the love of Beatrice — because he has been disloyal to his country and loyal to his daughter. Milly is real, England is unreal. Because he unwittingly knew this and acted on it, Wormold wins (is intended to win) our esteem and affection, and is rewarded with a happy ending. He is contrasted with the unworthy first husband of Beatrice who had such enthusiasm for UNESCO. The scorn Greene concentrates into those initials, the Aunt Sally he makes out of this dupe of political progressivism, is one of the most striking motifs of the book.

It is perhaps only a historical coincidence (one might call it hard lines on Greene) that those recurrent rebels in Oriente should turn out to be Fidel Castro, and that it should be Havana where nowadays, only ten years later, serious politics are more in the air than any other city in the world. But there is something almost sinisterly apt in the further coincidence that the major device of the plot, the major "event," is an international scare over missile sites in Cuba. The drawings of these sites, sent to London by Wormold, provoke all the other incidents of the book, because they make first the British Secret Service and then foreign services, take him seriously. In the novel, of course, the point of all this is the absurdity of international politics, for the drawings are in fact of vacuum cleaner parts, drawn out of scale. But in 1962, four years later, history caught up with the novel and passed it. That is something one is very conscious of in Cuba, events criticizing points of view. Especially our points of view.

Greene shows in his novel that he knows Havana well, and indeed his picture of the city then — of the whole island — is perfectly fair, granted the conventions of the satiric entertainment. Cuba now does not object to the portrait. Indeed, one can still see his Havana if one walks along Obispo or Obrapia, even though most of the characterizing features are gone, not to be found, like the banks and the American firms, or out of action, like the night clubs and the neon signs. One can see his people, though again the most characteristic ones are in Miami, or Madrid. It is still an entertaining pastime, to pick out in the streets of present-day Havana the individual who, with a sprucer suit, with a more knowing gleam in his eye, with more elaborate guile in his hands and haircut, might have been Lopez or Captain Segura.

The most striking case of this is the converted buildings, those embodied anecdotes. There is the UNEAC building — UNEAC is the Union of Cuban Artists and Writers — which was the home of a banker who after a financial reverse found himself with only eight million pesos left (the peso is officially worth a dollar), so cut his throat. The elaborate chandeliers still tinkle with that story while below the typewriters bang out Marxist editorials. There is a restaurant in the very millionairish home of a Minister of Public Works under Machado, who built the highway a foot or two too narrow. There is a laboratory in the home of another minister — perhaps that minister of education who went to Miami with two million dollars in his suitcases. "No, I'll carry them myself — they're hand-luggage." It is a city of anecdotes, and a lot of them are about people now in Miami. *Our Man in Miami*, written by a Cuban, could be a much better book than *Our Man in Havana*, because it could have a lot more variety and vigor of mood. That is the sort of literary criticism which present-day Havana puts into your mind.

But it is Hemingway who represents the Western writer to Cubans. For Latin America as a whole, it seems that Faulkner has been the greatest influence over the last twenty years. But that has no doubt something to do with the similarity of his situation to that of Latin American writers, the political dungeon in which he and they live, and the aesthetic spiders' webs he spun in reaction. As soon as the possibility of action is raised, the possibility of breaking out, Hemingway is bound to seem more interesting than Faulkner. No doubt his most famous treatment of Cuban characters and settings is *The Old Man and the Sea*, and there is a documentary which introduces you to a fisherman they claim to be the original. But the prestige of this story in Cuba as elsewhere is rather theoretical. And to the literary public now the use of Cuba as a setting for a fable, to induce a sense of timelessness, seems only a subtler mode of exploitation. Cuba is being used the way China was used in eighteenth-century fables, as a land outside time. But that Cuba is not timeless is in a sense the message of the Revolution. That with the Revolution, Cuba entered history, and is as much in time as American itself, is an important formula of theirs.

The paragraph quoted from *To Have and Have Not* expresses most directly Hemingway's challenge to Cubans. Both he and Greene found something in Cuba very sympathetic to their temperaments — two of the most clear-cut temperaments in contemporary literature. And Cubans return that feeling. The vigor with which both writers repudiated the pieties of their own countries and their native systems of politics and economics makes them spokesmen for the Third World. So the cynicism of the message quoted is not entirely easy for them to reject.

Nor is its directness, its crudity of expression. Hemingway is *the* Western writer for Cubans just because he is direct and crude. Hemingway was close to one old ideal of manhood in Cuba, in that he was *"muy macho,"* the *big* man, full of masculine sexuality and power. But he was very far from their traditional idea of the intellectual and literary man. Their authors have been characteristically belletrist, from José Martí himself to Alejo Carpentier and José Lezama Lima. Whether fiery like Martí or aloof like Lezama, they are rhetorical, formally elaborate, mannered. There is something of the Académie des Belles Lettres about them. And this manner, nowadays, seems inappropriately European, not to say colonial. Whereas Hemingway's manner, if it could be appropriated, would be just right for declarations of cultural independence.

Then Cubans these days feel the need to define themselves as individuals by more direct expressions of sexuality and aggressiveness than before. In this they are only like the rest of the world. It is, after all, Hemingway of all preceding writers whom Mailer and Bellow have found most fruitful, most necessary to imitate and react against. American Jewish writers as a group, Leslie Fiedler argues, have liberated themselves from the old cultural image of the literary Jew by making use of Hemingway. If this is true — to the extent to which it is true — American literature as much as Cuban has taken Hemingway to be *the* Western writer.

Above all, the Cubans like to define their position as a confrontation with the United States. They like to turn their backs on Europe, East as well as West, and to see themselves as challenging the United States for the leadership of the Third World, above all the leadership of Latin America. Therefore they like to divide the world up between civilization and barbarism, to claim the United States for barbarism, and to identify themselves with that. Europe, they often say, is played out. But in the Western Hemisphere life still runs to intensities, of opposite kinds. They understand the U.S.A., even while they fight it, better than European countries. This set of terms commands assent, perhaps, mostly as an expression of the determination to see things this way. But it certainly explains why Hemingway — a "barbaric" writer if ever there was one — should be so important for them.

And then of course he lived there, and lived there in style; the style of conspicuous consumption. His arrivals and departures from Havana Airport were big news in the old days. His finca, Vigia, in San Fernando de Paula, is still open to the public and is regularly visited by crowds of people. It has been used, in its function as museum, by one of Cuba's most interesting young writers, Edmundo Desnoes, in an essay, a novel, and the film made from that novel. A visit to the Hemingway house is a significant episode in *Inconsolable Memories,* and in *Memorias del Subdesarollo,* the Cuban film made from the novel, and using its Cuban title. *Memorias del Subdesarollo* could be translated as Memories, or Memoirs, of Underdevelopment, but something like Memorial to, or in Commemoration of, would give the reader a better angle on the story.

The visit to the finca is paid by the central character, a bourgeois, would-be writer, and his lower-class, scatterbrained girlfriend. Their various reactions to it, to each other in its presence, to the Russian visitors there at the same time, and to the guide — all this defines Hemingway's significance in terms of the novel's themes. The guide had been Hemingway's servant — in real life, too — and still reveres him as a superior being. The house, by being so limitedly a rich American's house in Cuba, so typically in all its furnishings a modern colonial villa, criticizes Hemingway on his own terms. But the central character cannot appropriate that criticism authentically, cannot repudiate Hemingway as a revolutionary should, because Hemingway's life — Ava Gardner and Marlene Dietrich and the parties, as well as the safaris and the wars and the best-selling novels — was also the life he himself lived in his fantasies.

This man believes in the Revolution, by means of disbelieving in its disbelievers; he is disillusioned with those who are disillusioned with it. But he is unable to feel and live in accordance with his new ideas. The novel has been misunderstood in America — to judge by what has been written about it — because reviewers have assumed that what a man feels, when it is in disaccord with what he believes, wants to feel, is his true experience, his true self; and that therefore this novel reveals the impracticability of the Revolution in experiential terms — is a statement of at least partial disillusion. But to Cuban Marxists, to the author himself, this is not true. A man may be trapped into feeling and living a life which falsifies him, which his true self disavows. And this may be true of his sexual life — which is to us the ultimate reality, the deepest bedrock of the self.

There is a short poem by Miguel Barnet which expresses the same feeling.

Revolución

Entre tu y yo
hay un montón de contradicciones
que se juntan
para hacer de mi el sobresaltado
que se humedece la frente
y te edifica.

You might say that the Revolution is the hero of *Memorias*, and that the central character is the background against which the action takes place. And the boredom the reader feels with the central character's boredom (because he is such a standard central character of Western novels of disillusionment) is employable in the service of the novel's enterprise, instead of being just a defect.

There are, I think, problems inherent in such an aesthetic conception. But most of my actual problems in reading may well have been the result of unfamiliarity with such enterprises. There are certainly moments in the story which are very interesting indeed. One that impressed me was brought out best in the movie version. Desnoes himself appears in both novel and film as a successful writer, a man with a public career, on whom the narrator comments cynically. He takes part in a panel discussion, which the central character attends. In the movie this sequence was shot in an official, newsreel style, as if we were to take the event at its official face value. The panel discusses the Revolution and culture, and Jack Gelber interrupts — in English — to make an impatient criticism of the whole proceedings for its stuffiness. Desnoes, smoking a cigar, translates this smilingly for the other members of the panel, who proceed to incorporate the protest into their deliberations. This episode, without making direct reference to the central character, leaves us feeling his kind of boredom with public and official activities. A major representative of those onto whom we project this feeling is Desnoes himself, whose face and manner are both slightly caricatured by the cigar and the smile and the translator's expertise. Then we see the central character again, on his way home. He is played by a Mastroianni type — Mastroianni at his most elegant. And in our reactions to that figure, so much more seductive, so much more "sincere," so much more expressive than that of the figure on the platform, and yet so hopeless, so self-absorbed, and self-indulgent, so preshrunk to the fitting of his elegant suits, so limited to the marginal graces of the boulevardier, the flâneur, we see the whole message of the film crystallized. And the more we explore the intricacies of Desnoes presenting himself, and commenting on himself, the better it gets. The public persona is after all more real, more alive, than the private one, however incompletely it may express a certain range of sincerities.

The film includes the episode at the finca, and shows us Rene Villareal, Hemingway's servant, enumerating and exegeting the great man's relics — explaining his work-habits — with reverent carefulness. How he understood his own role in the film is hard to guess. But in Desnoes's essay on Hemingway, *his* attitude to Rene, and to Rene's relationship to his master, is made aggressively clear. *"Creo que la revolución ha roto para siempre la posibilidad de que una relación semejante vuelva a producirse en Cuba."* And *"Hay*

*que rebelarse contra situaciones como la de Rene y declaraciones
como las de este famoso explotador de minas literarias."*
Wondering what Rene thinks about this is not an entirely accidental or trivial aspect of the film, or the essay or novel. One of
their most pungent effects is their documentary quality, their capturing of familiar reality from a slightly oblique angle. Havana,
with its two million people, is big enough to be a world-city, and
yet small enough to be private; when even its main buildings appear on the screen it is a shared experience, which could be true
nowadays of only suburban areas of great European cities, which
could generate only a clique privacy. Moreover, both the city and
the island see themselves from slightly oblique angles these days.
Everyone can remember when certain buildings, certain character-
types, had a different function, a different profile, from what they
have now. This is a redeemed, reborn city, still haunted by its unregenerate past; its profile is a double exposure. It is therefore
understandable that this effect should be very often aimed at in the
contemporary arts in Cuba, should be perhaps their major motif.

Desnoes's essay on Hemingway is the most interesting piece in
his volume of essays, *Punto de Vista*, which is, I think, his best
book so far. It is alternately personal and impersonal; he admits to,
asserts, the love-hate relationship to Hemingway which in the
novel he attributes to his central character. His tone swings between naïveté — a quite reckless self-exposure — and a formidable
knowingness about half a dozen other literatures, and a quite brutal Marxist orthodoxy. The changes of tone, indeed the tones
themselves, are quite strident, but the whole adds up to the voice
of a man embracing the Revolution passionately, but experimentally and distrustfully — self-distrustfully. He presents himself (all
he writes gives exactly the same impression) as a man strongly pre-
disposed to pessimism and cynicism, and to resentment against all
those who profess more lyrical qualities. The only child of a middle
bourgeois family — the social origin is mythically appropriate to
the sensibility and the ideology — he was educated, a typical Cuban
feature, partly in the Southern states of the U.S.A. And, an excep-
tional Cuban feature, strikingly Anglo-Saxon in skin, eyes, features,
build. This fact, his consciousness of his looks, turns up in his essays
and novels, it is such a richly problematic symbol of his fate.

Desnoes had in fact left Cuba — asphyxiated, as he says, by the political atmosphere then — before the Revolution. During the time of fighting in the provinces, he was in New York, working for *Vision*, a magazine financed by General Motors, Remington Rand, Shell, National City Bank, etc., for distribution in Latin America. A caption which the editors insisted be added to a photograph of Fidel on the Sierra, to the effect that if successful he would do away with democracy and with property in Cuba, was the final straw for Desnoes. He returned to Cuba, and has since embraced Marxism.

Cuban Marxism, carrying with it the theory of the "barbaric" Western Hemisphere, gives him a vantage point from which he can confront the whole world. He can be literature's Fidel. He can dismiss the U.S.A. for one reason, the older Marxist regimes for another, and Europe for a third. It is in Cuba, nowhere else, that the new consciousness is to be molded.

That is my interpolation, of course. What he says, and it is equally true, is that Cuban Marxism has given him an idea to live for that transcends himself, and that this alone makes life tolerable for him. But the other interpretation, the more aggressive function, of his ideology is equally valid. There are ways in which *Punto de Vista* reminds one of *Advertisements for Myself*. Cuban writers, as much as Jewish writers, needed to free themselves from the constraints of a too passive, too ironic, too "modest" cultural image. Desnoes himself dismisses Mailer as the court jester of capitalism; he sees himself, prefers to see himself, as closer to the Negro writers of America, with their violence, their cultural backwardness, their inferiority complex, their technical clumsiness. But — as with Mailer — the reader is invited by the naïvely excited rhetoric to add his own pinch of salt to such self-definitions. "*Mi aparencia, esta piel, me engaño,*" he says speaking of his blonde, blue-eyed, baby-skinned look. "*Ahora sé que aunque parezco blanco, anglosajón, y protestante, soy en realidad un negro sureno.*" And "*Quisiera sentir detrás de mi voz (aunque los propios condenados de la tierra me rechacen) un leproso de Bombay . . . etc.*" Spoken against so much predisposition to cynicism and languor, this enthusiastic energy of self-transformation, and this openness of self-confession, make a poignant and impressive dialectic.

Desnoes has so far published three novels as well as his book of essays. The first, *No Hay Problema*, is an easier book to read than *Memorias*, naïver in form and technique, but enjoyable and useful for anyone who wants to understand Cuba and the Revolution. The other, *El Cataclismo*, he has dismissed as *"un libro infamo,"* because it is a piece of socialist realism, which does not sufficiently transform its subject matter. All three books deal prominently with Havana. They are reports on the city, attempts to evaluate its "quality of life," in a sense. Such writing has been a feature of recent Cuban literature, in part for the reasons I suggested above, and now it is entering novels. The Revolution is taking place in the countryside, as they all say, but literature's best encounters with it are set in Havana. In the first half of this century, the years of Cuba's "independence," the dominant literary form was verse. And since the Revolution, in the opinion of the Cubans themselves, the best work has been done in poetry; the difference being that poets now aim at exact and expressive speech rather than at beautiful speech. But there have been some significant novels recently, dealing prominently with Havana, and it seems inevitable, in the present phase of world literature, that the novel should become the dominant form, provided the freedom of writers is not damaged.

One of these new novels is *Tres Tristes Tigres* by Guillermo Cabrera Infante. Cabrera Infante, at first the favorite son of the Revolution, editor of *Lunes de Revolución*, the weekly culture supplement to the official paper, now lives in London and repudiates the recent developments in Cuba. His novel is therefore in one sense not modern-Cuban. It has never been published there, though it won a literary prize in Spain. But its subject matter could not be more specifically Cuban, indeed Havanan. His disaffiliation from the Revolution must of course be a political event in some sense, but it seems to be no convenient palliation to say that it is not only political. The evidence of this lies both in the facts of the personal quarrels that also played a part, and in the petulance of his published complaints against the regime. And the novel itself could not be less political, could not seem more clearly the product of a nonpolitical mind.

It is a long novel, with a number of main characters, all of whom are active in the night life of Havana, just before the Revolution.

They are nearly all taken straight from life, and everyone in Havana who has read the book can identify them — and it seems as if everyone has read it even though it is not published there. (In Cuban culture this public-private ambivalence, so close to the gossip column, seems to have a different function and value from what it has with us. Of course it has that different function and value in Dublin too.) Most of these characters are still living there, though a significant number have left Cuba or are preparing to do so — one is currently working his passage by doing work in agriculture.

The novel clearly owes a good deal to Joyce, to *Ulysses*, which is the only non-American novel in English you will hear Cubans admit a debt to. (Britain scarcely counts for them at all.) More immediately, it clearly owes a lot to Leopoldo Marechal's novel of 1948, *Adán Buenosayres*, which gives a satiric-fantastic account of Buenos Aires life very like this account of Havana life. Its most brilliant feature is its language, which includes many varieties of Cuban, indeed of Havanan, Spanish. It is a series of disconnected first-person narratives, some of them stream-of-consciousness. But it is not markedly modern in formal techniques, and rather markedly nonmodern in subject matter. Considering the date and the genre, there is a striking lack of sadism, of sordidness, of pornography, almost of sexuality. Indeed, though one first becomes aware of the absence of these elements as a relief, by the end the novel feels empty. What we get instead in the last third of the novel is more kinds of verbal ingenuity, and arid kinds; tongue-twisters, private languages, codes, elaborate puns, etc.

The book is a brilliant (half the time) verbal extravaganza. The temperament behind it is the reverse of Desnoes's. Cabrera Infante comes across as ebullient, extrovert, loaded with cleverness and self-confidence, dismissive of all self-distrust. One sees more indisputable talent for fiction in *Tres Tristes Tigres* than in anything of Desnoes's. I rather expect to like Desnoes's next book better than any of his novels. This is to be a history of Cuba described half as a history of his own family, personal and impersonal alternating. The interrupting autobiographical voice, the self-interrogation, is too important a part of what he can do to let his fiction — any sustained single-level act of the imagination — be quite satisfactory. Whereas Cabrera Infante is a natural showman who can generate considerable energy within a system of elaborate artifices. It is understandable that it should be he who left revolutionary Cuba, even though Desnoes's constitutional cynicism might have made him seem a less likely candidate for faith in a social cause. But Cabrera Infante's temperament could make no use of the challenges the Revolution offers, could only chafe against the restraints; would Joyce have been any different? The fictional form toward which he tends is that of the autonomous aesthete. Whereas, in a recent questionnaire to Cuban writers, Desnoes answered the question, "Do you see a relation between your literary production and the Revolution?" beginning, "The relation between lovers . . ." As for the violence of Cabrera Infante's subsequent comments on Cuba, which still pain people in Havana, Joyce's political pronouncements were not worth being taken seriously either.

There have also been novels about Havana within the last ten years by two of the older and more well-established Cuban writers. Alejo Carpentier's *El Siglo de las Luces* contains a good many chapters set in the Havana of the French Revolutionary and Napoleonic era. And José Lezama Lima's *Paradiso* describes the life of a bourgeois family in Havana in the first part of this century. Carpentier's novel has been translated into at least English and French, while Lezama's is about to appear in both those languages and a German translation is mooted. Both have won their authors much international prestige, which is fully echoed in Cuba. Lezama's name particularly, we were told, is very high at the moment in all of Latin America.

But both these writers are recognizably, in their literary productions and personalities, of the old Havana, though both stand well personally with the new regime. Carpentier represents it in Paris. Both are "prize-winners," elaborate in style and form, and neither grapples with the politically problematic. In Carpentier's home when he was a child, we are told, Anatole France was the supreme writer and the supreme liberal mind, with his polished skepticism and ironic assurance and urbane elegance. France was an extremely popular writer all through Latin America in the 1920's, and Carpentier clearly belongs to his era rather than to Hemingway's.

Carpentier is a very learned writer, and his narrative is burdened with lore of every kind, while the subject matter is distanced by history. He provides. in effect a sumptuous tapestry of Havana then, of Cuba, of the Caribbean. The characters and events are figures in that tapestry. Our interest in them is subdued by, subjugated to, our sense of the total picturesqueness. His public pronouncements on literature and the Revolution have a similar amiable magniloquence. One does not feel he has "wrestled with the problems." In the questionnaire mentioned before, the first question asked, "What do you think is the best form in which the Revolution has expressed itself in Cuban culture?" Some people said documentary films. Desnoes listed the literacy campaign, etc. Carpentier said the freedom from compulsion of writers. Not a stupid answer, but symptomatic, I think, of a leaning backwards and away from, rather than forward and toward, the Revolution.

Lezama is a more extraordinary writer, in the sense of being more eccentric and probably also in the sense of being more talented. His novel owes a good deal to Proust and to Joyce — the Joyce of *Portrait of the Artist as a Young Man.* He too is learned, in recondite ways, but his elaborateness is more of sentence-form and sensibility, and the distancing effect comes from the operations of autobiographical memory, not those of "history." He celebrates the triumph of the imagination over the brute fact. He sees art in terms of such oppositions, and he tends to subsume history into the same terms. He has worked out a poetic cosmogony, not unlike Wallace Stevens's, of whom his work often reminds one; he belongs to that line of "gnostic" writers I discussed under the title of "rosewater Faustianism." In reply to the question last quoted from the questionnaire, he replied that the revolution has no forms, it has ecstasies; there is no form in Martí, only the promise of ecstasy. And he begins answering the second question (Do you see a relation between your production and the Revolution?) by saying, "In my opinion, the deepest relatable world is that of metaphor. For me, the revolution is a metaphor of man with his destiny." In the original, and in context, the obscurities are not lessened.

Lezama's father was a colonel who fought in the Revolutionary War, and one of the elite of the new Republic. Lezama and his literary friends' crucial political experience was of the disappointment of those hopes. Most of them poets, most of them assertively Catholic (including Lezama), they formed a distinct group in Cuban literature, the dominant group of the forties and fifties. They published in the internationally known review *Orígenes* (edited by Lezama) and all, in one way or another, created private poetic universes. There is a fine passage in a poem by Eliseo Diego, perhaps the best poet of them all, which expresses their political sadness.

> *Tendrá que ver*
> *como mi padre lo decia:*
> *la Republica.*
> *En el tranvía amarillo: La Republica, era,*
> *lleno el pecho, como*
> *decir la suave*
> *amplia, sagrada*
> *mujer que le dió hijos.*
>
> *Yo que no sé*
> *decirlo: la Republica.*

But this beautiful sadness the new Cuban writers must resist, as the Revolution resists that politics. Writers against the regime, like Cabrera Infante, resist it as much as those for it. In fact, the Catholic poets are for the Revolution. They work happily enough for the government, though rather out of the limelight, in the José Martí National Library. They still produce perhaps the bulk of the good poetry written in Cuba. But they haven't the ideological vigor of the new writers. In that sense they belong to the past, not to the present Cuba.

Of all Western writers, the one I most often thought of in the present Cuba was Conrad, because his mood — the mood of *Nostromo* — is closest to the mood that Cuba itself used to exhale. Look at any records of the old Cuba, literary or historical, and the contours of the present landscape will take on a Conradian meaning. He saw Latin Americans the way they used to see themselves. Alejo Carpentier is still very close to Conrad, in his huge perspectives of bay and mountain, of decade and of generation, those enclosing silences around even the fiercest action, of revolution or assassination.

But I thought of him also because of the way recent Cuban history refutes Conrad. Che's diaries and memoirs, for instance, often deal with situations exactly like those in Conrad's novels, but they give the incident an opposite outcome, an opposite significance. Think for instance of .all those idealistic enterprises in Conrad which come to shipwreck on the hard facts of nature and human nature. Then read this, about the beginning of the *Granma*'s historic trip from Mexico to begin the Revolution in Cuba.

We sang the Cuban national anthem and the "Hymn of the 26th of July" for perhaps 5 minutes and then the entire boat took on an aspect both ridiculous and tragic; men with anguished faces holding their stomachs, some with their heads in buckets, other lying in the strangest positions, immobile, their clothing soiled with vomit.

But that, instead of being the end of the story, was the most fleeting of episodes; the significant thing was not that they threw up, but that they sang the National Anthem. Or take Fidel's description of Che, "A man of total integrity, a man of supreme sense of honor, of absolute sincerity, — a man of stoic and Spartan living habits, a man in whose conduct not one stain can be found."

How hard it is for us, however much we admire Che, to join in such praise, which forbids the spirit of irony, forbids the spirit of Conrad. It is hard for Cubans, too, and doubly hard, no doubt dangerous, for Cuban writers, to forbid themselves that spirit. But their history has spoken — in some sense against literature; at least its irony this time is at the expense of irony itself; and they are making their fate out of their history.

Fidel's remarks about Che are typical Calvinist — stoic, Spartan — rhetoric. They remind me that half of my enthusiasm for Cuba derived from finding a place where that rhetoric could be used, where ears like mine could train themselves to hear it. The other half came from finding a Calvinist temperament active in the arts, working out solutions to aesthetic problems and experiments which are quite different from what we here know. The two coalesced in an image out of my past, and a sense of belonging.

Havana Now and London Then

The most extraordinary thing about Havana for me was the way I felt at home in it. That was extraordinary because Cuba couldn't be more exotic for an Englishman. When you fly into José Martí Airport, and see all the palm trees and that red soil and blue sea, you suddenly realize that you are in "the Spanish Main," while Havana itself is "the Caribbean," flamboyant hotels, night clubs and strip joints. And to realize that Caribbean should have meant "sea of the Carib Indians," doesn't, whatever else it may do, make you feel at home.

It was partly the nostalgic shabbiness of the city, which called itself British in my mind — some Britain of the past. The electric lights are dim, to save on the Russian oil that makes the electricity. There are very few private cars. You turn and stare at the two or three sports cars you see. You get where you are going by bus, the famous Leyland buses, now shabby and grinding. And the other main elements in the traffic are the official limousines, black and gleaming, and the trucks that every morning carry off loads of people to work in the fields. The driving is socialist, too. The traffic goes slowly as well as sparsely, and stops at every corner. Streets that were formerly one stream of speed — Havana had in 1954 a higher per capita purchase of Cadillacs than New York — are now pedestrian paradises. The sound of screeching tires and brakes is unheard, and a traffic accident is hard to imagine.

There are boarded up windows, patched doors, much peeling plaster. Lots of neon signs don't work. Lots of night clubs are closed. It is a city both occupied and abandoned. Abandoned in that the eyes of the country are no longer on Havana. The Revolution is taking place in the countryside. The physical signs of this are the shabbiness, the minimum repairs done to buildings, and those standing truckloads of people off to cut cane each morning. I've heard it calculated that out of two million inhabitants, as many as five hundred thousand are out of the city each day. And occupied in that the men in power are still transforming the functions of the buildings where they exert power. Somehow all this kept putting the idea of London into my head.

And yet this shabbiness is quite non-British, because it is of so picturesque a kind, painterly, sensuous, Latin. The pastel-painted stucco, the carved wooden doors, the wrought-iron balconies, with coverlets thrown over them, the peeling shutters, the second row of balconies, with perhaps a hen coop on them, some sheets of rusting iron, some plaster ornament, more balconies, with flowers, and a red-tiled roof; the streets of old Havana, particularly the waterfront, make the Impressionists' Paris look pale.

And the charm of the thing — to stay within aesthetic limits for the moment — is that all this picturesqueness is only one element, and not the dominant one. The other elements are not so well represented by buildings — the modern structures in Havana are by and large ugly — as by people. You can still see in the streets the people who correspond to the picturesque houses; a group of boys making their own bongo music and dancing their way along the Malecon. You can still see in Obispo the whole cast of characters out of *Our Man in Havana*, the people who correspond to the closed strip joints; late-night groups around the Nacional and El Patio, yearning for Broadway or the Village. But you also see the army and militiamen, who couldn't be more different; so serious, so taut, so young, so trained. And you see something less determinate, the mixture of racial types, the unselfconscious sameness of faces that to our eyes seem so different, pure Spanish next to pure Negro, and every sort of blend. That is, you see the nation solidifying in its new mold. It is because the picturesqueness is only a subordinate element that one can enjoy it. Havana is now not only the most picturesque city in the world, it is also the one in which the picturesque is most likable. The comparable change in London has had the reverse effect.

The essential seriousness in which the nation's new form crystallizes out, shows itself in the growth of reading. Books sell out on the day they are published, and literary reviews sell out in editions of ten thousand, whereas before the war *Orígenes*, which had an international reputation, sold three hundred to five hundred with difficulty. Cuba is a correction, or perhaps just an extension, of McLuhan's thesis. In politically serious cultures, the late twentieth century is not an age of decline in the dominance of print, but rather the reverse. Cubans are hungry and thirsty for reading. Bookshops often keep a library of perhaps fifty paperback volumes that people can sit and read. Because if you want to buy, you move along empty shelves spread — a very moving sight — with single dusty copies spread out flat to take up space, and still with empty areas between them. What you can buy are the *Obras Completas* of Marx and Martí, Russian-language textbooks, and engineering or medical works in English. But by Cuban writers, practically nothing. Almost the only readable books I saw in bookstores were one by John Strachey, and C. P. Snow's *Science and Government*. My hotel tourist shop had four books for sale — to tourists only. There were three translations from Spanish, and the fourth was *Cortico-Sub-Cortical Relationships in Sensory Regulation*. And in the buses you see people *absorbed* in equally heavy and forbidding texts. Cuba is busy transforming itself at the roots, growing, and Havana expresses, among other things, the sense of an organism, the sense of external danger and internal dynamism.

Perhaps that feeling at home was less a matter of recognizing familiar items than of missing them, of feeling the lack of things that alienate. It is an extraordinary rest to the eyes to get to Havana from New York, or for that matter from London, and to find that the most prominent figures on the streets are nonpornographic. We have got so used to provocative costumes and poses that even those of us who still stoke our indignations have forgotten what it is like without them. There are spots of color in Havana, but by and large the streets are sober. Some things are drab — some shop windows — and certainly the city must be called depressed. But then it was so gaudy, so overexcited; a certain depression — a certain number of dead neon signs — can only be good. A certain number of queues can be a sign of health, of voluntary social discipline.

Yes, of course I see, once I get the clue, the reason why Havana feels like home to me. The years of the war, 1939–45, I was twelve to seventeen, and London during the war is my idea of a city. I recognize, I positively like, the queues everywhere in Havana, the ration books, the lack of cars, the rather dull clothes, the appeals to conscience, the seriousness of intellectual taste, the sense of national purpose. Of course I should hate to spend my life queuing up, as Cubans must. Some men in Havana earn their living as queuers up for other people. But I should not, I think, change my mind about the Revolution if I had to. They don't. Because the Revolution has given them so many bigger things in return. Economically, culturally, politically, morally, they are giving up the immediately agreeable in order to get the ultimately valuable. And Cubans are luckier than Englishmen, in that they are not hagridden by the fear that they may be being puritanical again.

The bigger thing they get is the idea of a social authority which has moral authenticity. And it would be just as big a thing for England or America to get. For that is what is most disturbing about the orgiastic costume of American radicalism. It is a claim to moral authenticity which defines all such authenticity as in antithesis to social establishment. Even moderate American radicals can only recognize a good action by its defiance of power-backed authority. To know the two ideas only in antithesis neuroticizes both. Of course, the old Cuban bourgeois cynicism was no less a neurosis than the new American radical protest. But to find in the new Havana authority — and in Havana authority is everywhere to be found — which convinces you of its moral right, is like finding father again. One is back home indeed. Only of course it's not London today; far, far, from it; nor any place I live. But as an ideal realm, a home of the spirit, it is remarkably fruitful. Once one believes in authority, one can believe in justice again, and even in duty, not to mention reward and punishment.

It is a perfectly serious paradox, that for a visitor from the Western world, Cuba is the most conservative stimulus and encouragement he could find. But just for that reason, it presents the literary visitor with a special problem, and in a sense a discouragement. Literature may be said to be flourishing in Havana, and I personally welcome the sense it gives of observing limits. But still those limits are significantly there, are prominent in the Cuban picture when one looks from Havana to New York and back. There is a great deal a writer can do and be in a capitalist-corrupt metropolis that he cannot do and be in a city of faith. Think of Solzhenitsyn; think of Neiztvestny; all those bas-relief profiles of an artist. Over the skyline of New York one may imaginatively see the face of Norman Mailer hover as an emblem, but over Havana it would be a parochial paradox to conjure up the image of any writer. Only the face of Fidel himself has any right of imaginative possession there.

10 — AUTOBIOGRAPHICAL REFLECTIONS AND ANECDOTES: A JOURNEY

He was vaguely aware of the rage and chaos in the dark city around him, the terror of the clashing chaos. But what was the good even of being afraid? — even of grief? It was like a storm in which he could do nothing but lie still and endure and wait. "They also serve who only stand and wait." Perhaps it is the bitterest part, to keep still through it all, and watch, and wait.*

U.S.A.

In the summer of 1969 I got a grant from the Kittredge Foundation in Boston, to help me make a trip to London, Weimar, and Edinburgh, as part of my research into them as cities of culture. I combined this with my yearly trip home to see my parents, who still live in the village I grew up in, Weston Lullingfield, in Shropshire. I also combined it with a trip to Cuba, at the suggestion of a friend of mine who had been wanting to go there for some time.

The trip itself, as distinct from the research or the work done on it, made a difference to the decisions I came to, the judgments I formed. I ended up somewhere rather different from where I had intended to, and I think that the journey's small incidents, as well as its larger actions, added up to an argument.

The friend who went with me, Jim Harvey, has since written a very good account of what we saw, of the society we found, in Cuba. It was published in the Catholic magazine *Commonweal*, and though Jim long ago ceased to be a Catholic, what he was looking for in Castro's Communism was a new Church; that is, an idealistic organization of all life, setting itself in opposition to

---

* D. H. Lawrence, *Kangaroo*, Viking Compass edition, p. 323.

worldly corruption, manifesting itself immediately in authority and discipline, asceticism and prohibition, but ultimately in great men and great acts, in enthusiasm, faith, and love. You might say the same for me; we were both looking for, and found, the great culturally and morally conservative force to set against the forces of decadence and death rampant in our own society.

But there was a difference between us, in that I did not feel so confident of knowing what the quality of life of Cuban society as a whole was. I concentrated on the more accessible evidence — and more manageable, more reducible to theory — of what life was like for intellectuals, for writers. And this difference led to, and derived from, a difference between the ways we possessed all the knowledge, the judgments, we came to. Mine was more theoretical and detached, his more emotional and personal. He took Cuba unto himself; Cuba was now his, he was hers. This was not really a matter of more qualifications or criticisms or skepticism on my part; he had reservations too. Nor — essentially — was it a difference between our readiness to act. It was simply a difference between modes of knowledge; his more an act of love, an affirmation of life, setting the stamp of his personality upon the thing he knew, and appropriating it. It was a difference in intellectual temperament. When you transact a really far-reaching angelic bargain, you have to know how much "personality" you have renounced, how much you are now constituted by your participation in impersonal modes of knowledge. If you refuse to know that, you become an emotional fake, handing around slices of personality like cake you have iced yourself. But such a difference between constant companions breeds difficulties. One has to offer personality on social occasions, especially Latin social occasions; and it is unpleasant to feel oneself meagerly endowed by comparison with a friend. No doubt Erasmus knew many such difficulties on his journeys. They are written into his contract. Continual journeys, continuous exile, the dodging of responsibilities and confrontations, the running into irritabilities and discontents, it is all in the Erasmian horoscope.

My own journey began, of course, from *my* city, Boston; to which I belong, in which I find a home, despite the pathetic word exile, as much as Mailer does to New York, or Washington Irving to *his* New York. I have already described that city, in talking

Students confronting authority at Berkeley, and not, as at Brandeis, happy to unmask it. Their theory is that when you unmask the academy, the academician, beneath it you will find the armed policeman. But their feeling is that you will find a shamed and naked oldster. And so the realization of their theory, the fulfillment of their prophecy, still outrages and offends them. (United Press International.)

about teaching in Chapter 1, for if it is the capital of Massachusetts, it is also Academia. The two loci, with their different dimensionalities, coincide in my sort of life. It is a city of light, a Kulturstadt, a Weimar without a Goethe: but with plenty of Bertuchs and Böttigers — and also with its Knebels, and its Wielands, and even its Herders. The Sons of the Morning today feel the restrictions of that city more than its advantages. There have in all ages been many who lived there but aspired to be Sons of the Morning, aspired to fall. And nowadays the figure of Lucifer, which is the figure of Faust, of Mailer, of Simon Magus, is particularly refulgent on the battlements. Spiritual ambition, daimonic emulation, draws them on in their thousands, on and up and out, and we who stand pointing toward the center of the city are shouldered aside in the rush. And out through the other gate, signposted toward radicalism, the rush is maybe greater; though it is clear that very few really want to go far in that direction. But in the center of the city, in the actual classrooms, things are very quiet. Footfalls ring hollow. So I had decided to make a journey out too.

At Tufts I got most help in preparing myself for Cuba from a graduate student who had gone there the summer before for S.D.S. He lent me magazines, told me about official procedures, talked about what he had seen there. He is a tall, regularly handsome boy, short-haired, cool-voiced, Anglo-Saxon; moderation, regularity, incarnate in his handsomeness. He has the straight-shouldered but loose-limbed American adolescent look — not the sullen or sumptuous slouch, but the handy, ready-to-be-useful alertness — and in fact he even wears solid-color sweaters as a habit. In other words, an unmistakably, though quite unself-consciously old-fashioned myth-figure, the one hundred percent all-American boy, who used to be featured on the cover of *Life* magazine when I first came to this country. The flesh looks extra dense, the nostrils extra clean and waxen, as if they had never been picked, never needed even to be blown. But he also gives — also by his physique, and independent of what you know about him — the suggestion of another persona under the skin, steel under the wax, the suggestion of an unsmiling, unceasing organization of every ruthlessly emptied moment. A steel-gray eye, an unresponsive voice, the gray edge of a battleship prow. In some ways this accentuates the youthfulness of his face. Though they too look grayish — to the eye of the imagination — his features look boyishly untouched by time or anything else. How different his kind of impersonality is, I thought, how different the radical from the liberal. He has, it seems, quite simply expropriated his own personality and handed over the premises to the Party. He is now It.

A Calvinist's apartment, and his wife, tend to suffer the same process of alienation. Their subjective centers have shrunken, no tribute being paid to them. They have become objects. An aspect of bleakness and boniness over the face, a collapsed pile of mimeographed material on the straw matting of the apartment, a blight, a fall, a fallen condition. It is not unattractive, at moments, after so many overpampered and effulgent faces and rooms. But at other moments those scraped, stark, starved contours seem a warning. This is how revolutions get made, and get maintained. It can't be done without a cost, a bargain. You give up this and you get that.

I am not going to make any revolution, and this is one reason why. I am ready to acknowledge him a hero if he turns out to be one, which he well may; he is certainly more likely to than I. But he is close to the nerve of the reasons why I shan't be organizing.

On the other hand, what he is organizing will also express itself in spontaneous movements of the body politic, movements of joy and pride and generosity and indignation. Like the students' strike now on, May 1970, and the Tufts students' canvassing of Somerville and Medford for peace-petition signatures. It won't all be grimly disciplined, any more than Cuba is. But then spontaneous movements of the body politic, like those of the body carnal, those too easily jar on Erasmian nerves. Such self-conscious joy and generosity and pride — and how could they not be self-conscious, self-admiring, self-intensifying — provoke irony and skepticism. The participants too are barely escaping from irony and skepticism; the more intelligent they are, the more barely they escape; the more it needs an act of will which brutalizes their consciousness. The Erasmian does not escape, and can participate only sadly and constrainedly.

But to begin my trip. I needed, of course, many official papers to make a visit to Cuba legal. I spent a good deal of time in the new Federal Building in Boston, especially in the early morning, be-

cause the Sailing Permit Office opens at 8:30, and there are usually
seven or eight people waiting — with only seven or eight words of
English between them — by 8:45. It is a location for Fellini, the
Internal Revenue room, where one waits; an acre or so of shiny
pale linoleum floor, a theaterful of ballet music from *Swan Lake*,
our racially and sartorially exotic group of Permit seekers — South
American girls still wearing turbans with gilded curls bursting out
of the front of them, like Rita Hayworth — and the ladies who
work there sailing across the slippery floor on very high heels, quite
chicly corseted and coiffed, indeed quite chicly faced. Dressed in
rhinestoned blue or shocking pink, their hair hennaed or blued and
freshly set, a large bagful of makeup under their arms, the office
environment evokes and sustains their sense of themselves, their
style. Not that it is all one style, in clothes. Some may wear a dia-
mante brooch which spells their name — Cheryl — but others behind the same counter are in mauve tweed and cashmere and discreet cultured pearls. But they have a face, a head in common.
Alone, or with their husbands, on Sundays, or just before they have
put themselves together in the morning, they must be emblems of
alienation, every line in their faces a hieroglyph, all vain vivacity in
intention, all a slump of disappointment in effect. But in the office,
toward each other, their rhinestoned glasses reposing complacently
on Jayne Mansfield bosoms, they achieve gestures of delicacy and
boldness and freedom and — and all the other things that make up
style.

There in that office they are the lower spokes of the paddle
wheel of the American ship of state, its gaudy paint rusted and
flaking off, crunching over the sordid backwater detritus of the
mud flats, entangled with filthy cloths and broken bones, but still
moving, still sparkling, jerkily.

In the Sailing Permit Office itself, which is quite small, it seems
that there is only one man who works all day every day. He is
helped, irregularly, by a variety of others. They are all strikingly
different; fat or acned men, painted or satin-skirted women. The
regular man is rather short, neat-figured and neat-featured, very
straight-necked and straight-shouldered, with a dry and sweet-
smelling skin, and well-marked black eyebrows and black eyelashes
you can count as you sit before him, because his eyelids droop per-

manently. He will look you in the eye when that is necessary, but most of the time he is reserving himself within himself, conserving himself.

During the forty-five minutes I spent with him on my second visit, he had to answer the telephone five times, and on each occasion he had to give exactly the same information. The only time people call that number is when they want to know how to get a Sailing Permit. There are four or five documents you have to bring to the office, and one of them, a statement of your earnings so far in the tax year, is not easy for some people to get; so there are occasions for quite a few questions. I could hear a good deal of winsome personality being projected over the wires, strong bright voices making an act of life out of the dreariest chore; for instance, well-off ladies in Newton making the call on behalf of foreign help and baby-sitters with poor English. He merely gave the information required in a quiet guttural voice, never hurried, never impatient, never interrupting; the only dramatic thing about his manner was its quiet, antidramatic, tensionless, toneless, softness. He was, rather dramatically, expecting nothing for himself, asking nothing, wanting nothing. But if it was drama, it was not theater; clearly every gesture in his life expresses the same thing, *he* expresses it. He is a figure out of Gogol, out of Dostoevski, but not out of America.

And his official function corresponds to his personal style, for the Sailing Permit he finally hands you is useless — is unnecessary. No one is ever stopped from traveling because of it, no one has ever been asked to show it, in the experience of everyone I know. But he goes over all your statements and all your arithmetic. He checks all your documents, he insists (quietly) on seeing everything, he proves that you owe the government money, and then he finds a way to prove that you don't.

On the way to Mexico City, and ultimately to Cuba, we were interviewed at some length by a Customs and Immigration lady who boarded the plane in Chicago. *She* was out of America, Our Miss Brooks, all wisecracks and warmth in her short skirt and long but gallant face. But even she didn't ask to see my Sailing Permit. No doubt, back in the Boston Federal Building, my friend was even then going through someone else's scrawl of figures, feeling through his drooping eyelids the pressure of huge, black, not-speak-English eyes, explaining to them — so many explanations — that they must go back home to fetch some other functionless document before he could give them his functionless Sailing Permit.

I remember a New York Jewish friend telling me how she had to deal with a government clerk over the army allowance she drew for her first husband when he was sent to Korea. She is pretty and clever and small and childlike. She was nineteen then, a senior at City College, and she could do the arithmetic so much quicker than the clerk that she had to lavish a lot of girlish charm on him at the end of each visit to salve his pride.

There is more than one revolution brewing in America.

Mexico

In Mexico City my wife and I stayed in a hotel which featured a lilied fountain in its foyer, and our bathroom had antique tiles on the walls and a carved and paneled door. We were in the world of pleasure, concrete Muzak, where the first law is Unreality.

On the plane someone remarked that we should be flying BOAC, because their new VC jets have lockers over the passengers' heads; and that made me see the function of knowledge in our society as to provide a reason for preferring one product to another; to lubricate the machinery of buying and selling; and the function of intelligence as to pick up that knowledge and to implement those reasons. And that intellectuals, we of counter-America, are professional competitors and habitual winners in that competition; we clamber up and along the commercial rigging, hand over arm, glittering with pleasure in our own alertness; by which participation we live even while we claim to be standing outside and against the structure. Those ropes pass through us. Those hawsers are our minds.

We ate one evening at the Restaurant del Lago, a multileveled pyramid looking out on a multifountained lake (wherever Mexicans detect water it seems they start pumping a fountain) and at one moment we counted fifteen waiters on our level with a total of ten people eating. There was one to snatch away the vase of flowers from the table we were led to, another to snatch it up again from the table it had been put on and convey it out of the room. All had napkins over their arms and moved with notable grace. Naturally. They were all on stage, and we as much as they. Our bill, which grazed the lower limits of possible expenditure, was 226 pesos, which would perhaps keep a moderate-sized and moderate-minded family for a month. That puts the style in the waiters' elbows. There were of course no overhead lights, just soft pools of radiance here and there. When the trolley of desserts was rolled up to our table the room was too dark for the first waiter to see where to plug in its light. A second waiter had to play his personal, portable, pencil-slim flashlight on the floor to find the outlet. But that left two more waiters to introduce us — not haughtily, though, but winsomely, winningly — to the mousse and the crème and the gâteaux and the millefleurs. And when one goes to the Museo Nacional de Antropologia, an uncomfortable resemblance to the Restaurant del Lago haunts one. Public luxury belongs to the rich almost as much as private.

Next to the fountains, murals are what Mexico City features most, many by Diego Rivera, and some showing Trotsky. It comes as a shock, to meet that face, and to remember that life, and death, in colorful, bull-fighting Mexico. In this huge Hollywood patio, this hotel of tours and tiles, and burros and ponchos, the remote-control assassination of a heretic, the elimination by the Party of an ideological error. Can one afford a visual rhythm which inserts that face, that encounter, between buying a postcard and choosing a cafe?

We went one afternoon from one set of such murals at the Palacio Nacional to another at the Palacio de Bellas Artes, and avoided the rain by going to a free guitar concert there given by the pupils of Maestro Alirio Díaz. It was held in the Ponce Room of the Palacio, dominated by a medallioned profile of Ponce, who turned out to be a Mexican composer some of whose folk-song arrangements were played in the concert. The audience were obviously the relatives and friends of the pupils, the payers of the tuition. Ladies were wearing satin and taffeta coats, a lot of glitter on their handbags, hair dressed high on their heads, and earrings like silver claymores and diamond scimitars. It was provincial haut-bourgeois, Republican Convention-cum-Hollywood, but of another era; these people must, like everyone else, read *Time* and *Life*, but

368 CITIES OF LIGHT AND SONS OF THE MORNING

they can't, apparently, follow the directions. It was a vision of, say, Lyons in the 1930's, transported three thousand miles west, to where Paris discipline was weak, and the garden was tropical, and the hibiscus just naturally grew behind your ear.

The program notes had some very flowery tributes to Maestro Alirio, there were little speeches in his praise every so often — the United States students being pressed into this service particularly often — and at the end Maestro Alirio himself appeared, flanked by two functionaries, on what turned out to be a narrow balcony at the back of the stage. Not examining it, we had taken it for a mahogany panel running right across the back wall, for people entered it via some invisible door, and then were visible themselves as busts. The maestro was distributing prizes, though also receiving more tributes, and there was a lot of whispered consultation between him and the acolytes, perhaps simply about who these "pupils" were. For it seemed to be said by the program notes — in elegant circumlocution — that some assistant had done all the teaching, and Maestro Alirio had graciously lent his name, and allowed the prestige to accrue — had invested inherited capital.

We were being well prepared for Communist Cuba. We went also to a party whose guest list combined the head of Tass in Mexico and the head of *Reader's Digest* in Mexico. This was our taste of the life of international society; and it had, for me, much the taste that it has in novels. It seems to involve its participants in privileges for which they were bound to feel a bad conscience, unless they invested a tiresome amount of energy in not feeling that, in gaiety. They discussed a fancy dress party they had held, and another they were about to hold, and whether they came from Tass or from *Reader's Digest* didn't seem to make much difference. The realities of their life were those costumes. Just as the realities of Mexico were the foreign firms lining the main avenues, the new hotels and office blocks and showrooms and airlines, and the foreign residents' telephone directory.

The party was given by a young woman who was my idea of Jackie Kennedy. When I said this I was told that there were big differences, and maybe so. It is hard for me to see such differences, because it is hard for an Erasmian to *believe* in Jackie Kennedy; or Aristotle Onassis; or ritual murder or hydrogen bombs. A certain limited sense of reality goes with each temperament, and for me such facts as these are mere blurred profiles on my imaginative horizon, mere silhouettes. That is why Erasmians make poor journalists; Mailer, for instance, finds such facts as these prime imaginative realities; he would have found far more in that party than my prim "bad conscience" and the memory of other people's novels. On the other hand, some people who are good journalists, or good leaders of men, find the reality of books or music hard to believe in. Faustians tend to see only leaders in history, Calvinists only causes, Erasmians mostly the quality of life. Goethe thought Cagliostro responsible for the French Revolution, and would have thought Rasputin responsible for the Russian. Calvinist cause-men, like Robespierre and Lenin, struck less fire from Goethe's imagination.

Cuba

I was alone in Havana at first, my wife having gone back from Mexico to Boston; and Jim, who took a later flight to Cuba, was sent to a different hotel. My hotel, the Deauville, pronounced in Havana *el Dubil*, is perhaps the ugliest building on the whole Malecon promenade, made of concrete that looks like plastic, with foolishly acute angles. But it used to be a luxury hotel, and it is still "kept up," by standards just below what the standards of "keeping up" are in New York. There are discernible cracks in the plaster; they are filled in as soon as they appear; but they are not made to disappear.

The dining room has about twenty tables, permanently set for four or six, and one is always arranged for some six-course banquet, with enough cutlery and glassware to set up a newly married couple. No one ever sat there. As in the army, the management set out their equipment in a display of perfect cleanliness and efficiency, and then used other equipment. As if they expected inspection by the Maximum Leader himself. A large red plastic lobster is crawling up the dining room wall, as if trapped in a too-late attempt to escape to Miami.

The hotel is reserved for foreign visitors, and has quite a lot of staff, who were, when I got there, largely unoccupied. There were usually three or four girls behind the desk, being flirted with all day

long by three or four electricians or plumbers on the other side of
the desk; then two young ladies perched all day on stools in the
twin elevators — designed for Miami matrons — waiting for someone to take up or down; and two more languished behind the small
counter for the sale of souvenirs — cigars and rum, mostly, with a
few dolls, and three or four books. One of them was the copy of
Cortico-Sub-Cortical Relationships in Sensory Regulation. Jim told
me that at the Havana Libre you could buy a record of "Laugh
Along with Henny Youngman."

And in the dining room, and in the basement bar, I met, among
others, two Swedish musicologists, an Australian trade unionist, a
French boy hoping to learn his trade as a television engineer in a
Marxist society, an Italian (whose American wife lived in America) trying to get to the Isle of Pines for two years, and, at the end
of my stay, a group of French tourists and a group of West German tourists. The French tourists, whatever their political persuasion may have been, were no different in personality from what
they would have been in Batista Cuba. It was the Caribbean they
were visiting, and they unbuttoned their shirts to make the point.
They looked as though they might be schoolteachers by profession,
mostly still in their twenties; and in the bar at night they emancipated themselves together, and wriggled at each other to music just
as if it were a TV ad. The Germans were semiprofessional, lots of
them being journalists, of newspapers, radio, or television, though
traveling on tourist visas. They were less ardent for personal emancipation.

My flight out of Havana was to Madrid. As we waited to board,
we saw a highjacked TWA plane fly in, and all of us temporary
Cubans jeered as its cargo of San Franciscans were led into the
airport. "All of us" included three belligerent British businessmen,
one of whom was balding and satyrical, another young and cocky,
and the third I can no longer remember. They had already made
their mark in the crowded waiting room by demanding to know
why we were delayed, etc. I heard the second one insisting to a nice
stewardess that he must go out and get beer for the three of them.
"There is no such word as can't in my vocabulary, my friend." This
line was delivered loud and slow, with a glance at his audience.
They dealt in raucous and gaudy units of personality, all three of

them, in theater, though in fact they had no audience but me. Mostly they sat side by side on a sofa in the waiting room, their faces flushed and gleaming, and performed, into the general hubbub. I gathered that they had ended in Cuba a business trip that had covered all South America, and they had loud, boring opinions about how bad things were on the island. But even these three enjoyed the discomfiture of the Americans.

We ourselves had not been half an hour in the air, however, when the pilot told us we must return to ground "for twenty minutes"; and after we had changed course — rather *away* from Cuba, as it appeared from the map — American fighter planes started flashing across in front of us. We were told later that we had needed to dump gas in order to be light enough to land, and so the pilot had flown toward Florida to do that (why?) and so we had figured as an intriguing incognito on the U.S. Army radar screens. I presume we were, for some fraction of a minute, in some fraction of probability of being shot down. No doubt a low fraction, but when the whole number means headlines, prehaps history, such statistics are exciting. It was a brushing of our wings, however minimally, against those nightmare steel screens, forever bristling with the eagerness to explode.

After we had landed we were told that our difficulty had been with our landing gear — so that our mechanical danger had all been concentrated in the previous ten minutes — and that it would take several hours to fix. Then we were fed a nasty meal and sent back to Havana for the night. It was in fact twenty-four hours late when the plane took off, and by then everyone was very weary. We sat around the same small waiting room, eyes closed, hands spread idly over our baggage, limbs nerveless, faces flaccid, all energies concentrated, clutched, seized, in one or two knots of nerves. Worst off were the Cuban émigrés, the sympathizers with the ancient regime, the *gusanos*, flying to Spain to take up a new life. A lot of them were old and thin, shrunken inside ancient suits that could have held two of them, that once had held a man twice their size. Where *they* had passed the night I did not like to think, but they looked at the end of their tether. Their false teeth looked looser than the day before. They had had to give up all their possessions when they left the country — they were checked at the airport for things like gold watches — and some had had to work in agriculture for a period of from six months to two years to get permission to leave.

The three bears from Britain, the three wicked capitalists, were in an ecstasy of fury by lunch-time. They carried a clip-board with two sheets of paper attached, on which they entered all their causes of complaint. "Tuesday morning in London," the young one told a bland steward, "there's going to be a phone call from our building to wherever your London office is, and your boss is going to come over at the double. And he won't leave our building before he's made a pretty sad apology for all this." When we got aboard for the second time, he whipped a tiny thermometer out of his pocket, attached it to the roof of the plane, and entered the reading on his list. The plane had been standing in the sun all day, and it was, I think, ninety-four degrees Fahrenheit inside. There was indeed plenty to complain about.

But once in the air, and away from Cuba, and a bit cooler, a wave of relief swept over the plane, and in time euphoria. People started moving up and down the aisle, and talking to strangers. The three Britishers — salesmen, I presume, and not very highly placed — drank gin all night, and started to sing comic songs, and by the time we got to Madrid had convinced themselves that everything that had gone wrong was Cuba's fault and not the airline's. What they did with their list of complaints, I don't know. The Cuban consul in London would not have been much interested in the temperature of an Iberian plane. But as we rode to the airport waiting room at four in the morning, they were all smiles and praises for the little Iberia bus we were in, and various ordinary bits of airport machinery on view. By then I no longer disliked them. From most points of view — including the political — they were just naughty boys, black sheep of the Lower Fifth. It didn't seem possible after Cuba that one ought to take British capitalism seriously, however many more factories and guns Britain may have.

Germany

I took a train from Frankfurt to Weimar, which stopped at the border with the D.D.R., and I had to take all my luggage off the train to Customs and Immigration. A formidable woman inspector, very square and strong, handled my copies of Goethe and Mann judiciously, weighing them in her hand, and deciding with a nod of the head, "*Ist gut.*" I couldn't imagine that she would have recognized subversive literature in English if I had had it, so I was amused. But when I got back on the train I found everyone else in my carriage atwitter. I was congratulated more than once at having got off so light. For men and women alike, such an encounter with authority was a major event, a piece of public life, the material for a tragedy, or a comedy, something with powerful emotional potential.

In Weimar itself people several times referred to the Russians for my benefit as "our friends," with heavy irony. And they let me know, in English, that they had studied Russian eight years in school — perforce — compared with only four years of English, and yet they knew no Russian. One old lady I got talking to in the *Marktplatz*, a most pastoral and grandmotherly figure, took occasion to make a face when I showed her that I was reading a speech by Walter Ulbricht. She was of course perfectly right; after four days I found those speeches and editorials like unseasoned porridge; a minor headline one day announced excitedly "*Walter Ulbricht Hat Recht!*" Some trade union official in India had agreed with him.

Authority in Germany is so much more than just authority. Uniforms are so much more than just uniforms, even on ticket inspectors. Indeed, it is people in mock authority who are the worst of all — the waiters and porters and desk clerks. The heel-clicking, hip-swinging tenors in official positions exude such cold exultance in marking everything that divides and distinguishes man from man and group from group, whether the division leaves them personally above or below the man they face. The hotel in Frankfurt was worse in that way than the one in Weimar, and with an added capitalist grossness; such large, businesslike, middle-class ladies cleaning the rooms, instead of the poetically shy and blonde *Mädchen* of Weimar, and such heavy double doors to the rooms, and such huge, heavy keys. But both hotels were very "German." In the dining room at Weimar the food was elaborate and the orchestra played "Stardust" and "Smoke Gets in Your Eyes," and the men wore padded shoulders and the women plucked eyebrows, and everyone had a few gold teeth. It was a forties style of the sixties. Lots of the women wore pants suits, like inelegant Dietrichs, even those of Dietrich's age. Quite simply, it was a *coarse* style. All the poetry had been absorbed by the *Mädchen*, or by the old country ladies, with their white lawn caps tied under the chin, long black skirts, reaching to their ankles, blue cardigans, and starched white collars. For a moment, seeing such figures on the road from Weimar to Jena, you could see what Goethe had seen, and the poets' Germany of the whole century between him and 1914, the Germany that George Eliot and Matthew Arnold knew, the Germany of Frieda Lawrence and Margaret Schlegel.

Germany in 1969 made me realize that what I had not seen in Cuba was a middle class. I mean of course a middle class assertively enjoying itself, commanding its pleasures, filling its belly, satisfying its appetites, a category of behavior which somehow offends us more in them than in aristocrats and working men. In Germany, on both sides of the border, you saw the middle class all the time. The difference between the two countries was only in their degrees of smartness. On both sides of the border I heard the same self-accusation, "We Germans work too hard." It sounded as sinister as most such declarations of the intent to enjoy. A man who feels that is best advised to keep working. His pleasures are likely to be hideous.

In West Berlin, as in Frankfurt, I found myself in the heart of Western capitalism, though the Berlin hotel was full of American tourists, while the Frankfurt one was full of German businessmen, and indeed of Japanese, Indian, and African businessmen. Everyone had a briefcase full of specifications, schedules, cost-analyses.

In the lounge of that hotel a group of youngish businessmen assembled one morning, with a thirty-year-old blonde secretary in a twenty-year-old miniskirt: a strapping and competent physique packaged in a rather garish red, white, and blue ensemble. The men had that specially meaty German look, and she — though no doubt her shorthand also was good — was a sexual cathode for all those anodes, to make sure that they were all discharging powerfully and in parallel, not toward each other. Then another group appeared — it was to be a big negotiation, a takeover or something — and all the sitters-down reared up, and quantities of hearty jocular good will were piled up like detergent foam. And when things settled down a bit, it was revealed that this group had brought their own secretary — so much electricity might have been too much for the first girl — who was so young, so small, and so demurely, so primly frocked in black, that she seemed on loan from a child brothel, and it was clear that the second group started with a marked advantage.

Sexuality in Germany does seem dismayingly hearty, as substantial as meat and potatoes, a source of power to be plugged into as firmly as any other public utility.

On the train from Weimar to Berlin I was forced to sit nose to nose with an inordinately uxorious couple, who seemed determined — at least she was determined — to act out the roles of the middle-aged businessman and his popsy. She was herself middle-aged and plumply dowdy, but she acted illicit. She found a thousand questions to ask, and a thousand ways to respond to even the staidest reply with an irrepressible giggle and a stretched-mouth kiss. Then, overcome with sudden drowsiness, she would snuggle up and insinuate her hands inside his clothes or under his thighs, the only posture, she gave us to understand, in which she could find rest. Then she would cram a whole night's sleep into five minutes, and wake up needing a little kiss. He suffered her onslaught without much discomfort — no mean feat, considering under how many eyes all this passed — but quite passively. He seemed to find the role assigned him becoming enough to his own imagination, even when it had to be played in such diminished, such puppet, style. And she was plainly lost, lost, adrift in unreality, starring in some movie of her own direction, her quick-pulsed awareness of us as audience fermenting this potato love into ersatz champagne. She had brought a large lunch, ingeniously wrapped and ribboned and packed into a tin box, and it was while they were munching side by side that they seemed most as one, though even then she forced some big-eyed interchanges of gaze, their chomping jaws slowly coming to a halt under the intensity of it, until she broke down into a roguish giggle, and started choking.

That Germany, that hearty grossness, is certainly there in Luther, but Lutheranism has some aspects of very attractive austerity. I had found the Herderkirche in Weimar one good antidote to today's bulging mouthfuls, one way back and out to the Germany I was looking for. It has a magnificently sonorous organ and bells, and the interior reminds one of what Protestantism was supposed to be — icy stone floors, pale light, heavy wooden pews, and all that thunder. Yet the pulpit is rococo, and there are very elaborate tombs beside the altar, which doesn't contradict the austerity, but enriches it. People can mean two different things at the same time quite legitimately, as Herder himself did. It is a fallacy of radicalism to think that this is insincerity. Herder is a good example of that composite mind, with strong allegiances both to peasant piety and to aristocratic skepticism, as he preached from that pulpit to Goethe and Karl August. The different components of his mind counteracted each other in some sense, left him static, nonprogressive, circular, but only in the sense that a fountain is those things too.

The Franz Schiller University in Jena has a bust of Marx, because he got his degree there, and engraved in the hall is the famous sentence, "*Die Philosophen haben die Welt an verschiedenen interpretiert, es kommt aber darauf, sie zu verändern.*" As a slogan, that is surely the death of a university. To interpret always seriously, taking account of the changes this interpretation would bring if put into practice, that is intellectual life. (Though in fact free play of mind demands holidays from moral seriousness, too, demands pure theory and conscious cynicism and other things from time to time.) But never to interpret except as a means to changing, that would be more like intellectual death. Knowledge as the West has created it (and the arts, the sciences, the humanities) *is* a liberal illusion. It has roots and fruits in worlds that politics orders, but its own life is not in that world. It lives in a realm which, analyzed by political criteria, *will* seem unreal. But if you subdue the life of the mind to the discipline of reality as political radicalism knows it, you will be left with only a fragment of what we know as knowledge, as imagination, as mind. If you subdue *any* kind of life to that discipline, you are likely to diminish it.

For instance, during my few days there, I had several times found myself tripped up, semichoked, by red tape in Weimar. I could not change my D.D.R. marks back into American or British money, because the lady in the hotel had not given me the proper form when I first changed into marks — so when I got to Check-point Charlie my money just ceased to have any value. And I could not mail out of the country — in order not to have to carry them — the books I had brought in. After trying several officials, and waiting outside offices twice at 7:30 in the morning, I was told, with no note of regret or apology, but rather with the smiling suggestion that I should share in the pleasure of at last getting this intricate problem resolved — that there was absolutely no way for me to do so.

This is another kind of repression, of the individual in favor of the community; *not* the kind that appeals to my temperament. An Erasmian bitterly resents being compelled — especially being compelled to join in. Like Lawrence I want freedom for everyone else, so that I then have the right to reject their claims on me. This is the classic liberal betrayal of community. The East German political masochism is not a manifestation of community, perhaps, but it is the caricatural shadow thrown by that ideal, and such shadows are in some ways better criteria than perfect formulations, perfect images, of what is aimed at. Who will reject perfection? But when you see the shadows cast by two different images, you know which one you prefer, or which one you hate the most.

A teacher at Jena University whom I met there was about to go to England on research connected with his work, but during his summer holidays. He went to Berlin to apply for the official permission and arrangements for the travel while I was there; when he came back he told me that they took this form; on July 6 he would go to East Berlin prepared for the journey, pick up papers and foreign currency, and cross into West Berlin; there, on July 7, when his plane was to leave, he would get final word as to whether he could go or not. Later, in England, I got a card from him saying that the final word had been "No," and he had had to go back to East Berlin, hand back the papers and currency, and go home to Jena. He was of course apprehensive and pessimistic in advance, and did not claim to like that part of the system. But he did not merely biliously swallow it down, as I would have done. He said "Yes, sir" to it. He was an enthusiastic adherent of the regime in general, an enthusiastic citizen of the East German state. He believed in it, as a Peace State and a Workers' State, a place where judges entrust to a man's work-mates the responsibilities of reform-ing him when he has been antisocial. His mind was a good example of the Calvinist temperament at its sunniest; just as his social per-sonality was cheerful, naïve, impulsive, a man still with pen-pals, still fond of the sports he had played as an adolescent, who asked me what my hobbies were.

The group temperament imposed by the regime seemed to me to have in some sense simplified and blunted *his* mind, while on the only other person I got to know there it had had the opposite effect. She had been sharpened and soured by it into a habitual and ingenious nay-sayer. This was a difference of *mind*, for she was so-cially as gay and pleasure-loving as my other friend, being very pretty and lively. She was also clever, and quick and subtle of taste. But her opinions, not only of the East German regime but of all political setups, her expectations, not just for herself but of life in general, were bitterly contracted and acidulous. I don't think she herself realized how striking that was, how close to eccentricity she was, just because these traits were built into the structure of her world. I recognized the syndrome because it had been true of people like me when I was an adolescent. A lot of Englishmen of my generation bear the traces of it. The main thing America did for me was to show me an alternative, and make me realize how sharply characterized a phenomenon I was. I felt immediately at home with Anna, just as I had before, in Cuba. No doubt again because the war regime in England was also Calvinist — at least as focused by Authority inside a boys' grammar school.

The people I met in West Berlin talked to me about the student troubles in West German universities, and sent me to see the Pi-casso exhibition of new drawings. It was a neat pair of signs of the times. Communications, they said, have broken down almost com-pletely between faculty and students in the humanities subjects. Even between students critical discussion quickly becomes political abuse — in literature, the archetypal liberal illusion, there is practi-cally nothing that is a fact for people of opposed politics. While the Picasso drawings, wildly and fiercely pornographic, bore testi-mony to the only imaginative values capitalist society has left — flamboyant sexuality and the integrity of the artist as the supreme individualist — the extremist retreat to the body. Both are Faustian, not Erasmian, values, exaggerations pushed to the point of becoming denials of Erasmian compromise. They are the vices of liberal culture as much as political masochism and socialist realism are the vices of radical culture. West Berlin is a place of exaggerations. It has the reputation of being a great center of striptease, which is just right for its role as shop window of Western capitalism.

I flew from there to London, and as one rises up and looks down over Berlin one must always hear the Wagnerian music of the Nazis, the music of Faustian politics. American politics these days, particularly of the right, are Faustian enough; myth, mystique, and assassination; but our conditions still pale beside Germany in the thirties. The bourgeoisie remained a bourgeoisie, and within the Party, and the police and the Civil Service, the Calvinist virtues must have been highly developed, but the regime they were supporting was luridly different. As the head of Germany, Hitler was the Faustian temperament incarnate.

While in Russia there is a Calvinist temperamental mode in politics which seems able to control the style of even Faustian personalities. Struggles for power between individuals, even deadly struggles, go on in a muted way. Khrushchev is suddenly demoted from supreme power to insignificance without overt conflict. Both Stalin and Lenin (the evil saint, as Lawrence called him) seem to have been more able to adopt that mode than Trotsky, which may explain something in his failure. Trotsky was not a saint, being a man of various gifts and brilliant temperament. In Cuba, also, though Fidel is very dominant, that dominance operates within the Calvinist cooperative style. Whereas in England the cultural images seem to have been mostly Erasmian, with the exception of Elizabethan times and Cromwellian. The first offered Englishmen images with a stronger than usual strain of Faustian temperament; the second, images with a Calvinist strain.

I suppose I am thinking of images for men of reflection more than of those for men of action. Men of action must always be Faustian to some degree. But cultures differ from each other according to the complementary degree to which such men are also in one case Erasmian, in another Calvinist. I suppose my concern for men of reflection rather than for those of action explains why I don't include in my theory the connection — which seems to be easily and generally accepted — between the Faustian temperament and the West's technological hubris, in war, in ecology, in mental culture. I suppose that that hubris *is* Faustian, in some sense related to my sense of the word. But that relation is not clear to me; the H-bomb, and modern science generally, as the forbidden powers gained by the West's Faustian bargain with the Devil? I don't know; the connection other people see between our killing-power and our abrasive style of personality may or may not be, for all my intuition tells me, an important causal-explanatory link.

Britain

The stewardess brought me the *Guardian* to read, and I discovered that I was to arrive home on the day of the investiture of Prince Charles as the Prince of Wales. I discovered also that the *Guardian*, usually responsibility itself, had given up all attempts to stay clear of the flood of "news" inspired by the event. They had settled for irony. They gave quite full accounts of it all, but by snide commentators, and with irreverent insights into the personalities involved, into the Prince's intellectual prowess and Lord Snowdon's costume designs, by ironists like Alison Adburgham and Margaret Drabble. Naturally enough, they were also snide about the Welsh nationalists who threatened to disrupt the ceremonies, and about political events of an opposite character. The rules of the game of irony are that you must apply it all round.

But in a country like England, where so much irony has been directed for so many years at certain topics, like the Royal Family, to hear it all again — especially after an interval — feels like a madness. I felt we couldn't afford to *mention* the Royal Family again, except in drafting the law to abolish them. One can be ironic about the President of the United States, because he has power, and keeps exerting it, keeps changing our lives. One can't be ironic — if one claims to have left elementary school — about someone who lost his raison d'être so long ago. The Erasmian mode in England has grown so loose and slack that it amounts to temperamental inactivity, to diminishment. In America temperaments are still intensified by the nourishment offered them by their culture, by their cultural images; mostly because the economy is still expanding, but partly because the images happen to be Faustian.

In England there have been so many Erasmians in positions of maximum influence. For instance, Matthew Arnold. It occurred to me that it may have been from him that I inherited my temperament — via a thousand intermediary men and books and institutions, at school, etc. The mild, sweet uplift of Arnold's nondoctrinal Christianity was very much an equivalent to Erasmus's *Philosophia Christi*; all peace, harmony, simplicity, and calm. Both men were great admirers of classical literature, and found the same values and moral function in it — where Nietzsche found Faustian values. Hellenism, and sweetness and light, etc., are slogans of the Erasmian temperament. Both men made sharpness and clarity of mind, and elegance of style, into major intellectual virtues. Both wanted order maintained for them; they could not endorse any kind of disorder as preferable to even a corrupt kind of order. And of course both constituted for their contemporaries significant alternatives to the Faustians of their times (Luther in the one case, Carlyle in the other) and the Calvinists (Calvin and Marx). *Das Kapital*, like *Institutio Christianae Religionis*, is an intellectual Cheops pyramid, a stockpile of revolutionary explosives, beside which *Culture and Anarchy* seems small enough. And yet we continue to read, in schools at least, in England at least, Erasmians. England's best imaginative work is still the work of Britten and Auden and Forster, choirboy sopranos and historical pageants and the B.B.C., the liberal England of the Aldeburgh Festival.

Even in the seventeenth century, according to Melvin Lasky, English writers avoided the concept of revolution, and its attendant imagery of fire. The Puritan rebels spoke of "reformation," not of "revolution." And Locke, who used the imagery of fire always for ideas he wanted to warn people away from, tried to avoid "revolution" and all other "obscure, doubtful, and undefined words."

It is also striking how England in the nineteenth century differed from European countries in its response to Byron. E. M. Butler has pointed out that our word "Byronism" refers to everything in his writing and legend which makes him negligible; and that if we talked about him in terms of "daimonism" we should be forced to take him more seriously. In fact there are no Victorian equivalents for those writings and actions by Heine, Pushkin, Mickiewicz, Lamartine, which resulted from taking him seriously. The same is true of the British response, or nonresponse, to *Werther* and *Faust*.

Something self-protective — and favoring political circumstances — has guarded the English mind against all disturbances of its Erasmian balance. Our great Romantic was Coleridge, dedicated to orthodoxy, and our great Symbolist was Eliot, equally so dedicated. Our great modern sculptor, Moore, and his critical prophet, Read, are pastoralists and conservatives besides Picasso. In social life G. K. Chesterton was a fake-Faustian (Faust as Falstaff) but his Father Brown is very much an Erasmian. Dowdy simplemindedness has been the key virtue of the Catholic sensibility in England in this century — carried on after Brown by Waugh's Helena and Sayers's Harriet. (Sayers's Wimsey, like Waugh's gaudy aristocrats, is the nonserious obverse of the key virtues, like Chesterton's fake-Faustian persona.) The equivalent American myth, exemplified by Raymond Chandler and Ross Macdonald, points up the Erasmianism of the British by its differentness. Even the more adventurous representatives of the English imagination have recoiled from the Faustian enterprise the way Erasmus recoiled from Luther's. They have maintained a critical attitude toward everything, but in some sense a skeptical attitude toward their own criticalness; "I will put up with this Church until I shall see a better." But in order to see a better, says both the Faustian and the Calvinist revolutionary, you have to cease putting up with the present institutions. Erasmus claimed, against Luther, that man could not know whether or not he had free will; the issue is too complex and the biblical texts too obscure; we *have* to remain skeptical, critical, undetermined, in some sense ironical, forever, Luther accused him of having no religious faith at all, and warned him of the coming of the Day of Judgment. He recognized that ironical smile as the sin against his Holy Ghost.

Luther's test of the Christian teacher — the test that Erasmus failed — was "Does he know of death and the Devil? Or is he all sweetness and light?" So I hear Erasmus's voice again in Matthew Arnold, and it seems to me that I am hearing something recurrently and profoundly English. When I hear Arnold recommending disinterestedness, and directing his delicate irony against the world of violence, the world of ugly facts and unmanageable powers, I hear that despairing humor which has debilitated so many of my generation. The humor that disinfects, and debilitates, even our tragic seriousness. "And the final touch — short, bleak, and inhuman: *Wragg is in custody.* The sex lost in the confusion of our unrivalled happiness; or (shall I say) the superfluous Christian name lopped off by the straightforward vigour of our old Anglo-Saxon breed!" It seems to me that even such anti-Erasmian ironists as Evelyn Waugh and Beatrice Lillie and Noël Coward — all those lapidary phrase-makers whose metallic tones mistuned our ear, mistuned our voice, for all simply serious purposes — were only exploiters of Arnold's vein. And that he was only Erasmus reborn.

Even D. H. Lawrence, with his uneasy giggle at Mabel Dodge's houseful of objets d'art — "It's just like one of those nasty little temples in India." Thinking of some of his political pronouncements, one expects to categorize Lawrence as the most Faustian of all twentieth-century writers; and then one finds him defining himself in terms of Erasmus, the man by himself, in *Kangaroo,* the one novel where he confronts the issue of political action; and resisting the anarchic lure of Australia in the name of " 'the flag of our real civilized consciousness. I'll give up the ideals. But not the aware, self-responsible, deep consciousness that we've gained.' " One finds him calling Asquith, the Erasmian liberal, essentially English in a good sense, and Lloyd George, the Faustian radical, essentially not. (It was left to Joyce Cary, so lacking in Faustian fire himself, to make an English hero out of Lloyd George.) I have already mentioned, apropos of *Apocalypse,* Lawrence's affinity with the Congregationalists, his unease with the Primitive Methodists. But even more striking is his refusal, in pursuit of intuitive knowledge and power, to claim the right to be excessive, to assert his human sacrilege and monstrousness. There are cases of monstrous behavior and feeling in Lawrence; but he is distinguished from the real sacred monsters of modernist literature by his sense of himself as being, at his most Lawrentian, merely more alive than other people, more normal, more in touch with his own experience, more humanly integral and shapely. Proust, Joyce, Dostoevsky, Kafka, all admit, exploit for their art their own disease. But Lawrence claims to use his health. And clearly this sense of the healthy was very much like his mother's sense of the healthy, as represented in *Sons and Lovers* — was an English inheritance. (That is why so many readings of the novel, as an attack on Mrs. Morel, are bad misreadings.) The same is true of Orwell, when you put him beside, say, Malraux. England has been Europe's — not to mention America's — land of moderation. Charlotte von Stein, that apostle of clearheaded moderation, had British blood and a British temperament — I see her, in her white dress, as a more glamorous Jane Austen — and when Goethe signed the Erasmian contract at her behest he was becoming an honorary British citizen, bringing Weimar into the United Kingdom as the fifty-third county.

Indeed, England has been a land of moderation too long — to the point of stagnation. There is so much in England of the peculiar malice evoked by Erasmians as rulers, even among other Erasmians. Rulers of the Faustian or Calvinish temperaments have an iron in their grip which pacifies the ruled, because it satisfies their resentment at being led. If government is admitted to be a grim and cruel business, they need not want to do it for themselves. Tom Paine heard someone say that George III had enough of the Devil in him to be a good king; and that remark certainly reflected in a popular mirror the ethos of Faustian politics. But Paine argued that it was conclusive proof of the evils of monarchy that it should need such powers. Yet Paine's own Calvinist politics assign the Party a terrifying power role just as supernatural, though named after the *good* archangel, after Michael rather than after Lucifer. A man who leads us while claiming to have only our own sensibility and our own qualities rouses our envy and resentment. Democracy only works as long as its leaders have something of a Faustian personality, however controlled that is by a general Erasmian decorum. You saw that in the reluctance American liberals felt to vote for Stevenson, and in the peculiar malice directed at Woodrow Wilson to this day. The channels of English life are clogged with the sediment of those feelings, our veins are arthritic, our stomach is permanently sour, our gentleness is a fear of the ugly deposits which passion would flush out. And irony against the royal family is another such cop-out.

So I got off the plane thinking that the only news I wanted to hear about Buckingham Palace was about the installation of a black President there. If he represented the hegemony of the only vital force in British culture today, the immigrants, that would seriously seem a cause for hope. I was clear that the ideas, and the social forms, which I had seen in Cuba were far more alive than anything in England. And I thought that was partly because the Cubans had had their revolution, but partly also because they had a future, too. They felt themselves to represent the Third World and therefore to be at the heart of the contemporary international revolution. Even radicals in England cannot authentically feel that. Authentically they can only feel themselves in touch with the past. I had read in a German newspaper that bookstores in England reported selling either modern American novels, or nineteenth-century British memoirs; and it occurred to me that this was true of even the British New Left; that in its sense of *itself* it is looking back (to the Great Tradition and to nineteenth-century socialism) even while it points forward; that its consciousness of the new is as of something exotic, which it conscientiously subdues to its own categories. In the context of Mailer on the one hand, and Cuba on the other, the New Left is surely historically provincial, intellectually nostalgic, aesthetically necrophile.

It was then the figure of Raymond Williams I saw myself addressing, his face I saw personifying radical London, to counterpart Mailer in New York. His inspiration, and his discipline, are major facts of that movement. The year before I left Birmingham, I had gone to a conference there, which he had not attended, but at which he had been quoted by every speaker in confirmation or guarantee of his own opinions. It is an orthodoxy, and not just in such trivial ways as the citation of authority. It is an orthodoxy of thought; which in itself is a strength, and the group is one to take seriously. But in cultural matters, or more simply and demonstrably in literary matters, the orthodoxy is a weakness too. It intensifies that Calvinist tendency to demonstrate and organize truths rather than experimentally to respond to them. There is a hostility to the free play of the imagination deep in that temperament. By purifying themselves of the liberal taint in Leavis's critical approach, the New Left have sterilized themselves.

The imaginative and mythological equipment of the movement needs renewing. As the first step the old mascot of the working-class WEA bookman must be discarded. That image nowadays has purely nostalgic power; offered in reference to the present, it is an imaginative lie. The most obvious modernization would be to substitute the black or brown immigrant. It is he who, seen in the public libraries, has the poignancy of exclusion which the working-man used to have, carries the same promise of a seriousness of response to reading which the included man can never bring. When I sold my car the last time I left England, I advertised it in the *New Statesman*, and was written to by a man whose handwriting was unformed, who repeated words, who tore the paper unevenly off the notepad, who told me I could phone him at his work but must ask for him by a name different from the one he signed — a series of signs which seemed to be incongruous with his being a *New Statesman* reader, and cause for unease. When I saw him, I understood. He was black. All the signs now fitted into one pattern, and there was no cause for unease anymore. But that pattern is probably still too like the old workingman pattern, induces too much the old messages, the old voice. "Bookman" is fatal. For the Left to come to life again, the messages have got to be renewed, the voice has got to change. Not that an Erasmian will be the one to lift his voice into the new register needed. But he might be able to recognize the genuine new voice when it comes. That is his vocation, to keep cleaning out his ears, to keep listening.

I arrived in Edinburgh on the evening the astronauts landed on the moon. I found myself watching the early morning television pictures in the company of two Americans who were staying in the same boardinghouse. It was a startling reminder of where the wealth and power of the world are still invested — of where the hopes and imaginative energies of mankind are still invested, in a sense. The reminder was startling because I had been taking for granted exclusively other senses of that phrase for so long. And yet this lay within the realm I had been exploring; it was an alternative to, a contradiction of, those I had been dealing with.

A couple of nights later we went to see *The Sport of My Mad Mother* done by the Traverse Theatre. There everything, from the size of the auditorium to the idea of the play, was in a different contradiction of the moon landing. In other ages, I presume, it would have been absurd to talk about *these* things as being "in contradiction" of each other. On my second trip to Edinburgh, later that summer, we went to a Festival opera, and symphony concert, that were *not* in opposition to the moon landing. They were the same kind of enterprise. Though the concert was given by an Iron Curtain country orchestra, *they* understood the same thing by culture as a Western orchestra and as NASA. But the Traverse, the whole fringe of the Festival understands something in antithesis to that. They believe that the arts must subvert the established structures of society. In our day the battle lines are drawn, and the word "contradiction" is the only appropriate one. One cannot, I think, hold the two things together in one's mind, in any kind of synthesis. One has to reject one of them. This pressure produces much of the undirected radicalism of young people today. In the arts, and particularly in the performing arts, there is a lot of would-be Faustian radicalism; which in America aligns itself easily enough with the intellectual radicalism of Mailer, Fiedler, Sontag, etc., but in England is not really congruent with the New Left's radicalism.

As for the large, soggy, would-be Erasmian center, Edinburgh is a poignant monument to that. A year-round festival of fogs and kindness, of decent dampness and limitations. From the kindly landladies, with their enormous breakfasts and satin-frilled bedrooms, to the War Memorials, with their lists of kilted dead and memories of bagpipe marches. Like Canada, Scotland seems full of gray granite monuments to the regiments they sent to fight on England's behalf; ruling-class testimonials to the loyalty with which they have discharged the task entrusted to them. And the counterpart of those sad damp pseudo-Gothic crosses and pillars is the sad damp genre of dialect jokes and sentiment. Surely no city in England itself has a Greyfriars Bobby, the dog who came for its lunch every day to the Greyfriars Tavern, and after its master's death continued to come while spending most of its time on its master's grave. I remember reading such stories in gift books of the First World War, but none in the books of my own time. But Scotland, a kind of Greyfriars Bobby itself, continues to do the tricks its master taught it long after he himself lies underground.

The Greyfriars Tavern is just outside the Greyfriars Church, in whose yard the National Covenant was signed. It is hard to hold together in one's mind both Greyfriars Bobby and that supreme symbol of the Calvinist temperament, which inspired such acts of severe heroism and ideological hatred, which had to be sealed in so much blood and bitterness. And yet I think that the Calvinist temperament, by subordinating so rigidly the tenderer and more romantic feelings, produces such mousy manifestations of sensibility as Bobby, such psychic doll-fondlings, as a natural counterpart.

What Edinburgh meant to me was what Weston had meant, in between landing in London and going up north. It meant the constricted and tamed, the over-gentled landscape of the British Isles, and of the class I was born into, the lower middle class. It meant the land of the *Daily Express*. For an Englishman, England is always heartbreaking, because — like so many other things — it needs so much more love than it can arouse. It wears that subdued and diminished expression of a pet who hopes to deserve love by not demanding it, by obedience, by self-repression. I don't in fact remember the day I drove west from Birmingham to Weston, and I see the road in my mind as in early spring, with the sun out for the first time in weeks, rousing colors in the bricks and the grass and the sky which seem sudden and luminous, glowingly warm and bright. There is something spectral about it, the vaporous radiance of those small fields, with the high hedges, and the twisting lanes, and trees on rises soaring up like hieroglyphs, unfolding themselves, fanning out extended branches like fingers. There is something almost sepulchral about that gentle dampness and silence. The silence is so intense in this memory, I realize as I write, because I'm remembering the foot-and-mouth spring of 1968, when the fields were empty and the farms barely operating. But such gentle noises as one nowadays hears on that road make no difference. Life has never achieved a large gesture there. How intensely at home I felt; and how intensely I resented the ruglike comfort of it all. My journey had to result in something. It had to change something in that landscape. And it resulted — an implausibly apt coincidence — in my changing something I had written the year before, about Weston.

CONCLUSION TO PART I

Part II is the result of my journey, in some sense its fruit. It is the culmination of my argument in Part I, the solution to the problem proposed there, insofar as there is a solution. It admits the impracticability of the liberal position; in an age like ours, political radicalism is compulsory. But a radical temperament is not achieved so easily as a radical position. And for some of us, as I said, a change of temperament is particularly difficult. But then too a radical temperament means a disrespect for so many kinds of fact, and nonfact. It means the decay of the liberal illusion, the diminishment of imagination, of intellect, of sensibility. So I don't *want* a radical temperament. Fate and inclination, compulsion and preference, after all, run together. The disaccord of position and temperament persists but is not just dysfunctional, is not just a personal disability; one's private disharmonies have their public value. The problem is "solved," I no longer feel paralyzed and guilty, I no longer feel bad about myself-and-the-world.

What more can I claim for my argument? Not that it gives me or the world a plan of action, obviously. But that was never my enterprise. I already knew, I had accepted, that I was stuck with inaction. I set out to allay an anxiety — present in others as well as in myself — which derived from feelings *about* such inaction, or such inadequate and ineffective and incomplete action. And seeing now, in the light of these reflections, the alternatives of policy which others challenge us with, ours no longer seems specially guilty. In history it has not *been* inaction to see through the contemporary hysterias and hypocrisies, and to keep alive that cool clear medium in which truths live. It is liberals after all who listen, who respond, who understand, who sort out the grain from the chaff in the golden pile poured out by men of genius. It is Erasmians who mediate between them and the rest of the world, who treat with both as equals. Ages of revolution call for more than that, of course, call for radical commitment, but to respond to that call out of anxious responsiveness has been to produce ersatz thought and feeling, ersatz action, of the kind which is all around us now. Better, far better, to make an authentic refusal. No form of activism has ever proved to be guaranteed against disaster — and personal disaster as well as political — moral and intellectual self-falsification. The only thing that can justify a man in radical action is real conviction. And out of the most unpromising political policies — including inertias and compromises — have come things which *I* am bound to value as marvelous human achievements. *I* am bound to value the politics of men like Goethe and Lawrence. One must then follow out the uncertainties and falterings of one's instincts in politics, refusing to feel that to do so is a betrayal of moral seriousness. (For instance, I must say that within academic politics today, I think the conservative position — about the intellectual life, not about international policies — promises more than either the radical or the liberal.) And one must vigorously criticize the uncertainties and rashnesses of other instincts in those who claim to be clear about politics. There is as much harmful nonsense in the air today as there ever was, in matters of morality and social purpose as well as of taste and intelligence. Perhaps there is more than ever, among the active of conscience. Perhaps the thing *most* needed in the world is an *active* Erasmian temperament of mind; some forceful manifestation of that, some insistence on it, even while it is painfully compromised with the radical position in politics.

I'll end with a quotation from Max Weber's "Politics as a Vocation." This is a speech he gave at Munich University in 1918, which is full of stern but curative truths for today's distempers.

One can say that three pre-eminent qualities are decisive for the politician: passion, a feeling of responsibility, and a sense of proportion.

This means passion in the sense of *matter-of-factness*, of passionate devotion to a "cause," to the god or demon who is its overlord. It is not passion in the sense of that inner bearing which my late friend, Georg Simmel, used to designate as "sterile excitation" . . . that plays so great a part with our intellectuals in this carnival we decorate with the proud name of "revolution."

(Tr. H. H. Gerth and C. Wright Mills)

PART TWO

WESTON AND HAITI AND HISTORY

. . . that night (or the seven or eight nights while they huddled in the dark and watched from the windows the barns or granaries or whatever it is you harvest sugar into, and the fields too, blazing and smoking: he said how you could smell it, you could smell nothing else, the rank sweet rich smell as if the hatred and the implacability, the thousand secret dark years which had created the hatred and implacability, had intensified the smell of the sugar . . .*

August 1969

Spending a few weeks in Mexico and Cuba this summer, I began at last to hear those voices so long uplifted on the horizon of everyone's mind, the black voices of protest, of anger, of warning, of revenge. In such places, with the record of colonialism writ large all round one, the process of conversion moves fast. One begins to see all history, and the future, and one's own place in both, in terms of white men against black, of racial exploitation, of historical guilt and expiation.

Book after book showed me how the white man had brought upon the world's black, brown, red, and yellow peoples every variety of the sufferings of exploitation. I saw how since the 16th century, the so-called "Christian trader" white man began to ply the seas in his lust for Asian and African empires, and plunder, and power. I read, I saw, how the white man never has gone among the non-white peoples bearing the Cross in the true manner and spirit of Christ's teachings — meek, humble, and Christ-like.

* William Faulkner, *Absalom, Absalom*, New York, 1936, p. 249.

I perceived, as I read, how the collective white man had been actually nothing but a piratical opportunist who used Faustian machinations to make his own Christianity his initial wedge in criminal
conquests. First, always "religiously," he branded "heathen" and
"pagan" labels upon ancient non-white cultures and civilizations. The
stage thus set, he then turned upon his non-white victims his weapons
of war.

I read how, entering India — half a *billion* deeply religious brown
people — British white men, by 1759, through promises, trickery, and
manipulations, controlled much of India through Great Britain's East
India Company. The parasitical British administration kept tentacling
out to half of the sub-continent. In 1857, some of the desperate people
of India finally mutinied — and, excepting the African slave trade, nowhere has history recorded any more unnecessary bestial and ruthless
human carnage than the British suppression of the non-white Indian
people.

Over 115 million African blacks — close to the 1930's population
of the United States — were murdered or enslaved during the slave
trade. And I read how when the slave market was glutted, the can-
nibalistic white powers of Europe next carved up, as their colonies, the
richest areas of the black continent. And Europe's chancelleries for the
next century played a chess game of naked exploitation and power
from Cape Horn to Cairo.

— The Autobiography of Malcolm X

But I myself can't preach on the strength of such feelings, so recently acquired and only half appropriated still. I am as yet only
ready to reflect on the position I have just abandoned, and on why
and how much and whether I have abandoned it. That position
was a kind of obstinate pastoralism, a claiming the right to concern
myself with innocent and agreeable matters, to close my ears to
hysteria and violence.

> *Virginie. Tennessee. Géorgie. Alabama*
> *Putréfactions monstrueuses de révoltes inopérantes,*
> *marais de sang putrides*
> *trompettes absurdement bouchées*
> *Terres rouges, terres sanguines, terres consanguines . . .*
>
> *Ce qui est à moi*
> *c'est un homme seul emprisonné de*
> *blanc*

c'est un homme seul qui défie les cris
blancs de la mort blanche
(TOUSSAINT, TOUSSAINT LOUVERTURE)
— *Cahier d'un Retour au Pays Natal*

You don't open your ears to such voices till you are convinced you must. Those lines are by Aimé Césaire, the black poet of Martinique, the first black graduate of the Ecole Normale Supérieure in Paris. The theatrical occasion of my stay in Havana was a performance of his play *Lumumba*. Lumumba is a very contemporary figure of world history for Cubans — for the Third World as a whole. He belongs with Nasser, Ben Bella, Fidel Castro, Che Guevara, Frantz Fanon, who are all ideologically black, all heroes of blackness. These men represent the new history, and for Third World intellectuals the greatest hero of them all is Fanon, the ideologue of blackness, also from Martinique. He, like Che himself, left his native land, and left the profession for which he had been trained, psychiatry, left his social enclave and haven, the asylum to which he was entitled as an intellectual, to become a fighter in a foreign revolution, in another part of the Third World. He fought in the war there, the new heroism, and he died, the new martyrdom.

Fanon and Césaire together *are* the black revolution in Martinique. They are its poet and its fighting hero. In the theater program of *Lumumba* Fanon was quoted interpreting Césaire's work (along with Sartre interpreting Lumumba's politics) and in *Black Skin, White Masks*, Fanon himself often quotes Césaire in support of his own theories. They are intellectual comrades. James Baldwin says Malcolm X told him that *they* were the poet and warrior of *their* revolution, the black revolution in America. While in Cuba all the poets try to define their relation to Che as that, and even the whitest of novelists consider themselves ideologically black, and part of the world revolution against the European races. And in Jamaica the cult of Ras Tafari teaches that the blacks are the world's true Israelites — that Hitler was a divine punishment to the Jews for usurping that role — and that they want to return to Africa, to Ethiopia. They want no part of the white Babylon — Russia, the three-ribbed bear of *Revelation*, will crush Babylon, and revenge its crimes against the blacks.

Jamaica, Martinique, Haiti, Harlem; the cries of blackness and of revolution go up all around, and a white man in the Caribbean can soon feel frightened, can soon feel like Thomas Sutpen smelling the sugar in *Absalom, Absalom*. Just after the passage quoted as epigraph, he is depicted as intensely isolated on his

little island set in a smiling and fury-lurked and incredible indigo sea . . . And he overseeing it, riding peacefully about on his horse while he learned the language . . . not knowing that what he rode upon was a volcano, hearing the air tremble and throb at night with the drums and the chanting and not knowing that it was the heart of the earth itself he heard.

When I got home to England, home to Weston Lullingfield, I took out my Phillips School Atlas and tried to recapture what I had used to see under the heading Caribbean. And I think that the ordering principle in that proliferation of islands on the map was always the parenthesis behind each name, the initials (Br.), (Fr.), and (Du.). My sense of the islands themselves, from their own point of view, was just of welcoming white sand beyond the bright blue water. I had no picture of a people living there, of a culture. I had no sense of what had happened there between 1500 and 1800, between Sir Thomas More and Dr. Johnson, behind the backs of Bunyan and Newton and all the people whose names mean history to me. No sense of what they meant for us in England; what they mean for us today; and tomorrow. And I see now that this was knowledge of which one could not innocently be ignorant.

It is there, in terms of these realities, that our new destinies will shape themselves. Because it is there that our real past lies. It is there that we did what we did in the world, what bulks largest in the record of our achievements. It is there that we made our historical selves. Confined now to our own island, with so much to be unmade, to be undone, it is still to the Caribbean we must look for a sense of the future.

But I am still concerned to conserve as much as possible of the past, the old domain, of *my* intellectual haven, of "culture." Guilty though our culture is, poisoned though its roots are, demonstrable as are the effects of that poison in its high-culture fruit, that fruit nevertheless still seems to me the world's treasure, and to be preserved.

Along with my school atlas, I got out an essay which I wrote a year ago, about my native village and its relation to history. I wrote it in defense of my privacy, in protest against those angry voices I've now opened my ears to. Weston, it seemed to me, had had *no* relation to history, in the sense of melodramatic moral issues. It had been innocent, in the way I wanted to be. It had proved innocence possible. I now accept that innocence is impossible, and privacy morally impracticable. One must join in the ferment of accusation and self-accusation, however hysterical; one must ally oneself with the angry voices attacking our culture. One may still be able to achieve something more than anger, but it will not be by refusing anger.

Conflicting obligations must fulfill themselves as best they may, and the psychic cost of the conflict must be borne by the individual. Its reconciliation, the combination of liberal temperament and radical position, is a cause we can better serve, I think, by individual explorations like the present one, than by anything more theoretical and formulaic.

I reproduce the essay here, interpolating those of this summer's facts which constitute a comment. It is ninety-nine percent what it was. The one percent I have eliminated or altered was my attempt even then to admit to partial hearing, to take some account of, the other voices. That part seemed better replaced by some facts.

* * *

Weston and History

Weston Lullingfield, Shropshire, my home village, is not remarkable for either its landscape or its historical interest; though it has two pretty views, west to the Welsh hills and south to the hills from Wenlock Edge to the Breiddens, and though it has been there for hundreds of years. The field survey map of 1794 shows many of the same farms and cottages with the same field and garden boundaries as are there today, and back at least as far as that the same family names appear, the Adamses, the Birches, the

Dovastons, the Gittings, the Joneses, the Haycocks, the Kirkhams, etc. And there is an ancient British fortification, the Berth, visible, across the fields, from our front door.

But the striking thing to me is the impalpability of those hundreds of years, the way nothing in the village offers itself as old. Some things seem new, nearly everything not-new. What *is* old, like the Berth, is unrelatable to the present; does not *offer* itself at all. When I went to America, to the Midwest, I met a landscape in which everything man-made was *new*, and this seemed to me much more historical. I thought then that I must have missed what was there in Weston, custom dimming the eye like a cataract, but when I came back I could see no more.

It is disturbing to feel one's private experience unrelated to public issues, to feel oneself floating becalmed in an illusory country backwater, insulated from the storms of historical reality, behind glass, behind windows wadded with back copies of the *Shrewsbury Chronicle* and the *Shropshire Magazine*.

The nearest thing to history in Weston for me is an old family anecdote about Aunt Lizzie and Mrs. Cunliffe. It is through Aunt Lizzie, my mother's aunt, that we come to be in Weston; she, the first in her family to break into the professions, came here from Rochdale in 1893 to teach in the school, married here, remained thirty years headmistress, retired, and died here in 1938. Mrs. Cunliffe was Weston's principal landowner — though she herself actually lived in the neighboring village of Petton — and she wanted to be greeted as a kind of ruler by the village children she met as she drove the country roads in her yellow and black brougham, complete with silver-plated harness and coachman and footman in livery and cockaded silk hats. She wanted from the girls a curtsy and from the boys a salute which she seems to have designed herself — she was very artistic — the right hand to touch their caps and the whole right arm to be then extended from the shoulder. There was a touch of Mussolini about Mrs. Cunliffe. When she failed to get this acknowledgment of her status, she went home and wrote a severe note — she was forever writing severe notes — to the vicar of the village concerned, and he went to the schoolteacher, and the schoolteacher upbraided the whole school. In due course she communicated this way with Aunt Lizzie, via Mr. Tuke, the Weston vicar — as she communicated with the Cockshutt schoolchildren via the Cockshutt teacher and vicar, and the Petton and Burlton children similarly. Aunt Lizzie refused to scold the children or to train them in any such "bowing and scraping." She thought it "quite enough" if the boys touched their caps and the girls inclined their heads. Mrs. Cunliffe was angry and dispatched Mr. Tuke again, but Aunt Lizzie stood firm.

This was history to me because I could see Mrs. Cunliffe as representing Shropshire aristocracy and Aunt Lizzie confronting her as insurgent Manchester democracy. And this was satisfying because in her little gesture I could see my whole family's historical role. We, all our kind of people, though politically Conservative and even temperamentally conservative in most ways, all have a rather aggressive activism and common sense, a rather abrasive and reductive habit of humor, a Mancunian dislike for the pieties and pretensions or traditions that halo and beglamorize class conflicts and power structures. We are realists; we like the hard sharp edges of facts; above all we are risers — and not so much by means of money as by means of education. That made a difference I could feel between us and most other people in Weston. It was our character and I was glad to find its historical significance.

Aunt Lizzie's father, James Fitton, a baker and confectioner, was a great believer in education, who founded with two friends a literary society in Droylesden. Aunt Lizzie had quite a handsome portrait of him, presented to his family by the Society of Oddfellows; a long, bony face with hollow cheeks, a high forehead with quite a broad bulge of bone right at the top, just before the fine-spun hair began, a long, delicate, bony nose and chin, and well-set blue eyes, rather hooded by their lids. A delicate Lincoln — with something of Newman intermixed — a light, bright, Saxon Lincoln. Of his eight children, the three boys worked in a railway engineering shop in Gorton, and played in the Droylesden Reed Band, till they all emigrated to Australia. Aunt Jinny followed Aunt Lizzie to Weston and taught, without a certificate, till Aunt Lizzie married, when she followed her brothers to Australia. The other three sisters, including my mother's mother, Sarah, married locally. But all of them struggled, in their own lives or in their children's, to rise in the world, by mastering the secrets of the white collar and the white hand, the number and the word. My success at Weston school, my winning a scholarship to the grammar school in Shrewsbury, was attributed in the village to Aunt Lizzie. My whole career is seen as a logical development from that beginning. And essentially of course they are right.

Aunt Lizzie herself was a character by the time I knew her. Who wouldn't be, after thirty years' successful autocracy in a village school — and she was a very successful schoolmistress. She looked like her father, only less so, less dreamy, less delicate, less stern. She too had a high, broad brow, but her cheeks were rather full. She too had light-blue eyes but set in a pink face that flushed dangerously when she was crossed. Shrewd, sharp-tongued, practical, energetic, impatient, she was a very recognizable type, a characterological cliché, but she had — isolated there in Shropshire — made herself what she was more than most. Politically conservative, she was dazzled by Mr. Tuke, the last of Weston's high-style, high-handed vicars. He, after all, living at a vicarage which had three servants, the friend of county families, and with Brasenose College, Oxford, behind him, was a fine jousting partner for a woman whose schoolfriends went to work in the mills. Mr. Tuke's successor in 1915, Mr. Rugg, a sadder as well as a soberer figure, she was not dazzled by, nor by his still sadder successors. There has been small space for high-style living at Weston vicarage since 1915. Mr. Rugg had been at Oxford too, but perhaps she thought Oxford was no longer what it had been. And immediately after the war the Cunliffe estate was broken up. Nothing replaced Mrs. Cunliffe or Mr. Tuke; the countryside I grew up in was emptier than the one I heard about. The old system was visibly cracking all through Aunt Lizzie's headmistress-ship. History was on Manchester's side.

That is why I believe our family version of the conflict. Mrs. Cunliffe bowling through the villages in her brougham, her quieter and finer-bred husband left behind at home, Mrs. Cunliffe crowding Petton Church with pseudofeudal memorials to Cunliffes and Sparlings, Mrs. Cunliffe writing an autobiography with the title 53 *Years of Sunshine, Storm, and Rain* — in 1901 — Mrs. Cunliffe was a bit ridiculous. She could not impose herself on the imagination of any half-free soul, and Aunt Lizzie, with her sense

Mrs. Cunliffe. (From the *Shropshire Magazine,* July 1957, page 13.)

of the way the world was going, must have won an easy victory over her — within, for instance, Mr. Tuke's sympathies.

Mrs. Cunliffe, sixteen years older than Aunt Lizzie, was born in 1848 in Baden Baden, where her parents, on their way home from a European tour, were trapped by the revolution — an omen she should have heeded. She was the sole heiress of all the Sparling estates, the only child of a man who was himself the only sibling of eight to have children. And as her grandparents lived on till 1867 and 1870 respectively and then an uncle and then her father inherited it before it came to her in 1890, she had a long career as heiress, and every incentive to dramatize her own position, to anticipate the power and pomp to come. She is said to have spent as much as £150,000 on rebuilding the Hall and the lodges, and replanting the two-hundred-acre park, when she inherited. (Her uncle, who owned the property only briefly and only just before she did, had spent £60,000 on it. The Sparlings slid down the nineteenth century on the river of golden sovereigns tapped by the Liverpool merchant John Sparling between 1780 and 1800. It didn't, as we shall see, bring them happiness, but it eased them along in rather grandly plutonic style, decorating their dullness with festoons of gold.) Mrs. Cunliffe lived extravagantly, celebrating all family festivals — and she had ten children — very lavishly. When Brooke Cunliffe came back from the Boer War, she had triumphal arches with streamers built across the public roads from Petton to the railway station, three miles away at Baschurch, and all the schoolchildren from Weston, Petton, Burlton, Cockshutt, went to tea at the Hall, and there were swings and roundabouts in the park and a marquee full of presents, one for each child. By the time Mrs. Cunliffe died, in 1925, all the money seems to have been spent.

So she was generous; but she was also domineering, and in a gross and foolish style. I've heard anecdotes to her moral disadvantage all my life, and in all of them she got the worst of the conflict even in practical terms; that she sold a house in London and then had an Adam fireplace taken out of it and brought to Petton, but the house-purchaser forced her to return it; that she had Petton Church fenced off from the public, to make it a private chapel, but was forced to take the fence up again; and so on.

She must have been very self-willed and self-dramatizing; she always signed her written instructions to village people with her name in full, underlined heavily as much as three times. And her husband seems to have counted for nothing. She was totally unmastered. On rent-day it was to her that her tenants had to present themselves; Captain Cunliffe was not to be seen. She was very "business-like" (it was the one quality in her Aunt Lizzie approved) and very severe with her tenants. I've heard only one anecdote about the Captain. He appeared once to some children playing in the park (the children of a Sparling bastard, as it happens) and gave them a sovereign. They crowded round the one who had it in his hand, and when they turned back, manners remembered, to thank the donor, he had disappeared.

The only convincing picture of the lady is a photograph taken in old age. She looks there very like Queen Victoria — indeed she prided herself on the resemblance and perhaps enhanced it — with puffy, indeterminate features, a lace cap and fichu, black velvet ribbon round her neck and long jet earrings — a short, stout woman firing herself square at the camera, her purpose of self-projection so tense that her actual face is quite slack and inexpressive. Mrs. Cunliffe makes one understand Lytton Strachey.

She published four books, all privately. Besides her own autobiography, she edited — no doubt to unfortunate effect — her father's autobiographical notebooks, adding, among other things, a preface full of tedious genealogical boasting. The other two publications are called *Verses at Sunset* and *Seven Small Sermons*. The quality of the first can be gauged from this sample:

> *Fain would I leave one quick vibrating line*
> *To flash a message to some far-off soul*
> *When what was flesh is dust, and the divine*
> *And glowing spark flies upward to its goal.*
> *Oh for more trust, tho' Science cannot kill*
> *Men's craving for what has been, yet may be,*
> *As crimson sunlight o'er a darkening hill*
> *Sinks, but to rise again more gloriously.*

I know not what I am, yet cherish still
The inborn Hope of Immortality.

Obviously Mrs. Cunliffe had no great talent for verse, and her work in abstract thought, and in the visual arts — a wrought-iron screen she designed and several memorials survive in Petton Church — is similar. She was a typical fascist, ruling other people with a rod of iron and appropriating to herself quite illegitimately the realm of spiritual and artistic values. Order must be — *my* Order — so that Beauty may be preserved — *my* Beauty.

At the same time, I feel, in this matter, some sympathy for Mrs. Cunliffe and against Aunt Lizzie. Aunt Lizzie had books, and her taste in furniture and ornaments shows that she had an eye for such things — no better or worse, than Mrs. Cunliffe's. But Aunt Lizzie would never have risked writing such a poem, or even reading it. She had no thought of receiving a message about the soul or immortality, much less of leaving a quick, vibrating line. In our family the life of ideas and feelings is treated, in practice, with suspicion. Petty bourgeois democracy can be as bad as fascism in some things.

Anyway, I thought that finding out about Mrs. Cunliffe, and her father and grandfather, would be a way to see Weston and myself in relation to history. The Cunliffes and Sparlings had committed themselves, in books, in public office, in *records*, much more than the Fittons had.

I quite easily found some interesting things, but Mrs. Cunliffe's autobiography, almost the starting point of my quest (for I had known that such a book existed all my life) proved the hardest of all to lay my hands on. There is no copy in any library, nor in any private collection that I could discover. No local historian had even heard of it. It *had* been, I found out, in one private library, sold when the owner died; but I've no doubt that 53 *Years* was one of an auction lot of books which was bought for some other title, and Mrs. Cunliffe thrown away immediately. Over the last twenty years fifty or a hundred copies must have died that way around Shropshire, rotting under the laurel bushes of sold-up manor houses, wrenched from the bundle and flung out of sight before the purchasers drove away, or set to burning damply on bonfires of rubbish.

It was six months after I began that I finally got into my hands what may be the last copy extant, gorgeous in green leather and gold lettering. I was allowed to read it by a descendant of the family, in a London flat filled with the treasures of Petton, including family portraits I had seen reproduced but had thought long since destroyed, giant objects six and eight feet tall, crowding the apartment walls. I saw also the genealogy book, compiled by the College of Heralds, begun for Mrs. Cunliffe but still kept up to date, brilliant with coats of arms and artistic penmanship.

53 *Years* is not very interesting. The underprivileged mind, the underdeveloped life, behind it — her experiences as well as what she makes of them — are almost tragic. The Sparling money puffed up her vanity, withered away her seriousness. Her social position walled her in. Her intelligence and sensibility had no chance to grow freely, poisoned by gold at the root. The most vivid part was something she did not intend; the Lawrentian class-contrasts of her early life, in her father's parish of Eccleston in Lancashire; where the men, who earned their livings in the mines, were then leaving the Established Church in numbers for Mormonism, and emigrating to Salt Lake City. She used to go with her mother to visit these colliers' families in their sicknesses and family distresses. She sat at the deathbeds of drunken impenitents and of men "charred to a cinder in colliery explosions." And she tells us — apropos of a fine sermon her father preached on the occasion — that these colliers once got drunk a man they disliked and buried him alive standing up in a pit they dug for the purpose, stamping the loose dirt down over his head. Mrs. Cunliffe draws no connection, but the reader does, between such things and the life of the aria-singing, watercoloring, watered-silk thirteen year old who got her first crinoline in 1861 — "three ugly iron bars suspended from tapes."

For the rest she has little to tell us. She had many offers of marriage, because, she says, of her great expectations. She implies she was in love with one of them, but he was an Irishman, so her father forbade it, and she married a second cousin, who told her on their first meeting that he would never marry a girl without a fortune. His honesty impressed her. Perhaps his meekness did too. He was a veteran of the Crimean War and the Indian Mutiny, sixteen years older than her, but he was no match for her. She married determined to be an equal partner in every way (she declares the vow of wifely obedience an anachronism), and she retired him in 1890, when he was still in his fifties and had twenty-five years to live. He caught influenza in that year and suffered for long afterward from what she calls poisoned nerves. "Never at any time of a very energetic temperament, all business matters now became a weariness of the flesh to him, and I have ever since transacted them."

Perhaps she was impatient to become the local Widow of Windsor, reluctantly shouldering the burdens of Empire alone, in Balmoral bonnet and blacks. Besides being the year of his flu, 1890 was the year of her inheritance, and she had immediately set about the rebuilding of Petton. In her childhood she had resolved "that if ever Petton were mine, I would set my mark upon the place." Ellis Cunliffe soon became alarmed at the magnitude of the undertaking. "I would indeed he had my love for the place." But she had realized soon after marriage that he would never like *any* settled home.

Other people she talks about in the same strain, superficially generous. Simple faith may be more than Norman blood but, she tells us rather nicely, her mother had both. However, she lets it slip that the lady was great at small economies, and had a hasty temper and great family pride, so that she sounds like a Thackeray caricature. She herself, as a child, had difficult relations with her parents.

> A *silent, strange, and solitary child,*
> *Full of unearthly fancies. The unseen*
> *To me, was Real; God, unreconciled*
> *To Man, a problem, even at thirteen* . . .

Almost a third of her book is verse.

There are a great many illustrations, two photographs of her rose garden, one of her rockery, one of her sundial, one of her dog, but most reproductions of family portraits. She herself spent much time painting her children's pictures, and there are artistic photographs of the six daughters grouped in threes, Violet, Veronica, and Vanda Cunliffe, Verbena, Valencia, and Virginia Cunliffe. She tells us, and other people have confirmed it to me, that she denied her children nothing. Her severity to the rest of the world found its natural counterpart in indulgence to them. All ten of them grew up overprivileged, inhabitants of an enchanted garden where all the enchantment issued directly from the wand of that squat, gold-squatting, crinolined Circe.

The main part of her book begins with the first stanza of "Tears, Idle Tears," and ends with a quatrain from Longfellow, and there is an Afterword, congratulating the nineteenth century on its technological and scientific achievements (she lists them) and going on to give the details of Queen Victoria's decline. "January 20. The Queen is ill, and we go heavily . . . January 22 [after announcing the death] I have a dull foreboding that this may be the turning point in the history of the Empire."

Queen Victoria was a constant value-standard for Mrs. Cunliffe, and one which she relates explicitly to her idea of herself. In that diary entry for January 20, she observes, "Not the least part of what she has done for her people has been to exalt womanhood." And you can see the same idea in the Jubilee hymn she wrote to celebrate the sixtieth anniversary of the accession, sung at Cockshutt Church in 1897.

> *Thy servant, Lord, these sixty years*
> *Hath good and faithful proved,*
> *Through storm and sunshine, hopes and fears*
> *Victoria "the Beloved."*
> *And love as strong as death has she,*
> *And greatest womanhood.*
> *Her name throughout all time shall be*
> *"Victoria the Good." ***

Greatest womanhood is the giveaway phrase again; that is what Mrs. Cunliffe saw herself as, a plump, plush sackful of greatest womanhood. And no doubt there were a thousand such women — mothers, poetesses, patriots — in England then. Again, for a moment, one thinks more kindly of Lytton Strachey.

But I got less of the feeling of Mrs. Cunliffe from her long-sought book than from Petton Church, which I'd known ever since

---

* Her feeling for the Queen is said to have centered on that anecdote about the twelve-year-old Princess Victoria first learning her ancestry, saying, "There is much splendour, but there is more responsibility," and then, placing her hand in that of the Baroness Lehzen, earnestly, "I will be good, I will be good." Trust Mrs. Cunliffe to fix on *that* anecdote.

my grammar-school cycling explorations of the village churches round Weston. It is old, with some fine Jacobean oak, but as it stands now it is completely Mrs. Cunliffe's creation. "This Church was adorned and beautified/In the year of our Lord 1896/ By Emma Florence Cunliffe/Lady of the Manor of Petton." So says a brass plate in Gothic lettering, black with red capitals, and there are a dozen other such inscriptions, commemorating other gifts to the church. The most extreme case perhaps is "The three electric light pendants/With storage batteries/Were given in 1913 by/Emma Florence Cunliffe/As a memento of the 14 years ministry/Of the Reverend Edward Reith."

The walls are covered with memorials to Sparlings and Cunliffes, about fifteen of them, and no other name is to be seen in the church (well, there are two to servants and two to sons-in-law) except the one word Chambre on an otherwise illegible eighteenth-century marble slab near the pulpit. The Chambres owned Petton before the Sparlings, but every word of the inscription has faded, even to the touch, except the surname Chambre.

The most vivid things in the church are the stained-glass windows, quite elaborate and Pre-Raphaelite, and all seven of them Mrs. Cunliffe's work. The east window is The Light of the World, and there is a St. Francis dedicated to a son-in-law, mostly blue and purple, with mauve pigeons, some solid white lambs, and a group of realistic swallows flying through a panel of bright pink. But the most interesting and pretty is of an ample and majestic maiden in a white samite gown, girdled with a medallioned belt, and holding an armful of myrtle, quantities of flaxen hair falling down her shoulders. The composition is mostly silver and gold, but ferns and wild roses in red and blue grow round her, and the whole is enclosed in some shaky architecture, a column on each side supporting two smaller columns, supporting an arch. Underneath are two medallions, portraits of King Edward the Peacemaker and Queen Victoria the Good, and the inscription, "This window symbolical of Peace and Motherhood was placed here by Emma Florence Cunliffe."

But though that gives one a strong feeling of the bombazine Czarina, one might still feel that it had little to do with history, or with Weston, or with the Fittons.

*   *   *

What was troubling me was not only Mrs. Cunliffe's relation to history, but my relation to her, my tone about her — a trouble expressed in that barely acceptable phrase "bombazine Czarina." The facts of this sort of history demanded a tone. They could not stand by themselves. They demanded the tone of a professional entertainer.

The story of black power is full of domineering, self-intensifying characters who need no such tone. For instance, Toussaint Louverture, a Faustian hero of heroes. He was a small, wizened, middle-aged slave when the revolution in St. Domingue broke out. He had a grotesquely protuberant jaw, and his head was usually wrapped up in a scarf. He had doctored horses on the Bréda plantation, and he was first known as Toussaint Bréda. He could read and write a little, but had had no formal education.

On November 4, 1801, having repressed a revolt led by his nephew, he reentered Le Cap, which he suspected of disaffection, bringing with him forty prisoners. The people of the city had been collected in the center, the Place d'Armes, and the first and second demi-brigades, which belonged to the city, were drawn up there in a hollow square with Toussaint's personal guard behind them. Three cannon were dragged into the center of the square, their gunners marching beside them, carrying lighted matches. Then Toussaint himself appeared, unaccompanied. He rode around the square in a state of fury, cowing everyone with his eye, and shouting out denunciations of the rebellion, promising vengeance. Then he reined in his horse, pointed his finger at one of the officers of the brigades, and ordered him to step forward. The man stood to attention before him. "Traitor!" shouted Toussaint, "Scoundrel! Shoot yourself." And the officer drew his pistol, cocked it, shot himself, fell to the ground.

Toussaint rode on round the square, pointed again at another man, gave the same command, and the same thing happened; and again, and again to all the officers there. Not one man failed to point the gun at himself and fire it, much less tried to point it at Toussaint himself. When the officers all lay dead, the forty prisoners were brought in and were stood in front of the cannon. That side of the square was cleared, and the cannon were fired full at the men. The soldiers of the brigades, three thousand of them, were marched away under escort, and Toussaint rode off the square with his personal guard behind him.

Such anecdotes induce no note of the professional entertainer. And Toussaint was not just bloodthirsty; he was a man of brilliant ideas, in politics, war, administration, culture. Far from being a villain of history, he was one of its heroes, but in the style of an age of revolution. His first personal proclamation was drawn up in 1793:

Brothers and Friends,

I am Toussaint Louverture. My name has perhaps become known to you. I am bent on vengeance. I desire the establishment of liberty and equality in St-Domingue. I strive to bring them into being. Unite with us, brothers, and fight with us in the common cause.

Your most obedient and humble servant,

Toussaint Louverture

In 1794, after the National Convention in Paris had abolished slavery, he raised and trained four new regiments for France, assisted by Henry Christophe, then twenty-seven, and seconded from the French barracks at Le Cap for the purpose. Christophe, a black from Grenada, probably born free, had not until then served with the rebel bands. He had been a cook and then a head waiter, and he became the best disciplinarian, and self-discipliner, of all the great black leaders. His troops were always the best equipped and trained. And in 1797 he became friends with Colonel Vincent, the French engineer responsible for the colony's fortifications, and together they devised the agricultural system of *fermage* which (temporarily) saved the island's plantation economy. It might have restored that economy permanently if it had not been allowed to lapse by Christophe's successors. In eighteen months one of his plantations increased its production tenfold. By 1799 he himself was estimated to be worth $250,000. His fourteen-year, stable rule as King of Haiti, from 1806 on, was the high water mark of black progress in that age. But in 1820 he too was faced with a rebellion, and committed suicide, and blackness became again synonymous with backwardness.

In 1800 Napoleon had recognized Toussaint as commander in chief of the colony, and his rivals gave up overt opposition. In 1801 he captured the Spanish half of the island, the colony of Santo Domingo. He reorganized the country entirely, displaying a talent for administration which was, like his talent for war and negotiation, comparable with Napoleon's. He, like Christophe, tried to make the island stable, orderly, and industrious. He attended Mass regularly, tried to stamp out voodoo, and insisted on Christian marriage.

But in 1801, Napoleon sent his brother-in-law, Leclerc, to subdue the island, in an expedition which before it ended was to cost the lives of forty thousand Frenchmen alone. In May 1802 Toussaint submitted to Leclerc, and in June he was treacherously arrested and sent back to France to prison, where he died the following year amid the snows, the whiteness which Aimé Césaire evoked in the lines I quoted.

A few months later both the mulattoes and the blacks on St. Domingue rebelled again, and the French armies soon lost control of the situation. Leclerc died of yellow fever, and his successor, Rochambeau, sailed away under British protection in 1803.

The rule of Haiti went to Dessalines, the most savage and the least enlightened of all the black leaders. He really hated all whites, and all mulattoes, just for being white and brown. He really wanted — not steadily but recurrently — to kill them all.

The day of vengeance has come and the implacable enemies of the rights of man have received the fitting punishment for their crimes . . .

Like the torrent that bursts its banks and shatters everything in its path, the fury of your vengeance has dashed down all that resisted its impetuous career. Perish all tyrants of innocence, all oppressors of mankind! . . .

We have repaid these cannibals war for war, crime for crime, outrage for outrage. Yes, I have saved my country, I have avenged America! This avowal before heaven and earth is my pride and my glory! What do I care for the opinion of my contemporaries or of future generations? I have done my duty; I approve of myself; that suffices me . . .

In January 1804 Dessalines declared St. Domingue independent.
A great many whites were massacred. In May Napoleon declared
himself emperor; in September Dessalines declared himself emperor. The white population of the island was to all intents and
purposes exterminated. The island was renamed by the Carib word
Haiti, meaning high place, and all citizens were henceforth to be
known as *Noirs*. In drawing up the Act of Independence, one of
the committee shouted, "To set out this declaration we need the
skin of a white man for parchment, his skull as an inkhorn, his
blood for ink, and a bayonet for a pen."

In 1806 Dessalines was ambushed and assassinated, the soldiers
hacking off his fingers for the rings, and his clothes for the gold
lace, and then dragging his body a mile to Le Cap, to that same
Place d'Armes where Toussaint Louverture had exacted suicide
from his officers. There a crazy black woman called Défilée sat beside the disfigured corpse and wept, and when they buried it she
went each day to the grave with wild flowers.

Books about Haiti are full of stories like this, that seem fictional.
And their matter may well be doubted. But their meaning — their
right to command our pity and terror — that is not to be doubted.
The most statistical and impersonal facts of Haitian history have
the same meaning.

* * *

Weston Lullingfield covers about two thousand acres, and
throughout the nineteenth and twentieth centuries the population
has remained about three hundred. The school Aunt Lizzie came
to was put up in 1871 as a kind of geographical center. There are
three groups of houses and farms, Weston Village, Weston Common, and Weston Wharf, and the school was built just where the
road from the first divides in order to run to the other two. The
church, which was built just before — Weston only became a parish in 1857 — was sited in the same area and no doubt for the same
reasons, to provide an administrative center for the whole.

It was a compulsory Church of England school when she came
(average attendance thirty-six in 1895) but effectively it was a continuation of the dame school which had been maintained in Weston for a century and a half by the Harries Charity Trust. A will

drawn up by Mrs. Eleanor Harries in 1709 provided a school in Newtown, with a branch in Weston, for the children of poor families. The rents from 267 acres (amounting in 1851 to £323/10/ — annually) went to maintain schools teaching boys reading, writing, and accounts, and girls reading and needlework, until they were ready to go out into service or ready to be bound apprentices. Once a year they were all given a complete suit of clothing except for linen, and the same things, plus a Bible and a Prayer Book, when they left school. And if they stayed in their place with credit five years they then got a gratuity of £3, and if seven years, £5.

I can't guess quite what Aunt Lizzie must have felt about such heavy-handed paternalism. Perhaps she merely said to herself that times had changed. Her own conservatism was in quite a different style. When she and Aunt Jinny first came to Weston, they went for a walk after supper and said good evening to an old lady who stumbled as she returned the greeting. On the way back the same thing happened, and Aunt Jinny wanted to go to help her. "No, don't," said Aunt Lizzie, and Aunt Jinny looked again. "Oh, Lizzie," she said, "she's *curtsying* to us." The two Manchester girls clutched each other in disbelief, disapproval, and embarrassment. What Aunt Lizzie wanted — and what she taught the village to give her — was a different sort of acknowledgment of her superiority, a town-designed sort. She wanted to be acknowledged as a keener-witted and more vigorous player of the same game they were all playing; not as a member of a different class, a different species, to be deferred to, never to be measured against them in the side-by-side position. That other, country-designed, acknowledgment was just what Mrs. Cunliffe did want, of course.

But Aunt Lizzie was delighted to be an Establishment N.C.O. in Weston. She sat on the Parish Council, raised the money for the War Memorial, and made sure it was erected near the school. She sat in the front row in church and led the congregation in the responses and in standing up, sitting down, kneeling. She allowed herself the eccentricities of a trusted N.C.O. She rose impatiently from her hassock when Mr. Rugg delayed at the altar after Communion, muttering audibly, "I could clear the table and wash up while he's fiddling there." But this was the reverse of radicalism. She was the indulged and indispensable corporal of the unit — Mr.

Tuke was the garrison padre — and Mrs. Cunliffe was a second lieutenant who sat up nights designing Ruritanian epaulettes for herself, and thirteen-gun salutes.

The two women belonged in some ways to different nations. The year after Aunt Lizzie arrived in Weston, Valencia Cunliffe married a man called Loftus de Launay Mollerus le Champion. (She quite soon after ran away from him, and soon after that took laudanum.) Englishmen as Aunt Lizzie knew them did not have such names, nor go to such fancy schools, nor lead such aristocratic lives. And time was on her side and against them. When Mrs. Cunliffe died, in 1925, six surpliced clergy officiated, her body was drawn by six tenants on a wheeled bier from the Hall to the church, and her obituary described her husband as "fifteenth in descent from John of Gaunt." But in fact the estates had already been sold, in an unavailing attempt to avoid death duties, and in the official records Petton Hall soon begins to be described as a private school for nervous and backward boys.

Aunt Lizzie died in 1938, just before I won my scholarship to the grammar school. Neither lady can be said to represent history in any dramatic or public fashion. In themselves, both are objects only for the private eye.

*   *   *

And yet the cause which Aunt Lizzie served, and all the Fittons, was a most public one; the education she so forcefully dispensed in Weston was an induction of even that last pocket of peasantry into the service of the new industrialized culture, the Victorian state structure of competitive capitalism. Her school was an outpost of progress, one of the educational army advancing across the map.

In 1815 Henry Christophe, King of Haiti, wrote to Thomas Clarkson;

> For a long while my intention and dearest ambition has been to obtain for the nation which has entrusted to me its destiny the benefits of public instruction . . .
> I am completely dedicated to this project. The buildings required for the institutions of public instruction in the cities and in rural areas are under construction. I await the teachers and craftsmen for whom I asked, who will undertake the training of our youth.

The first of those teachers arrived in 1816, called Gulliver, and trained in the methods of the British and Foreign School Society of Borough Road, London. He took charge of the first National School, for three hundred boys, at Cap Henry (the new name for Le Cap). In 1817 John Daniell, who had been an instructor at the Society's training college at Borough Road, arrived to take charge of the Grand Central School at Sans Souci, for four hundred boys, and to teach the Prince Royal. There came also on the same ship a Mr. Sweet, who later proved a disgrace to the Society, because he drank. He was sent to begin another National School, at Gonaives. Prince Sanders, an American black who had been sent out to Haiti by Wilberforce in response to the king's first request for help, ran a school for one hundred at Port de Paix. And another school, at St. Marc, was opened by the end of 1817.

If God blesses my labours, and grants me time enough, I hope that the people of Haiti, overcoming the odious prejudice that has so long oppressed them, will astonish the world with their knowledge.

To follow on from the system of National Schools, the king purposed a number of Royal Academies, the whole to be completed by a Royal College. In 1818 the first Academy was set up under the Reverend William Morton. An Englishman called Richard Evans taught art there, and two Scotsmen were hired, Duncan Stewart to be professor of anatomy, and a Mr. Moore to teach mathematics. The king was drawing as best he could on all the advanced sectors of British culture; the Scottish universities were the best in the country, the Edinburgh medical school in particular. To improve Haitian agriculture, he had Arthur Young, the leader of the agricultural revolution in Britain, send out two ploughmen to demonstrate their craft.

But it was naturally the Abolitionists, headed by Clarkson and Wilbeforce, with whom he dealt most. William Wilberforce (1759–1833), the most famous philanthropist and reformer of his day, had forced the passage through Parliament of the abolition of the slave trade, in 1807, after twenty years of patient maneuvering, and in the middle of a war which drowned out most moral issues. And it was his efforts which were to be responsible for the abolition of slavery itself in British-owned territories. Thomas Clarkson

(1760–1846), was an abolitionist even before Wilberforce, his essay on slavery appearing in English in 1786. Wilberforce was the Parliamentary leader of the movement, but Clarkson was closer to events in Haiti, and to the king. The first mulatto uprising in St. Comingue, in 1790, was led by Vincent Ogé, who borrowed money from Clarkson and spent it on weapons for his rebellion. The king and Clarkson kept in close touch, the latter sending to Haiti news of Europe, and advice on how to win British recognition of the new kingdom, on which Christophe relied. He was engaged at the time of his death on two projects which Clarkson had recommended; the distribution of land to his soldiers, to integrate them back into the agricultural economy, and the acceptance into Haiti of some of the two hundred thousand American blacks who eventually all went to Liberia.

Behind Wilberforce and Clarkson stood Zachary Macaulay and James Stephen and others, all the Clapham Sect of reformers, who counted for so much in Victorian Britain. Haiti under Christophe was effectively in alliance with reformist England. He declared his intention to make Protestantism the state religion and English the official language; measures directed against the dominance of French culture, for France still claimed to own Haiti; but also directed toward assimilating Haiti to Britain, the leader of the world in the new processes of the industrialized state. The British and Foreign Schools Society represented a major aspect of that unofficial advanced England, and it largely determined the shape of English education too, and the national movement that brought, among others, Lizzie Fitton into teaching.

Their method was devised by Joseph Lancaster, whose name was perpetuated in Lancastrian schools all over England. Their 1798 *Manual of the System of Teaching Reading, Writing, Arithmetic, and Needlework*, prescribed all the details of the buildings and methods that would allow one master to "conduct a school of a thousand children with perfect ease." The crucial device was that he delegated his teaching duties to bright pupils, called monitors. The knowledge imparted had of course to be cruelly mechanized and quantified to make this possible. In the single classroom the master's desk must stand in the center of the platform, flanked by the smaller desks of the principal monitors. In front of these desks stand three sand-desks, of dark wood with white sand sprinkled on them. On these the children of the first class copy the letters of the alphabet wheel attached to the master's desk. Meanwhile the children of the second to the seventh classes, whose benches rose with the schoolroom floor, at an angle of one in twenty, were writing on slates to the dictation and correction of their monitors. The eighth class used pen and ink. The master had a bell and a whistle to control the whole, and some amusing and instructive books with which to reward the best pupils. It was a direct equivalent of the industrial revolution, an educational steam engine. You catch glimpses of the method in *Hard Times*. And I myself, at Weston school, sat in a room which held all the boys and girls between eight and fourteen (on the other side of the partition sat all those between four and eight), and we had one teacher for the lot of us.

Lancaster did not believe in corporal punishment; he hung badges of merit and disgrace round children's necks instead. But King Henry prescribed strokes of the cane. His schoolchildren worked from six to eleven in the mornings, and from two to six in the afternoons, and they learned both English and French. Thursdays and Sundays were holidays.

We will confound the calumniators of our race by proving ourselves in no respect inferior in moral and physical powers to the other inhabitants of the Globe, and by showing that we are capable of acquiring and practicing the sciences and the arts and attaining to an equal degree of improvement and civilization with Europeans.

On the testimony of the teachers, the schools worked well enough, during their brief existence. On the death of Christophe they were abandoned, and with them the whole attempt to bring Haiti into the nineteenth century. Nowadays the very landscape of Haiti displays the results of one hundred fifty years of neglect. Christophe's *code rural* had compelled very hard work on the plantations five days a week. Saturdays the workers cultivated their gardens and went to market; Sundays they went to church and relaxed. But every other day the rising bell went at 3:00 A.M. and summoned them to prayers and breakfast. At 4:30 they went to the fields and worked there till twelve, with an hour off between eight and nine to eat. From two to sundown they worked again. In return the plantation owner had to distribute among them twenty-five percent of his gross takings, feed and lodge them, provide nurse and midwife, and a weekly visit from the doctor. The whole was overseen and disciplined by the king's military police.

The result was a much higher rate of production than was achieved in the south of the island — under the rule of the mulatto Pétion — but also resentment and disaffection. The difference between the two regimes — a powerful cause of the rebellion against Christophe — seems to have been describable in terms of work versus play, or of moralism versus amoralism — though also in terms of control versus freedom. Christophe, like Toussaint, tried to stamp out voodoo, supported the Church, insisted on marriage — he married by force any couple he suspected of living together. He was himself a faithful, though severe, husband and father. Whereas in the south marriage was the exception, concubinage the rule, public affairs were known to be corrupt, and nobody had to work hard. Pétion and his successor, Boyer, shared a mistress. The former, a man of liberal principles, distributed the plantation land in fifteen-acre lots to his soldiers, which in itself ruined the efficiency of the sugar-based economy. Christophe had a force of four thousand gendarmes, recruited in Africa, who enforced public honesty by laying traps for thieves. They would leave valuables lying in the street and arrested anyone who picked them up, or who did not report them. Every arrondissement had an army officer as justice of the peace. And everyone, no matter how highly placed, was sent to work on the Citadelle if he did wrong.

The Citadelle, two thousand feet up an unscalable mountain, with its 365 cannon, is what everyone remembers about Christophe. It and his several palaces represent his dictator's vanity and wastefulness and cruelty to his subjects, in the typical dictator's form of a building mania. But put that aside, and the figure that emerges is not unlike the figure of Castro today; equally committed to education and productivity, moralizing and disciplining his Caribbean countrymen with equal severity, determined to bring his nation into history by appropriating for it the virtues of the dominating nations of his time. The image of Christophe in our books about Haiti often looks like Dessalines; but Dessalines is rather to be compared with Duvalier of contemporary Haiti.

* * *

It proved quite easy to get hold of *Pages From the Life of John Sparling*, which Mrs. Cunliffe had reduced from her father's three manuscript volumes and amplified with commentaries and genealogies. She took her epigraph, with her usual ill luck, from Disraeli. "In the structure, the decay, and the development of the various families of man, the vicissitudes of history find their main solution." This may well have seemed pompous enough to be appropriate to her enterprise, and vague enough to be safe. But she immediately juxtaposes her program, "Some account of the families of Sparling of Beaumont Cote, Trafford of Trafford, and Cunliffe of Cunliffe, Hollings, and Wycollar." And her relentless dog-star (perhaps she quite simply miscopied, and Disraeli wrote "families of *men*," which would have been safe enough) unkindly points the reader to the disproportion between the families of man and the families of Emma Florence Cunliffe.

Of course the enterprise itself is hopeless. She intends a piece of historical mystification, to disguise the fatal taint of the Sparling money, but even mystification demands skill. She never begins to find the true interest of her subject, such as it is, or the right tone to take about it. (Of course, this kind of genealogizing was common enough among families without that taint to hide — it could be born of sheer idleness or boredom, interacting with petty vanity and dullness of wit — but in Mrs. Cunliffe's case, as we shall see, one is bound to suspect the special motive of mystification.) When she admits the existence of a slave-ship-captain Sparling, she claims that he had "evidently descended in the social scale; he had probably in his youth 'run away to sea.'" But in fact there was small difference in the social scale (or in the moral scale) between this man and his uncle John Sparling the first, from whom all the Sparling and Cunliffe splendor *really* derived. There may have been a Sparling at Beaumont Cote under Charles I, as she says, but the family was humble enough in the first John Sparling's time for one of his uncles to be a seaman, another a tanner, and for him to start from scratch as a merchant. He was a self-made man, and the materials from which he made himself he found in the Liverpool slave trade, not in traditional British yeomanry. This is historical *fact*; it is something of quite a different order that the Traffords were — if they were — "Lords of Trafford what time King Canute sat by the seashore and reproved his courtiers," or that they could claim descent from Edward I, Edward II, Edward III, and John of Gaunt.

John Sparling II's own writing is disappointing. He has some interesting bits of information to offer. His first memory is of his fifth birthday — in 1820 — when he was given a bottle of brandy to regale the servants with in the evening. And he has a freshness of feeling and vividness of phrasing in his judgments. Of his father he says, "With all his varied stores of learning, he was never more than an intellectual voluptuary. Though capable of enlightening most of his acquaintances on most subjects, he never made his opinion to be sought, and he shrank from measuring himself with persons infinitely inferior in capacity to himself." Unfortunately this freshness of feeling turns out to be a function of his resentment — none of his other feelings comes alive in words — and his vivid phrasing is a matter of his "using a large vocabulary."

Born in 1815, the youngest son in a family of eight, he seems to have passed a lonely and unhappy childhood. "My father hated to be bored and, of course, saw little of me . . . To him the romping of a child was about as agreeable as the buzzing of a mosquito. My mother was so frequently suffering from neuralgia that my company would have painfully distracted her." So he grew up, he says, remarkable for a solitary contemplative disposition. "I loved to go and lose myself in the woods." He particularly loved the sound of storms in winter trees. But there is no distinction of sensibility in the adult personality, and most of his tastes are hearty and Philistine enough — for physical exercise and spending money — though he remained highly sensitive to affront and neglect.

He, as the third son of the family, was destined from the first to the Church (the second son went into the army) and was sent to Oxford at the beginning of the Oxford Movement, though he has nothing to say about that. In fact, he arrived at Oriel as an undergraduate while Newman was dean, in 1834. "When first I saw him I remember being struck by his strange resemblance to a Romish

Toussaint Louverture. (From *Black Liberator,* by Stephen
Alexis. Lithograph by Jack Matthew. Courtesy of Ernest Benn
Ltd., London.)

priest! He seemed as if he had emaciated himself to skin and bone by long fasting. His complexion was that of a resurrected corpse; his hair was dark and lank. He was short-sighted, and wore silver-mounted spectacles, through which his little viperous eyes twinkled remorselessly at those on whom he was preparing to spring." That is practically all he has to say about Newman, though he had some personal contact with him (Sparling was one of only six freshmen at Oriel that year) and again it is malice alone that gives the phrasing its zest. It is not malice in any significant alliance with understanding.

The most vivid passages in his book deal with his experiences at private school, where he was, like so many Victorian novel heroes, badly bullied. "N's was, on the whole, the basest nature I have ever encountered. He was vain, false, cruel, and spiteful almost beyond belief . . . For four wretched years I had to walk over hot ploughshares. I was daily and hourly beaten, *mercilessly* and *wantonly* beaten, for the sole and avowed reason that it was 'good fun' seeing me cry . . . It will hardly be credited that I was compelled often ten times a day to hold out my hands to be stung by wasps. Once they applied a wasp to my nose. My God! I think I feel the agonizing shock at this very moment throbbing on my brain!" This N was much Sparling's social inferior. His enmity was first engendered, we are told, by his being cut by Fanny Sparling, and there must have been a keen spice in the sadistic possession and brutalization of the squire's son only three miles away from both their homes, where their situations would be so different. Like his daughter and his father, John Sparling suffered for his money. He met N once after they had both left school. "N was ready to lick the dust from off my feet; *and then he died!* I wonder if thoughts of me troubled his last moments!"

Mrs. Cunliffe says of her father, "In whatsoever company he found himself, he was, nine times out of ten, head and shoulders above it intellectually. But he was a shy man, and keenly alive to anything like a slight." One can understand that he should have given the impression of a superior mind. He was certainly a special nature. But, at least on the evidence of this book, that was all an effect of this one abnormality.* Indeed, so vividly does every other

* At school, once the bullies had left, he was happy, and at Oxford, where

aspect of him resolve itself into a manifestation of that power of
affront and resentment, it is difficult to take him as a real person —
he becomes a comic character.

His illnesses — very vividly rendered — become affronts and injustices. "Ulcers formed, I believe, in both, but certainly alas! full
on the pupil of my right eye . . . As many as 200 leeches were
applied, principally below my eyes, and from time to time scarifica-
tion was performed. And all this while the pain in my joints was
the pain of a man who is being broken on the wheel." For weeks
and weeks, he tells us, he never slept, and his family hired a horrid
old woman to watch him, who smelled abominably and snored like
a score of bassoons, and each morning when *she woke*, after keeping *him awake* all night, she would congratulate him on his good
night's rest. But the characteristic touch comes in the next paragraph. "My sufferings were capable of some small measure of aggravation. That aggravation my father supplied . . . fussing and
worriting . . . persecuting me with a thousand questions . . .
when he left the room I always felt like a crushed worm." Need-
less to say, "Throughout my illness I believe the doctors grievously
mismanaged my case."

As has become clear, the person he most resented was his father,
William Sparling. The latter was a cleverer and more interesting
man than his son, and probably a colder one, but the former's resentment focuses on a feature they shared, the Sparling inheritance, ineffectuality. This, their inability to make their weight felt,
seems to have plagued them all, from the Liverpool merchant
down to Mrs. Cunliffe herself. They all failed in some significant
way to impose themselves on the world at their own valuation.
"Nevertheless," says John about his father, "in practical matters he
was almost a baby. At the moment of trial he was never equal to
the occasion. In dealing with all the graver interests of life he failed
signally . . . Socially, he allowed himself to be thrust to the wall,
and never made good his rightful position in the world . . . Were

---

he only just escaped a pass degree, he seems to have been quite dissipated,
gambling, horseplaying, getting into debt. In the vacations he traveled on the
Continent or hunted or shot or ratted or went to prize fights at home. The
impression is of a very normal, rather hobbledehoy squireen, only abnormal in
the ease and wholesaleness with which he might be put down.

I to be asked which was the most conspicuous infirmity of his mind I should without hesitation say it was indolence. It absorbed him. He would do anything to escape being plagued, and would live contentedly in a fool's paradise." The father is even blamed for the son's failure at Oxford; his yearly allowance was made so small that he lost all interest in the university before he even went up. "My father had undone in five minutes all that Mr. Burd had laboured to accomplish during ten years. In that room he effectively snuffed out all my ambition for academical distinction."

This power of simplifying resentment reduces the man's character, even in his own presentation of himself, down to a humor, a Dickens character. The one general interest of the autobiography, perhaps, is as a source book to be read alongside Dickens, to show just what Dickens needed to do, and did not need to do, by way of what we call exaggeration, in presenting his characters.

He married Catherine Sybella de Trafford — the de was added only in 1841 — and the story of their marriage is a fair example of this proto-Dickensianism. He tells us of various social occasions they were both present at while he could not think of her, because the de Traffords were Catholic. Then in 1843 at a party his sister told him Catherine had become a Protestant. The next day he wrote a letter to her father, offering himself, and went to see her, only to be told that it could never be. There was an insurmountable obstacle between them. She was already promised to another, a Protestant clergyman, to whom she had been secretly engaged for six years, and for whose sake she had gone through an agonizing and protracted conflict with her family over her religion. Her father still objected to the match but she was engaged. "It took me but an instant to grasp the entire position. The fact was, she had done and suffered far too much for this man already. It was childish to suppose that she was bound to immolate herself for the purpose of maintaining a *fruitless* fidelity long after her youth was passed in the face of her father's strenuous opposition. It suffices to say that I triumphed and the spell was dissolved for ever!"

It may have sufficed for him — and for her — but what the six-year-patient predecessor thought was probably different. Clearly Sparling's money would make him a better match in Sir Thomas de Trafford's eyes, but as far as the lady herself goes one can only suppose that she had already become eager to dump this first face-less suitor.

The marriage between these two rather sour and second-rate characters took place the same year. Both of them were a bit long in the tooth, and glad to settle for second best. At least he tells us his illness had so spoiled his looks that he had lost all self-confidence with women, and she was — as he points out — no longer young by Victorian standards. Of course, it is mostly his prose style that gives me this idea. Anyway, the John Sparlings set off on a three-year wedding journey, during which a child was born and died. In 1847 they set off again, taking a house in Paris to begin with. "The season drew to a close, but before we started, Catherine again had hopes of motherhood. Rather embarrassing, as we were starting on a tour in the East . . ." But it does not seem to have occurred to him to defer this tour. They went to Vienna and boarded a ship to go down the Danube. "We no sooner touched salt water than Catherine was nearly in convulsions with sea-sickness. A nice look-out with two thousand miles of sea-voyage before us." If he said that then, Mrs. Sparling may have had second thoughts about that first fiancé. They went to Smyrna, to Athens, to Corinth, and were on the scene for the Don Pacifico affair.* Sparling wrote jingoistic public letters about it, which were even published in Palmerston's paper, *The Globe*, calling for measures to make all the nations of the earth, and particularly all the weak nations, to tremble at the name of Britain.

We get little sense of Mrs. Sparling's character. We are told at one point that "the mountains scared Catherine so that I thought she would have gone into convulsions," but at other times he seems to hint at a coarse insensibility in her. Out on the Mediterranean in her advancing pregnancy, "It blew a hurricane for sixty mortal hours. How Catherine survived I cannot tell. My own nervous system was fearfully shattered, but as soon as we got into port Catherine demolished a quarter of a turkey and a bottle of porter . . ." Perhaps this toughness in her served them both well. In

* Don Pacifico, born in Malta, in trouble in Athens, claimed the protection of the British Empire as his birthright; and a Lord Palmerston, then Prime Minister, sounded all the trumpets of imperialism in a speech, "Civis Romanus Sum," recalling the Pax Romana.

Baden Baden, after she had nursed him through another illness ("My sufferings were frightful. Night and day I writhed in pain."), we read, "One evening Catherine was taken ill, and in an incredibly short time the child was born." This was Emma Florence, their only child, the last of the Sparlings.

Clearly John Sparling was no better than his daughter at creating a style for himself, in words or deeds. And in his case too one suspects the malign influence of the money; operating through all the busy preoccupations that it brought with it. The resentments and flatteries of other people, the competitions and machinations of the Sparlings themselves, the constant stimuli to self-assertion and public noisemaking, these, — granted a not very clear head or fine taste to begin with — surely these are the agents of the stupidity and self-falsification in them all. The money took up their energies and twisted their instincts, left them neither time nor taste for self-knowledge, ruined what might have been their temperament.

Like his daughter, John Sparling waited for his inheritance a long time — as the vicar of Eccleston — and he got it too late to enjoy it. His father died in 1870, but his elder brother, William, lived on until 1888, a disreputable old amorist whom the ladies of polite families could not visit, with an illegitimate son in the house. John Sparling lived only two years in possession of Petton, alone, melancholy, in ill health.

This elder brother William was in some ways colorful, but all I could find out about him was gossip, or rather memories of other people's gossip. It seemed best to concentrate on the father of both these brothers, William Sparling the first, though to find out about him I had to go to Liverpool, which I did rather reluctantly.

One of my problems in all this work had always been my attitudes to what I was finding out, and to the finding out itself. I had said I was relating myself to history, but what did history turn out to mean? Anecdotes; ornaments for the fringe of my own life; since these lives I was discovering were too dull to challenge me — acquiring interest only in their own fringing contacts with great names, like Newman and Palmerston — they could only console and confirm established habits of being in the listener. My facts were all released to me from the custody of white-haired and erect old ladies, apple cheeked and lemon voiced, charming, twinkling, though also delicate and severe, capable of asperity as well as of graciousness, but still old ladies. And in my custody those facts retained the same properties; they remained the building units of an essentially anecdotal sort of history.

* * *

So many kinds of fact constitute history — constitute so many kinds of history. When I flew into Cuba and saw the rows of palm trees and the bright red soil, and then felt that hot, wet air, and saw that vividly shapely harbor, I realized that I was in the landscape of my boyhood fantasies, the Spanish Main; the backdrop to the great British adventures, where plucky Devon seadogs had outsailed cumbersome armadas of the enemy; the bright blue sea of the pirates.

It is always there, at the back of one's mind, that one finds the really important kinds of history disregarded — pirates and smugglers, cowboys and Indians, Lawrence of Arabia and the Scarlet Pimpernel, chasing each other and one's crudest energies round and round the synaptic circuits.

There were, I had to learn, three stages of piracy, the corsairs, the buccaneers, and the pirates proper. The corsairs (originally French Protestants, later mostly British) did in some lawless sense represent their countries. They operated from 1562, when the Spaniards began to sail in convoys, in *flotas*, until 1618 when Spain became an ally of England. Drake is the man always taken to represent them, but he was not successful at the trade financially, while Hawkins was simply a slave-smuggler. Frobisher, Grenville, and Burgh are better examples. They really did exist, and did have the virtues of adventurers, but though they sailed the Caribbean so long and triumphantly, they never seriously disturbed the Spanish hegemony. In serious politics they hardly counted.

The next seventy years were the period of the buccaneers, based either on Tortuga, an island off Haiti, or Port Royal in Jamaica. Originally they were refugees from the settled islands, the failures of the Caribbean, and they were always outlaws. But in the sixties their combined fleets could have defeated the national navies in those waters, if they had been interested in anything besides plunder and torture. Many of them were compulsive killers, like L'Ol-

lonois, who took the town of Maracaibo in 1667, and subjected all
the inhabitants, one by one, to various kinds of torture. The most
famous name among them, one I remember from childhood
reading, was Henry Morgan, no seaman but a remarkable commander of men. His great exploit was to lead fourteen hundred
men across the Panama isthmus in 1671, with much larger Spanish
forces expecting them, and to defeat them in pitched battle, and
sack Panama City. He also invented the tactic of driving nuns and
priests in front of his army to take the enemies' fire as he advanced
toward them.

The pirates, entirely individual marauders, were the most degenerate of the three stages. Some had existed all the time, but they
attracted the myth-makers' attention at the beginning of the eighteenth century — due in part to Defoe's novel *Captain Singleton*.
This included an account of the adventures of John Avery, who had
taken a ship carrying the Grand Mogul's daughter, and had abducted her to Madagascar. All pirates were offered a royal pardon if
they surrendered themselves in 1698, with the named exceptions of
Captain Avery and Captain Kidd. This second is the name and the
legend Stevenson used. Defoe and Stevenson begin and end the
major period of British pirate fantasy — Yo ho ho and a bottle of
rum — the reality of which ended perhaps in 1729, with the death
of Woodes Rogers, the man who rescued Alexander Selkirk from
his island. He, as Governor, had driven the pirates from their bases
in the Bahamas. The most famous of the later pirates was Captain
Teach, Blackbeard, the central villain of Charles Johnson's *General
History of the Pirates* (1724), a very popular book. Teach died in
1717, shortly after taking his only sizable prize, but he lived on as a
hero of adventure stories, for instance, again, one by Stevenson.
And what Hollywood in the twentieth century has made of piracy,
though not on the same imaginative level as the Western, is still a
significant part of the psychological economy of our industrialized
culture. It is a stream of images that foster the Faustian temperament in boys growing up.

It is typical of economically exploited areas of the world that
they should also be made the setting of the most corrupt myths of
the exploiters, their most sentimental, lustful, boastful fantasies,

and it is also typical that the inhabitants of those areas, the exploited, should take over those myths themselves. The West Indian even today, observers feel, sees himself as flamboyant, swaggering, piratical, because of this pseudohistory and the cultural images it generated. Certain areas of the world thus become dedicated to dreams, to wish-fulfillment on a group scale, and whole nations live within the dominant nation's dream, acting out its fantasies, exiled from their own reality. That is the psychological meaning of the severe discipline which leaders like Christophe and Castro impose upon their peoples; it is a means to bring them back out of dreams into reality.

The most recent commercial development of this is the tourist industry, the logical result of the increasing gap between the developed and the underdeveloped countries of the world. As, in the U.S.A., automation spreads, holidays grow longer, wages climb higher, fares become cheaper; and in the Caribbean, unemployment increases, and the standard of living goes down, and nothing can be made or grown to sell to the world at competitive prices; the result is that more and more Americans spend more and more time, and money, in dream homes on dream islands. To ordinary tourism succeeds the holiday out of season, and then the residential visitor, who buys or rents a house for twelve months out of the year, and perhaps rents it out to friends. Whole countries, of the size of Caribbean islands, can be economically supported this way. Bermuda has a very high standard of living by Caribbean criteria, and very little unemployment. The Bahamas are not far behind.

But proud men do not want to belong to other people's dream islands. Men like Christophe and Castro, Jagan of Guiana and Williams of Trinidad, want to enter the world of reality, and bring their countries with them. They want to be taken seriously as independent nations, in the same sense as European nations are taken. But their relative inferiority is extremely difficult to change, with populations increasing and retarding the rise of standards of living and of standards of education. The world population in 1966 was 3,346 million; in 2000 it may be 6,000 million; and the area of fastest growth, since 1920, has been Latin America, due to the success of tropical medicine; population there increased by 136 percent over these last forty years. The present population of 120 million in Central and Tropical South America is expected to double by 1986. The inevitable consequence of this is that the number of illiterates in the world has grown by 200 million in the six years following 1960, and 70 percent of the world's school-age children are not in school. And it is of course in the underdeveloped countries that these effects are concentrated. In the developed countries the statistics move in the opposite direction, and the gap between the two gets wider. In the West Indies the proportion of those without regular employment is between 12 and 20 percent. But emigration to where there are jobs is easy only for those with the skills an industrialized society needs — who are the minority most needed at home. For the rest it gets harder in proportion as conditions at home get worse. The emigration from the West Indies to Britain rose from 2,000 in 1953 to 50,000 in 1960. The Commonwealth Immigration Bill to restrict entry was introduced into Parliament in 1961, and made law in 1962.

Eric Williams's first broadcast as Premier of Trinidad in 1962 took as its theme "Discipline, Production, and Tolerance," and in general his policy is as like that of Christophe and Castro as Duvalier's policy in Haiti is like that of Dessalines. Even nowadays, Caribbean islands have to struggle against a cultural inferiority complex, a dependency complex, which ruins the national life in ways that may seem remote from their cause. In Cuba these days they call this condition psychological and cultural "underdevelopment," because of the relation it bears to the cultural life of the developed nations. V. S. Naipaul's *The Middle Passage* gives vivid analyses of this condition of many of the islands, and particularly on his own, Trinidad.

It was a place where the stories were never stories of success but of failure: brilliant men, scholarship winners, who had died young, gone mad, or taken to drink: cricketers of promise whose careers had been ruined by disagreements with the authorities.

It was also a place where a recurring word of abuse was "conceited," an expression of the resentment felt of anyone who possessed unusual skills. Such skills were not required by a society which produced nothing, never had to prove its worth, and was never called upon to be efficient. And such people had to be cut down to size or, to use the

Trinidad expression, be made to "boil down." Generosity — the admiration of equal for equal — was therefore unknown; it was a quality I knew only from books and found only in England.

Yet Trinidad has perhaps the most viable economy of all the ex-British islands, because of its oil deposits, and the most able leader. The Prime Minister has taken an aggressive line, particularly toward Britain. He broke up the scarcely begun West Indian Federation in 1961, and in 1964 declared in London that his country had more in common with Egypt than with other members of the Commonwealth.

Naipaul also says, "We lived in a society that denied itself heroes." It is of course one of the comical aspects of life in Cuba now that the regime *imposes* heroes on you at every turn, in the names of every street, every club, every date in the calendar. But the islands must have heroes, and they must be their own, not Hollywood-provided, not Washington-provided. And these heroes of their own must be idealists, men of blameless honor and stoic virtue, like Martí and Che. Such implausibly heroic heroes are, paradoxically, the only ones who can guide their countrymen out of fantasy and into reality. They must not be, as Naipaul says Trinidadian heroes have always been, successful tricksters. This shows the corrupt influence of the pirate legends — or, as Naipaul says, of a slave culture. Which you specify does not matter very much. Both are equally aspects of the moral anti-world the West created in the Caribbean. Naipaul, going back, traced the influence of slavery everywhere; in this admiration for rogues, in the cinema laughter at newsreels of Belsen, in the vocabulary of racial hatred, in the beating of children, in the absence of family life, in the acceptance of physical brutality. Slavery is everywhere in the islands, he says; in the very food and vegetation — the sugar cane, brought to the islands by Columbus on his second voyage, the breadfruit, cheap fruit for slaves, brought by Captain Bligh among others, the star-apple, clumps of which in Jamaica mark old slave provision grounds. It is this, he implies, that keeps him from returning to live in Trinidad, even now: *slavery*.

* * *

William Sparling was born in 1777 and was sent to Eton and Oxford and then joined the Tenth Hussars, whose colonel was the Prince of Wales, an ultrafashionable regiment. This in itself is pretty gaudy, for a man whose father started with nothing. And more than gaudy, hubristic; one suspects — partly on the prompt- ings of his enemies' innuendos — a dangerously ambitious and dominant mother. She was the wife of his father's middle age, the wife of his wealth, and considerably younger; William was born when his father was forty-six. She survived her husband several years, the years of William's duel, the years of his danger.

He came back to Liverpool to live in 1800, when his father died, leaving his regiment, at twenty-three. He owned Santo Domingo, the grandest house in the city, with grounds that covered the whole north half of what is now Everton, plus Petton Hall and estate, plus a good deal of money — he spent £40,000 soon after on an adjoining Shropshire estate, the one that included part of Weston. In November 1802 he engaged himself to a girl called Anne Ren- shaw, the daughter of a Liverpool clergyman. Shortly after the en- gagement he went down to Petton, to make preparations, he says, for his marriage. On his return, on November 27, he found an anonymous letter waiting for him, which tried to discredit the girl's family. He disbelieved most of its accusations, he says, but thought that some others should be investigated, so he showed the letter to Mr. Renshaw, or he had his mother show it — the account is rather muddled on this point. Mr. Renshaw — allegedly amiable at this stage in the affair — promised to check on some facts that would constitute a definite answer to the accusation. But Sparling, after waiting twenty-four hours, wrote a letter breaking off the en- gagement. Renshaw then wrote back a letter full of furious resent- ment and insult, and Sparling left Liverpool, hoping the affair would blow over in his absence. But Mr. Renshaw's brother-in-law, Edward Grayson, a Liverpool ship-builder, was equally angry, and publicly described Sparling as a villain and a scoundrel and de- clared that if he could but find out where he was he would "chas- tise" him. He said all this to, among others, a Major Brooks, who went to London for Christmas (notice how quickly all these events happened) and told Sparling. The latter nevertheless took no ac- tion but went to France, in March 1803, the Napoleonic wars being

in truce. (One of Napoleon's armies was still active; in St. Domingue General Leclerc was trying to subdue the black republic set up
by Toussaint Louverture.) But when he was forced to return, in
September, by the war's breaking out again, he found that Grayson
was still threatening everywhere to "chastise" him. He therefore
wrote to him, declaring that he was available any time Grayson
wanted to meet, and requesting a withdrawal of the threat. Grayson refused, and things progressed to a duel with pistols. This only
took place at the end of February 1804 — note how slowly this
group of events happened — because Grayson needed time to set
his family affairs in order before risking his life. (A series of questions at the trial sardonically elicited the facts that he was a single
man, that no, he had never been married, but that yes, he had five
children, between eleven and nineteen.) So Sparling and Grayson
t in Toxteth Park, never having laid eyes on each other before;
ling shot Grayson in the right thigh, and a week later the latter
after having forgiven his murderer. Sparling was then ar-

etails of all this are preserved in a pamphlet printed April
ve days after the trial, which was held at Lancaster. It is
Trial at Large of William Sparling," and was printed
W. Jones of Liverpool. Mrs. Cunliffe made efforts to
f this destroyed, but two survive to my knowledge,
pshire County Archives, and one in the Liverpool
he former of these calls itself a second edition, and
itle page is missing, seems on internal evidence a
iled from the shorthand reports of two youths,
rinter because the affair had caused so much
This was particularly so, he says, because
n the increase just then. Its intention, there-
against Sparling, both because he was the
, and because he was the aristocrat of the
account, with no interpolated comment,
, and nothing sensational in the for-
scrupulous about his reporters' accu-
he same spot, but to the same pos-
essively in a court crowded beyond
which the most robust constitu-

tions found it difficult to support — it is presumed the candor of the reader will induce him to admit, that if there be anything surprising about it, it is rather that so much of it is preserved, than that anything should be found missing in it."

The anonymous letter itself is not printed in the "Trial at Large," nor paraphrased, nor do the references to it make clear what the Renshaws were accused of. The same is true of all subsequent accounts of the duel or the trial. But in 1965 a pamphlet was issued by the Liverpool Athenaeum, written by F. Harlan Taylor, and entitled "Liverpool and the Athenaeum," and in this we find — with no explanation of where it comes from — a transcript of the anonymous letter of 1802. (Renshaw, Grayson, and Sparling were all members of the Athenaeum, which was one of Sir William Roscoe's contributions to Liverpool culture.) The letter asks if Sparling knows that there is insanity on both sides of the girl's family; it says she is in love with his fortune, not himself, that she is in love with someone else, and, as if that were not enough, "Besides, why not a man of your fortune aim at something more genteel? Here you have the essence of everything that is vulgar, and believe me you may easily meet with one that is much more amiable." And later it refers to Anne Renshaw as an "artful and designing girl." very vulgar and very unconvincing epistle; why then did Willia Sparling, who seems to have been both refined and intelligent, t any notice of it?

The official case for the prosecution is that Sparling him *faked* a way out of the engagement; that he and his second, Sa Colquitt, a captain in the Royal Navy, then *conspired* to kill son, that they forced him into the duel coolly and deliberatel unofficial case is that they were Corinthian bullies, Regency aristocratic London dandies, acting out of the insolence of and class and youth. Much is made of their conduct after t Sparling drove off to a friend's house and left the messag my compliments to Mr. Benson and tell him that I hav walk this morning and that I am well." To another he sai put a bullet in Grayson this morning." The other said h wasn't dangerous. "No, I hope not; he made a great n Colquitt said as they drove away, "Gad! It did me good.

The defense countered with a long series of witness

fied to Sparling's milky mildness, quietness, gentleness, forbearing-
ness. These witnesses are very southern and aristocratic, friends
from the Tenth Hussars, or Eton and Oxford; Lord John Manners,
Lord Charles Manners, Sir Hungerford Hoskins, Lord James Murray, Lord Viscount Carleton, etc., etc.; The Prince of Wales himself sent a letter in Sparling's favor. To Liverpool such names must
have seemed, as connoisseurs of quietness and gentleness, as guar-
antors of virtue, pretty laughable. It is in notable contrast that the
witnesses to Colquitt's character are all either naval captains or
clergymen. It is also notable that they occasionally describe him as
cheerful, lively, good-humored, or manly, while Sparling's praises
are sung entirely in a choirboy soprano.

Nevertheless, my own judgment, for what it is worth, is that we
should believe them, that Sparling *was* a mild and peaceable young
man, and that the bourgeois melodrama presented by the prosecution — repeated in all subsequent accounts of the duel, and lavishly applauded in the Liverpool of the time — is a fake. Sparling's
remarks after the duel acquire, in the accounts of the defense witnesses, a context of agitation that alters their meaning; and that
context seems to me probable because of his conduct in general; for
instance, his avoiding all confrontations with Renshaw and Grayson whenever possible, and his continual disappearances. He wrote
out his own, very able, defense statement, but had his counsel read
it out for him. Whereas Colquitt delivered his own, much more
ordinary, performance. Sparling's letters to Grayson, heavily interpreted by the prosecution as masterpieces of sneering coolness, are
in a sense cool, but it is the coolness of clarity and moderation, of a
kind of caution. He is firm and clear, but almost impersonal. They
are the letters of an intelligent man, but a rather neutral personality. "I will not explain my conduct to you or to Dr. M'Cartney, but
briefly remark that female honour, virtue and innocence have nothing to do with the point in question; those qualities of Miss A.
Renshaw remain as I found them. It is an attempt on my part to
punish you for your insulting language, and this I will execute or
perish in attempting it." In reply to six- or seven-line letters of this
sort Grayson sent pages of self-righteous rhetoric, full of his idea of
himself breathing fire and slaughter, "In a word, I glory in my
expression, and if I had a thousand lives would rather forfeit them

all sooner than . . ."; full of long, hectic sentences spattered with
interjections ending, ". . . I know not and I care not"; and very
little to the announced purpose.

Grayson and Renshaw were both proprietors of the Liverpool
Athenaeum, and Grayson's second, Dr. Macartney, was a prominent local physician; naturally they looked to Liverpool like victims, the solid, honest, useful middle-class citizens oppressed by a
Cavalier or Restoration roarer (Liverpool had been consistently
anti-Stuart, pro-Hanoverian, merchant-class, respectable, throughout its history), but in fact the roaring was all on the Grayson and
Renshaw side. It is a typical detail that as soon as Grayson was
dead Renshaw put an advertisement in the paper that Sparling was
in hiding somewhere, and that anyone helping him escape would
become an accessory after the fact — and this *after* getting a message from Sparling that he was going to give himself up.

The most striking case of this is the letter Renshaw wrote to
Sparling when the engagement was broken off, which is deliberately as insulting as it can manage to be. He says he has investigated his family's health back through eighty-six years, and "my family has always been, as it now is, as pure in its blood, as it was till
lately superior to yours in fortune, and ever I trust will remain in
character and desert." His father's early indisposition (there were
apparently some marks on the old gentleman's neck which Sparling
had asked — in fear of hereditary insanity — to have explained)
had been "owing to the exertions of such an active mind and body,
as nature thought it unworthy of her to bestow on you." His sentences are long and hectic, full of furious parentheses like "born as
you were without one generous sentiment, and having imbibed insolence in its purest state at your mother's breast"; and full of ex-
clamations, "Mr. Sparling's esteem! gracious heaven, what a match-
less present! What a soothing assurance! What an obliterating
bonus is here offered, in extenuation of such dereliction of principle
and such turpitude of conduct, as it would not be possible, was all
you can command turned into gold and that gold beaten into the
thinnest plate; to conceal from the eyes of the world." The note
struck here, the note of almost obsessive resentment of the Sparling money, sounds throughout the letter. It is accompanied by a
very vulgar harping on the Sparlings' low origins, particularly those

of William's mother. "For butcher's curs are venom-mouthed," he quotes in a parenthesis, and in a footnote advises Sparling to go to his mother for an explanation. (Sparling replied that he gathered that "some Relation of mine keeps a Butcher's stall in Lancaster, this though I know nothing of it, may very probably be true, as many of my relations in Liverpool and elsewhere are in very low situations.")

Finally Renshaw declared that the famous anonymous letter was no mystery to *him*. It was "of homespun materials, of maternal texture or connivance." It is not too fanciful, I think, to trace a significant pattern in the letter's most striking metaphors, of manufactures, of bonuses, of gold, all of which surely derive from the commercial and industrial boom of which Liverpool was the center. The Sparlings were the robber barons of that boom to their enemies, its Morgans and Rockefellers, and that enmity itself was born of the city's bloodthirsty commercial competitiveness.

After such a letter, and after Grayson's deliberately public talk of "chastising" him, clearly Sparling *could* not afford either to appear in Liverpool, or to absent himself without taking some action. As he says, "I was pointed out as a person who was afraid to show myself." He had to ask at least as much as he did; that Grayson should say that the word "chastise" escaped him in the heat of the moment. But Grayson, intoxicated with his role in this bourgeois melodrama, fortified by the applause of a whole gallery of Liverpudlian merchants, refused to budge.

As for Sparling himself, what likeness of him can we today draw, as distinct from that role — Byron, Beau Brummel — which he was trapped into playing for this audience? He seems to me to have been a clever, refined, nervous young man, whom Renshaw and Grayson thought they could do what they liked with; the victim, in his nerves and emotions, of powerful parents and of the upward translation in class which they had wished on him; a victim on whom the class revenge could be wreaked with impunity. Their sense of their drama's shape is so clear in their letters that it may have come as a surprise to them that Sparling's actual bullet went home, while Grayson's missed — though of course the unhappy ending is popular with such dramas. (Literature and life are very mixed up here; Grayson and Renshaw thought they were in a play by Steele; Mrs. Sparling, or whoever it was wrote the anonymous letter, belongs in Jane Austen; and, by the prosecution at the trial, William Sparling himself was cast, most incongruously, as Rawdon Crawley.)

It fits this idea of him that reading that vulgar anonymous letter, even while disbelieving it, should nevertheless prevent his marrying the girl. The sense of someone, anyone, out there, powerfully wanting him not to, could paralyze the kind of man I'm thinking of. He would soon doubt the sincerity of his own feelings. He would soon feel the project not worth the effort. Naturally, such interpretations are mere guesses. He may even have written the letter himself, as a way out of a regretted involvement, in which case he was a different kind of man. But there is evidence for the interpretation I favor in the account of him given by his son. Obviously, this refers to William Sparling in a much later phase of his personality, and obviously the witness is prejudiced against his subject; but the diagnosis we glimpse through his resentment is the same as that we glimpse through the quite different resentment of Renshaw and Grayson. The "characteristic frigidity" they speak of, the inertia, the poverty of feeling and lack of generosity, are the same as what John Sparling calls "indolence" and "an intellectual voluptuary" and "he let himself be thrust to the wall." It seems to me a revealing touch, about both men, that the son accuses the father of having taught himself French and Spanish "to the point of almost theoretical perfection" and of having yet been afraid to venture speaking a word of either language.

In any case, whatever the psychological mechanism, William Sparling left Liverpool forever after he was acquitted, and came to Petton to live. If he was the man I think he was, the experience must have marked him for life. But he was still a great *parti*, and he was married within a year to a girl of good Lancashire family, a great beauty, and the toast of Bath, we are told, and within another four years he was High Sheriff of Shropshire. He lived until 1870, when he was ninety-three, and apparently in some splendor. We read of elaborate festivities, for instance, when his twin eldest sons came of age in 1834 — horse racing, ox- and sheep-roasting, oak-planting, and universal drunkenness for a fortnight. There was a procession of fifty tenants on horseback, in pairs, followed by forty

John Sparling's house in Liverpool — "Santo Domingo."
(Lithograph by J. McGahey, Liverpool, England.)

school-children with mottoes round their hats reading "Long life to the heir of Petton and his amiable brother, and Success to the house of Petton."

But the next interesting part of the story lies farther back, with John Sparling the first. Though he never lived at Petton, his money and his making of it are in some ways more real presences there all through the hundred and twenty-five years after his death than the actually living dispensers and administrators of it. And if he inhabits Petton, he is himself inhabited by, informed by, Liverpool. To us, knowing what we do about him, he can be only an aspect of the history of Liverpool. Certainly to me, looking for him and his house, Santo Domingo, in the Liverpool of 1967, he and his city seemed a joint manifestation of a much more forceful force of history than any of his descendants related to. Here at last I was escaping from anecdote.

But of course, I reminded myself, anecdotes are true too. People live in events as historically trivial as William Sparling's, events in which history is reflected rather than represented. Indeed, most English people's lives are a good deal less directly buffeted by history than his. In one way, William Sparling seemed very freshly relevant to me during that trip to Liverpool. Until I saw the buses for Penny Lane, I had forgotten that Liverpool is also the city of the Beatles, of all the pop groups, of the Mersey Sound in poetry, of the John Moore's Liverpool Exhibition, which I went to next morning. The home of the best things in modern British life since the war, and the home of the *modern* Corinthian buck, the working-class Regency rake, the proletarian Brummel. Against the gaunt and blackened streets of Everton, so hollowed out, so many vacant lots littered with bricks and flooded by the enormous sky, defined itself the composite figure in Mandarin coat of tangerine brocade, a head of gorgeous ringlets round an honest, snub-nosed, pimpled face, and legs and loins defined and flaunted, offered in frankest hedonism to be admired, to be loved, made bright and pure in skintight spotless pink. William Sparling was not so authentic a Mersey man as that, but if the Beatles are real, so is he.

*   *   *

I was doing my best for anecdotal history, but that frail tenor eloquence betrays a tension. It is full of pathos. I need soberer facts, severer meanings, before I find a comfortable vocal range. Of course, even Haitian history is full of anecdote. Which historian has been able to resist describing Pauline Bonaparte Leclerc's boudoir in Tortuga? — pure prostitute rococo. Incidentally, William Sparling may have been in Paris for Pauline's return as a widow. If so, he moved in the right circles to get presented to her.

But what I mean by history was always, despite my protests, a different order of fact from that. I needed to get back to something more solid, more silent, more savage, less human. The Caribbean islands are the tops of a range of mountains, taller than the Himalayas, which as late as 9000 B.C. formed an isthmus north from Venezuela, with the Bahamas a plateau linked to Cuba and perhaps to Florida. Three million years ago, in the Eocene period, they were entirely under water. In the Miocene, the Caribbean was a lake, with a land bridge from Florida to Trinidad.

The islands were first inhabited by the Siboneys, who had moved their settlements all the way down the continent of North America to Florida, and reached the Bahamas in dugout canoes. They went as far south as the island that was to be Hispaniola, later St. Domingue, later Haiti. The Siboneys had disappeared as a race by the time Columbus arrived; presumably they had intermarried with their successors, the Arawaks of the Bahamas. The latter had moved their settlements north along the archipelagoes from what is now Guiana in South America. Some Arawaks remained there, and their descendants are to be found in Guiana today, but most of them retreated northward along the islands, away from the neighborhood of the more warlike Caribs. The word Arawak means meal-eater, and they were a very peaceable people. They smoked tobacco and played ball games, and did not know iron or its uses. They fished by attaching a remora to a line and letting it catch fish for them, and they had learned how to eat the cassava, the islands' most common plant, by removing the prussic acid poison from it. The cultural character of the different islands were slightly different. The Arawaks closest to the Caribs, who were advancing north behind them, were the most adept at war. Those farthest north, in the Bahamas, were the most gentle and peace-loving.

It was these, the Lucayans, the island people, whom Columbus first met. They were exceedingly trusting and friendly toward the Spaniards, and they were quickly destroyed. The Lucayans, in fact, were all transported to Hispaniola, to work for their new masters, induced to cooperate by being told that they were going to Paradise; they died there in despair, and some drowned trying to swim back to where they came from. Meanwhile it was the Caribs, shooting their poisoned arrows, and eating their dead enemies, who made more impression on the Spaniards; an impression symbolized by the two words Europe took over from them, Caribbean, and cannibal. To them themselves the word Carib meant valiant man, and they fought Spaniards, English, Dutch, French, with a passion that justified the name.

In 1498, on his third voyage, Columbus enslaved Indians, and Queen Isabella had him arrested and brought back to Spain. The Governorship of the New World — the whole continent having been awarded to Spain by Papal Bull in 1493 — was given to de Ovando. He avoided slavery by inventing the two basic devices of Spanish colonialism; the *encomienda*, the dividing up of Indians among Spanish proprietors, for their conversion and instruction in useful habits; and the *repartimiento*, their laboring on his land grant. By these means the entire Arawak population was gradually exterminated. There were one hundred thousand on Cuba at the time of the conquest. By 1650 the population was seven hundred Spaniards, five thousand Indians, and — a significant addition — seven hundred Negro slaves.

The Church had protested against the treatment of the Indians from early on. The Dominican Montesinos had preached against Spanish brutality in 1511, and in 1515 Las Casas tried to end the encomienda system. Two hundred fifty thousand Arawaks had died by then, many committing suicide by swallowing the poison of the cassava, and some mothers strangling their babies to save them from the life that awaited them. Because freeing the Indians would create a labor problem, Las Casas offered the solution of importing black slaves from Africa. There were a few there already, but in 1517 royal orders permitted the importing of four thousand a year into the New World. In two hundred years that number had risen to one hundred thousand a year. On the ships the slaves were crammed in extremely close together, some merchants calculating a space of six feet by one foot four inches with two feet headroom; though one, being cross-examined, agreed that by those measurements his ship could carry only 451 slaves, and yet he always shipped 600.

Between 1500 and 1850, it is estimated, five million slaves were brought across the Atlantic — Mandingo, Fulani, Hausa, Ibo, Ijo, Yoruba, Joloff, etc. Two hundred men every day during those hundreds of years were taken from their homes in Africa. Suicide rates were high among these men too; men threw up their arms and ducked their heads under the water to drown; and among the Ibo, groups hanged themselves in the barracoons. And out of these dispersed groups, speaking different languages, worshiping different gods, was forged a race in the West Indies, the blacks.

The Pope had allotted Portugal the right to colonize Africa, so it was Portuguese factors who kept the first barracoons on the West African coast, to which the Arabs and Ashanti brought the prisoners of war, etc., whom they had for sale. They stored them till a vessel came with a license to buy them and take them to America. In the slave-ship manifests each person was invoiced as a fraction of one "piece of the Indies," which was the ideal slave, estimated to be seven quartas tall, a quarta being just over ten inches. So the total height, or length, of all the slaves was added up, and then divided by this measure to give the number of "pieces of the Indies" the ship was carrying. In this way human individuality was totally canceled out.

Prices went up fast, and by the end of the seventeenth century a slave cost £4 for a merchant to buy in Africa, and brought £40 when sold in Barbados. The demand and the profits from the trade were so great that many merchants went outside the official channels, both in buying and selling. This was the origin of so much smuggling and piracy in the Caribbean. It is the reality behind the romantic legends of British individualism.

Portugal and Spain having become one monarchy, Charles V granted a monopoly on supplying slaves to the West Indies in 1517, and in 1538 sold it to two German merchants. This, known as the Asiento, soon became an extremely valuable property. When Britain finally got it, in 1715, as a part of the Treaty of Utrecht, it was regarded as her main gain, economically, from that treaty. Soon after that, moreover, the sugar plantations began to boom. From 1715 to 1717 Barbados and Jamaica each exported to England goods worth as much as all North America exported. Sugar prices kept rising up to 1800. In 1805 Pitt calculated that of all the wealth entering the English exchequer from abroad, four-fifths came from the West Indies. The plantocracy was extremely rich, and totally despotic in its treatment of the slaves. To punish them, blacks were broken on the wheel and burned alive, and sometimes dropped into vats of boiling molasses, apart from the normal correction by whipping. The cart whip was wielded by men called Jumpers in Jamaica, who called in at plantations, asking if there were any slaves who needed whipping just then; and there are cases of owners finding the man a job in order not to reject a facility which was often desired in vain.

Britain's tenure of the slave trade Asiento was for twenty-five years, but the wars of the period interrupted that term, and at the peace of 1748 she won another five years. Meanwhile the merchants of Bristol and Liverpool went outside the Royal African Company. This company was so busy, due to the Asiento, that soon anyone was allowed to trade for himself, on paying a £10 fee. In the second half of the century, British merchants shipped forty thousand slaves a year, and the great ports of Bristol and Liverpool were renewed out of the profits. And John Sparling made enough money to buy an estate in Shropshire, and become a landed proprietor, a squire with faithful tenants, an ancestor.

Finally the institution as well as the trade was abolished. On August 1, 1834, five hundred thousand black slaves in the British West Indies became free men. This happened a few months after Wilberforce's death, as the result of his and Clarkson's efforts, and before them of the Moravians and the Methodists' preaching. With emancipation, in the larger islands, and Guiana, there was plenty of land to buy cheaply — sugar was no longer a boom crop — and the ex-slaves refused to work the plantations under the conditions offered. Almost immediately, therefore, Chinese coolies were imported, and then Indians, to prevent labor from imposing its terms on the planters. Between 1844 and 1917, when Indian national pride put a stop to mass emigration, five hundred thousand Indians arrived in the British West Indies, mostly in Trinidad and Guiana. They found there a racial rivalry with the blacks which still poisons life today, and with the whites terms of employment which have to be called economic slavery. So it continued. The Amerindians, the Africans, the Asians, brown, black, yellow, were all enslaved on these islands by whites, Europeans. That is what gives the islands their resonance in our imaginations — slavery. *That* is history.

* * *

But to return to John Sparling. He was born in 1731 (Mrs. Cunliffe gets both his dates wrong, of course) near Lancaster, the son of a yeoman, with one uncle a sailor, another a tanner. By 1759 he and a partner, William Bolden, were merchants in Norfolk, Virginia. In 1764 he returned to Liverpool and became a freeman, he and his partner then owning quite a few ships. In 1773 he bought the Santo Domingo estate for £3,470 (in 1810 William sold it for £20,300), in 1777 his son was born, in 1786 he bought Petton, in 1790 he was Mayor of Liverpool, and in 1800 he died. Luckily his firm's letterbook has been preserved, containing the accounts of the firm's trade with Virginia between 1788 and 1799. M. M. Schofield, who has analyzed the documents, estimates an expenditure of roughly £41,500 during that decade, and a profit of nearly £15,000, or 35%. They sent cloth, pottery, glass, metalware, and paint to America, and took back tar, turpentine, tobacco, beeswax. He owned property in south Liverpool, of which the name Sparling Street preserves the memory, and he owned the land on which Queen's Dock was built. Indeed he planned to build it himself, and then changed his mind and let the city do it. If he had not changed his mind, or if William had not sold the Santo Domingo estate, the Sparlings and Cunliffes might be reigning at Petton today. Mrs. Cunliffe remarks this, laughingly, in her book, and her present-day descendant returned to the point to me. It has perhaps bubbled to the surface of Sparling brains on average once a year since 1810.

John Sparling was apparently a picturesquely old-fashioned figure on the Liverpool 'Change, with gold-buckled shoes, three-cornered hat, gold-laced waistcoat, etc.; described only thirty years after his death as "one of those wealthy and upright traders of Britain, of the eighteenth century, whose attire and conduct were on a par, so far as plainness, precision, regularity, and substantial worth will suffer the comparison to be carried." There is a portrait of him by Romney, prominently displaying an aristocratic hand, implausibly tapering and transparent, the sort of hand the artist may have got an extra five guineas for. But he is dressed there too in an obstinately old-fashioned and plain style, which goes with the voice one hears in his letters to his Virginia firm, and in his will. He sounds genuinely shocked to find American merchants, after the War of Independence, not paying their British debts, and he cannot come to terms with the general financial looseness of the new States — he can foresee nothing but disaster for them. And in his will he not only forbids his heir to marry a Roman Catholic or a Protestant Dissenter, a native of Ireland or of North Britain, he requires him to reside in Santo Domingo — from the windows of which, incidentally, his own tomb was to be prominently visible. More exactly, whether or not they reside there, his heirs may neither sell the property nor let it for any term of more than seven years, and among possible tenants preference is to be given to any with the name of Sparling. I think a clear enough image is discoverable through these details of an obstinate, shrewd, cautious, masterful man, just the sort to produce, at the age of forty-six, a son who would grow up to be William Sparling.

But behind this harmlessly picturesque image looms a quite different order of facts. Although Mrs. Cunliffe attempts to conceal this, John Sparling in fact made his money in the slave trade. (It is typical of the Sparling bad luck that everyone in Weston knew this, and I never thought to question the assumption till I read Mrs. Cunliffe's disingenuous account.) In his later years, as we have seen, his firm traded in other things, perhaps because trade in slaves was highly speculative, and he was very prudent, his firm surviving when many failed in the fluctuations the American war brought. But in his early years in Virginia he certainly owned slave-trading ships, and bought and sold slaves. There are three bills of exchange for slaves sold in Jamaica (the main slave market) each for over £1,500.

What I hadn't realized before is that the prosperity of all Liverpool derived to a considerable degree from the slave trade.* Though that trade was of course a major source of British prosperity before Liverpool existed — before 1700, that is — still by the end of the eighteenth century the city had as much as nine-tenths of the English slave trade in her hands. In 1800 fifty-three thousand slaves were carried from Africa to America and the West Indies in Liverpool ships alone, and by the time of the abolition of the trade in 1807, it was calculated that three quarters of Liverpool seamen were engaged in it. Luckily the cotton trade was just then beginning to be big enough to replace the slaves. But this was so just because of the enormous slave profits, which had been invested in the canals and roads linking Liverpool with the rest of Lancashire, and in the city's docks, which were by then the finest in the world. Those profits were, as I said, speculative and variable, but one man, Thomas Leyland (William Roscoe's partner), made a profit of £100,000 in three years. And the Cunliffes, Ellis Cunliffe's family, in whose genealogy Emma Florence exults more than in her own, made their money the same way. Foster Cunliffe of Wycollar (1685–1758), three times Mayor of Liverpool, made an immense fortune at it, and is said to have introduced the trade to the city. He became an M.P., his son became the first baronet, Sir Ellis Cunliffe, and from him in due course came Mrs. Cunliffe's aristocratic husband, the Captain.

Of course they were not unique in this even in Shropshire. One of Mrs. Cunliffe's contemporaries, whom I consulted in writing this, warned me it was best to refer to the source of the Sparling money as "trade with the plantations," and reminded me how many people in the county had made money that way. And of course it was not only Shropshire or only Liverpool. It was all eighteenth- and nineteenth-century England.

Liverpool did well at the trade partly because it paid its captains

---

* I took several of these facts about Liverpool from an unpublished M.A. thesis of 1939 at Birmingham University Library by Harold A. Turner titled "The Making of Modern Liverpool, 1760–1820."

and seamen less than Bristol and London did, and so could afford to sell its slaves at twelve percent lower prices and still return a profit to its owners. The whole trade was of course one of the great crimes of history. The facts are sufficiently well known to need no repetition; the decks sometimes only three or four feet apart, the men manacled together, the rows of bodies touching each other on all sides, the branding on the buttocks. The mortality rate of the Middle Passage was admitted to be sixteen percent even in 1796, and that was after the Dolben Acts of 1788 and 1789 came into force. Every aspect of the trade was brutal and debasing. The sailors had to be shanghaied into the ships and were treated when aboard with a special brutality, and were often pressured into deserting at the West Indian end of the voyage, or just plain left there. And in 1789, out of three thousand seamen who should have been aboard ships returning into Liverpool, 630 were dead.

Just one anecdote, an extract from the will of another John Sparling, the son of James, who was the younger brother of John Sparling the first. "I, Captain John Sparling, master of the good ship Joseph, now on her way (with the blessing of God) to the Barbadoes, and afterwards to others of the West Indian islands, to dispose of a cargo of slaves, amounting to the number of 271, the privilege and commission of which (if sold) are as follows, say 4 in every 100 and four on the neat sales, and 2% on the gross sales which is my property. And if it should please the Almighty God, to call me from this earthly and wicked world, I, the said John Sparling, the younger, aforesaid, do give and bequeath unto my dearly beloved mother, Jane Sparling, all monies and other benefits arising from the above-mentioned voyage, together with £433/19/3d now in the hands of William Dean the younger." This percentage commission on the average price the slaves fetched when sold, made it of financial interest to the captains to have no weakly or sickly specimens on their hands when they arrived, to bring that average price down, and some took measures to make sure of that.

And this is the trade which is inseparable from Liverpool's prosperity. (The city's motto, *Deus nobis haec otia fecit*, takes on a lurid color in the light of these facts.) Liverpool is a creation of Restoration commercial rationalism, an incarnation of WASP middle-class success. Defoe — a very suitable godfather — visited it in 1680, 1690, and 1705, and rejoiced to find it doubled in size and trade each time. "Liverpool is one of the wonders of Britain," he declared, and "Heaven has Liverpool in its particular protection." The population in 1700 was five thousand, in 1760 twenty-five thousand, and by 1820 one hundred thousand. By that date its dock system was the finest in the world, it was connected to every part of England by the canal systems, and it had been the world's greatest slave port. And naturally the working-class life of such a city was disorderly and cruel. It became a city from which wealthy people retreated to Shropshire. In 1793 there were eighty-four hundred houses and twelve hundred of them premises licensed to sell alcohol; the proportion was said to be twice as high as the average in England. There were women's boxing, cock-fighting (the Earl of Derby owned three thousand fighting cocks in 1768), and bull-baiting (the last recorded occasion of it as part of a civic function was at the opening of that Queen's Dock of John Sparling's).

In the figure of John Sparling, Mayor of Liverpool, therefore, the harshest of historical forces do become relevant to Petton, do become visible from Weston. Consider his house alone, Santo Domingo. The name was given to the estate by the previous owner, George Campbell, to celebrate the capture by one of his ships of a rich prize from this wealthiest of the French possessions. And Santo Domingo meant also of course cigars, and mahogany, which became fashionable in Liverpool around 1750. But above all it meant the sugar trade, which was worked by slave labor. The name therefore flaunted the source of Sparling's wealth, and was surely an unlucky name for a slave-trader's house.

* * *

At the end of the eighteenth century, when first the mulattoes and then the blacks rebelled against the white plantocracy, St. Domingue was the richest colony in the world, after Java. In 1790 its exports and imports were worth $140 million, as much as the United States' exports and imports then. It accounted for two-thirds of France's foreign commerce, and in a good year seven hundred ships and eighty thousand seamen were employed in trading with it. It was only ten thousand square miles, but five of its cities had theaters, and there were fifty journals published in the colony, while the French provinces had only four or five each. The Freemasons had established a literary society there in 1784, *Le Cercle des Phila-delphes.*

It had therefore a high culture — for the *grands blancs.* There were among the forty thousand whites a large majority of *petits blancs,* who had revolutionary aspirations of their own. They declared themselves Jacobins, except during those periods when the National Assembly in France declared the mulattoes or the blacks free — the Assembly reversed policy more than once. Then there were twenty-seven thousand free *gens de couleur. Their* culture can be symbolized by the science of color; the 128 gradations the colony recognized between pure white and pure black, from *nègre* to *sacatra* to *griffe* to *marabou* to *mulâtre* to *quarteron* to *métis* to *mamelouc* to *quarteronné* to *sang mêlé.* And there were four to five hundred thousand blacks. Their culture was symbolized by the cart whip of plaited bullock hide, which bit into the flesh and sometimes had to be picked out again with the fingers; and by the holes dug in the ground to accommodate pregnant women's bellies while they were being flogged.

That of course was the culture imposed on them. But they brought, kept bringing, their own culture with them from Africa — a culture estimated to be of the complexity of medieval Christendom — and they kept that alive in mutilated form under the conditions of slavery. Judging by what survives in Haiti now, anthropologists think it was predominantly a Dahomean culture that was shared by the blacks of 1790, despite the great variety of the tribes who contributed to the slave ships. Voodoo itself is a Dahomean word. They maintained their manners of eating and preparing food, their singing while at work in the plantation, their dancing in religious worship, their attitudes to death and burial, and above all their religion. There were priests and a king and a class system in Dahomey just as in France — there were plantations and overseers and slavery. And since an important class of those sold to the traders was the political prisoner, the enemy of the state either native or foreign, there were probably many natural leaders, priests and princes, in the barracoons on St. Domingue. Certainly there was a long tradition of rebellion. The first black slaves reached

Haiti in 1510. The first slave uprising occurred in 1522; the next in 1533; another is recorded in 1537; another in 1548. The risings of the 1790's were the last in a long series. And every year many slaves escaped from their plantations, and hid in the hills. They were called *marrons*, or maroons, and there were quite large communities of them up there, preserving as best they could their preslavery culture. Above all, they kept alive among them the arts of war, which were to prove useful when the great rebellion came.

All the fighting in St. Domingue was hideously brutal, on the part of all concerned. General Maitland of the British — who tried for five years to add the island to their empire, and lost twenty thousand men there — introduced a form of execution he had learned in India, of firing a condemned man from a cannon. For the French, General Rochambeau imported a hundred man-eating bloodhounds from Cuba, because in Jamaica such dogs had been used with success in putting down the 1795 Maroon rising. But he used them for the public execution of black prisoners, and made each occasion a social event.

But the blacks' brutality must still seem (to me) not the worst but the most fearful. The black rising of 1791 was organized by a British-born ex-slave called Boukman, who used the voodoo network to synchronize the action in different areas. Voodoo centered in the worship of Damballah, the sacred serpent, served by papaloi and mamaloi (priest-kings and priestess-queens) who had the power to bring the dead back to life as zombies. They sacrificed chickens, kids, boars, drank their blood and smeared it on their faces, worshiped sexual idols, uttered frantic prophecies. When the drums beat, the congregation danced more and more frenziedly, and the *crise de loa* seized many of them, and they passed on the state of possession to others, grasping them by the hands and spitting in their faces. It was in these states of religious hysteria that they began their revolt. In one place they carried as their banner the naked body of a white child impaled on a stake. At another they put men between planks of wood and sawed them in two.

The black leaders, with one exception, tried to stamp out voodoo. Only Dessalines, with his hatred of all whites and all mulattoes, turned away also from everything in their culture.

After the failure of Christophe's attempt to make a nineteenth-century nation out of Haiti, the island stagnated at the point of collapse. For a hundred and fifty years now it has been one of the most backward and corrupt countries in the world. The per capita annual income is $70, and the illiteracy rate is ninety percent. Duvalier took over the presidency from Magloire in 1956. Magloire was a mulatto, and Duvalier has built his own image as a black man, as the father of a black illiterate people. He destroyed the armed forces, the source of possible *coups d'etat*, and built up his personal *Milice Civile*, known as the *Tonton Macoute*; this is a Creole expression for bogeyman, and alludes to the voodoo cult which he has also fostered. The Vatican, and the Catholic hierarchy in Haiti, have protested against the alliance he tried to make between Catholicism and voodoo, but these protests resulted only in the expulsion of Archbishop Poirier in 1960, and later of other bishops and priests, and the seizing of the Roman Catholic newspaper. Duvalier claimed that the church was allied with the mulattoes. In all this he is following the example of Dessalines, who is now Haiti's greatest historical hero.

* * *

Santo Domingo, the mansion, was very grand, with two flights of steps curving up to the front door and four huge columns in the front wall — it cost John Sparling more than he wanted to pay, though Mrs. Sparling was perhaps pleased — and had an eventful history. When it was vacated by William Sparling after his acquittal, it was rented to Prince William of Gloucester, who was commander in chief in the area; later it became a barracks, and later a school (in the forties a Pestalozzi school, run by a Swiss and patronized by Liverpool Unitarians); later still it became a Roman Catholic college and residence of the Catholic bishop of Liverpool. It was once planned to build the Catholic cathedral in the ground there, but in the thirties the mansion was pulled down to make way for working-class flats.

I rode out there, to what is now Sir Thomas White Gardens, on a bus, in the December dusk. Where the house stood is the beginning of Santo Domingo Road, and there is a Santo Domingo Vale, and a Santo Domingo Grove nearby. I could not find the old man's tomb in the churchyard across the road, but I could see what a magnificent position his house had. From that churchyard the land falls away steeply in a huge curve right down to the Mersey. Indeed all the way out from the center of Liverpool you are conscious of the position of the river and the shape of the whole city. You are riding above it, and you seem to have twice as much sky as you have in Birmingham, which redeems the blackened streets at least aesthetically. I thought as I rode of a black friend who had just gone back to Guiana after doing a Ph.D. at Birmingham, and who could well be the great-grandson of the great-grandson of one of the Sparling or Cunliffe slaves.

The profits of the trade were invested in Liverpool's communications systems, prominently in her canals. The most famous of these was the Duke of Bridgewater's Canal, built 1762–67 by James Brindley, which carried an enormous volume of traffic the thirty miles between Liverpool and Manchester. By 1792 the number of vessels going the journey had increased sevenfold, and goods had to be warehoused several months before they could be loaded. The tonnage on this canal alone was 450,000 in 1791, and 600,000 in 1792. Because of this, between 1790 and 1894, when the Manchester Ship Canal opened a direct link to Manchester from the sea, Liverpool was *the* great port for cotton imports and exports, and *the* market for spinning cotton. It was only after 1780 that cotton spinning became an important industry, and after 1790 that cotton became clothing material for the working class. So during that hundred years after 1790 the Liverpool-Manchester complex generated an intensity of industrial-commercial life, progress, and poverty, out of which came the Rochdale Aunt Lizzie knew, and out of which came Aunt Lizzie. While the Sparlings floated becalmed in the backwaters of Shropshire, the Fittons were whirling round in the very center of the industrial maelstrom, the very eye of the storm of the future. Aunt Lizzie's brothers went to work in the engineering shops at Gorton; my mother left school at twelve to work in the mills. My mother and her brothers spent their holidays in Weston, Aunt Lizzie having taken them under special protection because my mother's father died when she was two. Weston was a protective backwater for them, too, as indeed it was for Aunt Lizzie herself, who came here, from teaching in Rochdale, on doctor's advice. But Manchester-Liverpool remained real-

ity to them; unlike Mrs. Cunliffe, they played no historical tricks
on their own imaginations.

By an odd coincidence, the canals that spread out from Liverpool nearly came through Weston, nearly stopped it being a backwater. There is a map of 1795, printed in London, which shows
the Ellesmere Canal linking Liverpool with Shrewsbury via Chester, Wrexham, and Chirk, with Weston on the main line. If this
had been built — and if the railways had not ousted the canals
— Weston would have become a much more important village,
or town, than some now five times its size. Part of the canal
was in fact built, with a terminus at Weston, running to Llany-
mynych, where it joined another that ran to Welshpool and Newtown, a total of forty-one miles; and on the way it linked with
another that ran from Chester to Chirk. In 1797 a wharf was built
in Weston, with a basin, four lime kilns, a pub, a warehouse, a
clerk's house, and a weighing machine. Lime and slate were sold
there to local farmers, while cheeses and timber went back to
Wales. But a report of 1805 declared that the subscribed funds
were exhausted, and nothing more got built. In fact, by the end of
the century the canal had been disused so long its course was barely
discoverable. The huge paw of history touched Weston but gave it
only a slight jolt.

By a further coincidence, the canals had an almost direct bearing
on Aunt Lizzie's life. She married a Weston man whose family
came to the village as employees of the Ruabon firm that sent the
lime and slate by the canal, the firm that owned the warehouse and
the clerk's house. Moreover, it is a hundred to one that the canal
crossed Mrs. Cunliffe's fields somewhere. But of course the real
connection for both is with the historical force which the canals
represented. The canals *brought* both sturdy, lean, sharp-yapping
Aunt Lizzie, and the bloated puff-ball of Petton; both ladies advanced upon Weston in the wagon train of an army whose advance
guard was that branching artery of tamed and serviceable water,
that triumph of lineality over topography.

So Weston now stands in the shadow of history for me. But
what I feel most is still how remote from the reality it is. Having
reached the Niagara of Liverpool teaches one the size of the differ-

ence between that and the backwaters. Weston *is* out of history, out of the action, out of the battle. The shadow of history lies across its fields as a shadow, something which can be worked into the view, worked into one's enjoyment of the scene, something amenable to imagination, amenable to liberal hedonism. To try to give that shadow substance and bulk, to make it *matter*, would be to my sense to falsify. That is of course because my sense is liberal, a function of a liberal temperament; but though I've said that before the argument is not circular. It is spiral. Passing the same point again at a different level, I confirm my sense of the design of the whole, I confirm my self.

The rumors of violence — of slave ships and slave markets — remain rumors in Weston; the smell of blood is a smell. The very dullness of the Sparlings as individuals insulates us from all that; because their individuality was dull, and individuality is factual, and facts are to be respected. History, in Weston, remains ultimately pastoral, remains ultimately as quiet as the actual pastures of Petton, dotted only with standing cattle. Out of that quietness I grew up, and down into it I thrust my roots again.

*   *   *

Yes, I still believe that. I'm not prepared to pull myself up by the roots, to forego the nourishment that comes from this quietness, even knowing how much of it is dullness, is insulation, even knowing how much of it was paid for by other people in the Caribbean. After all, John Sparling's house was named Santo Domingo by its *previous* owner; and my family only lived in the *next* village to the Sparlings. These are facts, as much as any other. The chain of connection moves crabwise, like a chess knight, not link immediately and viscerally in link. This is historical complicity. I don't inherit, in any personal sense, the guilt of John Sparling. And that guilt itself was not personal in the ordinary sense of the word. Moreover, even if it were guilty, this quietness would still be valuable. What is good is good, and my luck is something to be guarded, to be cultivated, as long as it can be. But of course there are other things one wants to do besides preserve and cultivate. Besides keeping a temperamental readiness to respond variously, honestly, and cherishingly to all the facts of life equally, one wants also to acquire the power to act, to take up a position, and to change some of those facts. And the only position to take up these days, so my argument runs, must be radical, no matter how Erasmian one's temperament.

BIBLIOGRAPHY

Only books mentioned, but incompletely identified, in the text are included

CHAPTER 1

Mannheim, Karl. *Ideology and Utopia.* New York, 1936.
Walzer, Michael. *Revolution of the Saints.* Cambridge, Mass., 1966.

CHAPTER 2

Hedge, F. H., ed. *Prose Writers of Germany.* Philadelphia, 1847.
Butler, E. M. *The Fortunes of Faust.* Cambridge, 1952.

CHAPTER 3

Morton, A. L. *The Everlasting Gospel.* London, 1958.
Gilchrist, Alexander. *Life of William Blake.* London, 1863.

CHAPTER 4

Gray, Ronald. *Goethe the Alchemist.* Cambridge, 1952.
Berlin, Isaiah. "Herder and the Enlightenment," *Aspects of the 18th Century.* Earl Wasserman, ed. Baltimore, 1965.
Friedenthal, R. *Goethe: his life and times.* Cleveland, 1965.
Frantz, A. I. *Half a Hundred Thralls to Faust.* U. of N. Carolina Town Press, 1949.
Jantz, H. S. *Goethe's Faust as a Renaissance Man.* Princeton, 1951.
Butler, E. M. *Byron and Goethe.* London, 1956.

CHAPTER 5

Huizinga, Johann. *Erasmus of Rotterdam.* London, 1952.
Zweig, Stefan. *Erasmus of Rotterdam.* New York, 1934.

Daiches, David. "Christopher North," *Literary Essays*, Edinburgh, 1956.

CHAPTER 6

Howard, Leon. *The Connecticut Wits*. Chicago, 1943.
Brooks, Van Wyck. *The World of Washington Irving*. New York, 1944.

CHAPTER 7

Scholem, Gershen. *Major Trends in Jewish Mysticism*. New York, 1954.
Hill, Christopher. *Puritanism and Revolution*. London, 1962.
Cohn, Norman. *Pursuit of the Millennium*. Fairlawn, New Jersey, 1957.
Woodcock, George. *Anarchism*. Cleveland, 1962.
Knox, Ronald. *Enthusiasm*. Oxford, 1950.
Watt, Ian. "Two Historical Aspects of the Augustan Tradition," *Studies in the 18th Century*. R. F. Brissenden, ed. Toronto, 1968.
Frye, Northrop. *Anatomy of Criticism*. Princeton, 1957. *Fearful Symmetry*. Boston, 1962.

CHAPTER 8

Yates, Frances. *Giordano Bruno and the Hermetic Tradition*. Chicago, 1964. *The Art of Memory*. London, 1966. *Theater of the World*. London, 1969.
Walker, D. P. *Spiritual and Demonic Magic*. London, 1958.
Jones, Ernest. *The Life and Work of Sigmund Freud*. New York, 1953.
Jonas, Hans. *The Gnostic Religion*. Boston, 1958.
Krieger, Murray, ed. *Northrop Frye in Modern Criticism*. New York, 1966.
Butler, E. M. *The Myth of the Magus*. Cambridge, 1948.

CHAPTER 10

Lasky, Melvin. "*The Birth of a Metaphor*," *Encounter*, Feb. 1970.
Butler, E. M. *Byron and Goethe*. London, 1956.

INDEX

The index refers to both book-titles and authors' names, but it gives page references for discussions of an author only outside the chapter mainly devoted to him. Goethe, Schiller, Herder, for example, are indexed only for discussions of them outside the chapter on Weimar.